Publications of the
MINNESOTA HISTORICAL SOCIETY

RUSSELL W. FRIDLEY, Director

*JUNE DRENNING HOLMQUIST, Assistant Director
for Research and Publications*

WOMEN
of MINNESOTA
Selected Biographical Essays

Edited by Barbara Stuhler
and Gretchen Kreuter

MINNESOTA HISTORICAL SOCIETY PRESS ● *1977* ● *ST. PAUL*

Copyright © 1977 by the Minnesota Historical Society
Corrected reprint, 1979
International Standard Book Number: 0-87351-112-3

Library of Congress Cataloging in Publication Data

Main entry under title:
Women of Minnesota: Selected Biographical Essays
 (Publications of the Minnesota Historical Society)
 Includes index.
 1. Women — Minnesota — Biography. I. Stuhler,
Barbara. II. Kreuter, Gretchen. III. Series:
Minnesota Historical Society. Publications.
HQ1438.M6W65   301.41'2'09776 [B]   77-3361

To the memory of our mothers
MARVYL von LOEWE
MAE GALBRAITH STUHLER

ACKNOWLEDGMENTS

There are many to praise for making this book possible, and only ourselves to blame for any shortcomings it may have. Russell W. Fridley, director of the Minnesota Historical Society, counseled and encouraged us from the project's conception three years ago to its completion. The Northwest Area Foundation supplied the generous financial support that stimulated both the editors and authors, and the state of Minnesota granted funds to defray partially the costs of publication.

A number of women provided research and other editorial assistance — among them Ramona Burks, Dallas Chrislock, Lillian Jensen, and Jo Anne Ray. The Society's assistant director, June D. Holmquist, and Jean A. Brookins, managing editor, were, as always, dependably critical and creative. Anne A. Hage had a major responsibility in the final stages of editing, and she performed that task with skill and enthusiasm. All but four of the photographs used in the book are in the collections of the Minnesota Historical Society's audio-visual library. That of Ada Comstock Notestein was kindly supplied by the Comstock House Society, Moorhead, and those of the Larson sisters by Henrietta and Nora Larson.

Finally, we would like to thank our friends and authors who shared our interest in restoring, in some measure, women to their proper place in Minnesota history.

St. Paul, Minnesota   *Gretchen Kreuter*
February, 1977   *Barbara Stuhler*

ABOUT THE AUTHORS

Nina Marchetti Archabal is assistant director for humanities, University of Minnesota Gallery, and a Ph.D. candidate in music at the university in Minneapolis.

Winifred D. Wandersee Bolin received her Ph.D. from the University of Minnesota. She teaches history at St. Cloud State University, St. Cloud.

Arvonne S. Fraser is a political and woman's rights activist.

Elizabeth Gilman, the granddaughter of her subject, is a worker at Chrysalis Center for Women and a counselor at Hope Transition Center, St. Paul.

Rhoda R. Gilman is supervisor of research for the Minnesota Historical Society.

Patricia C. Harpole is assistant chief librarian for the Minnesota Historical Society.

Sue E. Holbert is deputy state archivist, division of archives and manuscripts, Minnesota Historical Society.

Carol Jenson is associate professor of history, University of Wisconsin — La Crosse.

Dolores De Bower Johnson works for the Saint Paul Chamber Orchestra.

Sister Karen Kennelly C.S.J. is professor of history and academic dean at the College of St. Catherine, St. Paul.

Gretchen Kreuter is assistant professor of history and co-ordinator of women's studies at St. Olaf College, Northfield.

Abigail McCarthy is the author of *Private Faces/Public Places*, a memoir of Washington, D.C., and the Midwest, and is a columnist for *Commonweal* and *One Woman's Voice*, distributed by New York Times Features.

Eileen Manning Michels is assistant professor of art history at the College of St. Catherine and the College of St. Thomas, St. Paul.

Jo Anne Ray is editor of the *Minnesota Horticulturist*, a magazine published in St. Paul.

Nancy Freeman Rohde is assistant professor of library science, University of Minnesota, Minneapolis.

Geraldine Bryan Schofield is a former instructor in English at the University of Minnesota. She now lives in Minneapolis.

Susan Margot Smith is a Ph.D. candidate in American studies at the University of Minnesota, Minneapolis.

Barbara Stuhler is professor and associate dean of continuing education and extension, University of Minnesota, Minneapolis.

CONTENTS

INTRODUCTION

By Barbara Stuhler and Gretchen Kreuter

WOMEN were long invisible, or nearly so, to American historians. Traditionally concerned with power and the powerful, scholars either ignored women or discussed only the ones who were associated with "women's rights" and consequently impinged on power and politics, or those who were sufficiently colorful or notorious to provide good anecdotal material. The historical profession, interested in change over time, assumed that women were immutable and changeless and, therefore, of little relevance to the serious scholar.

In recent years, however, there has been great interest, among both professional historians and the general public, in the history of women. That interest is, in part, a consequence of the social revolutions of the 1960s. The civil rights movement evoked a new sense of black consciousness, and in short order this same search for identity was emulated by other racial and ethnic minorities. The appearance in 1963 of Betty Friedan's *The Feminine Mystique* marked a resurgence of the women's movement which had, to a large extent, lain dormant since the winning of the vote in 1920.[1] Often grudgingly, people and politicians responded with changing attitudes and new laws. Conventional accounts of American history which had excluded minorities would no longer do so. The historical profession agonizingly reappraised its omissions, and new and more inclusive histories began to appear.

This collection of essays derives from both of these social and intellectual experiences. It is closely related to the women's movement of the 1960s, and it also represents an effort to make amends for past exclusions — to add in a modest way to our knowledge about the contributions of women in our society.

The essays are "feminist" in the sense that nearly all our authors

1

have been concerned with "women achievers" — state legislators or college presidents, for example — and how they succeeded in having full professional lives at a time when society said only men could be truly professional. The essays are feminist in some of the kinds of questions the authors have asked of their subjects: did these women receive equal pay for equal work? Were they promoted with the same frequency as men? Did they have the right to own property, obtain custody of children in the event of divorce or separation, hold public office? The achievements of the women in these pages can be marked in some measure by the number of "firsts" they represent — among them the first woman candidate of a major party for the United States Senate, the first woman on the faculty of the Harvard Graduate School of Business Administration, possibly the first single white adoptive parent in Minnesota.

Some of the authors, however, have written about women who were *not* achievers by the traditional definitions of historical importance. Their lives raise questions about the completeness or the legitimacy of those definitions. For example, can we continue to talk about American religion as though it were man's province when we realize that, from the 1830s on, religious education was almost completely managed by women? Can we continue to extol only "professionals," when we know that women as volunteers not only won the vote but, in a variety of ways, have made their communities better places to live in?

This collection of essays does not purport to include every woman of interest or eminence in Minnesota history, nor do the individual essays constitute the final definitive word on their subjects. Limitations of space alone would preclude that, and in some cases the papers of the subject are not yet fully available or are under some restrictions on their ` sage. In other instances, individuals fully worthy of inclusion have been omitted for want of a biographer, or because to include them would seriously distort what the editors see as the balance of the book. There are, for example, eight Minnesota women listed in the three-volume biographical collection, *Notable American Women,* but only four of the eight are included in these pages. They are Harriet Bishop, Hannah Kempfer, Maria Sanford, and Jane Grey Swisshelm. Those who are not are Wanda H. Gág, artist and author; Martha G. Ripley, physician and humanitarian; Clara H. Ueland, suffragist and reformer; and Julia Wood, newspaper editor and novelist. We have listed them in Chapter 17 along with more than a hundred other women whose lives should stimulate scholars and writers to do further work in the field.[2]

We have tried to span Minnesota history from territorial days to the present, and to indicate the diversity of women's achievements and interests. Given the restrictions of circumstance and attitude faced by women, it is perhaps not surprising that many of them were found in the helping professions, in education, serving as volunteers in civic enterprises, or in some way working to improve the moral tone and conscience of society. Whatever their primary occupation or avocation, several were involved in the suffrage movement, ranging from Harriet Bishop, a school-teacher in the fledgling community of St. Paul, to Fanny Brin, nearly a century later, a civic leader in that upstart sister city, Minneapolis. Each in her own way was a distinctive personality: Jane Grey Swisshelm was a talented and persuasive journalist. Catheryne Cooke Gilman was a moralist of the first order. Eva McDonald Valesh was an early union organizer. Frances Densmore was an ethnomusicologist, a pioneer in the study of American Indian music. Kate Donnelly was the proverbial "woman-behind-the-man," who might be termed the Abigail Adams of Minnesota. Maud Hart Lovelace is a "scribbling woman," whose tales of family life in Mankato are rich in warmth and humor.

Minnesota women involved in higher education were especially distinguished: Maria Sanford, Ada Comstock Notestein, Mary Molloy, and the Larson sisters of Northfield. Some ventured onto the elective political scene — like Anna Dickie Olesen and the more than thirty women who held office in the state legislature. Gratia Countryman and Alice O'Brien made significant contributions to the civic and cultural life of the Twin Cities.

Although there are great differences among the women described in these pages, there are similarities as well. Most were well-to-do by reason of birth, marriage, or achievement, and all were educated beyond the average for their day. The parents of these women were eager to have their daughters educated, some even moving from one community to another to provide easier access to institutions of higher learning. At a minimum, the women were high school graduates and more than half were qualified as teachers. Some were college graduates, and a few earned doctorates. They participated to an unusual degree in organizations, particularly women's groups, and, for some, that experience was a training ground for leadership in other activities. Several were associated with causes of one sort or another, and, of these, a significant number were interested and active in the peace movement. They were articulate as speakers or writers, some as both. A few were successful on the professional lecture circuit. Religion, in varying ways and degrees, was important to many of them.

More were married than not, but the margin of wedded over single is not great. Not all the marriages were happy, and there were divorces and separations. The married women did not have large families. Only three had as many as three children, although Kate Donnelly lost several more to disease and miscarriage. Four had one child apiece and two had none — Harriet Bishop who was divorced and Ada Comstock Notestein who married at sixty-seven. Gratia Countryman, although not married, became a single parent through adoption. Excluding for a moment those active in politics, all of the women in these pages, except Kate Donnelly, Alice O'Brien, and Fanny Brin, earned their own livings, or contributed in significant measure to the family income. Some of the women elected to the legislature were also gainfully employed, and Anna Dickie Olesen was eventually appointed to a salaried position because of her service to a political party. In the case of these wage-earning women, their financial independence and middle-class occupations were related to their high educational level. In all these respects, they differed greatly from the average American woman of their day.

Most remarkable was the longevity of these notable women. None of those who are no longer alive died before they were sixty; four died in their seventies; three in their eighties, and three in their nineties. Even among the living, except for those currently serving in the legislature, their ages range from the late fifties to the eighties. Although one may explain this longevity in terms of the better nutrition and health care that middle-class persons enjoy, it is tempting to conclude that a productive life augurs well for a long life.

We have not been rigorous in defining how one qualifies as a Minnesotan for the purposes of this collection. Many of the subjects were not born in the state; Maria Sanford did not arrive in Minnesota until she was forty-three. Some spent only a few years there: for crusading journalist Jane Grey Swisshelm, Minnesota was only a way station on her lifelong itinerary. Others were born and reared in the state but spent their professional lives elsewhere: Henrietta Larson and Ada Comstock made their reputations in Cambridge, Massachusetts, not Minnesota. Nevertheless it is appropriate to include them in a book about Minnesota women. Maria Sanford was the closest thing to an official "heroine" that Minnesota has had thus far. Jane Swisshelm rocked early state politics and left her journalistic mark long after she moved on to other locales. Henrietta Larson and Ada Comstock always thought of themselves as Minnesotans, shaped by the state's people and traditions and, in the case of Larson, by the Norwegian-Lutheran heritage that characterizes many Minnesota communities.

Minnesota, because of its diversity, offers a particularly rich field of exploration for women's history. Since the territorial days of the 1850s it has been both urban and rural, industrial and agricultural. It has been populated by a wide variety of people of several races — Native American, black, Mexican American — and by many ethnic groups representing the "old" immigration and the "new." It has long had a vigorous intellectual and cultural and political life. One would expect to find, among its women past and present, a wide variety of ambitions, achievements, and life-styles, and indeed this is the case. We must add, however, that this collection does not reflect the full range of Minnesota's diversity. All its subjects are white; many had New England or Anglo-American antecedents. Fanny Brin is the only Jew. Brin and Hannah Kempfer are the only immigrants. Other ethnic and racial minorities are represented only in Chapter 17, and several there included are deserving of wider attention. We might also note that there are no notorious women in this collection — although one "lady of the night," at least according to legend, was a leading businesswoman of the 1920s in St. Paul.

One cannot, we hope, read this collection without realizing that the "eternal Eve" — the stereotype to which all women were once assumed to conform — is a figment of the imagination. The characteristics that were defined in the "Cult of True Womanhood" — piety, purity, submissiveness, and domesticity — were not nearly as universal as historians once thought.

In former times, the function of biography was to describe persons worthy of emulation. Today we call such individuals "role models." In the early days of the American republic, the figures of the American past were supposed to embody all that was good and worthy in human life and fill the reader with loyalty and pride. When those figures did not, in fact, possess every possible virtue, their biographers graciously invented them. The alabaster George

Washington known to generations of schoolchildren was the creation of Parson Weems.

We have attempted to avoid the excesses of that old school of biographical writing and to evaluate fairly both the strengths and weaknesses of our subjects. If some of the women described in these pages seem to be rather extraordinary personalities, it is because they were. If many in the cast of characters seem single-minded, purposeful, and even humorless, the reasons are obvious: in a man's world, a grim determination and persistence were often necessary to advance a woman's cause or accomplish her ends.

We hope this collection will make familiar to a wider audience the achievements and interests of a group of Minnesota women. But beyond that, we hope it will inspire both the historian and the general reader to ask some broader questions about the history of the state — whether, in fact, we have truly known Minnesota's history when we have omitted the experience and accomplishments of at least half its population.

In 1902 the Minnesota Historical Company published *Men of Minnesota,* a volume containing 2,060 portraits of men of influence in the state. Its stated purpose was "to preserve for future generations the features and characters of men upon whom the destiny of the State of Minnesota depends." The first recognition that women might also have a part in shaping Minnesota's destiny came with the publication in 1924 of *Who's Who Among Minnesota Women.* Reviewing the book for *Minnesota History* in December, 1925, historian Theodore C. Blegen wrote: "A comprehensive study of women as a factor in the development of Minnesota will probably some day be made. . . . The great importance of the part played by women in history is universally admitted, but it is almost never brought out adequately in the published histories. Certainly a real contribution to American history could be made if some competent historian undertook a thoroughgoing study of the influence of women in the history of a single state, say Minnesota."[3]

The "thoroughgoing history" Dean Blegen called for fifty-two years ago has not yet appeared. The present volume attempts in a beginning way to call attention to the influence of some women of Minnesota in the development of the state and nation.

1. HARRIET E. BISHOP
Moralist and Reformer

By Winifred D. Wandersee Bolin

IN JULY, 1847, the steamboat "Lynx" churned its way up the
Mississippi River toward what was soon to become Minnesota
Territory. From its deck Harriet Bishop, a young woman from
Vermont, admired the wild forests and rocky crags as they slid past
her gaze. She was not, however, a tourist; she was a schoolteacher
with a mission. Missionaries were not new to Minnesota in the
1840s. Schoolteachers were. The combination of both in a single
female person was a nineteenth-century innovation, the product of
a changing society that endowed womanhood with special responsibilities for maintaining civilization in the towns and cities of the
East and for establishing it in the rude communities of the West.[1]

One glimpse of St. Paul was enough to persuade most visitors
that civilization — even at the lowest denominator of morality and
religion — had not yet arrived. A few hundred inhabitants lived in
a jumble of log huts along rutted streets that were muddy in spring
and fall, dusty in summer, and impassable in winter. St. Paul was
for the most part a male society made up of soldiers, Indians, fur
traders, land speculators, and merchants. There were only three
white American families in the town when Harriet Bishop arrived.
Liquor was sold in every store and drinking was one of the few
available recreational activities. The town's founding father, if it
had one, was a whisky dealer known as "Pig's Eye" Parrant. When
the pioneer missionary Thomas S. Williamson visited St. Paul in
1846, he was struck by the town's deplorable educational and religious conditions. Twelve to twenty families with school-age children lived in the surrounding countryside and half the parents
could not read. Dismayed by what he had seen, and entreated by
one of the mothers to find a teacher for the community, Williamson immediately began to seek a "civilizing force."[2]

A shortage of competent teachers was common throughout the West, and in the 1840s a new organization was established to help solve the problem. For years Catharine Beecher, daughter of a notable New England family and sister of Harriet Beecher Stowe, had attempted to arouse interest in the cause of popular education. It troubled her that a generation of children was growing up beyond the reach of educational facilities. She sought out wealthy individuals who could contribute to her efforts, and she made frequent speaking tours to advance her ideas and to provide financial backing for her cause. Beecher played upon the feelings and fears of her audiences as she tried to gain their sympathy for what she described as the masses of children suffering under cruel teachers in degenerate environments.[3]

Her efforts were at least moderately successful, and in 1847 William Slade, a former governor of Vermont, established the National Board of Popular Education with Catharine Beecher in charge of the selection, training, and placement of teachers. That very spring, Beecher engaged a group of thirty-five young women in a monthlong program that emphasized the social skills and attitudes needed to uplift a frontier community.

She lectured them on difficulties that were bound to arise — the dangers to their health, the shortage of schoolbooks, the moral weakness and lack of spiritual training in the community. She also expanded upon ways that these young teachers could exert an influence outside the schoolroom. "The Christian female teacher," she declared, "will quietly take her station, collecting the ignorant children around her, inspiriting the principles of morality and awakening the hope of immortality." Harriet Bishop was one of those thirty-five trainees, and she took every word to heart.[4]

Beecher's concerns, as a matter of fact, went far beyond educational matters. She was troubled by the ambiguity and contradictions inherent in the inferior status of women in a nation that prided itself on its egalitarianism and democratic spirit. Perhaps the subordination of women, as Beecher's biographer has suggested, was a convenient solution to the social strains of antebellum America: "In a democracy as agitated and tension-filled as the United States in the 1840's, some form of hierarchy was needed to avoid a war of all against all . . . by removing half the population from the arena of competition and making it subservient to the other half, the amount of antagonism the society had to bear would be reduced to a tolerable limit."[5]

Harriet E. Bishop

Basically, Beecher tried to reconcile women's inferior position in a democracy by ennobling the sphere that society was willing to allot to them. For she saw the home as an integral part of the life of the nation, reflecting and promoting American values. Women were to assume a central role within a web of institutions that included the family, the school, and the church. In the interest of social harmony (an elusive goal at best) women were to embrace self-sacrifice and become the exemplars and teachers of a national morality. The elevation of the teaching profession was closely related to the extension of women's domestic role. Teachers in the classroom, like wives and mothers in the home, would be the guardians of morality, the purveyors of moral uplift.[6]

All this was a tall order but to many of Catharine Beecher's pupils, and certainly to Harriet Bishop, the mission was an exhilarating one. For men and women alike, the 1840s were a time of religious enthusiasm, romanticism, and humanitarian reform. Conscious of the inadequacies of their social institutions, Americans cherished a spirit of optimism and hope that wrongs could be made right, souls could be made clean, the nation could become perfect. Ralph Waldo Emerson in his quiet book-lined study might write his essay, "Man the Reformer," but Catharine Beecher's students, living in haylofts and spare bedrooms in tiny frontier hamlets, teaching from a few tattered volumes, would personify Woman the Reformer.

Harriet Bishop was thirty years old when she took up the challenge. Born on January 1, 1817, in Panton, Addison County, Vermont, she was the third daughter of Putnam and Miranda (Wright) Bishop. She had developed a serious sense of purpose early in life. Converted and baptized in Lake Champlain at the age of thirteen, she was for several years the youngest member of her Baptist church. In early adolescence she read the memoirs of two missionary wives, Harriet Newall and Anna H. Hudson, who had been sent to Burma by the Baptist Home Missionary Society, and she determined to follow a similar career. After taking a course at the Fort Edward Institute in New York state, Harriet began teaching there in the public schools of Essex County. But she soon discovered that there were far more teaching opportunities in the West than in the Northeast, and in an effort to improve her chances for a western position, she enrolled in Catharine Beecher's teacher-training course in Albany, New York.[7]

Meantime a letter to Slade from Thomas Williamson had been forwarded to Beecher explaining the desperate need for a female teacher for the young children of St. Paul. This was the opportunity Bishop had been seeking, but her decision to go west was not taken lightly. Friends warned of the hazards of the journey. Williamson himself admitted that St. Paul was on "the utmost verge of civilization" and that a woman who took up the challenge would have to forego most of the comforts and pleasures of the East. "Every possible obstacle was presented," Bishop recalled years later, "but they were to me as so many incentives to persist in my decision . . . because I was more needed here than at any other spot on earth, and because there was no other one of my class who felt it a duty to come." Perhaps she recalled those missionary wives who had gone halfway around the world to pursue their calling in Burma. Surely Minnesota could be no worse.[8]

Bishop had hardly embarked on her journey when an incident convinced her that a special Providence watched over her and worked for the success of her mission. Not wanting to travel on the Sabbath, she stayed over with friends in Palmyra, New York. If it had not been for this delay she would have sailed on the ship "Chesapeake," which shortly went down in Lake Erie with the loss of all passengers.[9]

The last leg of her long trip brought Bishop on July 16, 1847, to the steamboat landing at Kaposia, a Dakota or Sioux village a few miles downriver from St. Paul. Here the portents were more distressing. As she disembarked her eyes fell upon a scene that was, she wrote later, "novel and grotesque, not to say repulsive." A band of curious Indians, members of Little Crow's village, stood on the shore, their blankets and hair streaming in the wind, their limbs uncovered. The older children were nearly naked, the smaller ones completely so, and nearly every woman held an infant in her arms. The steamboat captain had advised the new schoolmarm on protocol before they docked — *"'kiss the pappooses,'* and *thereby secure the friendship of the band"* — and indeed she found "the greasy, smutty face of every mother's child . . . presented to afford me my initiatory lesson." Her revulsion was frank, and though she made some effort to conceal it in future dealings with Indians, she never felt her distaste was a defect of either her nature or her training. No good Victorian mother would want her child kissed by a stranger, and Bishop could see no charm or purpose in this rude custom. It seemed only proof, if any were needed, that her work was cut out for her.[10]

Thomas Williamson and his sister Mary met the new schoolteacher at Kaposia and made her welcome in their home, while she recovered from her journey and prepared for the trials that lay ahead. Several days later she was taken nine miles upstream to St. Paul in a canoe paddled by two young Indian women. By the time she arrived she was seasick and homesick. After resting on a blanket under a tree, she climbed the path up the steep cliff and caught her first glimpse of the town. "Here was a field to be cultivated," she declared, "a garden of untrained flowers to be tended, and the heart raised a thank-offering to heaven and cheerfully entered upon its work."[11]

Bishop's first schoolhouse was a mud-plastered log hovel, formerly a blacksmith shop, on the corner of Third and St. Peter streets. Rats and snakes scuttled about the corners, and each day a hen came in to lay an egg. "Dark faces," she reported, occasionally peered in the door and windows. But the crudity of her surroundings only enhanced her sense of the importance of her work: "Why should I pine for halls of science and literature, when such glorious privileges were mine. . . . There was not a spot in earth's broad domain that could have tempted me to an exchange."

She brought in evergreen branches to decorate the walls of her classroom, and before starting formal lessons she insisted that each pupil receive a good scrubbing with a bar of soap. Her civilizing mission clearly included an attention to detail, though there is no record of the lessons she taught or the books her pupils learned to read. Nevertheless, as one early settler of St. Paul observed, "Miss Bishop was thoroughly impressed with the belief that she had a work to do — a destiny that must be filled." [12]

Almost immediately, Bishop began to extend the sphere of her moral influence through religious and social activities. Two weeks after her arrival she established the town's first Sunday school, and though she was then the only Baptist in town, it became the foundation for the First Baptist Church of St. Paul. Seven pupils came the first Sunday. The racial mixture was such that an interpreter was needed who could speak English, French, and Dakota. By the third Sunday, the school had increased to about twenty-five pupils. [13]

Despite her zeal, Bishop was uneasy in her role as a religious leader with the multiple responsibilities of superintendent, teacher, and quasi-minister. She seems to have worried that she was exceeding her womanly prerogatives: "For a singlehanded and lone female to occupy a distinct and decided position in such a community," she wrote in a mixture of pride and self-effacement, "was no trifling work. Her actions would be misunderstood, her words misinterpreted, and the devices of Satan would beset her on every hand. . . . But for an invisible presence, she would have shrunk entirely from the new duty." Her prayers for qualified help were answered in the summer of 1848 when Deacon Abram H. Cavender, a Baptist, and the Reverend Benjamin F. Hoyt, a Methodist, arrived in St. Paul to tend the flock that she had gathered. [14]

Bishop felt no qualms, however, about participating in movements for social reform. Like many of her female contemporaries, she was an outspoken advocate of temperance, and her observations in St. Paul heightened her hatred of the "devil's water." She wrote later: "The *bottle* was the unfailing attendant on *every* occasion and stood confessed the *life of every company.*" The effects of drink were frequently seen: a white-haired widow died of delirium tremens, drunken Indians fought and fatally injured each other, and a young man froze to death on the prairies in an alcoholic stupor. [15]

She made her position on temperance known at once. During her first days in St. Paul, a group of citizens took her on an outing to the Falls of St. Anthony. All went well until one of the escort rode up to Harriet's wagon to get a bottle from it. She told him sternly that she had never been in company where liquor was used. She recalled the incident later:

"'Then,' replied the gentleman with great suavity, 'you are entitled to the first drink,' at the same time presenting the bottle.

"'No, sir, thank you, unless you deliver it into my sole charge.'

"'That could not be done,' and of course a hearty laugh was raised at my expense. . . .'"[16]

Ridicule notwithstanding, a division of the Sons of Temperance had been established, due in part to her efforts, by the spring of 1849. Other similar groups were organized not long after, and temperance soon emerged as a political issue. "The banner of temperance was now unfurled in auspicious breezes. The drunkard was reclaimed and young men were saved from following in his steps," Harriet Bishop announced prematurely. "But the destroyer of domestic peace — the murderer of the soul, could not sleep. Efforts were made to win the drunkard back to his cups: to overthrow the resolves of the young; to entrap the unwary." In fact, temperance won a victory at the polls in 1851, only to face defeat when the next legislature repealed the law. The cause, however, remained close to Bishop's heart throughout her life. Her volume of poetry, *Minnesota Then and Now*, published in 1869, had as one of its major themes the battle for temperance, presented as a clear-cut struggle between good and evil.[17]

What made her comfortable in the role of temperance advocate and social reformer was her acceptance of Catharine Beecher's convictions about the role of women. Bishop dwelt on the achievements and potentialities, not on the oppression or subordinate status of her sex. In every community, she declared, there were anonymous women whose lives made up an essential chapter in the history of the country. Men might level the forests, plant and harvest crops, and contest for political power, but "To woman is entrusted the future destiny of Minnesota. Her influence is to determine the predominance of vice or virtue; whether the 'powers that be' shall, in the future, be men 'fearing God and working righteousness', or men choosing 'darkness rather than light.' . . . And this influence is not to be wielded by dissension, strife and the ballot box, but by precept and example."[18]

Bishop's well-defined concept of women's role was in the
Beecher tradition. Although she went beyond her teacher in supporting equal suffrage, her feminism was restrained, and she
probably would have been uncomfortable in the company of her
contemporaries, Elizabeth Cady Stanton and Susan B. Anthony.
But in 1881 when the Minnesota Woman Suffrage Association was
established, Harriet Bishop was among its organizers.[19]

In her early years in Minnesota, however, Bishop's efforts at
community improvement were more appropriate to women's conventional spheres. She helped form the St. Paul Circle of Industry,
a group of eight women who raised funds for a new schoolhouse.
She also helped establish the Baptist Sewing Society to defray incidental expenses of the church. Appointed a committee of one,
she drafted articles for the group in August, 1851, and during the
next several years held a number of executive positions in the society.[20]

In 1867 Bishop, with several other Protestant women of St. Paul,
organized the Ladies Christian Union, which aimed to provide assistance to nearly every kind of needy person, whether destitute,
homeless, friendless, or (saddest of all) immoral. When the women
of the Christian Union discovered that their goal was too ambitious, they focused their efforts on a residence for the homeless, and
in 1869 they purchased a house for the purpose. Branch societies
met frequently, however, to sew clothing for the poor and to engage in "instructive" reading.[21]

Frontier society devoted little attention and fewer resources to
the luckless and unsuccessful. The efforts of Bishop and the
women she recruited for worthy causes undoubtedly had a
humanizing effect in an otherwise rough and heedless environment. Bishop's style in these endeavors was suited to the demands
of her surroundings. An early settler described her as "angular,
positive, determined — such a woman as is necessary for frontier
life." No diplomat, she attacked evils in an uncompromising spirit
that antagonized some of her closest associates. She was not to be
deterred from the accomplishment of deeds that only good Christian women could perform, for she truly believed in the moral
superiority of women in general and, most likely, of herself in particular.[22]

Bishop's enthusiasm for moral reform through social activity
reflected one aspect of American social history in the nineteenth
century, but in other less positive ways she was also a creature of

her times. Her attitude toward Native Americans, at least with respect to the Sioux who lived near Fort Snelling, was adversely critical and by today's standards racist. When she arrived in Minnesota, she confessed years later, she was filled with a "book knowledge" of Indian life and character that she soon found to be largely incorrect: "The world has been taught to admire [the Indian] for his noble traits, his manly bearing, and his alleged remembrance of trifling acts of kindness. The latter, it is true, are remembered, but more with the expectation of repetition than a return."[23]

Her first glimpse of the Sioux at Kaposia had begun her disillusionment with the picture of the noble savage. Indians, she wrote in her autobiographical volume, *Floral Home,* were cowards, thieves, and liars, and she believed that her own observations supported such judgments. In her reminiscences she described the greediness of Old Bets, an Indian beggar in St. Paul, the squalor of Indian camps she visited, and the presumptuousness of the tribesman who offered to make her his second wife. "Instinct more than reason is the guide of the red man," she concluded sadly. "He repudiates improvement and despises manual effort. For ages has the heart been embedded in moral pollution."[24]

These were, to say the least, unhesitating and unsparing judgments, but they were typical of the racism and ethnocentrism found nearly everywhere on the American frontier. Settlers failed to understand why Native Americans were not eager to embrace the white man's version of progress and enlightenment. Nor did they appreciate that an ancient culture was being destroyed by the establishment of farms and the destruction of forests and game. Worst of all, few settlers even thought of Native Americans as human beings — they were only obstacles to progress. And Bishop had arrived in Minnesota only fifteen years after the Black Hawk War in Illinois, where Indian women and children were massacred by white soldiers.

Bishop was more tolerant than many settlers. She was prepared to take up what later imperialists would call the "white man's burden." "In face of dangers and violent deaths," she wrote, "the Indian must be sought and saved. His redemption has been purchased, and he must be instructed in the 'way of salvation.'" She had known an unpromising little Indian girl who had hung about the mission premises as wild as could be. The child was finally adopted by a mission family and within a year she had become tidy and clean, had learned to read and write English fluently, and could perform many domestic duties. "Indian children are universally quick in perception," Bishop noted in concluding this happy anecdote, "and when the mind is *thoroughly enlisted,* they make rapid advances in any course of improvement." Like many of her white neighbors, Bishop believed the Indian could make great strides if only he would give up his blanket and cut his hair. Occasionally, however, she showed a streak of compassion for the tribes who were obliged to retreat from the land that had once been theirs. One of her poems concerns an Indian man of "proud and majestic mien" whom she had seen standing alone on a bluff:

> The pale faces come, so potent in skill!
>   His own race were dwindling away;
> The remnant doomed, how brief the hour,
>   They might on their hunting-ground stay.
> And sadly, oh sadly, his spirit was stirred,
>   For life was bereft of its charms —
> Since these flower-clad plains and crested bluffs
>   Were marked for the white man's farms.[25]

But her sympathy vanished completely when the Sioux Uprising of 1862 took place. The revolt was brutal, and so were the government's reprisals. Bishop was horrified and minced no words in her book, *Dakota War Whoop,* published in 1864: "above the shrieks and groans of their victims rose the terrible war whoop of the government-pampered Dakotas, furious from a taste of blood, and panting for more." Bishop dismissed the possibility that the Indians had been wronged — their lands taken, annuity payments delayed, food supplies withheld. Good Victorian that she was, she believed the government had spoiled the Indians, not oppressed them. In her view they were at fault for refusing to take advantage of the opportunities generously offered by the white man's government. Perhaps it is too much to expect that a woman bred in nineteenth-century American society could understand the values of another culture. Certainly Harriet Bishop did not.[26]

Although Bishop expressed herself freely on any number of issues she believed important, she was notably reticent about her own personal life. A mature woman of "marriageable age" when she arrived in St. Paul, she was described by a contemporary as tall and comely, with a good figure and a bright expressive face. Earnest, decided in manner, and quick in speech, she had a bus-

tling, businesslike air and seemed always in a hurry. Until late
in life she wore her hair in curls that made her look much
younger than she really was.[27]

Frontier schoolteachers were expected to marry eventually and
exert their influence through the normal course of family life, "for
it is believed that in all cases, the schoolroom is the truest avenue
to domestic happiness."[28] This formula almost worked for Bishop.
About three years after her arrival in St. Paul she became engaged
to a young lawyer named James K. Humphrey, who was eight
years her junior and, according to friends, not her equal intellectually. During one whole summer — probably that of 1850 though
the date is uncertain — the couple made plans for a fall wedding.
Humphrey built a cottage, Bishop completed her trousseau, and
all went smoothly. Then Humphrey's sister, Stella Selby, returning from a trip to the East, forbade the alliance on the grounds that
Harriet was too old for her brother. The prospective bridegroom,
either weak-willed or not very deeply in love, broke the engagement.[29]

According to the one account that survives of this romance,
Bishop was overwhelmed by disappointment, and left Minnesota
Territory for an unknown destination in November, 1850. It is un-
clear where she went or when she returned, but the following
summer found her again involved in church affairs. She did not
return to teaching. Seven years later — hardly on the rebound —
she married John McConkey, a harnessmaker and widower with
four children. The marriage was unhappy and after nine years it
was legally dissolved in March, 1867, on the grounds that McConkey was a habitual drunkard who treated his wife inhumanely. At
the age of fifty Bishop resumed her maiden name, although she
continued to preface it with "Mrs."

Because Bishop never wrote about her private life, it is difficult
to judge the effects of these unhappy romances. A friend and contemporary claimed that her life was ruined by the love affair with
Humphrey and "she seemed to lose her fine mental balance," but
neither her community life nor her writings indicate that she suffered from a broken heart. All her published work was completed
between 1857 and 1869, and little of it suggested that she was
unhappy. Instead, it displayed an optimistic attitude toward life in
Minnesota. Her first book, *Floral Home*, was a kind of travelogue,
an attempt to sell Minnesota to easterners: "I have known Minnesota from its infancy, and have loved it as a parent does a child,

till my very being is entwined with her interests; and to me it is fit
for a paradise. Come to Minnesota, but bring with you principles
firm and unyielding." Her preferences were all western, she
wrote, and nothing could induce her to return to the East. She
even admired the climate of Minnesota, which she called one of
its greatest attractions. "For healthfulness it is unsurpassed. . . .
The atmosphere is bracing, exhilarating, invigorating, and
pure." She admitted that in winter the "extremities do occasionally suffer the bitings of frost," but this was because one was
"scarcely sensible of cold" in the dry atmosphere. There was no
need to suffer if one were well prepared for the season.[30]

Bishop often reflected upon the wisdom of her decision to go to
Minnesota and the sense of satisfaction she gained from her accomplishments there. She never lost the belief that her life had
been shaped by noble ideals and that she had fulfilled them: "The
true secret of happiness is to live for the good of the world and the
glory of God, making the best of whatever trials and privations
betide. No where is there a more favorable field for the cultivation
of a spirit to be useful, and to accommodate oneself to circumstances, than upon the frontier of a new and sparsely populated
region."[31]

She died in 1883 of "general asthenia" at the age of sixty-one.[32]
By that time she was almost unknown in the burgeoning city of St.
Paul. Schoolhouses dotted the state, numerous schoolteachers had
arrived, there were two fledgling normal schools, and many more
textbooks than the few that Harriet Bishop had carried with her on
her mission into the wilderness.

Harriet Bishop's place in history is small but significant. In her
strengths and weaknesses she displayed the fervor of nineteenth-
century moral reform and the important role of women in advancing
it. Nearly every major reform movement of the period received her
attention — religious benevolence, the improvement of education,
temperance, and equal suffrage. The one major issue of the day
upon which she was silent was slavery. Perhaps she did not feel
its effects on the Minnesota frontier.

Her writings are useful historical documents, reflecting the concerns of an intelligently aware and socially conscious woman coming to grips with a pioneer environment. As literary works they
are unimportant; as history they are biased. But they remind us
that Harriet Bishop fell into another category typical of many
middle-class females of her day — that of the "scribbling women"

who devoted themselves to prose and poetry that often revealed more soul than talent.[33]

Bishop is chiefly remembered for establishing the first public school and the first Sunday school in St. Paul. In many ways, however, these achievements were less important historically than what she stood for. With her strength and energy, her high moral purpose — and her narrow-mindedness — she personified a whole generation of women who sought to fulfill their own manifest destiny within the "Cult of True Womanhood" and the precepts of a white Christian civilization.[34]

2. KATE DONNELLY versus the Cult of True Womanhood

By Gretchen Kreuter

ONE OF THE MOST colorful and ambitious figures of Minnesota's early history was Ignatius Donnelly, who came to be known as the "Sage of Nininger." From the first days of statehood to the turn of the twentieth century Donnelly pursued a half-dozen careers that took him from civilized Philadelphia to pioneer Minnesota, from respectable Republicanism to agrarian radicalism, from farming to Shakespearean scholarship.

In 1895, however, the sage sat down at his desk in Nininger, Minnesota, to write a memoir of his wife of forty years who had died a year earlier. The book was called simply *In Memoriam: Mrs. Katharine Donnelly,* and in its pages Ignatius recorded the bittersweet memories of his spouse, the mother of his three surviving children, his companion through a dozen political campaigns. He set forth her noble qualities so that they might never be forgotten. She was, he recalled, always happy and cheerful, but above all he wished to chronicle "her magnificent *goodness.*" When he first took her to Minnesota, the condition of the Catholic church there was pitiful and its missionary priests "inefficient or worse," but she had succeeded in uplifting them. She formed a Sunday school and a church choir in Hastings. She awarded trinkets, religious tokens, and books to her pupils to encourage them in the ways of righteousness. When illness struck the community, she served the sick with the "physician's instinct." In time of trouble she was everyone's counselor. When she visited Washington as the wife of young Congressman Donnelly, she was "the center of the choicest social groups." [1]

She had a beautiful voice with a three-octave range, Ignatius fondly recalled, and "mingled the simplest household duties with bursts of triumphant song." Had he done wrong to gather such an

artist into his home? he asked rhetorically. No indeed. She chose
to abandon a musical career, for she was without vanity or ambition. "She would rather listen to the crooning of her children on
her knee than win the thunderous plaudits of swarming theatres." [2]

After describing these virtues, and a few chaste incidents from
their early married life, the bereaved husband shifted at once to
Kate's final illness and the deathbed scene, in which she displayed the courage, modesty, and forbearance that had characterized her whole life.

Donnelly's contemporaries who read *In Memoriam* probably
found the book's descriptions familiar indeed, because those qualities illustrated the literary and moral conventions of the "Cult of
True Womanhood." [3] Through most of the nineteenth century
popular magazines and gift books, platform orators and pulpit sa-
vants from shore to shore preached the doctrine of the True
Woman. Piety, purity, domesticity, and submissiveness were her
distinguishing characteristics, and these were the qualities Ignatius declared most distinctive in his departed wife: the piety
that led her to establish Sunday schools in the wilderness; the purity that inspired her to reform the lives of dissolute missionaries;
the joy in domesticity that made her prefer the gurgling of an infant to the applause of music lovers, and the submissiveness that
kept her cheerful in the face of her husband's reverses, family
hardships, and ultimately her own impending demise. The qualities
Ignatius chose to admire in his deceased wife exemplified a Middle
Western variety of Victorian morality, a middle-class notion of
what was proper for women, and an idealized conception of the
female.

They did not, however, sound much like Kate. Perhaps she was
indeed pious and pure, but if piety meant a constant attention to
religious duties and if purity indicated an unwillingness to talk
about "delicate" matters, she was neither. Domesticity, it is true,
was her chief interest, but she was unsentimental about the traditional joys of family life. She did not like Christmas dinner "in the
family way," she observed after one holiday spent among a crowd
of relatives: the tables were all pushed together, no one had
enough room, and everybody got cold food. [4]

As for scorning the world's applause, her letters to Ignatius
suggest otherwise. "I sang . . . *magnificently,*" she wrote him
proudly after she had taken part in a funeral service in Philadelphia. After it was over, "every one was speaking of the singing."

Less than a week later she sang in public again — "it was a very grand occasion & I sang equal to it," she informed her husband.[5] She continued to perform for many years in Philadelphia, Washington, and St. Paul, and she never told Ignatius she sounded anything less than splendid.

In the matter of submissiveness it is hard to see how even her grieving husband could have used that term to describe his wife. Kate McCaffrey Donnelly was not the submissive type! She seldom concealed her hatreds and jealousies, nor did she turn the other cheek. She despised her mother-in-law for years and had no hesitation about telling Ignatius so: "the more I hear & know of her — the less do I desire any further acquaintance." She regularly let Donnelly know what was wrong with his political speeches: his Fourth of July oration "was too far fetched & too infidel," she wrote him in 1859. "Why don't you fellows harp more upon the '*free soil*' question than waste your time in talking foreigner & Catholic business — '*free soil*' is what the west will swallow." Once, when he sent her some of his poetry, she called it "*slop*" and urged him not to publish it. "You will yet be very much ashamed [of] it," she concluded.[6]

Far from being preoccupied with the ideal and the spiritual, Kate constantly reminded Ignatius of the stern realities of life — especially those that had to do with money. When he was nominated for lieutenant governor of Minnesota in 1859, she was pleased, but she asked at once, "give me particulars concerning the salary . . . money is my weak point." When Ignatius was renominated for Congress in 1864, Kate wrote that little Iggy had jumped for joy at the news, clapped his hands and cried out, " 'Now . . . papa will get lots of money.' " She noted wryly, "your innocent child looks with a practical eye to your great honors — which side of the family does he take the trait from[?]"[7]

Kate McCaffrey Donnelly was born in Philadelphia in 1833 of Irish stock. She began teaching at sixteen, and when Donnelly married her in September, 1855, she was a school principal. Even in his True Womanhood eulogy, Ignatius described some jolly, undignified times she had had with her pupils — she went sledding with them in the winter, he wrote, without losing their respect.[8]

Ignatius' mother disapproved of the match, and for fifteen years the two women did not speak. Kate missed no opportunity to put down her mother-in-law and, for that matter, all of Ignatius' female

Kate Donnelly

relatives: "your confounded mother & sisters are perfect asses," Kate observed, when she learned that the elder Mrs. Donnelly had brought "her two marketable daughters down to Cape May — determined to push them off her hands . . . in all cases using your name as a herald of herself." The daughters were giving nightly concerts at hotels on the cape. "Your sisters sing to show off their ugly selves & their eggregious [*sic*] vanity," Kate wrote. "The audience pay nothing to hear them — & go to make fun of them — & to conjecture," she continued, twisting the knife a bit, "if it is not the same brass that has thrust you forward in the world." [9]

Ignatius was a lawyer when he married Kate and he wanted to be rich and famous. A trip west in the 1850s had persuaded him that fortunes and reputations could be quickly made there. Arriving in Minnesota with his new bride — "Wifey," he always called her — he found the area in the midst of an economic boom. He formed a partnership with John Nininger for the development of a townsite south of St. Paul. "Two heads are better than one," Kate observed, "even if one should be a 'Sour Kraut' " — Nininger's ancestry was German — "and the other a 'Paddy.' " [10]

At twenty-six Donnelly was briefly a millionaire. Then the Panic

of 1857 struck, ruining his town of Nininger and leaving him heavily burdened with debts. Fortunes were as easily lost as made in
those days, but young Ignatius was resilient. He turned his town
lots into wheat fields, built his residence at Nininger, and ever
afterward considered himself a farmer. A few months after this
conversion, believing his grasp of his new occupation adequate,
he lectured before the Dakota County Agricultural Society on
the significance of agriculture.[11]

Kate, however, found him an indifferent farmer and often a non-
resident one. Frequently left to deal with farm matters herself, she
quite unsubmissively reminded him of his neglected duties. She
sometimes informed Ignatius of agricultural problems that needed
public attention: "do something — about this freight matter," she
urged him in 1861. "Write an article & get it in one of the papers.
The Prairie du Chien & La Crosse lines in opposition to one
another take grain from Hastings at 5 cts per bush & charge all
other places from *St. Paul down* 12 cts." [12]

When domestic drudgery at Nininger was compounded by the
illness of both herself and the children, she was not above writing
her husband in the martyr's mode: "As I had no help to do the
work for me I could not take your advice about the complexion &
hands & have them now in such a state that I do not suppose you
will want me. The rain has made the work very hard to do but as
you insisted upon it — I thought it would not do to postpone it
until you could come home & do it." Usually her style was more
forthright. When Ignatius, newly elected to the national House of
Representatives, proposed bringing some of his colleagues out to
Nininger for summer visits, Kate put her foot down: "I am not
going . . . to make a slave of myself for all the Congressmen in
Washington." [13]

Ignatius was far more a politician than a country boy, and his
ambitions were not extinguished by the Panic of 1857. The first
elective post he sought was the lieutenant governorship of the
new state of Minnesota, and Kate, although uneasy about the
financial uncertainties of an officeholder's career, encouraged him.
Like any good nineteenth-century wife, she assured him he was
destined for "great parts in the drama of life," but added, that if all
did not go well, "wifey & you will have a good time studying
economy." [14]

Kate kept a sense of detachment and humor during the hullabal-
loo of political campaigning. In 1862 she accompanied Ignatius to

a Fourth of July celebration where he was the featured speaker. Later she described the pomp and ceremony involved: Their carriage was preceded by marshals in uniform and followed by a band in a wagon; ahead, two hundred mounted men "opened a line & saluted as we passed through." And, she wrote, "I almost bit my lips off to preserve a proper dignified composure." [15]

Ignatius' political campaigns and offices made for long separations from his wife and children. These were never easy for Kate. "Do you miss . . . your own bedfellow[?]" she characteristically inquired. Occasionally she grew desperate awaiting his return. The Sioux Uprising of 1862, though it occurred far from Nininger, unnerved her. "I have been trying to be courageous," she wrote, "[but] it seems to be reaching a crisis with me. . . . I am downright sick & feel that it is impossible to stay here in this state any longer. . . . So do come if but for a day." [16]

"Everything going right," Ignatius replied cheerfully from the state capital to her entreaty. The legislation he had backed, enabling soldiers to vote before they left for the battlefield, "will place my election beyond doubt." [17]

A woman, Kate declared after another month of Ignatius' absence, should have two husbands — one to stay at home while the other was away; but she quickly added, "I could find plenty of reasons why women should have two [spouses] but none for men to have more than one." When Kate discovered that her husband had asked his cousin Mary what his wife had been doing on a trip to Hastings, she replied with indignation, "how dare you pimp after me." [18]

After his term as lieutenant governor, Ignatius Donnelly ran successfully for Congress on the Republican ticket. He served in the House of Representatives from 1863 to 1869 through some of the most tempestuous days of the Civil War and Reconstruction. Kate chose not to accompany her husband to Washington. They could not afford a second home, nor could she abandon a mother's duty and leave the children behind while she went to the capital during legislative sessions.[19] Instead, she moved to Philadelphia where she lived with her own family and avoided at least some of the hardships of Congressman Donnelly's absences.

The situation was not ideal. "Five weeks are elapsed since I saw your dear fat face," she wrote, "and if you do not come this week I will surely elope with some one." Her spunky wit, however, was not impaired: "I am afraid people will commence to think you are larking it in Washington and keeping out of your wife[']s way. If *I* thought so — you would see a stout substantial looking person — take the next train for Baltimore. . . . But I have every confidence in my own superior attraction, & don't think it possible that any one could take my place." When, on one occasion, Ignatius' return to his family was delayed by an invitation to the White House, Kate wrote ironically: "you have *honored* the Lincolns — I suppose you had to *notice* them — well I hope it will be for the best — but really they are the *kind* of *people one would scarcely desire in one's sett* [*sic*]. You poor little modest man — how did you behave yourself in company[?]" [20]

As the Civil War continued, new problems troubled Kate. In an age when the rate of infant mortality was high and a childhood ailment might last for months, she was always concerned about the health of her children. Her anxiety mounted when three-year-old Elizabeth sickened and died in January, 1864.[21] The illness, she thought, was some sort of dysentery, and the other Donnelly children also suffered from it for many weeks. Kate believed the war had increased the prevalence of infectious diseases. Philadelphia was filled with Union soldiers newly released from hospitals or strolling about in hopes that fresh air would aid their recuperation. "Of course so much putridity causes a great deal of disease," she observed shortly after Elizabeth died. "Years ago — chills & fever were unheard of in a city like this — yet I have heard of a great many cases of it." She thought that a "very fatal" epidemic of "spotted fever" going around Philadelphia could be traced to the woolen factories where cloth for army uniforms was made, and she urged Ignatius to stay away from places where there were soldiers about.[22]

Not always taking her own advice, she went to sing at the Christian Street Hospital in Philadelphia, where hundreds of Civil War amputees were being treated. "There was not one in the place with two legs," she reported. "It was awful." [23]

Political fevers were also widespread as wartime passions raged throughout the United States. At first Kate did not take the heightened conflicts seriously. "I noticed a motto passing the house," she wrote during the election campaign of 1864, "' 'Death to traitors' it seemed like a joke to me." She soon learned that the slogan was meant to be taken seriously as prowar and antiwar factions struggled within and between the two major parties. As election day neared, a mob of Republicans disrupted a Democratic parade in Philadelphia. Two men were killed in the ensuing fracas. "Politics *locally* here are matters in which men are the tests not principles," she concluded. "I would be a Demo[crat] in this city without taking the interests of the nation at large to heart."[24]

She never discussed in her letters what those interests might be, never commented upon the larger purposes of the Civil War. After two years of Union reverses she grew mistrustful when optimistic reports of Northern victories were disseminated in the press.[25]

Ignatius became associated with the Radical Republicans and, in the early years of Reconstruction, enlisted on the side of civil rights for the freedmen. Though he changed many of his political ideas over the years, he never retreated from his advocacy of full civil and political rights for blacks. Kate did not think the black minority of Minnesota repaid this loyalty. "Damn the colored," she wrote in 1869. "Not one word about your services to them — still unrecognized."[26]

Local politicians in Minnesota mistrusted Donnelly and denied him not only a fourth term in the House, but also the Republican party's nomination for the Senate in 1868. Out of office in 1869 his thoughts turned once more to possibilities for great wealth, and he became a lobbyist for Jay Cooke, banker and financier. While Kate remained in Nininger, Donnelly, in the guise of Washington correspondent for the *St. Paul Dispatch*, went back to the capital to lobby for the passage of land-grant legislation. A man returning to Washington society after his official career has ended feels like a ghost coming back to earth, he told Kate. "He sees new people going through the same round of eating, drinking, joking, dressing, striving, which he and his went through, and he is painfully impressed with the hollowness and unreality of the whole thing."[27]

His lobbying was unsuccessful, his dreams of riches slipped once more out of reach, and he returned to Minnesota. Over the years Kate responded to these reverses with a mixture of encouragement, critical reflection, and cautionary advice. When Ignatius toured the Mississippi River towns in 1866 attacking President Andrew Johnson before enthusiastic crowds, Kate told him to tone down his behavior. "It is too bombastic . . . you are loosing your modesty cloak," she warned. When Alexander Ramsey emerged as Donnelly's bitter opponent after his try for the Senate in 1868, Kate's temper was up: "Beat him no matter what happens — he would break the party to break you — in this case party be hanged — I would stand at nothing to defeat him." When a for-

merly pro-Donnelly newspaper turned against Ignatius in 1869,
Kate wrote indignantly, "The Winona paper must be sick over its
own vomit — how can men do such things[?]" Three months later
she concluded that newspaper correspondents were "almost all
black mailers." Then turning to her husband's prose she told him
in 1870, "Your letter about Washington society &c was flatter than
a pan cake." On these occasions, his wife was not quite so happy,
jovial, and cheerful as Ignatius later remembered her.[28]

During the 1860s Kate Donnelly was beset by various physical
problems that weakened her carefree joviality. She described her
ailments to Ignatius in detail that was, if not clinical, at least vivid
and by Victorian standards indelicate. In the summer of 1864, a
few months after Elizabeth's death, she was pregnant with a child
that died *in utero* but was not expelled. "You know my disposition[,] I hate to give up anything I once get hold of," Kate wrote.
After another month of discomfort and various diagnoses from her
doctor, she began to hemorrhage — "I was flowing like a
hydrant" — and after another three weeks went into labor and
miscarried. She described the fetus: "The head was large the body
long & slender rather shrunken but in no way decayed — around
the neck there was a black & green line — the tongue was rather
large and protruded a little — maybe it was strangled by the um-
bilical cord."[29]

All this occurred amidst preparations for moving to a different
house in Philadelphia, and while the children had severe cases of
whooping cough. But none of it prevented Kate from complaining
about Ignatius' relatives and her own financial embarrassments, or
from entreating him for minor political favors on behalf of friends.
After the miscarriage Kate bore no more children. She seems to
have suffered continuous abdominal problems. Her physician advised surgery to remove uterine polyps, and in 1870 she underwent several operations from which she apparently never fully
recovered.[30]

In the 1870s Ignatius Donnelly left the Republican party and
became successively a Liberal Republican, a Granger, and a
Greenbacker. He served for several years in the Minnesota Senate
and sponsored, with only moderate success, an array of legislation
designed to benefit the farmer. In 1878 he made another effort to
return to Congress, this time as a Greenback Democrat, but was

unsuccessful. All the while Kate kept up a flow of advice about both home responsibilities and politics. No longer did she look with amused detachment upon the hoopla of political campaigning. Get your posters up, she urged, as he set out on the hustings as a third-party candidate, otherwise "your appointments are not known as they should be — and you have not the regular newspaper channel." She reminded him grimly, "There [are] no friendships but those of interest and success *only* makes friends." [31]

"We are five days behind all our neighbors cutting grain," she reported from Nininger in 1878 while Ignatius was thinking about becoming a congressional candidate again. "The Globe has something about your being a candidate. . . . If they want you let it be at *their expense* not *yours* & [let them] show they are willing to help you." [32]

In 1884 a similar effort by Ignatius to run as a Democratic and Farmers' Alliance candidate was greeted with similar bluntness by his wife: "*Do not* lose your head[.] Remember [Horace B.] Strait [your opponent] has money — owns Scott county — the district cut out to beat Donnelly, strongly Norwegian — And when Presidential voting arrives — party lines will be drawn & these very fellows who are wanting you now will go back on you." She had done a little research on the matter: "Strait I see voted for the Morrison Tariff bill & that is capital for him. Look over the Spofford Almanac for 1884 & see the vote last Presidential year[.] Look well before you leap. . . . Tell Emma she can[']t afford to sell eggs just now as she will need them to keep for hatching." [33]

In her political commentary Kate Donnelly almost always concerned herself with strategy and tactics, not issues. With considerable accuracy, she saw the same forces at work whether the politics concerned Democrats, Republicans, Greenbackers, Alliance men, or Populists. When Ignatius did hold political offices, Kate made an occasional request for patronage for some relative, friend, or acquaintance. "Did you get Johnson[']s daughter her clerkship[?] — you know it is of more importance to get your own county folks what they desire than St Paul people," she wrote in 1891. She claimed that she did not discuss politics socially, unless someone else started it: "Some people attack me purposely (*men* always) on account of your opinions. I never open such a subject myself & wait with patience till it becomes almost insulting & when thoroughly roused I am overwhelming." She never felt it necessary to stay mute on political matters nor allow her immersion in domesticity to keep her uninformed about practical politics.[34]

Domesticity did, however, take its toll. For forty years Kate was deeply involved in the joys and sorrows of nineteenth-century family life. Sometimes she was anxious about the possibility of an unwanted pregnancy: "I have *not* received that visit & I fear — I fear — I fear — more than ever it will just break my heart to wean my poor baby. . . . it is now a week over time & no symptoms yet," Kate wrote in 1861. There were the frequent and often unfamiliar illnesses that beset children in a new land: meningitis appeared in Nininger in the winter of 1870. "I am frightened about it," Kate confided to Ignatius. "I will telegraph the instant any symptom comes in my family." When Elizabeth died, Kate mourned that she could not even visit her daughter's grave for a time, because she had to care for the children who remained. Kate, after her own offspring were grown, assisted at the birth of grandchildren, cared for nieces and nephews when their parents were ill, and comforted aged relatives. "I am getting old[,] daddy[,] & I miss you greatly," she wrote sadly to Ignatius in 1890, during a particularly trying visit to Philadelphia. "If I was very rich I could make things more tolerable but always to find so much trouble & the means to alleviate so far off, makes me want to hide away in a corner of the world."[35]

She never did, of course. She remained full of spunk and advice. The same letter included several pages of studied political commentary dealing with the forthcoming state auditor's race in Minnesota and what Ignatius and the Farmers' Alliance ought to do about it. "Threaten no one. Act cautiously & secure *yourself* first, for on that depends the rest." Her earthy frankness was unimpaired. After describing a gruesome operation her daughter had undergone, she reported she was so upset by it that "my bowels have been going for five days."[36]

And she continued to look after Ignatius' interests. The elusive prosperity they had sought for so many years finally came to the Donnellys in the 1880s, not from politics or business but from literature and oratory. He wrote several books that brought him wide attention and considerable royalties. Kate, in Philadelphia on a visit, was indignant to find that one of his works, *The Great Cryptogram*, was on sale at a reduced price. She reported this atrocity to Ignatius, but urged, "I want you to keep cool & do nothing for

the present. I am going there [*to Wanamakers*] & I am going to
find out how many they have had."[37] She had fought a harsh climate, a rude land, indigence, and infectious diseases, but she still
had enough zest to rail against the publisher's remaindering of her
husband's book.

The 1890s brought Ignatius into the political limelight again,
this time as a founder of the Populist party. He ran unsuccessfully
for governor of Minnesota on the Populist ticket in 1892, when he
was sixty-one. By this time Kate was in failing health. In June,
1894, after a series of strokes that left her partially paralyzed, she
suffered a fatal one. She was sixty-one. A year later Ignatius began
to write the little book, *In Memoriam*, which turned out to be such
a fond but inaccurate description of his wife.[38]

It would be a mistake to think that *In Memoriam* was a reflection of what he wished his wife had been, or of his view of women
in general. Highly idiosyncratic himself, Ignatius took pleasure in
his wife's strong-mindedness. Occasionally he even sought her
advice, though he did not always take it. When he thought his
Senate nomination a sure thing in 1868 — he was nearly always
more optimistic than she about such events — he wrote her, "keep
up a brave heart and *you* shall be Senator yet."[39]

He was not intimidated by her frequent advice and criticism.
When, for example, she flew into a rage because several hens had
starved on their nests through his neglect, he replied jovially that
it was splendid to learn she was in good health — her capacity to
scold proved it. "I knew that if ill you would fall into the tender
and the sentimental."[40]

The rhetoric of their correspondence was flavored far more by
the Battle of the Sexes than by the conventions of the Cult of True
Womanhood. He twitted her about her need for new corsets and
her desire to conceal her age. For one birthday he sent her a
prayer book, saying, "With great delicacy I left blank the number
of your birth day, so that you could fill it in as you saw fit." She
received the gift with good humor: "I cannot fill up the *blank* in
the front page with propriety as it is a holy book & warns us
against deceptions."[41]

Ignatius fell away from Catholicism early in his life, but Kate
remained in the church. He was not above teasing her for her religious convictions. After he had been to hear a "Spiritualist Lec-
turess" he wrote that she had revealed "a great deal of feminine

eloquence — long interminable involuted sentences — full of
poetry and flowers and fire works — with a great deal about your
old friend the Pope of Rome. . . . You . . . would have enjoyed
it, especially if you could have been allowed the privilege of pull-
ing her hair afterward." He concluded, "She is a mighty smart
woman."[42]

Through the years Ignatius saved clippings on nearly all aspects
of the women's rights movement. Fragmentary essays, never published, on "Marriage" and "The Woman Question" are included
in his diaries. He read John Stuart Mill's essay on the subjection of
women and made notes on it. When in 1869 a New York convention of the People's Industrial Order reported on the condition of
women workers, Donnelly took notes on that too. He was interested in the common law disabilities of married women, and he
saved a clipping from "A Lady Correspondent" criticizing the
double standard of morality. He mused upon the "fact" that, in
proportion to their numbers, far more queens than kings were distinguished.[43]

When he set down his own thoughts on the "Woman Question,"
they emerged as a combination of what feminists today would
consider liberal and conservative ideas. "I do not think women are
ready for the ballot," he wrote, "but 'the pear is ripening
rapidly.'" He did not believe that women would be degraded by
politics: "Women attend our political meetings in the West in
great numbers," and "I never heard it alleged that they were cor-
rupted or depraved thereby." But he also spoke of women's conversation as mostly "mere chit-chat and gossip," and of the need to
elevate their minds.[44] He was interested enough in the subject of
women to begin an essay on the topic, but not sufficiently absorbed to finish it. His manuscript soon wandered off onto hard
money, tariffs, and tree planting — other subjects in which he considered himself ahead of his time.

Kate Donnelly, so far as is known, never set down her views on
the "Woman Question" or the New Woman of the late nineteenth
century. On the contrary, she once wrote, "My great regret is that
my life is frittered away in minor matters & I have not time
enough to give my own children." But that remark was designed,
at least in part, to tug at Ignatius' conscience. She pursued a modest singing career and, during the early years of the Civil War, did
volunteer work sewing shirts for Union soldiers. It is perhaps
more interesting that she sometimes imagined herself in office or

on the public platform — always as a jest but never as an absurdity. "What office are you going to get me!!!" she asked Ignatius in 1864 when she told him how nobly she had defended his interests. And in 1870 after hearing about the lecturer Kate Field, she told Ignatius she was thinking of embarking on the lecture circuit herself — then told him to do so.[45]

She was quick to chastise her husband when she thought he ridiculed women or subscribed to the double standard. For example, she complained of an analogy he had made in a speech: "I do not think you should have said 'there are bad women — therefore do away with women' — it is a vulnerable point for ridicule. . . . You might more appropriately speak of men — it takes two to make a bargain."[46]

In her whole life she repudiated some common stereotypes about what women were or should be. She had no independent reputation except as the wife of a public man, but in her letters she left a record of an articulate, witty, and irrepressible personality who defied ordinary categories of description. It was not her fault that after her death bereavement caused her unconventional husband to fall into the conventions of the Cult of True Womanhood.

If he had wanted others to understand a little better what Kate was really like, he might have printed the last quatrain from the Valentine she sent to him in 1870:

> Look on her, and behold your heart's delight
> In the full bloom of lasting *Twenty-Nine* —
> Your little Hero of a hundred Fights,
> Your cherished Wife, your charming Valentine![47]

3. JANE GREY SWISSHELM
Marriage and Slavery

By Abigail McCarthy

IT IS STRANGE that the name of Jane Grey Swisshelm (1815–84) is not a household word in Minnesota or in the nation in this decade of the new feminism. When Jane Swisshelm arrived in Minnesota Territory on June 22, 1857, she was in her early forties and one of the best-known women in the United States. For more than ten years she had been the editor of the *Pittsburgh Saturday Visiter*, a leading liberal newspaper that "had thousands of readers scattered over every State and Territory in the nation, in England and the Canadas." Her ability as writer and journalist was such that Horace Greeley had employed her as Washington correspondent for the *New York Tribune*. A dispatch she wrote for him was credited with ending Daniel Webster's hopes for nomination to the presidency in 1852. She has been described as an abolitionist, a feminist, and a reconstructionist, but her talents and interests were so varied that she does not fit neatly into any one category.[1]

Although she went to Minnesota with her six-year-old daughter in search of health and peace — "the tyrannies of an unhappy marriage, endured for almost twenty years, had left her weary and ill" — she soon took on the editorship of the *St. Cloud Visiter*, which quickly became as well known as her first paper. Within a decade she herself was known as the mother of the Republican party in the West.[2]

At the very beginning of her Minnesota years, she challenged Sylvanus B. Lowry, a sympathizer with the slave states and the Democratic political "dictator" of central Minnesota. Her victory in the struggle with him was the beginning of the decline of his power. Thereafter, Mrs. Swisshelm, as a writer and lecturer, praised, scolded, mothered, and guided the citizens of Minnesota until 1865. She was enthusiastic about her adopted home and aware of its possibilities. She did much to shape Minnesota's political direction in those formative years. During the Civil War she went to Washington to strengthen eastern sentiment for severe punishment of the Indians after the Sioux War of 1862. As a friend of Secretary of War Edwin M. Stanton and, later, of Mrs. Lincoln, she was close to the center of events. She was a volunteer Civil War nurse and an effective critic of the hospital service. At the end of her public career, she was one of the first women to work in government — as an employee of the War Department. Few women today can claim an equal influence on the course of the United States.[3]

Hers is in every way a woman's story. Contemporaries described her as a woman of "slight figure, of less than medium height, with pleasant face, eyes beaming with kindliness, soft voice, and winning manners." And also as "quite a Jenny Lind in appearance . . . with an unusual expanse of forehead, dark brown hair, combed over her temples, light blue liquid eyes, nose rather prominent, mouth small and disclosing very fine teeth — countenance pleasing, and smile truly enchanting."[4]

But Sylvanus Lowry, the man she vanquished in the greatest battle of her life, saw behind this beguiling exterior a spirit equal to his own. In the last years of his life he called upon the woman who had brought his career to an abrupt halt. She wrote of this encounter in her autobiography: "'I am the only person who ever understood you,'" he said. "'People now think you go into hospitals from a sense of duty; from benevolence, like those good people who expect to get to heaven by doing disagreeable things on earth; but I know you go because you must; go for your own pleasure; you do not care for heaven or anything else, but yourself.'

"He stopped, looked down, trace the pattern of the carpet with the point of his cane, then raised his head and continued: 'You take care of the sick and wounded, go into all those dreadful places just as I used to drink brandy — for sake of the exhilaration it brings you.'"[5]

It is interesting to note that Jane Swisshelm does not dispute General Lowry's assertion. In fact she says, "I was more than ever impressed by the genuine greatness of the man, who had been degraded by the use of irresponsible power." In her heart she must have recognized the truth of his assessment.[6]

In the paradox apparent in these descriptions of Mrs. Swisshelm
by men who knew her lies the whole problem of woman's history.
Because of her physical appearance, her biology, if you will, it
seems impossible for historians — even women historians — to
deal with her personhood. It seems extremely difficult for them to
believe that the rage for identity and accomplishment which
characterizes Western man should be part of Western woman as
well. It has been the easy course to ascribe any evidence of this
fact to masculinity; indeed, one of Jane Swisshelm's admirers says
of her, "What was masculine was her intellect and courage." [7]

One of the calmest assessments of what it is to be a woman is to
be found in her own autobiography, *Half a Century.* Jane Grey
Swisshelm's feminism was a by-product of her life. In her early
years of adulthood she was careful to distinguish herself from the
doctrinaire feminists of her day. When she wrote her autobiography, *Half a Century,* published in 1880, she listed as her reasons
for doing so: one, the desire to give the inside history of "the great
Abolition war"; two, a desire "to give an inside history of the hospitals during the war of the Rebellion"; and only third, "to give an
analysis of the ground which produced the Woman's Rights agitation, and the causes which limited its influence." To the reader
today, however, her fourth objective is closely allied to the third.
It was, she said, "to illustrate the force of education and the muta-
bility of human character" by means of a personal narrative — her
own.[8]

In 1836, she tells us, like most of the women of her time, she
would rather "have broken an engagement" than "permit her
name to appear in print, even in the announcement of marriage."
By 1850 she "had as much newspaper notoriety as any man of that
time, and was singularly indifferent to the praise or blame of the
Press." In 1837 she could not "break the seal of silence set upon
her lips by 'Inspiration,'" — by which, of course, she meant the
admonition of Paul in the New Testament that women be silent in
the churches — "even so far as to pray with a man dying of in-
temperance, and who yet, in 1862, addressed the Minnesota Senate in session, and as many others as could be packed in the hall,
with no more embarrassment than though talking with a friend in
a chimney corner."

Her autobiography is a remarkable chronicle of one woman's
liberation. The vehicles of that liberation seem to have been, by

Jane Grey Swisshelm

the author's account, an extraordinary sense of selfhood and God-given gifts, a strong sisterhood among the women of her family and friends, the relative freedom of pioneer life for women, and, strange as it may seem, her religious convictions. The obstacles to that liberation were the age-old condition of woman, law and the institution of marriage, and, again, paradoxically, her religion. The catalysts in the struggle were slavery and the Abolition movement.

It is strange that so few of Jane Swisshelm's biographers have commented on the fact that she showed unusual intelligence and precocity in learning. Her autobiography begins with her first memory of her consciousness of herself as self. She remembered that she was sitting under a blossoming apple tree on a beautiful day with a blue sky "over which white clouds scudded away toward the great hills." She was at that time only two and a half years old. Yet she could, she says, already read and sew, say her catechism and prayers. Her second memory is of her awakening to sin. "On a warm summer day, while walking alone on the common which lay between home and Squire Horner's house, I was struck motionless by the thought that I had forgotten God. . . . I

seemed to stand outside, and see myself a mere mite, in a pink
sun-bonnet and white bib, the very chief of sinners, for the probability was I had been thinking of that bonnet and bib." She
thought that this experience occurred in her third summer. Before
the end of her third year, she had learned to read the New Testament and "went regularly to school, where I was kept at the head
of a spelling-class, in which there were grown young men and
women. One of these, Wilkins McNair, used to carry me home,
much amused, no doubt, by my supremacy." [9]

Born on December 6, 1815, at a time when children were
treated like miniature adults, it is apparent from her own comments that Jane Grey Cannon's prowess as a three-year-old must
have been thought striking even then. She also points out what
kind of childhood these memories implied: "To me, no childhood
was possible under the training this indicates, yet in giving that
training, my parents were loving and gentle as they were faithful." [10] It meant also that the mite in the pink sunbonnet was
constantly with the mother and father, who took such great pains
to teach her, and whose conversation with her must have been
precious to the child since she absorbed their religious concerns
so fully and completely.

She was brought up in the newly settled Appalachian region of
western Pennsylvania, then frontier country. Her father and
mother were "both Scotch-Irish and descended from the Scotch
Reformers." Her grandmother, Jane Grey, for whom she was
named, was "of that family which was allied to royalty, and gave to
England her nine days queen." This grandmother must have made
a happy impression upon Jane because, as she said, her
grandmother, a true Calvinist, believed in "the total depravity of
all" but was always doubtful about the "actual transgressions" of
any. [11]

Her childhood was also remarkable in the fearlessness she displayed and the way she seemed to find excitement in life. Much of
this excitement was provided by the church, a fact equally true in
the stern lives of many Presbyterians and Methodists on the frontier. She enjoyed the ceremony which surrounded the Sabbath for
which a great preparation had to be made among people who kept
it so strictly. There were rare outings, to what was called "occasional hearing" at a nearby meeting house, which involved a
two-mile walk, two long sermons, "and in the intermission, a
church sociable, in fact if not in name. Friends who lived twenty

miles apart, met here, exchanged greetings and news, gave notices and invitations, and obeyed the higher law of kindness under protest of their Calvinistic consciences. In this breathing-time we ate our lunch, went to the nearest house and had a drink from the spring which ran through the stone milk-house. It was a day full of sight-seeing and of solemn, grand impressions." [12]

Before Jane was seven her father, who had fallen on evil times, moved the family from Wilkinsburg, the scene of her first memories, back to Pittsburgh. There in 1821 they lived opposite the Trinity Church. The "thickly peopled graveyard" of Trinity and that of adjoining First Presbyterian Church were favorite places for walks, and the children played on the borders outside the fences. Jane heard many tales from her grandmother, and also from an uncle "who delighted in telling us tales of the supernatural" about ghosts. She believed in them implicitly, she said, and was consumed with a desire to see them. When the Trinity graveyard was dug up to provide a foundation for a new church, she heard about the body of a woman who had been buried three years and "found in a wonderful state of preservation, when the coffin was laid open by the diggers. It was left that the friends might remove it, and that night I felt would be the time for ghosts. So I went over alone, and while I crouched by the open grave, peering in, a cloud passed, and the moon poured down a flood of light, by which I could see the quiet sleeper, with folded hands, taking her last, long rest. . . . Earth was far away and heaven near at hand, but no ghost came, and I went home disappointed." [13]

Jane Cannon was tiny and pretty, and accustomed to admiration and success in her early life. (Perhaps the very fact of her tininess and her prettiness made her less the object of envy and more the object of admiration.) After her father's death in 1823, when her mother found it necessary to set the whole family to work to make ends meet — not at all unusual in that time — she had little Jane learn lace making. She was soon so proficient that her mother procured pupils for her to teach, as she tells us, "usually sitting on their knee." Lace work as a "furor" of the time gave way to painting on velvet and this, too, she learned and sold the resulting pictures. When she was sent for six weeks to boarding school, the only possible source of postelementary education for a girl, she was quite evidently the pet of the school, dubbed "Wax Doll" by the other students. When Jane's mother was no longer able to send

her to school, the director offered to furnish board and tuition if
she would teach the little girls. She was then twelve. "I was allowed to amuse myself drawing flowers, which were quite a surprise, and pronounced better than anything the drawing master
could do — to recite poetry, for the benefit of the larger girls, and
to play in the orchard with my pupils." [14]

She was brought home from school because it was feared that
she was in the first stage of tuberculosis, that scourge of America
in the nineteenth century. Her sensible and intelligent mother
brought her back to health by a regimen of light exercise and
dancing and plenty of fresh air, milk, and eggs. By the time she
was fourteen she was again a teacher, operating the only school in
Wilkinsburg, to which the family had returned. In 1830 she taught
seven hours a day and also on Saturday morning, which she devoted to Bible reading and catechism. "I was the first, I believe, in
Allegheny Co., to teach children without beating them. I
abolished corporeal punishment entirely, and was so successful
that boys, ungovernable at home, were altogether tractable. This
life was perfectly congenial, and I followed it for nearly six
years." [15]

Up until her twentieth year Jane Cannon's story was one of
progressive enlightenment, experience, a gradually widening
world, with happy results in work and association at every turn. It
was the story of the development of the potentiality in a human
person. This pleasant progress was soon to change, and that
change brought her into public life.

As an indirect result of her marriage Jane was precipitated
into the forefront of the antislavery struggle. She had been
brought up an abolitionist. The Covenanter church, the branch of
Presbyterianism in which she was raised, had in the year 1800
agreed in synod that slavery and Christianity were incompatible
and had never relaxed the discipline which forbade fellowship
with slaveholders. As a child she had gone about the township
collecting names for a petition to abolish slavery in the District of
Columbia. But it was not until a fierce storm broke in her unhappy
marriage — a storm which caused her severe physical and nervous
breakdown — that she became a public fighter against slavery. Before her illness she saw, "as by a revelation," that the trouble in
her marriage had been sent to her because she had neglected her
mission in life. "Christ's little ones were sick and in prison, and I

had not visited them! . . . I had been false to every principle of justice; had been decorating parlors when I should have been tearing down prisons!" After her illness and the resultant depression had passed, she set to work.[16]

Jane Cannon Swisshelm's marriage on November 18, 1836, has been a puzzle to all her biographers. It was more than the typical misalliance. Jane had woven romantic dreams about James Swisshelm since she was a twelve-year-old. He was the son of a Revolutionary War soldier and prosperous farmer who had owned most of a valley near Wilkinsburg. He had limited education but she thought he had "good abilities."

On the way to boarding school at the age of twelve, she had first met James Swisshelm in what seemed perilous circumstances in which he played an heroic role. A timid and inexpert driver ran the wagon in which the children were riding into a raging river in the dark of night. Out of the darkness had appeared a dark, young, cheerful giant who rescued them. Years later when a stranger was presented to her at a party, Jane recognized her rescuer. Her host "presented a man whose presence made me feel that I was a very little girl and should have been at home. He was over six feet tall, well formed and strongly built, with black hair and eyes, a long face, and heavy black whiskers. He was handsomely dressed, and his manner that of a grave and reverend seignor. A Russian count in a New York drawing room, then, when counts were few, could not have seemed more foreign than this man in that village parlor, less than two miles from the place of his birth. . . . I next saw him on horseback and this man of giant strength in full suit of black, riding a large spirited black horse, became my 'black knight'." [17]

It was not unusual on the frontier for a woman to be better educated and more cultivated than her husband, as in this case. Men were occupied only in subduing the wilderness. Therefore, Jane hoped initially that her husband would remedy his lack of education but she found that, among his other defects, he had no love of books. Moreover, his religion "derided human learning and depended on inspiration." She decided sternly that she must be the mate of the man she had chosen. If he would not come up to her level, she must go to his, so she gave up study and for years did not read any book except the Bible.[18]

A more serious disparity between them lay in religion. Her Presbyterianism with its emphasis on election, on long theological sermons, and logical argument based on the Scripture, was in contrast to his emotional frontier Methodism. Her mother opposed the union, as did his, because of this difference. But he seems to have been most persistent in his suit, promising that they should live apart from his family, that he would never interfere with her rights of conscience, and that he would take or send her to her meeting when possible. "He proposed going up the Allegheny to establish saw-mills, and if I would go into the woods with him, there should be no trouble about religion." Immediately after their marriage he foreswore these promises on what seems very petty grounds: that Jane had offended him by crying while dressing to be married and shedding tears again when she left home. If she cared so little for him, he said, he would not leave his friends and go up the Allegheny with her.[19]

He proposed that she live with his mother, whose farm he managed, and add to the family finances by teaching in a small building on the property. He also announced that she was to "get religion" and preach. John Wesley had called women to the pulpit and in the Methodism of the time, women were still allowed to preach. (It was an interesting *contretemps* with Jane quoting Saint Paul, "Let women keep silence in churches and learn of their husbands at home" against her husband.) She clung to the teaching of her own church. She would not preach, would not live in the house with his mother, and stayed with her own. She continued teaching and taught his two brothers for whom she developed a great affection. She served as teacher, tailor, and dressmaker for her husband's family, she tells us, and he visited her once or twice a week. On these visits he ignored her mother's presence. All this in the first months of marriage! It was a rude awakening from her dreams. Soon afterward, during her mother's long absence on a visit to relatives, he bought a wagonmaker's shop and employed a workman whom he sent to board with Jane at her mother's house. He then fitted up living quarters behind the wagon shop and set Jane up in housekeeping there.[20]

While she was living in this strange way, Jane rediscovered her early talent for painting. A traveling artist visited Wilkinsburg and introduced her to the world of portraiture. She started to paint with whatever materials she had on hand. Bard, the wagonmaker who boarded with her, made her a stretcher and with unbleached muslin, tacks, and white lead, she made canvas. She mixed paints with "lampblack, king's yellow and red lead, with oil and turpentine." It has been pointed out about her later writing that she was uninterested in mere description but excelled in discussing ideas, finding the weak points in argument, and in delineating character. It was her fascination with the latter which seemed at the core of her love of portraiture: "I felt I had found my vocation. What did I care for preachers and theological arguments? What matter who sent me my bread, or whether I had any? What matter for anything, so long as I had a canvas and some paints, with that long perspective of faces and figures crowding up and begging to be painted. . . . I forgot God, and did not know it; forgot philosophy, and did not care to remember it; but alas! I forgot to get Bard's dinner, and, although I forgot to be hungry, I had no reason to suppose he did."[21]

She was overcome by what she saw as a conflict between her art and her duty. And she saw her duty as housekeeping. "I tried to compromise, but experience soon deprived me of that hope, for to paint was to be oblivious of all other things." In retrospect when she was writing her autobiography she saw this as folly. "I put away my brushes; resolutely crucified my divine gift, and while it hung writhing on the cross, *spent my best years and powers cooking cabbage.*" Nor was she comforted by the fact that she had achieved a remarkable life work by the pen. She insisted that she did not care for literary fame, had never cared enough for writing to find it in conflict with her domestic duties, but that she had never visited a picture gallery without feeling a sense of "repentance for the betrayal of a trust." It was in the waste and abuse of women's talents that she was later to find her strongest argument against the church and its teaching on women. "Is that Christianity which has so long said to one-half of the race, 'Thou shalt not use any gift of the Creator, if it be not approved by thy brother; and unto man, not God, thou shalt ever turn and ask, "What wilt thou have me to do?"'"[22]

In later years Mrs. Swisshelm insisted that her husband had never been unkind to her. "Here let me say, that in my twenty years of married life, my conflicts were all spiritual; that there never was a time when my husband's strong right arm would not be tempered to infantile gentleness to tend me in illness, or when he hesitated to throw himself between me and danger. Over streams and other places impassible to me, he carried me, but could not understand how so frail a thing could be so obstinate."[23]

It is difficult to reconcile this statement with the apparent stubbornness and callousness of a man who could ally himself with his mother against his young bride, and subject her to the indignities described above. (She had noted sadly that even in that first year, he had not visited her any more often when she moved from her mother's house to the wagon shop quarters than he had before.) And more than callousness is suggested by his refusal to recognize the damaging effect of the terror in which she lived — because of two bears and a panther he insisted on keeping as pets on the farm! No wonder her health began to fail.

It is hard to understand how they could have fallen in love and chosen each other in the first place. Psychohistorians might see clues in the intensity of Jane's nature and the fact that she had at an early age lost a loved father, and subsequently, a strong and loving older brother.

It is clear Jane had invested her Pennsylvania farmer-suitor with a chivalry and heroic qualities he did not possess. Her infatuation is understandable, but his decision to marry her is more incomprehensible. He seems to have had a genuine admiration for her intellectual gifts. Perhaps, of practical and thrifty stock, he saw them as marketable qualities. She says of him on the occasion of their second meeting: "He had elected me his wife some years before this evening, and had not kept it secret; had been assured his choice was presumptuous, but came and took possession of his prospective property with the air of a man who understood his business."[24] He, too, may have had illusions — of winning a pretty, pleasant, and tractable wife with unusual virtues.

In any case, Jane Swisshelm's biographers find her curiously reticent about her difficulties in marriage. Margaret Farrand Thorp says, "The emotions and events of girlhood and marriage emerge obliquely, by implication, in strange half-lights." Helen Beal Woodward says, "It was not Jim Swisshelm's fault that a beauty-hungry girl in a crude American village had looked at him and seen a black knight, a Russian count, and Lord Mortimer superimposed upon the likeness of a passive Pennsylvania farmer." In her sixties, looking back at her marriage, Jane wrote: "Had he and I gone into the pine woods . . . had we been married under an equitable law or had he emigrated to Minnesota, as he proposed . . . there would have been no separation; but after fifteen years in his mother's house I must run away or die, and leave my child to a step-mother. So I ran away." James Swisshelm, she went on, was "not much better than the average man. Knew his rights, and knowing sought to maintain them against me; while, in some respects, he was to me incalculably more than just." Curiously enough, her final decision to leave him seems to have stemmed from the time of the birth of their daughter after fifteen years of marriage. It is generally assumed that this daughter, born in 1851, was the only child to whom Mrs. Swisshelm gave birth, but her reference to the litigation which surrounded her divorce — to the fact that having "a living child" complicated her suit — may indicate that she might have had stillborn children. Her decision to leave seems to have been based on the conviction that she would die if she remained with her husband. She might not have been referring to the nervous strain alone, and now, as the mother of little Mary Henrietta, called "Zo" or "Nettie," she had a compelling reason for living.[25]

In the early years, however, when James Swisshelm, finally moved by the evidence of Jane's failing health, took her in 1838 to Louisville, Kentucky, where he planned to join a brother in business, she still had great faith in him and his possibilities.

It was in Louisville that "she came face to face with slavery in some of its most heartless aspects." She described it in terms of *men* as slaveholders, *men* "whose business it was to insult every woman who ventured on the street without a male protector, by a stare so lascivious as could not be imagined on American free soil," *men* who "lived, in whole or in part, by the sale of their own children, and the labor of the mothers extorted by the lash." She was always, after that, to refer to slaveholders in that fashion, as "women-whippers" and barterers of their own children. She could never see slavery as an abstraction but always in terms of the familial relationships involved. The examples she gives us in *Half a Century* horrify even today.[26]

Across the street from the boardinghouse in which she and her husband had taken rooms lived a grocer who owned a woman, the mother of five children, of whom he was the father. "The older two he had sold, one at a time, as they became saleable or got in his way. On the sale of the first, the mother 'took on so that he was obliged to flog her almost to death before she gave up.'" Jane's own landlady lamented the loss of two slaves her brother had meant to leave her before he died intestate, his children by a quadroon slave whom he had bound to the whipping post and lashed until she yielded to him and became the mother of those boys. Incident after incident flows from her pen: "a man was beaten to death in an open shed, on the corner of two public streets, where the sound of the blows . . . and unavailing prayers for mercy were continued a whole forenoon." [27]

It was not only the condition of the slave that distressed Mrs. Swisshelm but the deterioration of character in the slaveholder. She came to know one man whose entire support came from the sale of his children and the wages of nineteen women. She found that the principal Baptist preacher owned and hired out one hundred slaves. When he wanted to sell one, he himself took the slave to the auction block and acted as auctioneer. An elder in the Presbyterian church punished a small boy for running away by fitting him with an iron collar with "four projections and a hoop" over his head. To Southern white women, "work was a dire disgrace." Even to go outside to pump water in order to have a cool drink was to lose caste. [28]

She does not draw the parallels, but reading between the lines and noting the juxtaposition of incidents in her autobiography makes it clear that Mrs. Swisshelm saw a comparison between the institution of slavery and her own situation as a married woman. She had noted earlier that she was left without support or compensation for her services to her husband's family in that first year — and was sent only food. She observed that the wives and sisters and daughters of Pennsylvania farmers were expected to gather in the fall crops while their men "pitched horseshoes to work off their surplus vitality." When a woman fell at her post from lack of strength, "there was always another to take her place." Now in Louisville, when her husband failed in business, she set to work and became successful as a dressmaker. He was content to act as her agent, spending long hours away from the house in which she was virtually a prisoner. It was too much. She had made sacrifices to be her husband's housekeeper and to keep herself "in woman's sphere." "I wanted to be back on free soil, out of an atmosphere which killed all manhood, and furnished women-whippers as a substitute for men." [29]

The situation was brought to a head when Jane received news that her mother was dying and urgently needed her. Her husband was reluctant to let her go: he rested his case on Saint Paul's epistle to the Ephesians: "Wives submit yourselves unto your husbands as unto the Lord." For the first time Jane saw this as con-

tradictory to the mind and will of God. "Was every husband God
to his wife? Would wives appear in the general judgment at all, or
if they did, would they hand in a schedule of marital com-
mands? . . . Then and there I cast it from me forever, as being no
part of divine law, and thus unconsciously took the first step in
breaking through a faith in plenary inspiration." Her religion had
matured. She saw herself as totally responsible for her own actions. She went to her mother's deathbed.[30]

Her husband's reprisal was to say, after her mother's death, that
he was the owner of her "person and services" and that he would
file his claim against the executors for wages for the time spent in
nursing her mother. Jane was completely overwhelmed by the
discovery that a law made this possible. "Why should the discovery of its existence curdle my blood, stop my heart-beats, and send
a rush of burning shame from forehead to finger-tip?"[31] The parallel is so obvious that the reader needs no answer. To avoid the
humiliation she seems to have compromised by letting him use
the income from her mother's estate, left to her in trusteeship, for
improvements on *his* mother's property in which she said she had
not even dower rights. But, later, when he refused to allow the
sale of some of her mother's property unless the money were
given directly to him, she rebelled — but not directly against him.

The method of her rebellion was typical of that she was to use
throughout her life in the cause of women's rights. She and James
had returned to Pennsylvania and she was already well known as a
correspondent to the *Pittsburgh Commercial Journal,* the most
widely read publication in the area. She borrowed books, studied
the law, and began a series of letters on the subject of a married
woman's right to hold property. She said nothing of her own affairs
and kept to the abstract until she came upon a dramatic example.
A husband had refused to give the father of his dead wife even a
few of her personal possessions as souvenirs, selling them at public auction and thus forcing the father to buy them there. "I turned
every man's scorn against himself, said to them: 'Gentlemen, these
are your laws!'" She transmuted her personal problem and her
deeply felt sense of injustice into a victory for all women. She did
it cannily by demonstrating to men that injustice for their
daughters was injustice for themselves. In that same year of
1847–48, the Pennsylvania legislature secured to married women
the right to hold property, a product, in fact, of her vigorous editorials. Lucretia C. Mott and Mary A. Grew of Philadelphia had la-

bored assiduously for the same project, she noted in passing. (She was always to believe that the best way to labor was hers — by influencing public opinion through writing or speaking.)[32]

Jane Grey Swisshelm is not universally admired. Lester B. Shippee categorizes her as an agitator, one of those "who can never be content to leave things as they find them . . . seers, prophets, reformers . . . stormy petrels of society . . . gadflies." In summing up her life work, he wonders whether it was constructive or destructive. Her writings were "diatribes."[33] But he is thinking of her only as an abolitionist. She is much more complicated.

For example, her approach to feminism is, considering the quality of debate in her time, logical and far from shrill. She "confined herself to general principles," choosing personal example carefully for the sake of illustration. She refused to make men the enemy. She had experienced too many deep and supportive masculine friendships for that. Nor did she think the solution to women's problems lay in gaining every right men enjoyed. She outlined her own policy as follows: "The policy of the *Visiter* in regard to Woman's Rights was to 'go easy,' except in the case of those slave-women, who had no rights. For others, gain an advance when you could. Educate girls with boys, develop their brains, and take away legal disabilities little by little, as experience should show was wise; but never dream of their doing the world's hard work, either mental or physical; and Heaven defend them from going into all the trades. . . .

"Women should not weaken their cause by impracticable demands. Make no claim which could not be won in a reasonable time. Take one step at a time, get a good foothold in it and advance carefully. Suffrage in municipal elections for property holders who could read, and had never been connected with crime, was the place to strike for the ballot. Say nothing about suffrage elsewhere until it proved successful here."[34]

Her method in attacking slavery was entirely different. She felt a deep, subconscious identification with the slave. Moreover, she found in her attack on slavery an answer to the problems in her married life, as well as an acceptable outlet for her intellectual energy and talent. She had a cause compatible with her conscience; the neglect of that cause had brought about the troubles visited upon her. (At the time of joining her church she had promised God that she would be content to spend her whole life "in any labor he should appoint" — and had been sure that He had accepted her as one who would be "set to tasks from which other laborers shrank.") Finally, Abolition was a subject on which she and her husband were in perfect accord; she tells us that "he always voted a straight abolition ticket." Whatever need for repression she felt, she need not feel it in this struggle.[35]

She began her work against slavery by writing letters and poems for abolition papers and then for the *Pittsburgh Commercial Journal and Spirit of the Age.* Her method of attack was to use sarcasm, of which she remained a master all her writing life, ridicule, and personal attack, all larded with quotations from authorities. By the time she wrote her memoirs, she seems to have become aware of the deficiencies in this early style for she goes to some length to explain it.

"Of slavery in the abstract I know nothing. There was no abstraction in tying Martha to a whipping-post and scourging her for mourning the loss of her children. . . . This great nation was engaged in the pusillanimous work of beating poor little Mexico [*it was the time of the Mexican War which abolitionists saw as an effort to extend slave territory*] — a giant whipping a cripple. . . . Each one seemed to stand before me, his innermost soul laid bare, and his idiosyncrasy I was sure to strike with sarcasm, ridicule solemn denunciations, old truths from Bible and history and the opinions of good men. I had a reckless abandon, for had I not thrown myself into the breach to die there . . .? My style I caught from my crude, rural surroundings, and was familiar to the unlearned, and I was not surprised to find the letters eagerly read."[36]

Eagerly indeed. By the time she was thirty-two, she was famous as a writer throughout Pennsylvania, and by January, 1848, she was able to bring out the first copy of the *Pittsburgh Saturday Visiter,* a paper she owned and edited herself.[37] She might half-apologize for her irony and sarcasm, but they were formidable weapons in the polemical nineteenth century. Her skill with them — and her fearlessness — brought her unprecedented success.

In 1857 Mrs. Swisshelm left her husband and went with her small daughter to join her only sister and her husband, Mr. and Mrs. Henry Mitchell, in St. Cloud, Minnesota. By that time she was accustomed to fame and to victories. It is true that she was exhausted and ill, and firmly intended to lead a quiet life on the forty acres claimed for her on a lake near St. Cloud. It is also true that this dream was thwarted by the removal of troops from Fort Ripley because of the threat of Indian uprisings to the south. (It was unthinkable that a woman should live alone in Indian country from which military protection had been withdrawn.) But she herself ascribes her willingness to start another paper in St. Cloud to her own nature. When on her initial trip from St. Paul to St. Cloud she first heard that Sylvanus Lowry, the virtual dictator of central Minnesota, was also a slave sympathizer, she thought: "This is a broad country; but if this be true, there is not room in it for Gen. Lowrie [*sic*] and me." When she had thought of an idyllic prairie life, "I had not yet learned that every human soul is a Shunamite, 'a company of two armies,' and wherever there is one, there is strife. 'To live is to contend.' " She had no sooner settled down with her sister and brother-in-law in St. Cloud than she accepted the proffered backing of a few leading citizens and began publishing the *St. Cloud Visiter*. [38]

Her chosen adversary was formidable. Sylvanus Lowry was a Tennesseean, a slaveholder, who lived on the river above St. Cloud in "semi-barbaric splendor." Even Jane Swisshelm admired him, in a way: "He was one of those who are born to command — of splendid physique and dignified bearing, superior intellect and mesmeric fascination. His natural advantages had been increased by a liberal education; he had been brought up among slaves, lived among Indians as agent and interpreter, felt his own superiority, and asserted it with the full force of honest conviction. . . .

"The territorial government under [President James] Buchanan was a mere tool of slavery. Every federal officer was a Southerner, or a Northern man with Southern principles. Government gold flowed freely in that channel, and to the eagles Gen. Lowrie had but to say, as to his other servants, 'come,' and they flew into his exchequer."

The battle was joined almost immediately. The new community could not really support a paper except as a subsidized advertiser to draw settlers to the region. Lowry agreed to be one of the subsidizers if she, the well-known abolitionist, would support Buchanan. And she agreed! [39]

Her friends and supporters were scandalized, but they underestimated her. Her goal was the opposite; she intended to defeat Buchanan with irony and sarcasm. She became, as she put it, Buchanan's "only honest supporter. All the others pretended he was going to do something quite foreign to his purpose. . . . The one sole object of his administration was the perpetuation and spread of slavery, and this object the *Visiter* would support with the best arguments in its power." She attacked Buchanan by pretending to praise him for his support of slavery. Her descriptions of the president were examples of her rhetoric at its sarcastic and vitriolic best.[40]

Most reports of the ensuing action follow Mrs. Swisshelm's account of the affair, as does the following: "Then action became perceptibly accelerated. A speech by Lowry's lawyer, [James C.] Shepley, on the place of woman; an editorial [*by her*] praising the lecture but calling attention to the omission in his classification of types of the gambling woman not unknown . . . in the fifties; the lawyer's pretense that this was an allusion to his wife; General Lowry's rush to the defense of an abused lady; and a decision to mob the paper and its editor, all came in rapid succession. St. Cloud, however, would stand for no such method of breaking up a fair fight. Nevertheless, by night, three men broke into the printing establishment, smashed the press, scattered the type . . . and so sought to put an end to the whole issue. This aroused the indignation of the portion of the populace inclining to Mrs. Swisshelm's way of thinking; a public meeting, where she gave an account of the whole affair, produced resolutions of support . . . and new equipment was rushed from Chicago."[41]

Mrs. Swisshelm reported the raid in the renewed paper and identified the three men as Lowry, Shepley, and Dr. Benjamin Palmer, fiancé of Shepley's sister-in-law. They sued the paper for libel. To protect her backers, she apologized, suspended the *Visiter*, and revived the charges the next day in the *St. Cloud Democrat*, a new paper of which she was the sole owner. Lowry was defeated. It was the beginning of his slow political and financial decline.

But is the account totally accurate? For example, is her description of the gambling woman really a general one? — "the large, thick-skinned, coarse, sensual-featured, loud-mouthed, double-fisted dames, whose entrance into a room appears to take one's breath, whose conversational tones are audible at the furthest side of the next square, whose guffahs resound across a mile wide

river, and who talks with an energy which makes the saliva fly
like — showers of melted pearls. . . . Her triumphs consist in
card-table successes, displays of cheap finery, and in catching marriageable husbands for herself and her poor relations." [42]

Or is this the description of a person Jane Swisshelm had reason
to dislike very much? The identification with his wife does not
seem to have been mere pretense on Shepley's part. Elizabeth
Shepley Sergeant, granddaughter of the lady in question, wrote a
fictional account in which she takes it for granted that the description was a caricature of her grandmother. Moreover, she credits
Mrs. Shepley with devising the strategy to destroy Mrs. Swisshelm
in the community by means of a public lecture on Woman — "I
have sought to present to your gaze a new species with whom
some of us poor males as yet scarce feel at ease — the Strong-
Minded Woman — . . . who leaves the sheltered domestic hearth
. . . to enter the bitter invective and competition of politics." She
puts into her grandmother's mouth the words, "We know she
deserted a husband, and dragged a babe from its Father's arms, to
come out here." [43]

Very close to the bone. In nothing had Jane Swisshelm been as
defeated as in her effort to make a success of her marriage. Her
position in the small pioneer community must have been difficult,
despite the protection of the Mitchells. And she had elected, because of her convictions, to eschew the sponsorship of General
Lowry, "the friend of my friends, the man who stood ready to set
me on the pinnacle of social distinction by his recognition." [44]
Surely the night of the lecture was not the first time she had
endured Mrs. Shepley's scorn.

Jane Grey Swisshelm did not wage battles like these without
cost. Her public reply to the Lowry attack was the first speech she
ever made; she had a guard standing by to shoot her "through the
brain" in case the mob set upon her. The day after that meeting
she became ill and was "thought to be dying." [45] In St. Cloud for
the second time in her life, circumstances and her own nature
prevented her from living the normal life of a woman of her times.

After the Lowry affair, however, she was established in the public mind as a prominent citizen. The meeting referred to above
was her very first public appearance. She discovered, during that
experience, that she could communicate just as well through
speaking as through writing, and in the ensuing years she became
a popular lecturer. At the same time she continued her trenchant

and informative writing. Her newspaper letters, appearing from
1858 through 1865 in the *St. Cloud Visiter* and the *St. Cloud
Democrat* (both papers are on file at the Minnesota Historical Society), are "a sharply etched record of what an observant and emotional woman saw, heard, thought, and felt as she journeyed about
the young state of Minnesota and as she labored in the nation's
capital in the time of Abraham Lincoln." But descriptive as they
are, these letters are, like all her writing, letters of advocacy.
"Wonder when the people of Minn. will find out that her wealth is
in her soil; and that those who are not directly or indirectly engaged in digging it out are little better than loafers?" she wrote on
April 6, 1860, while on a trip through southern Minnesota. She
praised the German settlers of Stearns County for doing just that
and suggested that they write home to the " 'Father Land' and see
if it cannot spare us two or three thousand more." She could not
understand why more settlers did not come from New England: "I
cannot tell why men stay and struggle in the East, with low daily
wages, when they might make themselves magnificent homes, on
the banks of our beautiful lakes and rivers." She detailed the virtues of Minnesota: Wheat 25 or 30 bushels to the acre compared to
10 in Pennsylvania; beef, mutton, and wool raised for one-third
less than in Illinois; "no cattle diseases"; grass more "nutricious";
sheep "yield more and finer wool." [46]

No doubt her enthusiasm for thrifty farming and for self-
dependent homesteads surrounded by gardens, fruit trees, and
berry bushes stemmed from her Pennsylvania girlhood. It was
their aversion to farming which originally made her dislike the
Indians. She decided that they were "a set of lazy, impudent beg-
gers" supported by the government. On this subject she was historically and culturally blind and some of her graphic descriptions — such as that of a ragged band of Chippewa playing
football with the heads of some decapitated Sioux in the dusty
streets of St. Cloud — make the reader understand her blindness.
When, late in the summer of 1862, the Minnesota frontier was ter-
rified by the bloody revolt of the Sioux, in which hundreds of
white inhabitants were slain, she felt vindicated. Her dislike
turned to fear and hatred. One of her reasons for going East in
1863 was to arouse eastern opinion in favor of drastic punishment
of the Indians. She spoke before audiences in Chicago, Philadelphia, Brooklyn, and Washington. Once in Washington, she stayed.
Through her friend Secretary Stanton she was offered an appointment as a clerk in the War Department. Her nephew and assistant

editor, William B. Mitchell, took over the management of the *St.
Cloud Democrat*. It was while she was awaiting the summons to
begin her new work that she discovered the shortage of nurses at
the government hospitals in and around Washington.[47]

Margaret Thorp wisely observes that Jane Swisshelm devoted
more than a quarter of her autobiography to her Civil War nursing,
a matter of months, but months when she literally brought dying
men, cases depaired of, back to life. "That period of nursing was
the only time in Jane Swisshelm's life when she worked in an
atmosphere of approval. . . . No relatives criticized her doings
and lamented them, no newspapers bombarded her with angry
paragraphs; to have encouragement, not opposition in well-doing
was restful and very sweet." In addition to that, the work made
use of all her powers — the knowledge of anatomy "derived from
her habit of looking at people with a portrait painter's eye, and the
dexterity of her painter's hands." A valid insight, but an injured
soldier quoted by Mrs. Swisshelm herself goes even deeper. He
and his fellow wounded agreed, he said, that she nursed them because she loved to, not just out of duty, but that she lost interest in
them once she had saved them. She was contending, at last, with
the greatest of adversaries; she was fighting death itself for the
lives of young men.[48]

Jane Grey Swisshelm set many precedents, and women of the
late twentieth century benefit by those precedents. Minnesotans
have benefited from offshoots of her struggles — by the university
founded as a coeducational institution, by the fact that, with innate
practical wisdom, she led central Minnesota pioneers to see that
their future lay in agriculture rather than speculation. She was
feared and respected as no American woman before her — and
few since. It was true that her battles were sometimes unworthy of
her. (She was savage about the Indians — but she had seen the
victims of the Sioux War. She was crudely anti-Catholic. She was a
fierce reconstructionist.) But her fearlessness served her grand
causes well.[49]

Self-fulfillment was a goal she did not recognize. Yet more than
any other feminist of the time she established the fact that the
talents and strengths of women were equally as important as those
of men; that women had an obligation to use these attributes in
the service of humanity; that they must fight for the right to do so.

4. EVA McDONALD VALESH
Minnesota Populist

By Rhoda R. Gilman

DURING the turbulent years of the late 1880s and early 1890s, when Minnesota's awakening labor movement first made common cause with poverty-stricken farmers and shook the state's two-party system to its foundations, a feminine comet flashed across the political sky. In the literature of Populism Eva McDonald Valesh is often mentioned along with the more famous Mary E. Lease of Kansas and several other articulate women who spoke for the People's party across the nation. But in Minnesota her light, like the third-party movement, soon flickered out. In 1896, finding her hopes for reform dashed, her vaulting ambitions disappointed, and her marriage unworkable, she turned her back on the state and its politics and launched a successful but little publicized career as a journalist in New York City and Washington, D.C.

Annie L. Diggs, a fellow worker in the National Farmers' Alliance which spawned the People's party, described Eva McDonald as "the jauntiest, sauciest, prettiest little woman in the whole coterie of women in the Alliance. . . . A fun-loving, jolly, prankish elf of a woman, quite as much at home on an improvised store-box platform on the street corner . . . as in the drawing-room, radiating sparkling wit and repartee." A contrasting impression was received by a Minnesota farmer who heard her speak at Kasson in 1890: "Miss McDonald in a very unassuming and lady-like manner took up the speeches of the previous evening and logically proved the fallacy of their conclusions. . . . all were charmed by her eloquence, convinced by her logic, and melted to tears by her pathetic description of the poor of the great cities." Dr. Everett W. Fish, editor of the Alliance newspaper, the *Great West*, saw yet a different Eva in the course of in-fighting for control of the organization's Minnesota executive committee, where she defended her election to the office of State Lecturer on the grounds that a two-thirds vote of the members overrode the Alliance constitution. "To say that her fiery temper got the better of her would perhaps be a slight excuse," wrote Fish in 1891. "But the statement was made and sustained with a spirit that would drive an ironwood fence post through frozen sod."[1]

To Ignatius Donnelly, whose leadership of the Minnesota third-party movement Eva ultimately challenged, she was a "vicious little pest," and an even harsher judgment came from her own younger sister. Embittered, perhaps, by long years of family responsibility and ill health, Blanche MacDonald wrote of Eva in 1956: "She was the most selfish and self-absorbed person I have ever known." Although Eva was repeatedly described by herself and others as fiery and emotional, the few pieces of her own correspondence that have survived reveal a woman with an inward distrust of emotion who struggled, as she put it, to maintain the "mental balance that is so essential to the philosophic temperament."[2]

From this composite picture one can glimpse the talent, the shrewdness, and the relentless drive necessary for a woman to achieve political power at a time when suffrage for women was seldom seriously discussed even by radical third-party groups. It also suggests some of the personal costs entailed by being a "new woman" of the 1880s. For those with education, economic security, and family backing, the price may not have been so high, but Eva McDonald had few advantages beyond what she seized for herself.

Born in Orono, Maine, in 1866, Eva moved with her parents and a flock of younger brothers to Stillwater, Minnesota, about 1875. In 1877 the family relocated in Minneapolis, where she entered high school. Already her responsibilities were heavy, for her mother "was the sort of woman who adored her latest baby" and left the care of the others mostly to Eva. Eventually the family numbered eight, five of whom were boys. Higher education was unthought of for the daughters, and after Eva graduated from high school in 1881, weighing only eighty-five pounds and looking even younger than her fifteen years, it was taken for granted that she would continue to help at home as well as in a small grocery store that the family opened a year or two later.[3]

John L. McDonald was a carpenter by trade and a capable family provider. He was also a lover of learning. Although he had re-

Eva McDonald Valesh

ceived little formal education, he read widely and had a lively interest in politics and community affairs. Eva recalled him as "a tolerant man" who "lived on a higher spiritual level than we did."[4] It was he, apparently, who sensed the restlessness of his precocious, tomboyish daughter. Aware that she was clever with words, he took a sample of her writing to the editor of a small weekly newspaper called the *Saturday Evening Spectator*. She was not hired as a reporter, but through the introduction she got a job in the print shop where the paper was produced. With quick fingers and an even quicker mind, she soon mastered typesetting and proofreading, earning the substantial wage of six dollars a week and eventually joining the typographers' union.

In 1886, at the age of twenty, she became dissatisfied once more and enrolled in a one-year teachers' training course, but her juvenile appearance combined, possibly, with a certain cocky irreverence for authority, kept her from getting a position. Characteristically, she did not take the rebuff without protest. A year later she told how "I received a certificate and a diploma from the teachers' training school, but was not given a school to teach, although the superintendent of the training school said I was eligible. I went to [Minneapolis school] Superintendent [John E.] Bradley and asked him why I was not given a school. He did not give me any satisfaction one way or the other, so I asked for the board of education to investigate the matter. The board declined to investigate, evidently not caring to bother itself. I dropped the matter and have never asked for a position since and do not expect to again, as I have discovered a more congenial occupation than teaching." [5] Her new occupation was the result of an unusual proposal that came her way early in 1888.

The 1880s had been years of rapid industrial development in Minnesota. The decade saw the population of both Minneapolis and St. Paul more than tripled, and it also saw an upwelling of labor organization and union activity. Isolated craft unions had existed in Minnesota since the 1850s, but it was not until the early 1880s that the movement for labor solidarity became widespread. Then, somewhat as the Grange had swept among poverty-stricken farmers in the 1870s, the Noble Order of the Knights of Labor gathered industrial workers into a tidal wave of protest. Nationally it crested in 1886, then declined sharply, but in Minnesota the peak of its activity came somewhat later, and in 1888 the Knights still dominated the labor movement with a vigorous state organization and a notably far-seeing group of leaders. [6]

At about the same time, Minnesotans became aware of another new phenomenon: for the first time large numbers of women in the state were being employed in factories and stores. The Knights of Labor recognized their presence by chartering two "Ladies Protective Assemblies" and by calling as early as 1886 for equal wages to women who performed the same jobs as men. [7]

Early in 1888 the innovative editor of the *St. Paul Globe* proposed to run a series of stories on women workers in the Twin Cities. But getting such stories proved to be a problem. Employers refused to co-operate, and the young women themselves were fearful and reticent. Feminine reporters were less than plentiful in 1888, and the assignment had an element of risk. At this impasse someone in Minneapolis labor circles suggested John McDonald's daughter, who had at one time been vaguely connected with the *Spectator*. Eva immediately agreed to take on the job, and her father made no objection, although she was certain that if her mother had been present the plan would have been vetoed. [8]

Her first article appeared on March 25, 1888, under the headline

" 'Mong Girls Who Toil" and was signed with the pen name "Eva Gay." In it she promised to "carry *Globe* readers with me through a series of articles and show the life, home life and shop life, of the working girls and women of Minneapolis." Starting with visits to three firms that manufactured overalls and cheap work clothes, she described the conditions she had observed and reported conversations with three or four girls who had been willing to answer her questions. With observant eye and chatty style she made her way on through bag and mattress factories, woolen mills, shoe factories, steam laundries, cigar factories, print shops, book binderies, and into the service trades. In a few places she was actually hired, and here she turned her youthful appearance to advantage. "I wore old clothes," she recalled, and "I had my hair cut very short like a boy. . . . No employer ever discovered me . . . because they were looking for a tall, grimly efficient spinster." [9] The series, which continued to appear on the Minneapolis page of each Sunday edition for nearly a year, established Eva as a professional journalist. In time she broadened the scope of the articles to humorous observation of things outside the usual working world, including seven episodes on her misadventures while posing as a lady's maid. By then, however, she had already been swept into a wholly different and more absorbing field of work.

Less than a month after Eva's visit to the clothing factories described in her first article, the 250 women employed by one of the firms went on strike. Eva had found that they were paid three and a half cents for a shirt and seven cents for a pair of overalls — rates that enabled the majority to make no more than three dollars a week. Slow workers got considerably less. Whether or not her description of the unventilated loft in which they worked and the abusiveness of their foreman had aroused public sympathy, there was widespread support for the strikers among clergymen and citizens' groups in Minneapolis. [10]

Many of the women were members of the Knights of Labor, and although the Knights did not officially endorse the strike, Timothy W. Brosnan, Master Worker of the Minnesota district, and John P. McGaughey, an organizer and national officer of the order, were present at most of the strike meetings. Eva also attended several of them, and at one she was asked by some of her factory acquaintances to address the group. The earnestness and fluency with which the tiny pixie spoke impressed McGaughey, and he took her aside afterward.

What followed assumed in Eva's later memory almost the proportions of a Pygmalion legend. McGaughey undertook to train
her in public speaking and make of her an orator and labor
agitator. Night after night they attended small union gatherings
where she spoke briefly and he later instructed and criticized. She
often resented his relentless drilling, but after an explosion of
temper she would think it over and come back again, impressed
by his skill and fascinated by the excitement and glamor of the
effort. Her first public speech was given in Duluth, where she and
McGaughey addressed a gathering sponsored by the Knights of
Labor and Eva dwelt on the unfair plight of the working girl. "Let
the girls band together," she urged, "so that no girl need be in-
sulted because she works; let her be paid what her services are
worth; . . . let the men and women band together and give [work-
ing girls] their share of this world's goods." [11]

Meanwhile McGaughey introduced Eva to the ferment of radical and reformist ideas that was shaking the complacency of the
late nineteenth-century world. He prescribed a course of reading
in the literature of economics and social criticism that no doubt
included such well-known American works as Edward Kellogg's
Labor and Other Capital, Edward Bellamy's *Looking Backward,*
and *Progress and Poverty* by Henry George. Treatises on the co-
operative movement may also have been recommended, since
McGaughey himself was chairman of the Knights' national committee on co-operation, and Eva recalled making her way through
"some translations of French economics" — possibly the works of
Pierre Joseph Proudhon and Louis Blanc. [12]

With McGaughey Eva also attended the gatherings of a select
group within the Knights of Labor leadership — a sort of ideologi-
cal steering committee that met frequently to study and discuss
current industrial topics and the various financial, economic, and
political prescriptions for the ills of the working classes. They also
assumed responsibility for educating the rank-and-file membership through lectures and study groups, and in general they comprised the intellectual leadership of the movement in Minnesota. [13]

It was a heady atmosphere for a young woman of twenty-one.
McGaughey's tutoring ended when, at a meeting they were both
to address, she gave his customary speech as well as her own,
leaving him with nothing to say. Following this prank, he informed her that she "had graduated." [14] By then, however, her glib
command of radical social thought, coupled with her effective

writing and speaking, had won her a firm place within the inner circle of Twin Cities labor leadership.

Eva's first exposure to politics took place in the fall of 1888, when she was nominated by the Democratic party for a vacancy on the Minneapolis school board. Minnesota women had been allowed to vote in school elections since 1875, but Eva was the first woman to run for a school board seat in Hennepin County. She was also the first woman candidate in the county ever nominated by a major party.[15] It was a presidential year, however, and Eva lost when the Republicans took Hennepin County along with the rest of the country.

By mid-spring of 1889 Eva's assignment on the *Globe* had changed. She still wrote occasional articles under her "Eva Gay" byline, but her major job was editing a column of labor news that appeared weekly in the Minneapolis section, usually under the title "The World of Work." There was plenty of labor news to report, for the month of April, 1889, saw a strike by the street railway employees of both cities. Mass importation of "scabs" and some resulting violence made it the most serious labor disturbance Minnesota had yet known. McGaughey and Eva were both actively involved through the Knights of Labor. Agitation for the eight-hour day also increased that year. At its national convention in December, 1888, the American Federation of Labor had given high priority to the movement for shorter hours, possibly to divert attention from the rivalry between the declining Knights of Labor and the rising federation for control of the union movement. In Minnesota, at least, it had that effect. A state Eight Hour League was soon established with leadership that drew from both groups, and as winter released its grip, a successful series of public meetings was held in Minneapolis, many of which Eva organized and addressed.[16]

Her sudden absorption by the labor movement and her constant involvement in activities that were at best unconventional for a young woman of her age quickly brought strained relations with her family. She recalled: "My people nearly turned me from home. In those days a young girl couldn't go and take an apartment or live in a hotel. That wasn't respectable." Her mother complained that the family had come "to a nice pass" when she had to read the morning paper to learn of her daughter's activities. Her father "seemed to realize that there was nothing he could do, so he rarely made any objection." John McDonald was by that time deeply involved in the labor movement himself and spoke before at least one eight-hour rally in the summer of 1889. Early in August, when Eva organized a mass meeting at the corner of Cedar and Washington streets, he lent her his wagon to use as a platform and stationed himself on the tailboard to see that no one annoyed her. She, however, saw in this his belief that girls should have parental supervision rather than any intention of supporting her, for "he seldom said an encouraging word." [17]

In later years she wondered that she had not been more seriously affected by her family's disapproval, but she maintained that "I loved all this activity. Nothing worried me. I didn't care what people said. It didn't bother me a bit." She may have been sustained by a youthful sense of mission and a genuine dedication to the labor movement. "I always felt that I really belonged to the workers," she recalled, "and would be willing to make any sacrifices for them if necessary." [18]

The growing militancy of organized labor in Minnesota as the decade of the 1880s drew to a close was matched, or even surpassed, by unrest among the state's farmers. The protest role played by the Grange in the 1870s had been assumed in the mid-1880s by an organization called the Farmers' Alliance. At a state-wide convention in 1886, members of the Alliance resolved "That there are really but two parties in this State to-day — the people and their plunderers," and "That the interests of all producers are identical; the millions who work on the farm find their chief market and natural allies among the millions who toil in shop and factory." Soon after this declaration the Alliance met in conjunction with the Knights of Labor, and the two groups agreed to submit a joint set of legislative demands to both major political parties. Minnesota Democrats and Republicans paid lip service to the demands and incorporated a number of them in platforms adopted that year. But when the legislature met in 1887 the grievances of both farmers and labor were ignored. [19]

In the elections of 1888 the farmer and labor forces endorsed an independent ticket with disastrous results. Their candidate for governor was Ignatius Donnelly, Minnesota's well-known and perennial spokesman for agrarian reform; for lieutenant governor they chose John McGaughey. There was dissension, however, and financial backing for the ticket never developed. Donnelly withdrew and threw his support to the Republican candidate — a course Twin Cities labor leaders found hard to forgive.

The year 1889 was a period of regrouping and rapid growth for the Farmers' Alliance, both in Minnesota and nationwide. With Donnelly as State Lecturer (an office somewhat analogous to organizer for a labor union) chapters mushroomed throughout the state, and the movement gained an aggressive newspaper voice when the *Great West* began publication in St. Paul under the able editorship of Dr. Everett Fish.

It was Fish who first drew Eva McDonald into the Alliance orbit. He recalled it later in these words: "We heard her make a delightful speech in a labor meeting, and invited her to call on us at our office. We had a very long talk with her, both at the office and various tea-table talks with our family — told her of a future before her if she would aim high! That the great spirits who had almost created the on-coming destiny of her sex were passing away — Mrs. [Mary A.] Livermore, Miss [Susan B.] Anthony, Annie Dickinson and a long list of brilliant and powerful names." [20]

The doctor's rosy dreams for Eva's future in the women's movement faded a bit when she stated that she was a skeptic and opposed to both Prohibition and organized churches, but he consoled himself by reflecting that "the moral [sense] might easily be developed if she were thrown in contact with her great sisters in the field." Grandiloquently, he announced: "We can open the door wide open. We will put you on the lecture stand over the state — and will open the columns of a paper that goes over the entire country."

But Eva was not dazzled. She told him, in effect, "The city workers are the only people for whom I work without pay." They agreed on five dollars a lecture and guaranteed expenses. [21]

The same issue of the *Great West* which announced that "This well-known literary lady and eloquent champion of labor will go out in the state to lecture for the Farmers Alliance" also carried a double-column feature by Eva entitled "The New Political Economy." In it she stated her intention to examine the reasons why farmers "are the hardest working and poorest paid class in the country. . . . why the railroad corporations, real estate speculators, stock gamblers and professional politicians grow enormously wealthy without doing any work at all. . . . why farmers' wives are so often broken down and fill the insane asylums and hospitals." The column continued to appear somewhat irregularly for three months, discussing such topics as the history of the eight-hour-day movement and the arguments of single-taxers and Greenbackers.[22]

In one column Eva took up Fish's earlier challenge and threw it back at him in a manner that may have dismayed him as well as other Alliance leaders. The article described her impressions of the Alliance state convention held in March, 1890. "I felt rather subdued on seeing over five hundred delegates assembled to represent the farmers' interests and not a woman among them," she wrote. "Is it because Minnesota farmers' wives and daughters don't have to work and consequently know nothing of the evils to be remedied? . . . If I were convinced that the women of the rural districts of this state are carefully educated, well clothed, well fed and not overworked — I wouldn't say a word about their absence from the convention. But . . . if the average farmer is a slave then his wife is the slave of a slave. Her position is fixed by his and is always a little the worse of the two." She pointed out that there had been arguments for forming ladies auxiliary societies and that a few members had even advocated admitting women to full membership in the Alliance. "And why not?" she asked. "In industrial organizations women have proven themselves the equal of men in every respect. . . . They will quickly show their ability if given the opportunity."[23]

By the end of April Fish was convinced that Eva was not a tool to be controlled and that she had political objectives of her own. They seem to have quarreled, and he dropped her column from his paper. Enthusiastic letters about her lectures continued to appear, however, written by local Alliance men throughout the state. She was well received by the farmers and even more so by their wives. Her aggressive impudence was carefully hidden beneath a demure manner and severely plain clothing. Donnelly, with whom Eva shared platforms through much of June and July that year, noted in his diary: "It was interesting to observe how the women gathered around her at the close of the meeting — a curious exhibition of feminine sympathy." Eva herself was surprised by their eager questions about factory conditions — until she realized how many of them had seen daughters leave to take a job in the cities.[24]

Ignatius Donnelly, though nearing sixty and scarred by a lifetime of political battles, had not yet learned to share Fish's wariness of the twenty-three-year-old upstart. Nevertheless, he seems to have sensed a certain steeliness in her makeup. On June 18, 1890, he committed to his diary a charming picture of their drive together to a meeting ten miles south of Winona. It was a lovely morning and the road wound slowly up a long gorge beneath the towering Mississippi bluffs. "The great variety of verdure, the different scents that filled the air, all made the drive most enjoyable. I quoted poetry by the yard. Miss McDonald is a very bright girl — quick and apt; not poetical; her mind bearing the traces of the hard battle by which she has raised herself from the living grave of the factory-room."

Her message to the farmers, repeated continually, was of the common interests between farm and factory and the need for mutual political support. She also continued to broaden her own contacts with the city labor organizations. In mid-June she addressed the plasterers' union of St. Paul on the need for organization, sharing the platform with her old partner, McGaughey, with A. O. Grigsby of the Duluth *Industrial Age*, and with Frank Valesh, a young Czech cigar maker who had just been elected president of the St. Paul Trades and Labor Assembly.[25]

Minnesota labor at this time was feeling its way through a delicate period of transition. The nationwide decline of the Knights of Labor had caught up with the movement in Minnesota, and craft groups in the cities had withdrawn right and left. A few of these groups had ties to national unions that were already affiliated with the American Federation of Labor, which had been formed in 1886, but there was no state-wide organization to replace the nearly defunct Minnesota district of the Knights of Labor. For a while the state Eight Hour League served as a stop-gap rallying point, but by the summer of 1890 the need was felt for a new organization.[26]

The first meeting of the Minnesota Federation of Labor, held in July, included representatives not only from the trades and labor assemblies of Minneapolis and St. Paul, but from the Eight Hour League, the Knights of Labor (what was left of it), and even the Farmers' Alliance. General principles and a system of representation were agreed upon, and political discussion was banished from all future meetings. Eva attended as a representative of the Eight

Hour League, and she also was present at the second convention, held in December, 1890, when a permanent organization was formed and Frank Valesh was elected president.[27]

On the political front, the farmer and labor forces tried third-party action once more, and under the name Alliance Labor Union party held a convention in July, 1890. Donnelly sought the nomination for governor again, but the labor people, still angry at what they considered his desertion to the Republicans two years before, favored R. J. Hall of Morris, president of the state Alliance. In the end Sidney M. Owen, a compromise candidate, was named. The party waged a vigorous campaign that fell short in the gubernatorial race but elected an Alliance congressman and made important gains in the state legislature. Pushed to the sidelines, Donnelly ran successfully for the Minnesota Senate and laid careful plans to take over the presidency of the Alliance himself.[28]

Eva's close ties with the labor faction placed her in the anti-Donnelly camp, but in seeking support throughout the state, Donnelly was apparently willing to continue courting labor. And perhaps, like Fish, he made the mistake of thinking he could control Eva with a paternal hand. On November 27, 1890, he wrote to her: "I am a candidate for president of the Alliance at our meeting of Dec. 30th. If I am elected I propose to push the work. Are yr engagements such that after Jany 1st you could take the field?"[29] It was a delicately worded offer, open to more than one interpretation, but the suggestion could hardly be avoided that he might support her as his successor in the office of State Lecturer.

On the first day of the Alliance convention Eva gave one of the opening speeches, and when balloting for State Lecturer began on the afternoon of the second day, her name stood at the top of the list. Her only serious rivals were Dr. Fish and James H. Baker. Donnelly had swept triumphantly into the presidency, and if he had wanted to prevent her election, there is little question that he could have done so. There were convenient grounds for rejecting her, as Fish promptly pointed out: Alliance membership was not open to women, and without membership she was ineligible for any office. Fish withdrew in favor of Baker, but Eva's popularity with the rank-and-file outstate membership proved decisive. She was elected by a vote of 436 to 209.[30]

The convention had scarcely closed when Fish declared war on Eva in the columns of the *Great West*. His first attacks were sidelong and cautious. While protesting that she "is in quite all respects an admirable young lady, and a talker of exquisite ability," he nevertheless felt that she was "identified with the political atmosphere of these two cities, of the state house, and of the daily press." A few days later he professed horrified disbelief of "a statement" that she was leaking confidential reports of Alliance business to the *Globe,* while on another page of the same issue he took pains to point out that "Miss McDonald is a salaried reporter for one of the most contemptible plutocratic sheets in the world — the St. Paul *Globe* — and is not, and cannot be, a member of a local alliance." [31]

In the meantime Eva had achieved another coup. The annual meeting of the National Farmers' Alliance was held in Omaha at the end of January, 1891. Eva went as a reporter for the *Globe.* Being, however, an officer of the Minnesota Alliance, she was admitted to the convention when the rest of the press was excluded. She also succeeded in getting appointed an assistant national lecturer — a post which involved no particular responsibility but offered the opportunity to go on speaking tours for the national organization. And it carried prestige. [32]

Back in Minnesota, Eva cornered for herself the clerkship of the House appropriations committee, a job that kept her in close touch with legislative developments and also paid five dollars a day. Since the office of State Lecturer carried no salary, she could hardly have been criticized for this, but she nevertheless pledged her earnings to the Alliance. She recalled that one member of the appropriations committee, a brewer from South St. Paul, announced loudly in her hearing, "I could get a much better man clerk for half that price." Quick as a flash Eva shot back, "I've heard people say they could get much better legislators than you for half the price, too." She soon became indispensable to the chairman, Hans P. Bjorge, of Otter Tail County, whom she described as "a cultured Norwegian gentleman farmer, not too practical," and Bjorge in turn became one of her staunchest friends on the Alliance executive committee. [33]

In the Alliance a move was afoot to dump Fish as the semiofficial spokesman for the organization. It was not the first time this had been tried. The doctor's feverish loyalty to Donnelly and his talent for vituperation made him a constant center of dissension. Moreover, the *Great West* was aimed exclusively at farmers and contained little or no labor news. Various plans were rumored for starting an independent farmer-labor paper, and perhaps, as Fish maintained, Eva hoped to become its editor. Donnelly countered by proposing that the Alliance purchase the *Great West* outright. It was over this issue that Eva first clashed openly with Donnelly and gradually emerged as the most outspoken opponent of his leadership.[34]

While sparks and accusations flew in the executive committee, Fish fumed and moaned. The *Great West*'s issue of February 13 was devoted almost exclusively to Eva, giving the impression that the editor had spent the whole week meditating on her and dashing off diatribes as new grievances occurred to him:

"The entire difficulty now existing, which is more bitter than ever before, is due to Miss McDonald, who has been a fighter every moment of her presence on the committee."

"It was sickening to see a grave man like Bjorge traipsing through the streets of St. Paul from place to place, at the tap of his girl committee-clerk."

"Surely there is a great deal of manhood disguised by a hairpin."

"It makes us tired of our own Irish ancestry — and, as a prominent lady said, 'makes us distrustful of suffrage.' How long, Oh Lord, must we bear the burden?"

And mournfully recalling the high hopes he had once held for Eva, he was led at last to a fine flow of masculine condescension: "We entertain no malice towards this young lady — not a grain. Her abilities are such that if she will come out from behind this presuming on account of her sex, cultivate the womanhood which has distinguished the eminent members of her sex, and above all let the sad wants of humanity inspire her to more of the tender, and less spitfire, a grand future will yet await her."

As Minnesota Alliance leaders quarreled and feuded, the long groundswell of protest among the nation's disinherited was slowly building toward a climax. From its beginnings, the national Alliance movement had been divided between northern and southern sections. In 1889 an attempt was made to unite them. It failed, but the effort did result in transforming the southern Farmers' Alliance into a powerful organization known as the Farmers' Alliance and Industrial Union, which reached to the West Coast and into some of the northeastern states. Kansas and the Dakotas opted to join it also, but Minnesota remained with the smaller and more conservative National Farmers' Alliance, which was rooted in the Middle West. At a convention held in December, 1890, the Farmers' Alliance and Industrial Union called for a national meeting of farm, labor, and reform groups. The place was to be Cincinnati and the date was to be May, 1891. Election victories had been won in 1890 by many state Alliance parties, and with the prospect of a presidential year in 1892, the time seemed coming to unite them in a national third-party movement.[35]

Each state Alliance was to send a delegation to Cincinnati. In Minnesota the question remained open of which organization it was to represent: the state Farmers' Alliance, dominated by Donnelly, or the Alliance Labor Union party, controlled by his enemies, of whom Eva McDonald had become the leading voice. Donnelly had national prestige, not only for his long record in protest politics, but as the author of *Caesar's Column*, a radical novel which had become a runaway best-seller in 1890. So when he announced that he would lead the delegation, there seemed little chance that dissidents from the Alliance Labor Union party would be able to unseat him at the convention.[36]

They tried, however. Several spokesmen for the opposition accompanied Eva to Cincinnati and challenged Donnelly's right to represent the state. The credentials committee turned a cold shoulder and also denied Eva when she made a special appeal on her own behalf. In the meantime she had invaded a caucus of the regular delegates, who at first voted magnanimously to seat her. She responded with such peppery words that they changed their minds immediately. Her name was placed in nomination for assistant secretary of the conference but was withdrawn when the Minnesota delegation protested, and when, at the suggestion of a group of newspaper people, she addressed the convention after its adjournment one evening, she was introduced as representing the Knights of Labor. Her persistence led Fish to grumble that "the only two troubles the vast convention had were the proper adjustment of the temperance question and Miss McDonald."[37]

In fact, the convention proved to be an overwhelming personal triumph for Donnelly, who succeeded almost singlehandedly in uniting the motley crowd and persuading those who still hung back from third-party action. A national committee to organize for a People's party was proclaimed, and the meeting ended with a surge of crusading emotion that washed back across the country with the returning delegates and sowed the seeds of Populism in state after state. Eva also returned, and on June 2, less than two weeks later, she and Frank Valesh were married.[38]

The first summer of Eva's marriage foreshadowed things to come: she and Valesh scarcely saw each other. Politically, if not personally, it was an ideal time for Eva to accept an out-of-state lecture tour. Donnelly's first move on returning to the state was to eliminate the Alliance Labor Union party. Alliance endorsement was given instead to the new Minnesota People's party, in which Eva and the labor group were as much outsiders as he had been in the campaign of the year before. But Eva was not to be silenced. The new national committee for a People's party was recruiting speakers in a campaign to convince reform groups across the country of the need for third-party action. In the small army of speakers recruited, Eva hit the trail along with such notables as "Sockless" Jerry Simpson, Senator William A. Peffer, Mary Lease, and Annie Diggs of Kansas, Leonidas L. Polk of North Carolina, James B. Weaver of Iowa, John H. Powers of Nebraska, and Dr. C. W. Macune of Texas.[39]

Her first engagements took her to Allegany County, New York, a key area in the state where an infant People's party was fighting to get off the ground. In a letter to Albert Dollenmayer, a young reporter for the *Minneapolis Tribune* who was her confidant and closest friend, she noted eagerly that "Jerry Simpson, Peffer, Polk, Weaver and all the celebrities stray into this country occasionally. They seem to think I'm a good speaker and predict a future for me. I lose no opportunity of studying their style and am putting in some hard study, both on the materials of my speeches and the manner of delivery." She was also charmed with the country and said prophetically: "I don't think I shall ever be contented to live on the prairies again."[40]

After a brief return to Minnesota, she left once more. On a steamy August night in Springfield, Illinois, she addressed a gathering of diverse farm and labor organizations that still hesitated to unite under the People's party. "It was amusing to hear Peffer and Pres. Powers of the National Alliance," she wrote. "They are straight out third party men, but they tried to adapt the new gospel to the people to whom they talked. I didn't worry about that. Just preached the gospel same as usual and told them I wouldn't be offended, should they desire to go out and cool off occasionally. I spoke in the court house where Abe Lincoln had often spoken and I think the inspiration still lingers." In Ohio she was the main attraction at a mass meeting during the state convention of the People's party. There she defended the right of a woman to speak in public "as long as there were homeless, voiceless women, helpless to cope with the hard conditions of life." The audience was rapturous.[41]

Her horizons were expanding. On August 20 she wrote to Dollenmayer from Corning, New York, that she had been invited to join the "aristocratic inner circle" of Alliance leadership on the Atlantic shore near Chesapeake Bay to "hold a council of peace on the industrial problem and incidentally to catch crabs and go surf bathing." She was also cultivating a friendship with Simpson, who "can do a good deal toward putting me a few rounds higher on the ladder if he chooses." In a revealing passage, she burst out: "I expect you to sympathize with my growing ambitions, Doll, for I'm afraid Frank will begin to fear that I'm getting so interested that it will end in my staying away from home right along. It is a hard struggle. I hate to leave him and I'm unhappy all the time away, yet I can't bear to let slip the opportunities that offer to get to the front. . . . now I have met the best of them I think without egotism that I could stand side by side with them and hold my own."

But the great summer of campaigning ended, and Eva returned to the prairies, her husband, and her neglected duties as State Lecturer of the Minnesota Alliance. With its most effective leaders absorbed by internal quarrels and national politics, the organization had suffered. Even more important in its decline, perhaps, were the bountiful harvests that midwestern farmers had reaped that year and a sharp rise in wheat prices.[42]

Speaking in the rural communities of Minnesota was hard, gritty work, and no doubt it seemed less exciting than it had the year before. Passenger trains usually ran only once a day, and sometimes, Eva recalled, she had to ride the caboose of a freight in order to make her schedule. The train crews were friendly, and on occasion she shared coffee and sandwiches with them, but the pounding and jerking of the uncushioned caboose only added to the wearying pace of speeches, organizational meetings, and one-night stopovers in small-town hotels or boardinghouses.

She did some lecturing around the state in the fall of 1891, but her efforts to organize chapters were undoubtedly handicapped by the lack of a state-wide press outlet. Having got Eva out of his system, Fish resolutely ignored her in the columns of the *Great West,* claiming blatantly that the office of State Lecturer was vacant. Although an attempt was made to start another Alliance paper, it petered out quickly.[43]

In November Eva attended a convention of the Farmers' Alliance and Industrial Union held in Indianapolis, where the national committee for a People's party was also assembled. "I got more honors than I was expecting," she wrote to Dollenmayer, "being selected to speak with Mrs. Lease and Mrs. Diggs on the evening devoted to woman's work. I also received some flattering offers to make a trip through the Southern states next spring." But she did not accept them, nor did she make any effort to retain the office of State Lecturer when the Minnesota Alliance convened in January. It would have been useless, for Donnelly was virtually unopposed for the office of president, and the decline in active Alliance chapters from nearly a thousand in 1890 to 377 at the end of 1891 was laid at her door. Moreover, Eva was by then six months pregnant.[44]

So, chafing and impatient, she sat at home waiting for her baby's birth, while the national Populist party came into being at a stirring convention held in St. Louis in February. Prevented from public speaking, she turned to writing and was encouraged when *The Arena* accepted her analysis of "The Strength and Weakness of the People's Movement" for publication in its May issue.[45]

With clear perception, the article examined the two major elements that made up Populism: the farmers, with a vast but ephemeral organization, hotly demanding political action; and labor, with better organization and discipline, but reluctant to grasp the political tool. She pointed out that participation of the Knights of Labor in forming the People's party did not mean that of workingmen generally, for the Knights were no longer a mass organization and represented only a residual group of "intelligent and far-seeing leaders." Bread-and-butter unionism, embodied in the American Federation of Labor, still held aloof. She rehearsed, as she so often had on the platform, the common interests of the two groups and reiterated her faith that "this new movement will unite the industrial forces of city and country." In closing, Eva noted with sharp insight: "It is a peculiarity of the People's movement that it has not yet produced a leader. It has teachers, — earnest, thoughtful, and progressive. It has statesmen of good parts. But a leader, in the true sense, is yet wanting."

This lack became only too evident at the nominating convention held the following July in Omaha. The People's ticket was made up of two aging Civil War generals — Weaver for president and James G. Field of Virginia for vice-president. In the fall the Populists polled over a million presidential votes and elected three governors and a number of congressmen, but impressive as the showing was, it did nothing to dent the American two-party system. In Minnesota Donnelly was again nominated for governor, but despite truly heroic efforts, he ran a poor third, receiving only about 16 per cent of the vote.[46]

In the meantime, as Annie Diggs wrote, the "crowning glory of motherhood" had come to Eva. It did not come easily. The birth of Frank Morgan Valesh nearly cost his mother's life, and she remained an invalid for months afterward. The experience probably left her with a terror of pregnancy that contributed to the disintegration of her marriage. In other respects, the story was dismally predictable. Eva hated housework and flatly refused to stay at home, nor did she think it necessary to consult her husband about her career decisions. She appears to have been fond enough of little Frank, but she was scarcely a doting mother. Valesh, who had immigrated from Bohemia at the age of nine, worried that her work would reflect on his own ability as a breadwinner. In 1892 he had resigned the presidency of the Minnesota Federation of Labor to take a job with the state Bureau of Labor Statistics which required travel and kept him away from home much of the time.[47]

As soon as her health permitted Eva accepted a position with the *Minneapolis Tribune*, editing a labor column as she had for the *Globe*, and in time doing more varied reporting. She also resumed lecturing for the Farmers' Alliance from time to time, for early in 1893 Donnelly broke with Fish and set about trying to heal the old wounds in the organization.[48] The year 1894 saw deepening depression throughout the country, and Populist hopes revived. Sidney Owen, who had been the defeated candidate for governor of the Alliance Labor Union party in 1890, ran again. He received a more substantial vote than before, but still far from enough. Eva's last political appearance occurred in 1896, when she was among a string of well-known Populist and Democratic party figures who were recruited to introduce presidential candidate William Jennings Bryan to Twin Cities crowds. With Bryan's decisive defeat, both in Minnesota and the nation, the Populist era came to an end.

At some time in the same year Eva and her husband decided to go their separate ways. Frank Valesh quit the labor movement and moved to Graceville, a small town on the open prairies of western Minnesota. Eva, with her four-year-old son, went to New York City. For several years she had been bored and frustrated with her job at the *Tribune* and with life in Minnesota. As early as 1893 she had written envyingly to her friend Dollenmayer of his assignment in Washington, and had complained: "I'm dreadfully weary of this section and spend more time planning to get away from it than I do at work." [49]

During the national AFL conventions that the Valeshes had attended together they had formed a warm personal friendship with Samuel Gompers, and he immediately offered Eva a job as an organizer. She preferred to stay with journalism, however. Friends on the staff of the *Tribune* provided her with a tenuous contact in the city room of William Randolph Hearst's *New York Journal,* and she challenged the streets of the metropolis and the competition of hard-bitten city reporters alone and almost unknown. She proved herself more than their equal in brashness and determination. By 1898 she was one of Hearst's top reporters and even managed to go along on a mission to Cuba. She had no illusions about her job security, however, and when a colleague warned her that she would be "thrown aside like a squeezed-out lemon" when Hearst had used the best of her talents and energy, she decided to quit. [50]

Moving to Washington, D.C., she supported herself with a variety of free-lance assignments, including ghost-writing articles for prominent political figures. At the same time, with borrowed money, she established an independent political newsletter which served a syndicate of papers around the country. This she recalled as "the happiest work I ever did in my life." [51] Nevertheless, she took time out from it in 1900 to join the staff of the Democratic National Committee as a paid consultant on labor affairs during Bryan's second campaign for president. Shortly after the election Gompers approached her about helping him with his personal periodical, the monthly *American Federationist.* She agreed, and for the next eight years she stayed with Gompers. In her recollection the job consisted of total responsibility for editing and publishing the magazine. She quit at last when he refused her request to put her name on it along with his.

Going to New York again, she immediately became involved with the Women's Trade Union League. About a year later she married Benjamin F. Cross, scion of a wealthy New York family, and in 1911 she and Cross began publishing a magazine known as the *American Club Woman.* Although never an official organ, it had close ties to the General Federation of Women's Clubs, and a large part of the magazine's contents consisted of news and announcements of that organization. Thanks to a liberal subsidy from Cross's family, the *Club Woman* survived for seven years. When it ceased publication the United States was in the midst of World War I, and Eva was already deeply involved in organizing charitable and relief work.[52]

A few years later her second marriage ended. Eva retained a country home that she and Cross had bought in the Catskills but faced the necessity of supporting herself once more. In 1919 a heart attack at the age of fifty-three had left her unable to sustain the pace and the pressure that had always been her way of life, but characteristically she scorned the idea of retiring to an old age of poverty and dependence. Since 1900 she had been on the honorary withdrawal list of the typographer's union, and in the mid-1920s she reactivated her membership. The long-standing seniority entitled her to top wages. For four years she worked as a proofreader for the *Pictorial Review,* then she moved to the *New York Times,* where she did proofreading until her retirement in 1951 at the age of eighty-five.[53]

The last member of her family with whom she maintained contact was her sister Blanche, fourteen years younger than Eva. Blanche had accompanied her to New York and had cared for five-year-old Frank during Eva's hard first year on the *Journal.* Thereafter the child was sent to a boarding school, but Blanche often joined Eva for vacations, and later she served as a contributing editor of the *American Club Woman.* According to Blanche, Eva returned briefly to Minneapolis in 1910 to divorce Valesh. Her family's view of this is perhaps suggested by Eva's own reluctance forty-six years afterward to admit there had been a divorce. John McDonald was killed in an accident in 1911, and in 1916 Blanche moved to New York, where she worked for ten years. In 1926 a complete break occurred between the sisters after Blanche suffered a nervous breakdown from the strain of caring for their aged mother.[54]

When Eva McDonald died in 1956 at the age of ninety, Minnesota's Populist past — and her own — were distant memories, and her name was scarcely recalled in the state where she had made her deepest mark. New generations of feminists and suffragists had succeeded where she had failed, and while she re-

treated steadily into conservatism on labor issues, midwestern radical leaders associated with an even more powerful wave of
farmer-labor protest had taken her place.

But the Populist women of the 1880s and 1890s were the first
American women to achieve political impact outside the strict
boundaries of the feminist and Abolition movements. Unlike many
of their contemporaries, they saw the cause of women integrally
bound to the cause of economic and social justice for the working
classes, and they challenged their fellow radicals to accept them as
equals in the struggle. In Eva's case the toughness and independence that challenge required may have hardened in time into a
single-minded ambition and a love of power for its own sake. But
if so, who can judge her? The bright sword of wit and the shield of
impudence were slender weapons with which to challenge the
prejudices of the 1880s.

5. MARIA LOUISE SANFORD
Minnesota's Heroine

*By Geraldine Bryan Schofield
and Susan Margot Smith*

A MEMORIAL SERVICE for Maria Louise Sanford was held on May 9, 1920, in Saint Mark's Episcopal Church, Minneapolis. It was one of the first of many tributes paid to the teacher, friend, and community figure who had been called the "best-loved woman in Minnesota." A few weeks later, the University of Minnesota dedicated its final convocation of the year to her memory. Maria Sanford would have loved the memorial pageantry and the rich vocabulary of eulogy that flowed from university faculty, alumni associations, and community organizations. Above all, she would have relished the public recognition of her work by governors, regents, and college presidents.[1]

It would probably not have occurred to her or to her admirers that the decorum of memorial made her less complicated than she had been or left any significant part of her unmentioned. But there was, in fact, a romantic, turbulent, undisciplined side of her which went all but unnoticed. Nothing was said about her tendency to gamble with time and money or about the inconsistencies of her powerful will. Her long struggle with the academic community was graciously ignored. If her troubles were mentioned, they were treated like the burdens of a modern pilgrim's progress. Her contemporaries thus made her more legendary than lifelike. It was left for the biographer to try to recover her full dimension.

Maria Sanford was born in Old Saybrook, Connecticut, on December 19, 1836, to Henry E. and Mary Clark Sanford. Her ancestors had settled Saybrook and been pillars of its community for three generations. It did not matter that her shoemaker father had returned to the family homestead after a business failure in Georgia or that his debt kept the family on the edge of perpetual poverty. Theirs was a heritage that adversity could not sully, and the children were reminded of it by their mother over and over again.[2]

77

Maria was an intense and active child. A family story had it that
she snatched a cup and drank from it unassisted at the age of two
months. She walked with her father, read with her mother, and
absorbed the domestic imagery of kerosene lamps, chopped wood,
and bubbling soap. From her mother she learned inspirational
stories of Revolutionary War heroes and worthy women; together
they talked about literature and recited poetry. On Sunday afternoons the family repeated Psalms and studied the Bible. Maria,
entranced by the diction and imagery of the King James version,
set out to read ten chapters or more each Sabbath.[3]

Her early formal education was by contrast bleak and stifling.
She remembered it, first in a country schoolhouse and then an
academy, as a barren activity without singing, literature, or history.
In the classes she attended children were reprimanded for drawing pictures on their slates and required to do a lot of "useless"
memorization. Services in the Congregational church were
equally grim, appealing neither to her imagination nor her intellect.[4]

The intellectual influence of her mother overcame dull
classrooms, however, and Maria used her dowry to attend the New
Britain Normal School. She completed the course with honors in
1855. Her graduate essay set forth a code of stern idealism: "The
future lies before us," she wrote, "and we can make it what we
will; no deed, no word, no thought of ours but leaves its deathless
record there, and blots once made can never be effaced." Her
commencement motto was: "Fear not! faint not! fail not!"[5]

Full of energy and ambition, she began her teaching career forty
miles from home at a country school in Gilead. Her first salary of
ten dollars a month was improved upon as she moved from Gilead
to a graded school in Glastonbury and afterward to the upper
grades in New Haven. There, on the advice of historian John
Fiske, Maria continued her education by reading a selection of
basic works in history and science. She was teaching in another
Connecticut town, earning thirty-six dollars a month, when her
talent as a teacher came to the attention of W. W. Woodruff,
superintendent of schools in Chester County, Pennsylvania.[6]

Their meeting was a happy circumstance, for Maria had been
teaching for twelve years and was looking for another job. Not
long afterward she wrote to Woodruff, expressing her interest in
becoming a school principal. She thought, she said, that there
might be less prejudice against a woman holding such a post in

Maria Louise Sanford

Pennsylvania than in the "land of steady habits." Woodruff was impressed with her and persuaded the county school board to hire her as a classroom teacher for a four-month term at forty-five dollars a month. In 1867 Maria left Connecticut for the first time at the age of thirty-one.[7]

Her success in Parkersville, Pennsylvania, was a matter for superlatives and Superintendent Woodruff was lavish with them: "During the last eight years I have examined about 3000 teachers, and have made 2500 visits to the schools of the county . . . and I have no hesitancy in saying, as I often have said, that I consider Miss Sanford the best teacher that I have ever seen in a schoolroom. In this opinion, I am sustained, so far as I have heard, by the 127 teachers, school directors, and friends of education who visited her school during her first term of four months." Moreover, attendance in her classes rose above the average 60 to 70 per cent to an extraordinary 93 per cent. The school board raised her wages by a third and hired her for the summer term. She was so popular with the students that a number of them followed her to an academy at Unionville, Pennsylvania, paying a double tax rate to do so. Her motto at the time was: "Nothing is impossible to him who wills."[8]

It was not long before the young teacher's interest in education extended beyond her own classroom. She addressed a teachers' institute and saw her lecture published in the state school journal. In due course a number of leading citizens began a campaign to win her election as the county superintendent of schools. An eager candidate, she diligently visited voters and collected signatures. But even Pennsylvania was not ready for something as radical as a woman superintendent, and she lost in a close vote.[9]

As a lecturer on the art of teaching and the objectives of education, however, she was much sought after. Crisscrossing Chester County, she spoke on such topics as "Moral Training in School," "How Can We Elevate Our Public Schools?" and "Lessons in Manners and Morals." Her persistent theme was that training in decorum and character was the first task not only of each teacher but of the educational system in general. Unless manners and morals were shaped, she thought, the mind was unlikely to be accessible. She argued that the prevailing definition of education was so narrow that it dulled the students' minds. She sought transformation and reached out to the stifled imagination and latent sensibility.[10]

Swarthmore College invited the dynamic Miss Sanford to replace one of its faculty members on a temporary basis in the fall of 1869. The following year she accepted a permanent appointment and was given responsibility for instruction in history, political economy, and public speaking. Her style in the classroom was electrifying, her impact on students enormous. She turned dry names into vital personages and dates into points of departure. If she thought it would elucidate meaning, she turned poetry into prose. If a subject was worth introducing in the first place, she made it alive, intense, and urgent. She walked as she talked, gave surprise tests, and usually forgot to take attendance. Edward Hicks Magill, president of Swarthmore, once asked her whether she was sufficiently aware of absentees to stop her lectures if all the seats were vacant. The point was moot because her classes were always full.[11]

Her enthusiasm inevitably brimmed over the edges of the campus, for she had things to say about the educational enterprise that required wider audiences. She began at teachers' institutes, where for many years she was the only woman speaker. Then she discovered that people outside the teaching profession were interested in lectures on composition, history, teaching, and social issues.

She advertised her services quite frankly, announcing three days and an evening of lecturing for fifty dollars and expenses. The response was overwhelming.[12]

Although President Magill may have been disposed to count Miss Sanford's outside activities among Swarthmore's accomplishments, some disgruntled faculty and board members were not inclined to do so. Mild academic jealousies soon turned into bitter friction. An uneasy peace was made by reducing her salary from $2,000 to $1,500 for the academic year 1876–77. President Magill was unhappy with this solution but apparently powerless to do anything about it. He did, however, refuse to ask her to take on additional duties at the college. Her relationship with the Swarthmore community was not improved by her weekly three-day absences from campus, reduced salary, and decreased responsibilities.[13]

Maria was not indifferent to her situation: she suffered from the accusations of her enemies and was shunned by others who were uncomfortable with either her style or her activities. Still, she not only enjoyed public lecturing but needed the extra income it provided. She was supporting her orphaned niece, as well as repaying a loan of $1,000 for which she had stood surety to help finance an unsuccessful business venture in which two of her young relatives were involved. There could be no practical thought of abandoning her speaking engagements. As long as students flocked to her classes her professional life seemed to be in good order. But she knew that her loose-fitting black dresses made no concession to style, her hair was turning gray, and her inner resources might be limited. In 1875 she expressed a moment of desolation: "I feel that I am losing hope, I feel less strong, less confident, less sure of what I am, of what I can do, of the good in what I have done, and even sick — a wood robin's note is the only sound that breaks the silence. Can you hear it?"[14]

Her melancholy was sharpened by unhappiness in love. Early in her Connecticut teaching career, she broke her engagement to a promising theology student who claimed to believe in the theory of evolution. The righteousness of her position softened her regret. But the consequences of being in love with Edward H. Magill were far more serious. The two were intellectual companions and kindred spirits. Both had powerful personalities and ardent dispositions. They shared triumphs and exhausted depressions during long hours in one another's offices until a crisis of need and desire at last forced them to cope with the fact that he was already married.[15]

Since the world view they shared required them to give up any hope of a permanent relationship, they painfully set about to impose the discipline of the decision upon themselves. Early in 1876 Maria channeled her passion into a dramatic declaration of how she intended to manage her grief and shape her life: "I thank thee, oh my God, for light. 'Till death us part' it shall be true. I can work for him, seek his happiness, live for him; and receive no sign. Shall I not then be his good angel? That will not be coldness, but the fullness of unselfish love. O God help me! My heart shall not grow cold for I will keep it warm with sympathy and love for others. I will throw my whole soul into my profession." This stern resolution had the necessary effect. She met her classes, maintained her speaking schedule, and began looking beyond Swarthmore. A year later there seemed to be an opportunity at the University of Michigan and President Magill sent a glowing letter of recommendation. "She is truly a remarkably gifted teacher," he wrote. "I have never seen her equal in an experience of more than a quarter of a century." In spite of this testimonial, Michigan was unwilling to take on even so gifted a woman. Maria remained at Swarthmore until 1879 when she resigned her position with little more than hope to sustain her.[16]

A year passed before the University of Minnesota offered her another academic home. Its president, William Watts Folwell, who was recruiting new faculty members, wanted a woman to fill a vacancy in the French department. Maria Sanford had not graduated from college, lacked advanced degrees, and could read no foreign language. But Edward Magill said she had talent, and Folwell himself saw something exceptional in her. So he appointed her an assistant professor of English at a salary of $1,200. She arrived in Minneapolis in 1880 with her niece, Emily L. Hough, who had been boarding with her.[17]

At last she seemed to have found a place large enough for her talents. She had access to a student body of three hundred, from subfreshmen to seniors, to whom she could introduce her ideals and expectations. Her teaching load included large classes in composition, rhetoric, elocution, and oratory. She had no particular concern about class size or regard for customary practice, and she overwhelmed them with work. Upperclassmen could expect two written essays or one carefully prepared recitation a term, requirements that escalated over the years. Student orators could expect to be drilled at ruthless 4:00 A.M. coaching sessions no matter what convention might say about women who instructed young men in oratory.[18]

Her concern for the welfare of her students was not limited to the hours she spent in her office or the dingy, little classroom in Old Main. Sixteen of them lived with her in the house she purchased near the campus. They shared household tasks, made it their home away from home, and were swept along by Maria's enormous energy and optimism. Knowing that there was little social life on campus, she often had parties at her house. She encouraged students to roll up the rugs for dancing and once gave a "Bal-Masque" for sophomores. The whole arrangement proved so popular that she soon bought a second house to accommodate more roomers.[19]

The new professor's fine disregard for precedent and conventions did not, surprisingly, immediately alienate her from her academic colleagues. She was promoted to the rank of full professor of rhetoric and elocution in her second year, and during her third she served as acting head of the English department. If her new post created any uneasiness in her mind, Edward Magill was there to set it at rest. "Oh my friend," he once wrote, "if thou could know how eagerly and anxiously I have watched thy career, and how proud I am made of every new success that comes to my ears — would it be *some* compensation — for hard labor, for anxious and wearing cares?" A flourish was added to her success by the knowledge that Minnesota also had audiences for the public lecturer. She gave her first lecture outside the university in October, 1880.[20]

The latent capacities of a youthful university provided just the scope that Maria's expansive nature required, and she loved it. To Cyrus Northrop, then under consideration as successor to President Folwell, she wrote: "I think you will find this a most delightful place to work. Our Regents are liberal in thought and act, and if they are a little slow they have the good of the Univ. at heart. As a Faculty we are united and cordial and we will give you our hearty support. . . . We are not accustomed to much supervision but we understand that 'new masters make new laws.' Our students are remarkably obedient and law-abiding; and I can think of no reason which should deter you from coming *to rule over* us."[21]

Her personal affairs were far from happy. In the late 1880s, persuaded by the success of a former student to make a considerable investment in local real estate, she asked several friends to pool their resources for the venture. Then the boom collapsed and she faced the specter of a staggering financial loss which one biographer estimated at over $30,000. Although she was advised to declare bankruptcy, she insisted on holding herself responsible for the losses of those who had parted with their money. Her personal integrity was at stake, she felt.[22]

Since her small salary made little impact on this burden, she began to seek outside income. Lecturing was the most obvious source, and she had no trouble finding engagements. Many groups were already acquainted with her through her university extension work. Others were attracted by her lively advertising. Soon she was traveling around Minnesota and into neighboring states, saving money by walking and, when she had to ride, by sleeping in day coaches. Such small economies not only became part of her routine, but made substantial inroads on her energy. Gathering and chopping her own wood, picking up wastepaper to burn in the classroom stove, and sweeping out railroad cars for grain to feed her chickens were more than incidental activities. Necessity, as she saw it, forced her to deal with a major problem, and to deal with it in painfully small increments. The only way her expansive temperament could tolerate the cramping situation was to make it part of a virtuous life plan. Thus the smallest saving for herself or the university was as important as a speech on moral education or a class session in composition. To neglect one aspect of the work was to dishonor it all.[23]

Her students and colleagues began to think otherwise. Although she was still drawing large classes and building up a program in oratory, many thought her teaching was suffering. The "sunrise class" she held at 7:30 A.M. may have been composed of honor students, but it was hard to overlook the probability that the unusual hour was chosen by the instructor to accommodate her outside work. She already had an image of singularity because of her unfashionable black dresses and social aloofness. Now associates began to wonder if she was motivated by self-interest. Even the yearbook and the junior class play caricatured her practices and appearance. Finally a group of students organized themselves in order to ask for her removal from the faculty.[24]

She was crushed by such explicit animosity, but she refused to be deterred from the objectives and the style that she had worked out for herself. By 1890 the complaints became specific. Edward Magill may have wondered who could doubt "the Queen" but Cyrus Northrop knew only too well. Students and faculty members complained that the work in the rhetoric department was in excess of that stipulated in the catalogue. In any case, one essay a week was too much. It was also said that Professor Sanford made money from her students by giving private lessons and renting books which she had assigned as required reading. It was a bad year.[25]

Still she continued the relentless pace. She carried full teaching loads in the early 1890s, taught during summer sessions, and conducted an unusual course called "Senior Literary Criticism." At the same time, she tended her expanding lecture circuit. Gradually criticism gave way to tolerance and cautious esteem. A poem that appeared in a student publication was an offer of friendship, though it hinted at some of the difficulties.

> Though sometimes her little dealings may not
> soothe a person's feelings,
> And he lets his temper fly beyond recall;
> Still these deeds are done in blindness, and
> her heart is full of kindness —
> She's a pretty good Maria after all.

A former student, disillusioned by his experiences in graduate school, wrote to her: "I have often heard you say in the classroom that you did not consider it your only duty to teach Rhetoric and composition but also to help us become better men and women. . . . I wish that all teachers had your theories and lived up to them as you do, professor." Indeed her mail was full of letters thanking her for encouragement and inspiration. Even her colleagues seemed to be having a flash of appreciation for her efforts. One of them wrote to her affectionately while she was on a vacation: "I hope that you will be moderate in your industry and not work more than thirty six hours out of the twenty four."[26]

She flourished under approval and threw herself into even more activities. The struggling debate program was one of her pet projects, and she regularly called upon selected alumni to donate prize money for debate contests. Some thought the request was inappropriate, but most of them responsed enthusiastically. The success of her efforts was clear when the University of Minnesota was invited to become a member of the Northern Oratorical League. Meanwhile, her classes continued to be rich and colorful. Her course called "Reading," focusing on Shakespeare, had long been popular. But when she used lantern slides to illustrate her lectures, the response was overwhelming. Students from rural backgrounds suddenly had an opportunity to become acquainted with the art and architecture of the ancient world. The exotica of Rome, Carthage, and Egypt became staples of classes in rhetoric. The university may not have had a department of art history, but it had instruction in the subject. Maria saw nothing illogical in the pedagogy. The good, the true, and the beautiful were, after all, the single object of education.[27]

As a lecturer in the public sphere, she seemed to be more and more in demand. She took her extensive and adaptable repertory to public schools, civic organizations, and town meetings. Cyrus Northrop provided her with a generous letter of introduction, if not the blessing of the university. "Professor Maria L. Sanford," he wrote, "has had great success in the University of Minnesota in teaching . . . her classes being very enthusiastic over their work. She has great power in stimulating her students and in awakening the liveliest interest."[28]

Community leaders really did not need to be convinced. The Minneapolis superintendent of schools doubtless spoke for many. "No other woman in Minnesota," he maintained, "has done so much in the interests of the common schools of the state and is always so willing to give her time and strength to the teachers . . ." In fact, she was a friend not only to the educational community, but to anyone who cared about the quality of life in the city. An early president of the Minneapolis Improvement League, she organized projects "to promote the cleanliness, health and beauty of the city." This involved work to improve garbage and snow removal, prohibit spitting in streetcars, and stimulate the planting of flowers. She encouraged children in the public schools to participate in a city-wide competition for prize flowers, a project which won national attention.[29]

Her students had a chance to display their loyalty when the *Minneapolis Journal* conducted a favorite-teacher contest. The first prize was a trip to Europe. Although Maria won the third prize, a group of undergraduates persuaded the *Journal* to let them make up the difference for the trip to Europe. In 1899, at the age of 62, Maria had her first and only opportunity to see the art treasures whose beauty she had tried so hard to capture in the classroom. She thought it was one of the most exciting things that had ever happened to her, but true to form, she spent most of her time at art galleries in London and Paris collecting slides for her illustrated lectures. After two months, she returned home with twenty-seven dollars of her prize money unspent.[30]

It was not long before she was again at odds with the university. A student complained that he had to accept tutoring from her in order to pass her course and that she charged him five dollars. It was rumored that her art students were required to pay a fee of a dollar a year. And someone said that she had given two seniors marks for work they had yet to complete. In March, 1900, the president addressed her in a rare attack of frustration: "Now when you were struggling and pleading for a full salary [of] $2400, you said if you got it you would be the happiest woman in Minnesota. You did get it. All the time that you give to students belongs to the University. It is paid for by a full salary. The charging here and there five dollars or one dollar is wholly wrong and ought not to be done in any case. There is a good deal of excitement over it in certain quarters, as the fact has been brought out in one of the Faculties. I hope you will never take another cent from any student for teaching — except your salary." He did not exaggerate the excitement. Ten days later the regents had before them a resolution to discharge her and three other members of the faculty at the end of the 1901 school year.[31]

The proposal to terminate the appointment of Maria Sanford, thrown almost immediately into the public forum, brought swift and fierce reaction. Civic leaders made inquiry. Former students offered their support. The Woman's Council of Minneapolis, in a resolution to the board of regents, voted to extend to her "its heartiest thanks, and as mothers . . . express our confidence in her as a guide and inspiration to all those who have come under her instruction." It appeared for a time that the problem might be solved if she were selected for the presidency of the University of Idaho. In 1900 glowing letters of recommendation went to Idaho. John Pillsbury, president of the board of regents, described her as a woman of "rare ability" with "the faculty of commanding the respect of all those with whom she comes in contact." Cyrus Northrop went a little further. "She has the gentleness and refinement of the true woman united to the firmness and decision of the

man. . . . I know of no one in the Faculty of this University
. . . who possesses such power to interest the people in the
value of education as she." Unfortunately, the University of Idaho
was not interested.[32]

The regents finally yielded to Professor Sanford's supporters.
Her job was saved, but a year later, perhaps in response to faculty
criticism of her ideas and pedagogy, her salary was cut from $2,400
to $1,800. This reduction was an insult she felt keenly. Age was
given as the reason for not raising her salary — she was past
sixty-five — but she was taking eighteen hours of recitation a week
and supervising debates and oratorical contests. Bitterly resentful,
she wrote to the board of regents: "My pride in my professional
reputation is very great, and the degradation which I have suffered
has been far harder to bear than the privation which the change
has brought . . ."[33]

The skirmishing over her salary continued year after year. In
1905 she presented the regents with a report comparing her work
with that of five other department heads. Her rhetoric department,
she concluded, was the largest, she taught the largest number of
classes, and she had the largest number of students. The data did
not impress the regents. So she resumed the argument the following month: "Inasmuch as I am managing the largest department in
this college, and teaching a larger number of students than any
other professor, I respectfully request you to make my salary more
nearly commensurate with my work. . . . As evidence that I have
not lost my power to teach I call your attention to the large
number of students in my classes, nearly all my work being elective. I will assure you that when by this test I am growing old,
when the number of students seeking my instruction falls off, I
will cheerfully submit to any reduction of my salary you may see
fit to make."[34]

In the spring of 1907, changing her tactics, she took her case
directly to the governor. She was determined, she said, to make
her department outstanding. This would mean salary money for
everyone. As for herself, she was weary of the hectic round of outside lecturing to supplement her income. She wanted $3,000 plus
vindication of her work and her record by the regents. The dean of
the college took her part. "Miss Sanford is doing vigorous and valuable work," he assured the regents' salary committee, "more
concentrated and systematic than formerly." Whether his argu-

ment was persuasive or whether the whole affair had become too annoying to pursue further, the regents finally relented. Miss Sanford's salary was increased to $3,000 a year, making her eligible for a Carnegie pension of $1,500 when she retired.[35]

The regents may have been reluctant to recognize Maria Sanford's accomplishments as a teacher, but she was earning wide recognition beyond the campus. It was no longer sufficient to say that she accepted some speaking engagements outside the university. She had become an accomplished entrepreneur on the lecture circuit, speaking to university extension students, schools, farmers' clubs, civic and social organizations, and honorary societies. One winter she lectured four or five nights a week. She could discuss poetry or social issues, art or politics. She often traveled fifty or a hundred miles to give a lecture, sometimes walking part of the way.[36]

Maria Sanford had by now become a prominent and respected public figure. The governor appointed her as Minnesota delegate to the 1903 Congress of the National Prison Association. Civic leaders consulted her on matters of importance to the city of Minneapolis. Students continued to write to her. "I had a picture in my mind of you as you used to sweep into the lecture hall brimming over with enthousiasm [sic] . . ." wrote one. Said another, "I doubt if you yourself fully appreciate the value as an example to your students, that the courage and industry of your life have been and are."[37]

In the fall of 1906 preparations were under way for her gala seventieth birthday party. The Women's League obtained contributions from ninety-one individuals and twenty-four clubs. A reception was held on campus in the new women's building, Alice Shevlin Hall. In the receiving line were the governor and many of the university's chief officers. The alumni presented the university with a portrait of Maria, and she herself received a coat and muff. The occasion was important to her in both a personal and diplomatic sense. It helped to narrow the gap between mere popularity and academic respectability.[38]

The occasion of her retirement in June, 1909, in her seventy-third year, was the crowning event of her academic life. The regents made their peace by naming her professor emeritus of rhetoric. She was adopted into the graduating class and asked to give the main commencement address. Her oration rang with all the ideas about duty, morality, and inspiration that had shaped her professional career.[39]

Retirement for Maria Sanford was really no more than a resolution, but an important one, of her conflicting interests. She was now free to devote her energies to what she liked to call "general helping." Before long she was committed to a round of public engagements on behalf of education, religion, and the public welfare. A favorite project, and one that went on for many years, involved black churches and educational institutions in the South. It began with a dedicatory address at the First Congregational Church in Atlanta. Then in 1910 with the help of its pastor, Henry H. Proctor, she arranged a speaking tour to secure funds for the church. It soon became clear that in this way she could serve the interests of other black churches, teacher training schools, and universities. At one point she even persuaded President William H. Taft to endorse her fund-raising efforts for the Haines Normal and Industrial Institute of Augusta, Georgia.[40]

Fund-raising was still a matter of personal concern. Her debt was reduced but still substantial, and her relatives had needs that she was determined to help support. Her pension and lecture fees were not enough. In the fall of 1910, attracted by another real estate venture, she purchased thirty-five acres of land in Largo, Florida. Thus at the age of seventy-four she stood in the Chicago railroad station with a spade, a hoe, and batch of celery seedlings, convinced that a rare opportunity lay at the other end of the track. The land turned out to be covered with palmetto scrub and quite unsuitable for celery. But she and her fifteen-year-old grand-nephew spent half a year there, living in a one-room shack, before she gave up farming and returned to Minneapolis. Eventually she exchanged the farm for some property in Lakeland, Florida. Land management was not one of her talents.[41]

Leadership from the speaker's platform was. Early in 1912 Minneapolis club women asked her to address the biennial meeting of the National Federation of Women's Clubs in San Francisco. The intent was to thank and honor her, said the invitation, for "in a long public and private life you have stood every test, and been true to the highest ideals of womanhood." Her speech, "The Value of Moral Power in the Schoolroom," was an unqualified success. A newspaper report was lyrical: "Seventy-five and active; seventy-five with a voice that has the power and resonance

. . . to move with enthusiastic admiration and devotion the immense audience of club women that packed the auditorium
this morning . . ." She was overwhelmed with dinner invitations,
had all kinds of attention, and throve on it. "I am having a delightful time," she wrote to her niece. "Everyone is praising my speech
and all treat me with marked respect." Moreover, she had made a
little extra money along the way by speaking in Tacoma and Port-
land.[42]

Requests for her time and talent became more numerous with
each passing year. She was regarded not only as a seasoned
speaker but as an educator with ideas worth listening to. President
George E. Vincent of the University of Minnesota asked her to
join seventy-five other lecturers in a newly developed extension
program. The women's clubs of Minnesota called on her for lectures that took her back and forth across the state. In 1914 she
represented Minnesota at the tenth annual conference of the National Child Labor Committee and the National Conference on
Unemployment. The following year she joined a campaign to
make Minneapolis dry. The *Minneapolis Journal* even sent her to
assess the merits of a new school system in Gary, Indiana.[43]

Private interests took her even farther afield. By 1915 she had
created a lecture circuit that reached west to California, Montana,
and North Dakota, and east to New York. Nor did she make any
concession to age. On one trip to Montana she found the railroad
station disagreeably noisy and full of flies. So she moved to a truck
out on the platform where she settled comfortably for the night.
She was seventy-nine at the time. From New York, she wrote, "I
am very busy. I lecture every day in different places, and between
the traveling and preparing my lectures there is hardly a minute
left."[44]

This hectic schedule was dictated by need as much as by interest, for she was still struggling with money. The debt was diminished and manageable, but still several thousand dollars strong.
Meanwhile, her many relatives had lives and debts of their
own. Over the years she paid for their educations, their taxes, and
additions to their houses. Still she could not refrain from investments. She gambled on a marble quarry in Colorado, a rubber
plantation in Mexico, and a copper mine in Montana. None of
them worked to her benefit. Though it remains unknown how she
finally paid off her debts, that she did must be assumed from the
fact that after her death not one claim was made on her estate.[45]

There was no doubt, however, that her life and work had been of very great value. Her birthdays were for many years occasions for public celebration, but her eightieth surpassed them all. At a convocation in the armory at the university, the guest of honor was presented with eighty pink roses and tributes from some of her oldest friends. Professor Oscar W. Firkins, the university's one-man comparative literature department, was characteristically poetic:

> Praise her not with smug obeisance,
> Sleek and millinered complaisance!
> Save your peppermint and raisins
>   For the dupe of sugared lies!
> Praise her, travel-soiled and dusty,
> Praise her, vehement and gusty,
> Praise her, kinked and knurled and crusty,
> Leonine and hale and lusty,
> Praise her, oaken-ribbed and trusty,
>   Shout 'Maria' to the skies.

Maria was touched but unwilling to be laid to rest by occasions with a commemorative flavor. "Work is life to me," she said. "I am hoping that my health and strength will hold out for another ten years, to enable me to do things for others that I have always longed to do but never had the time."[46]

She did not have ten more years but she made the most of those that remained. An aneurism of the aorta made hardly any impact on her life-style, and she continued to lecture from a full schedule. During World War I she became involved in patriotic war work and participated in historic pageants. Her last public address, "Apostrophe to the Flag," was given at a national convention of the Daughters of the American Revolution in Washington, D.C. She died there in her sleep the next day, on April 21, 1920, with, it was said, a smile on her face.[47]

Maria Sanford's accomplishments were catalogued so often by her admirers that they are easy to recall. She was an unusually gifted teacher, an inspiring lecturer, a tireless worker for civic causes. A staunch adherent to the nineteenth-century faith that education could not only transform the individual but cure social ills, she thought of herself as an educator responsible to a public trust; her loyalties went beyond any single institution.

Her ethics were associated with patriotism, religion, frugality, and self-help, and for these values she was respected and loved.

She was wary of labor unions, strikes, or anything that smacked of "socialist" philosophies. Although her life was a struggle for professional advancement, she came only in her later years to support women's suffrage. Even then she thought of it as a privilege rather than a right.[48]

Little notice has been taken, however, of the disharmonies that seemed to run through her life. Her faculty colleagues often criticized her, her students periodically revolted, she was repeatedly accused of self-interest and impropriety. Her activities alone could not have been the cause of so much criticism.

Perhaps it was after all simply a matter of temperament. She was strong-willed, unmethodical, often quixotic. Her aesthetic sensibility was at odds with prevailing academic practices; her energies took her beyond the bounds of conventional female activities; her restless spirit constantly looked for new opportunities. She was an entrepreneur, whether or not she intended to be. Discord and explicit dislike were inevitable results. Perhaps it is remarkable that she should have been the recipient of so much ungrudging praise.

6. FRANCES DENSMORE
Pioneer in the Study
of American Indian Music

By Nina Marchetti Archabal

FRANCES DENSMORE was a distinguished Minnesota scholar
who for over half a century worked to record and interpret the
music of American Indians. At a time when most Americans were
interested in eradicating Indian culture, she labored with a sense
of urgency to document their customs and music. Essentially self-
taught and with little institutional support, she tirelessly collected
and transcribed native music, conducting field studies among
tribes from the Pacific Northwest to the Florida Everglades.
By the time of her death in 1957 she had made about 2,500 sound
recordings, published more than 20 books and 200 articles, and
lectured throughout the United States on Indian customs and
music. Although her musical analyses reflected a training in
eighteenth- and nineteenth-century European music, her scholarly
interest in the music of Native Americans made her an American
pioneer in the field of ethnomusicology.

Frances Densmore was born on May 21, 1867, in the Mississippi
River town of Red Wing. Her paternal grandparents, Orrin and
Elizabeth Densmore, had migrated westward from New York state
to Wisconsin in the 1840s. In 1857 they moved on to Minnesota
and settled in Red Wing, where Orrin became the superintendent
of a sawmill and a citizen of some prominence. He had strong
interests in educational and scientific topics and recorded local
weather data for many years, sending off monthly reports to the
Smithsonian Institution.

Orrin and Elizabeth's oldest child Benjamin — Frances'
father — was born in New York in 1831 and moved west with his
family. Trained as a civil engineer, he served with the Sixth Minnesota Regiment during the Civil War and then returned to Red
Wing, where he and his brother Daniel founded the Red Wing

Iron Works. In 1866 Benjamin married Sarah Adalaide Greenland and the next year their first child, Frances, was born.[1]

During her early childhood Frances frequently saw Indians on the streets of Red Wing. As she recalled many years later, her curiosity was aroused and she became eager to learn more about these "strange people."[2] She also remembered that her interest in their music was stimulated when she was very young: "our home commanded a view of the Mississippi River. Opposite the town, on an island, was a camp of Sioux Indians and at night, when they were dancing, we could hear the sound of the drum and see the flicker of their camp-fire. In the twilight I listened to these sounds, when I ought to have been going to sleep. . . . So I fell asleep with my mind full of fancies about the 'interesting people' across the Mississippi."[3]

Frances' formal musical education began early and was, she recalled, "Spartan in its severity. I was taught harmony on the keyboard while I still lisped, and took 'time out' if I played anything as frivolous as Pleyel's German Hymn with variations during a practice period." On the strength of this foundation she went on to undertake the most extensive and rigorous musical training then available in the United States. In 1884, at the age of seventeen, she entered Oberlin Conservatory in Ohio, where she worked on piano, organ, and harmony. Returning to Minnesota in 1887 after her studies, she gave piano lessons at a St. Paul music store and served as a church organist. During the winter of 1888 she began further musical training in Boston, studying piano with Carl Baermann and counterpoint with the distinguished Harvard composer and professor, John Knowles Paine. After two winters of study in Boston, she settled again in St. Paul and rented a studio to teach piano.

In a brief autobiographical sketch Frances Densmore recalled that her scholarly interest in Indian music probably began while she was in Boston. About that time she had learned of the research being done by Alice Cunningham Fletcher on the music and customs of the Omaha Indians. Densmore acquired a copy of Fletcher's *A Study of Omaha Indian Music* shortly after its publication in 1893, and it inspired her to begin her own lifelong study of North American Indian music and customs.[4]

Fletcher's book was an important early work in its field, as well as a model for Densmore's own studies. When Densmore started her work, the music of non-Western cultures, previously of inter-

est largely as a novelty, was just beginning to develop as a subject
for serious study. Of critical importance in this development was
Thomas A. Edison's invention in 1877 of sound recording, a
technology which provided a means of preserving unwritten
music for study and analysis. Alice Fletcher's account of Omaha
music was based on sound recordings made with a primitive but
sturdy device suitable for prairie travel. Her book stimulated considerable interest in Indian music and firmly established the importance of sound recording for future work in the field.[5]

Fletcher's study included descriptions of Omaha customs and
presented the Indian songs as transcribed by her collaborator,
John Comfort Fillmore, director of the Milwaukee School of
Music. Fillmore transcribed the songs with piano accompaniments, a procedure he explained in an analytical "Report on the
Structural Peculiarities of the Music" which was appended to
Fletcher's study. In the course of working with Fletcher's collection of songs, Fillmore had become convinced that Indians possessed an unconscious sense of harmony, by which they even conceived modulations from one key to another. He therefore
presented Fletcher's Omaha songs with elaborate harmonizations
not unlike those of nineteenth-century gospel hymns. Fillmore's
theoretical work on native music was to have a considerable
influence on Densmore's own ideas about the structure of Indian
music.

In 1893 Densmore visited Fillmore in Milwaukee in order to
become fully acquainted with his theory. She remembered that he
explained his work in detail, "playing the harmonized songs on
the piano and describing his experiences with the Omaha."[6]

Returning to Minnesota, she studied Fletcher's book and began
to read systematically on the subject of Indians. "For the next ten
years," she recalled, "I soaked my receptive mind in what army
officers wrote about Indians, and what historians wrote about Indians, [along] with some of the publications of the Bureau of
American Ethnology. . . . All this was preparation for my life
work."[7]

During the early years of her study of Indian music Densmore
continued her career as a professional, performing musician. She
was active in St. Paul and Red Wing as a piano teacher, church
organist, church choir director, and professional lecturer on various musical subjects to local clubs. In 1895 she added a novel
lecture to her repertory. Now, in addition to her talks on Wag-

Frances Densmore, right, with Susan Windgrow, a Dakota

nerian operas and other conventional musical topics, she offered a lecture on Indian music based on the research of Alice Fletcher, with whom she was corresponding and who was offering her direction and encouragement.[8]

On December 4, 1895, Densmore delivered her first lecture on Indian music before the Schubert Club of St. Paul, which had assembled for the occasion at Conover Hall. The talk was illustrated with Omaha songs. Many years later Densmore recalled that she played the piano accompaniment while one of the Schubert Club members sang the songs. In later lectures Densmore sang the songs herself and provided her own accompaniment.[9]

From the beginning Densmore took her work as a lecturer seriously and paid meticulous attention to the manner of delivery. She took elocution lessons, and an undated lecture manuscript from about this time shows careful underscoring to indicate details of pronunciation and inflection. Between 1895 and 1904 she gave at least fifteen talks on Indian music in Minnesota, North Dakota,

Illinois, and New York. Her appearances were promoted with printed circulars which included complimentary extracts from a variety of press notices and personal endorsements. In these early years she sang the Omaha songs from Fletcher's book, using the piano at times to "simulate a drum" as well as accompanying herself by striking two sticks together and clapping her hands. Then in 1903 she acquired a drum and four birch-bark medicine rattles used in Chippewa medicine rituals. Soon mastering the rudiments of performance on these devices, she expanded her repertory to include a talk on native musical instruments. She lectured in addition on such topics as "The Indian's Natural Sense of Harmony," "Primitive Rhythms," and "Indian Life Expressed in Music." [10]

About this time Densmore also began to use two Omaha songs in an arrangement by St. Paul-born composer Arthur Farwell, whom she heard late in 1903 in a lecture-recital entitled "Myth and Music of the American Indians and its Relationship to the Development of American Musical Art." She subsequently obtained a copy of Farwell's "Dawn," a piano fantasy on two Omaha songs, and used it to demonstrate the possible application of Indian music to modern composition. [11]

In 1903 Densmore began her long and prolific career of writing on Indian music. In May of that year the *Minneapolis Journal* published her article, "The Song and the Silence of the Red Man." The piece was based on James Mooney's *The Ghost-Dance Religion and the Sioux Outbreak of 1890* and was accompanied by photographs from the book. In this and other articles written about the same time, she treated the experience of Native Americans in a highly romanticized fashion, more as drama than as history. While her early writings are by today's standards sentimental and patronizing, they nevertheless display a genuine and sympathetic interest in Indians and their culture. This attitude continued to characterize her work as she moved into more rigorous studies, and perhaps it helped her to earn the confidence and co-operation of Indian acquaintances. [12]

In 1905 Frances Densmore made her first extensive acquaintance with Indians in their own cultural setting. Accompanied by her sister Margaret, who was to join her on many later field trips, she visited the Chippewa at the villages of Grand Marais and Grand Portage on Lake Superior. To reach them the Densmores boarded a small passenger boat which left Duluth on August 9 and sailed up the shore to Grand Marais. Upon arriving Frances hired an Indian guide named Caribou to show her the sights of the town. With Caribou she also trekked through the woods to call on Shingibis, the Grand Medicine man, from whom she hoped to learn more about Chippewa music. "I asked Shingibis if he knew the hunting songs that have magic power over the animals," she wrote. "A quizzical smile crossed his kindly face as he replied with appropriate gestures that when he went hunting he did not sing, but kept very still, took good aim and shot the game. Slightly crestfallen I changed the subject." Later "after considerable circumlocution I returned cautiously to the subject of Indian music. 'When do you sing?' I asked most politely. Shingibis waved his hand in the direction of a church spire which pricked the distant green, and replied, 'White man goes to church over there. I don't go to church. Have Indian church at home. I sing when I have Indian church.'"[13]

Shingibis agreed to hold a religious ceremony that night, and after making arrangements about price and the length of the session, Densmore went back to Grand Marais. That evening she returned with four chaperones. She later described the ceremony: "Shingibis was watching for us, and ushered us into one of the wigwams, motioning us to seats on a cot which extended along one side, and introducing us to Blue Sky and one or two other Indians who sat on the opposite side. Around the fire in the center were fresh sprigs of arbor-vitae laid carefully on the ground. Shingibis seated himself upon some bright splint mats at the end of the wigwam. Beside him was a wooden box, upon which stood a nickel alarm clock and a small kerosene lamp. Before him stood his Grand Medicine tom-tom, with its top of soft brown deerskin.

"We sat in respectful silence until Shingibis was ready to begin.

"The songs were full of wild beauty, but I did not attempt to use a note book, — it would have seemed a sacrilege. Shingibis sang one after another, beating the tom-tom with the curved stick in his right hand and shaking steadily the Grand Medicine rattle in his left."[14]

This ceremony and its associated songs were of great interest to Densmore and marked the beginning of her research on the Midewiwin, or Grand Medicine Society of the Chippewa. When she visited the Grand Portage band, she gathered enough material for two short articles. She also made a number of lantern slides at the Chippewa villages which she later used to illustrate her lectures.[15]

In the summer of 1906 Densmore collected songs from two Sioux women at the Prairie Island village near Red Wing. Although she had written down Indian music from memory on earlier occasions, Densmore remembered this event as the first time an Indian singer actively co-operated by performing songs for transcription. One of the Prairie Island women sang a song of the Haethuska (Warrior) Society which was a variant of an Omaha song Densmore had often performed in her lectures. The following year she published the two Sioux songs with a brief account of the occasion and an explanation of the social significance of the songs. She embellished her transcriptions with piano accompaniments similar to those made by John Fillmore for Alice Fletcher's study.[16]

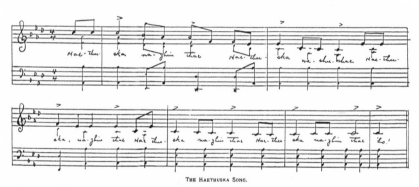

THE HAETHUSKA SONG.

This Omaha warrior's song was taught to Densmore by her Dakota friend Wapatanka. It was sung "softly, in the sweet mezzo-voce which the Indian women use when singing alone." From Indian School Journal, April, 1907, p. 32.

During the same summer of 1906 Densmore made an extended visit to Indian communities in northern and western Minnesota. At White Earth in the western part of the state, she attended on June 14 a Chippewa celebration marking the anniversary of the tribe's removal to that reservation. Accompanied by the Reverend Benjamin Brigham and Mrs. F. C. Wiswell, an Episcopal missionary who was teaching lace making to the Chippewa, Densmore witnessed the ceremonies. "The celebration was colorful and picturesque, with the Indians dancing in full regalia," she wrote.

"Chief Wadena and Joe Critt were there and let me take their pictures. Chief Mejakigijig was among the dancers, with prominent chiefs and men from other reservations. There were war dances in which veterans of wars with the Sioux dramatized their victories, and 'squaw dances' in which an invitation to join was accompanied by a gift of beadwork or a few yards of calico. I heard for the first time the throb of the huge drum and the lusty songs of the men who sat around it. My new friends explained it all to me, described the participants and interpreted for me."[17]

The next year Frances, once more accompanied by her sister Margaret, again attended the White Earth celebration of June 14. Afterward one of the Indians agreed to sing the songs into a recording machine. Thus arose Densmore's first opportunity to make recordings of Indian music. Borrowing the necessary equipment from a local music store, she set up a temporary recording studio in the store's backroom. The Indian Big Bear (Kitchimakwa) sat in front of the recording machine and filled twelve cylinder records with his songs.[18]

The summer's work was by no means finished. From White Earth the Densmores went on to the Red Lake Reservation where they spent three weeks gathering further material about tribal life and customs. Frances then went alone to the Leech Lake Agency at Onigum. She arrived to find that Flat Mouth, hereditary chief of the Pillager band of Chippewa, was gravely ill. Medicine men were performing rituals in a desperate last effort to save his life. Frances Densmore was permitted to witness the extraordinary events: "Hour after hour I stood outside the circle of Indians, watching the medicine men and listening to their songs. As the end approached, Flat Mouth was carried into a teepee and a gun was fired when his spirit passed away. A funeral feast was held the next day and the Indians let me go into the lodge while it was in progress. They drew back the curtain that concealed the body of the dead chief and let me take a photograph. In all my experiences I have never felt so much alone!"[19]

On her return to Red Wing, she wrote to the Bureau of American Ethnology at the Smithsonian Institution, reporting the events she had witnessed at Onigum and soliciting support for her efforts to record Indian customs before they disappeared forever. William H. Holmes, chief of the bureau, responded with a grant of $150 to support her work. With these funds Frances purchased an Edison recording machine. She returned to Onigum in September and persuaded the Chippewa to repeat the songs for her. "The Indians remembered my presence there at the time of Flat Mouth's death," she wrote, "and the medicine man who was in charge of the ceremony recorded many of his best songs. Several others recorded songs of the Grand Medicine and drew the pictures that represent the words of these songs. I tested the accuracy of this system of mnemonics by showing the pictures to members of the Grand Medicine Society at White Earth, a few weeks later, and they sang the same songs." In her account book for 1907 Densmore noted her travel expenses to Onigum and White Earth as "Trip No. 1 — September 25th–October 19th — average cost per day — $3.70." Thus began her professional field work and her association with the Bureau of American Ethnology.[20]

Early in 1908 the bureau summoned Densmore to Washington, D.C., to report on her work. She presented her recordings and information on the Chippewa Grand Medicine ceremony, for which the bureau paid a fee of $300. This was the first investigation of native music supported by the bureau. Its annual report for 1907–08 described her work enthusiastically, noting that "the collection of phonographic records thus far obtained is extensive, and the investigation promises results of exceptional interest and scientific value."[21]

Densmore's association with the bureau immediately brought her research to the attention of her professional peers. The Anthropological Society of Washington, taking advantage of her presence at the bureau, invited her to lecture. When she addressed the society on February 18, 1908, Alice Fletcher was in the audience. Thus Densmore finally met the woman who had been the greatest inspiration to her work.

The Bureau of Ethnology continued its financial assistance, and in 1909 she returned to Washington for a second report on her continuing research and to announce the completion of her manuscript on Chippewa music. In a second address to the Anthropological Society she described in detail the method she had devised for recording and transcribing, and the system she had developed for analyzing the songs. She also spoke of the sense of mission which inspired her work. "The purpose of the present work is the collection and classification of data with a view to determining the natural laws which govern musical expression. . . . It is as though one set out to chart an unknown land. Another has blazed the trail . . . It is not mine to prove that there is beauty and poetry in Indian music — that fact was established years ago by Miss Alice C. Fletcher. It is ours to follow. . . . In a few years the valuable Indian songs will cease to exist . . . We have taken from the Indian his land and his hunting ground but he is carrying his song with him, on his last long journey. Strange as it may seem the Indian is willing to give his songs . . ."[22]

Densmore's *Chippewa Music* inaugurated a long series of scholarly studies based on her own field recordings and interviews and modeled after Fletcher's *A Study of Omaha Indian Music*. In her book Fletcher had argued that music showed the influence of social life and thus she presented the Omaha songs according to their function in tribal life. With a similar anthropological orientation Densmore described Indian music in the context of specific ceremonies and social customs, the particular circumstances in which she witnessed a ceremony, and information provided by her informants, illustrating her material with photographs of persons and artifacts.

She also provided analyses and transcriptions of 180 songs which she had collected in 1907, 1908, and 1909 at the White Earth, Leech Lake, and Red Lake reservations. These included songs of the Midé (Grand Medicine) and social songs — dream, war, love, and moccasin-game songs. Along with descriptive analyses of individual songs, she gave detailed information about their significance and tribal context. Tables summarized her analyses of the music in terms of six aspects of melody (tonality, tone material, beginnings of songs, endings of songs, first progressions, and accidentals), two aspects of rhythm (accent and metric unit), and structure — melodic or harmonic. These categories emphasized melody rather than rhythm, reflecting Densmore's fundamental orientation toward nineteenth-century Western music, in which the qualities of melody are substantially more developed than those of rhythm.

Although Densmore was later to vary the specific parameters of her tabulated analyses, she continued to use the basic methods and organization she had developed for *Chippewa Music:* a system of tables summarizing the occurrences of various musical characteristics of the songs, descriptive analyses of individual songs in relation to their function in the life of the tribe, and transcriptions of the songs in conventional notation.

In a second volume, *Chippewa Music — II* published in 1913, she began to express the results of her analysis in percentages as well as in tabulated figures.[23] In addition she expanded the number of parameters of analysis from nine to twenty-two, fourteen of them concerned with aspects of melody and eight with aspects of rhythm. She continued to use these twenty-two parameters until 1923, when she reduced them to eighteen in her publication on *Mandan and Hidatsa Music*. Thereafter she gradually simplified the tabulated analyses by decreasing the number of parameters until in her last book on *Music of Acoma, Isleta, Cochiti and Zuñi Pueblos* (1957) she included only eleven. Parameters of analysis were eliminated, she explained, when the "results of analysis were practically uniform" or when "tables did not seem of sufficient importance to be continued." In several books she eliminated tabulated analyses entirely, although these studies included descriptive analyses which were in fact based on unpublished tabulations.[24]

In her monumental study, *Teton Sioux Music*, published in 1918, Densmore made an important addition to her analysis. Here she included cumulative tables which compared the characteristics of the music under study — in this case, Sioux — with the cumulative characteristics of all the music she had studied to date. As a corollary, she also began to include a descriptive comparative analysis interpreting the information provided by the cumulative comparative tables, a practice she continued in her later books. Regrettably, however, she did not take the logical next step of transferring this information to maps which would have indicated the geographic distribution of specific characteristics in North American Indian music.

Beginning with *Chippewa Music*, and in all her subsequent publications, Densmore transcribed Indian songs in conventional Western notation as unaccompanied melodies. In this important respect she departed from Fletcher's model and from her own earlier work, in which she had embellished the renderings of Indian melodies with realizations of what she heard as implicit harmonies. These early transcriptions were in fact more arrangements than transcriptions. But in *Chippewa Music* Densmore notated only the *melody* of the songs.[25]

Throughout her career Densmore was aware of the problems involved in using traditional Western notation to transcribe Indian music. In listening to Indian singers she had noted that they often sang certain "irregular" intervals, deviations from the tones of the tempered scale, some of which were smaller than a quarter tone. In *Chippewa Music* she introduced special signs to indicate these slight variations of pitch and note duration which defied conventional notation. As she explained in the preface: "It is acknowledged that ordinary musical notation does not, in all instances, represent accurately the tones sung. . . . If a new and complete notation were used in recording fractional tones it should be used in connection with delicately adjusted instruments which would determine those fractional tones with mathematical accuracy. The present study is not an analysis of fractional tones, but of melodic trend and general musical character; therefore the ordinary musical notation is used, with the addition of a few signs in special cases." Here Densmore assumed that her background in Western music would enable her to distinguish "general musical character" and did not consider the possibility that the fractional tones might themselves be the essential characteristic. Moreover, she overlooked the fact that while a given system of notation may successfully capture the character of music produced by one culture, such a system may be relatively ineffective when applied to that of another culture.[26]

Despite her conclusion that the fractional tones were not an essential feature of Indian music, Densmore remained curious about singers' deviations from the tempered scale, and in 1915 she went to Carl E. Seashore of the psychological laboratory at Iowa State University for help in devising a way of testing the accuracy of pitch discrimination among Indians. With Seashore's guidance Densmore developed a test using a set of tuning forks which produced tones of only slightly different frequencies. She gave the test to a number of Mandan, Hidatsa, Chippewa, and Sioux, hoping to learn whether they intentionally produced the minute intervals when they performed their music. Seashore's analysis of the test data verified her suspicion that Indians were capable of singing the tiny intervals deliberately. This information did not, however, persuade her to develop a more sensitive notation. Rather, throughout her career she continued to defend her transcriptions in conventional notation as generalized representations of the Indian songs.[27]

Early in her career Densmore experimented with the potential of graph notation for transcription. She never intended, however, that her graphic representations of Indian melodies should replace the use of conventional notation but rather that the two types of transcription be used concurrently. She first developed a system for making graph transcriptions in conjunction with her study of Teton Sioux music. This work included graphic representations introduced, as she explained, "for the purpose of making the trend of Sioux melodies more apparent to the eye than in musical transcription."

By plotting only the tones which her analysis had identified as accented, Densmore hoped to reveal the general course or trend of the melodies. Her examination of the graphic transcriptions of 240 Sioux songs revealed five primary melodic types. She used this information to explore a possible correlation between melodic type and songs having similar uses or titles, a correlation she had already tentatively suggested in *Chippewa Music — II*. She found

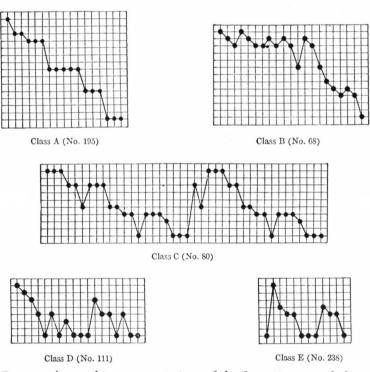

Class A (No. 195)   Class B (No. 68)

Class C (No. 80)

Class D (No. 111)   Class E (No. 238)

Densmore's graphic representations of the five primary melodic types observed in her plotting of 240 Sioux melodies. From Densmore, **Teton Sioux Music,** *53.*

that two of the melodic types occurred throughout the series of songs studied, but that comparison of the plots to the titles of the three remaining types revealed that songs having similar uses or titles resemble each other. Densmore's use of graphs is one of the earliest experiments with an alternative approach to transcription in the history of ethnomusicology.[28]

Although Densmore was primarily interested in studying the melodic trends and general character of Indian music, she showed considerable interest in various electronic instruments which could provide more exact transcriptions of sound than were possible by ear. These instruments were of particular interest to her as a means of testing the validity of her own transcriptions. In 1918 she contacted Dayton C. Miller, chairman of the department of physics at Case School of Applied Science in Cleveland. Miller had recently invented an instrument known as the phonodeik which was capable of making a film record of sound. The phonodeik operated by means of a conical horn which focused sound on a diaphragm; the resulting movement of the diaphragm was then photographed and projected on a screen. Densmore hoped that the phonodeik could be helpful in verifying her observation of a strange incongruity between the rhythm of the singer and that of the instrumental accompaniment in much Indian music. In her study of Chippewa music she had first observed that the musicians seldom struck the drum and sang a tone simultaneously. She wished, however, to confirm this incongruity of song and accompaniment which was foreign to Western music.[29]

Her analysis of ninety-one Chippewa songs with drum accompaniment had revealed sixty-three songs in which the voice and drum had independent metric units. Although she had attempted to transcribe this phenomenon by ear, she hoped that the phonodeik would provide a means of determining the exact relation of the drum beats to the voice. Miller made a film record of part of a cylinder record in which the voice and drum seemed to have independent rhythms, using about twenty-three seconds of the recording to produce about thirty-eight feet of film. His reading of the film record verified Densmore's discovery that there were indeed two independent rhythms, but he felt on balance that the results of the experiment hardly justified the great amount of work involved.[30]

In 1934 Densmore again visited Carl Seashore's laboratory to discuss the latest developments in phonophotography. As a demonstration of his apparatus, Seashore produced a tone-photograph of one of Densmore's cylinder records. A graphic analysis was then made from the tone-phonograph and Densmore was reassured to learn that the graph gave essentially the same results as her transcription by ear.[31] Although Seashore's equipment could produce more detailed and accurate transcriptions than those made by ear, Densmore persistently clung to her position that the object of transcription was to show the musical essentials, not minute details which might obscure the larger picture. Thus she continued to make transcriptions in conventional notation by ear.

Densmore intended her transcriptions to provide a generalized picture of Indian music, using intervals, or steps of the scale, borrowed from the vocabulary of Western music. She gradually became aware, however, of the limitations of a theory of Indian music which explained musical phenomena wholly in terms of Western music. Early in her career she began to raise questions about Fletcher's and Fillmore's theories based on the Indians' unconscious sense of harmony.

Fillmore had looked to accoustical principles to support his theory, noting that the *"essential thing in all music is the relation of tones to a tonic or key-note;* and the tones most nearly related accoustically to any given key-note *are the tones of its triad."* [32] Here Fillmore was referring to the accoustical fact that a vibrating or sounding body produces not only the fundamental tone but also a series of overtones which are less distinctly audible. The first four overtones above the principal C, for example, are the tones of the triad C-E-G. While Fillmore was correct in noting that the triad is generated accoustically, he was incorrect in assuming that this phenomenon provided a comprehensive, rational basis for the relationships among tones as they occur in all music. Acoustics do not in fact even provide a satisfactory explanation for the relationship of tones and chords in eighteenth- and nineteenth-century Western music. Fillmore, however, went one step further and argued that the tonal relationships exemplified by Western music with its key structure and harmony were universal and thus he justified his practice of harmonizing the Indian songs with tonal chordal accompaniments. The resulting arrangements sounded strangely like gospel hymns.

Densmore first expressed her uneasiness about interpretations of Indian music based on European musical theory in a short article published in 1906. While she praised Fillmore's work enthusiastically, she also observed that harmonizations made by others less skilled than he were often unconvincing. She hoped that someday an Indian musician would "take the melodies which we are collecting, and . . . translate for us their hidden harmonic thought, expressing it in terms of the white man's culture. He will do by intuition that which our most conscientious work cannot accomplish." [33]

A year later, when she published the two songs sung for her by the Prairie Island women, she mentioned the enthusiasm with which the women had greeted her harmonized versions of their music. Fillmore, observing similar reactions, had interpreted them as proof of his harmonic theory. He noted that whenever the songs of the Omaha "were played for them on a piano or organ, *they were not satisfied without the addition of chords to the melodies.* . . . It seems proper to draw the conclusion that the sense of harmony is an innate endowment of human nature, that it is the same for the trained musician and for the untrained primitive man, the difference being purely one of development." [34]

Densmore, however, drew a rather different conclusion from the favorable response to her harmonizations. She suspected that it provided more information about the Sioux singers' desire to please her than about their unconsious sense of harmony.

When she published her study of Chippewa music in 1910, she made several important modifications in Fillmore's theory. He had argued that melody in native music was shaped by the Indians' *"natural perception of the harmonic relations of tones."* Densmore took a less dogmatic stand, observing: "The sequence of tones in Chippewa songs show that certain songs are harmonic and others melodic in structure. . . . Songs are classified as harmonic if their accented tones follow the intervals of diatonic chords, and as melodic if their contiguous accented tones have no apparent chord relationship." By melodic Densmore referred to melody completely independent of any implied harmony. Of the 180 songs analyzed in *Chippewa Music*, she identified 139 as melodic in their structure. [35]

In her second study of Chippewa music, she retreated more overtly from Fillmore's position, observing that the "sequence of tones in many of the songs is such that the 'harmonic relation' is extremely complicated, if indeed (in some instances), it can be said to exist." By 1943, when she published a book on Choctaw music, she eliminated the category called "structure — melodic or harmonic" as a basis for analysis. Although she gave no reason for this change, it is apparent that she simply no longer thought of Indian music in terms of harmony.[36]

In an article that appeared in 1917 Densmore's deviations from the ideas of her mentor are most clear. Although these deviations are interesting as theoretical modifications of Fillmore's concept of the keynote or tonal center, they are more important as they reveal Densmore's understanding of Indian music in terms increasingly independent of Western music. Her discussion was still heavily indebted to Fillmore, but she carefully avoided any specific reference to the keynote and tonality in the sense in which he had understood them. Instead she vaguely defined the keynote as the tone which was apparently most important and which functioned in some way as the focus of the melody. She avoided any reference to a tonal relationship between the keynote and the other tones of the Indian songs, stating simply that the keynote could be identified by the "test of the ear" thus leaving the matter to intuition. She suggested a variety of standards for determining the keynote, such as frequency of appearance, rhythmic stress, placement at the beginning or final tone, and function as the lowest tone. Instead of using criteria based on the theory of Western tonal music, she expanded her perspective and considered ways of organizing musical sounds other than those with which she was familiar.[37] Throughout her career Densmore continued to generalize about Indian music. Unlike Fillmore, however, she based her generalizations on actual counts of various musical phenomena. On the basis of these data, she grew increasingly doubtful of the existence of a universal tonal system based on acoustics.

As she examined the music of various Indian tribes, Densmore observed several other patterns of melodic organization in addition to the triad structure seen in much Chippewa music. Indeed, in *Chippewa Music* she had identified a few songs in which the interval of the fourth was particularly prominent. In songs collected during the 1920s among the Nootka and Quileute of the Pacific Northwest, she noticed the frequent occurrence of the interval of the fourth and of phrases comprised of the tetrachord pattern (as in C-D-E-F or E-F-G-A) as prominent structural elements. (She later observed this same characteristic in Menominee, Winnebago, Cheyenne, and Arapaho songs.) When she published *Nootka and Quileute Music* in 1939, she classified the Indian songs based on the tetrachord as a group analogous to those based on the triad. She wrote: "Two types of melodic structure occur in songs of the American Indians, the tetrachord (complete and incomplete), and the triad formation. Combinations of the two are also found, as well as freely melodic songs that have no frame work and songs that are said to have been composed in imitation of the sounds produced by a wooden flute." [38] Her analyses of Nootka and Quileute music finally put to rest Fillmore's theory of the harmonic structure of Indian music.

In studies of the Tule Indians of Panama and later among the Yuman, Seminole, and certain Pueblo tribes, Densmore found an elaborate patterned type of melodic design which she referred to as "period structure." By this term she meant a definite form consisting of several periods or discrete musical phrases which were repeated in regular order. In *Yuman and Yaqui Music* she explained the complex period structure of many of the Yuman songs: "In describing the form of Yuman songs the interpreter said, 'There is always a chorus near the end of a song that goes up higher.' He said it is the custom that 'the song shall be sung four times and the chorus twice,' also that 'if the chorus is sung a third time the ending is on a high note.' The term 'chorus' is derived from a knowledge of the white man's songs and indicates a pleasing part of the song but not a change in the number of singers. It usually contains about eight measures and is not repeated. The other portions of the song are sung from 2 or 3 to 11 times and are accurately repeated." [39] The periodic structure was thus defined in terms of internal repetitions of phrases without reference to any particular intervals such as Densmore had noted, for example, in the Chippewa melodies based on the triad and in the Nootka and Quileute melodies based on the tetrachord.

When *Music of the Indians of British Columbia* appeared in 1943, Densmore reported that in the more than 2,500 Indian melodies analyzed up to that time she had found four basic patterns of melodic structure: "(1) a formation on the simplest overtones of a fundamental, generally called a triad formation, (2) a formation based on the interval of a fourth, (3) a typical folk-song structure . . . and (4) a period formation." [40] Giving only passing attention to the patterns already described in earlier studies, she concentrated her attention on the folk-song structure, which she introduced here for the first time.

She used the term "folk-song structure" to describe a large group of Indian songs in which the whole-tone interval was particularly prominent. It is significant, however, that she did not refer simply to the "whole-tone structure" in Indian music but instead borrowed the phrase "folk-song structure" from an apparently alien music. She was not unaware of the implications of this terminology as she intended to suggest a relationship between Indian music and English folk song. As she explained, "The Indians of British Columbia have been in contact with people from Scotland for many generations. . . . it appears that the songs recorded in British Columbia bear interesting resemblances to the songs recorded at Neah Bay and on the Mexican border, as well as resemblances to Scotch songs and to the accepted basis of English folk song. The foregoing observations are offered as an aid to further study, not as presenting any hypothesis or theory. . . . These observations suggest influences from the east, across Canada, and also from the south, along the coast of the United States." [41]

In an effort to provide background for her argument, Densmore quoted a passage from the English folk-song scholar, A. H. Fox-Strangways: "'the folk singer has not only no harmony . . . but no feeling for it . . . one note of the tune has an affinity for (or an antipathy to) some others; connections are thus formed, and structure is made possible. Shortly, the folk-songster is satisfied with *affinity* between notes. . . . The nucleus of his scale is three notes a tone apart (F, G, A, for instance) which have this affinity; above and below this are two outliers, C, D, which also have it; beyond those five he takes notes tentatively.'" [42]

This extract notwithstanding, Densmore made only limited use of Fox-Strangways' conception in her subsequent discussion of folk-song structure and completely ignored his reference to tones within the context of a pentatonic scale (C, D, F, G, A). Indeed, she applied the concept of folk-song structure as she understood it to Indian melodies with a total compass of only three tones. Her application of Fox-Strangways' definition constituted a redefinition of the term. Although her analysis would have been stronger and more in keeping with her usual approach if she had simply noted the frequency of whole-tone progressions in some Indian music and then postulated the influence of English and Scotch folk song, she apparently felt that Fox-Strangways' explicit denial of a universal feeling for harmony would reinforce her own ideas as they had developed over the years.

Through the process of recording, transcribing and analyzing thousands of Indian songs, Densmore gradually evolved a theory of Indian music based on the objective data. While she continued to use notation and terminology originally developed for the interpretation of Western music, she developed an increasingly sensitive appreciation of the limitations they imposed. Perhaps most important, she moved from her initial conception of Indian song as melody with implied harmony to an understanding of Indian song based on only the actual linear melody heard. This freed her to discover the principles which actually functioned in Indian music and indeed to appreciate it on its own terms.

Densmore's efforts yielded major published studies on the music of the Chippewa, Teton Sioux, Northern Ute, Mandan and Hidatsa, Tule Indians of Panama, Papago, Pawnee, Menominee, Yuman and Yaqui, Cheyenne and Arapaho, Santo Domingo Pueblo, Nootka and Quileute, Choctaw, the Indians of British Columbia, Seminole and Acoma, Isleta, Cochiti, and Zuñi pueblos. With the exception of her work with the Cheyenne and Arapaho and the Indians of Santo Domingo Pueblo, which were conducted for the Southwest Museum of Los Angeles, all her research was done under the auspices of the Bureau of American Ethnology. She was employed by the bureau from 1907 until 1933, when over-all government economy measures necessitated severe cutbacks and it was no longer possible for the bureau to continue its assistance. In 1939 the bureau resumed its support and Densmore, although seventy-two years old, took up her field activities with the same intense enthusiasm which characterized all her earlier work.

In July, 1940, Densmore began work for the James J. Hill Reference Library in St. Paul on a brochure to accompany the Hill collection of Seth Eastman's watercolors of American Indians. She arranged the paintings so as to reconstruct as nearly as possible the sequence of Indian history during the period of Eastman's work and wrote an introduction to the collection. More than half the forty-six paintings were scenes near Fort Snelling, where Eastman had served as an army officer from 1841 to 1848. Densmore's introduction included frequent quotations from Mary

H. Eastman's books, especially *Dahcotah; or, Life and Legends of the Sioux Around Fort Snelling.* As Densmore explained, "It is a privilege to present her work beside that of her husband after so many years."[43]

In the 1940s a generous private gift to the federal government made it possible to preserve Densmore's collection of more than 2,400 wax cylinders in more permanent form. In November, 1941, she was appointed to work with the collection and to prepare a handbook, a task she completed in 1943. In 1948 the enormous task of transferring the recordings from cylinders to discs was begun. With characteristic tenacity Densmore, now eighty-one years old, supervised this project from her home in Red Wing. Her correspondence for this period is proof of her full participation. In a letter written on July 20, 1951, for example, she apologized for the delay caused by what she described as a "slight bronchial pneumonia." She continued, "I must maintain my reputation for complete work." In addition, she reviewed the entire collection to select representative songs for transfer to long-playing records which were made available to the public. Between 1951 and 1953 the Library of Congress released seven of these records with the accompanying booklets she had prepared.[44]

In 1954 Densmore, now eighty-seven, gave a series of seminars on Indian music at the University of Florida in Gainesville. She also took advantage of the opportunity to carry on further field studies among the Florida Seminoles. On March 24, she wrote back to her friend Mary Biederman in Red Wing: "I am getting to the end of my first month at the University of Florida and the month has really been more successful than I had dared to expect, in the interest that has been aroused in Indian music. I have given six short lectures . . . I will probably go to the town of Dania at the end of the week to begin more observations on the Seminoles." In April, after a month of field work, she wrote again with indefatigable enthusiasm, "Here I am — back in civilization . . . The trip yielded valuable results — some entirely new data."[45]

Three years later, on June 5, 1957, Frances Densmore died at Red Wing not long after her ninetieth birthday. During her lifetime she was a tireless recorder of Native American music. Her extensive and original work contributed significantly to the study of non-Western music. It was important not only as one of the earliest efforts to study music in its cultural context but also as one of the first efforts to recognize and understand Indian music as profoundly different from Western music. Unfortunately, however, within the discipline of ethnomusicology some contemporary scholars, noting her use of the vocabulary associated with the theory of Western music, have tended to overlook the significance of her work. They have assumed that because she retained some traditional terminology she was not aware of the fundamental differences between Western and Indian music. Nothing could be further from the truth.

The current scholarly interest in American Indian cultures should bring new attention to her work. Restudy of her writings and recordings would not only bring long-overdue recognition to Densmore's pioneering scholarly accomplishments but also stimulate further study of her beloved Indian music. Such an enterprise would be in the spirit of Frances Densmore.

7. MARY MOLLOY
Women's College Founder

By Karen Kennelly C.S.J.

THE QUESTION of women's capacity for college education was still being seriously debated by Americans at the close of the nineteenth century. Minnesotans were not immune to doubt on the matter. Was there not, a St. Paul newspaper asked in 1891, a serious "physiological question regarding the undeveloped and therefore uncomplicated state of the average woman's brain as compared with man's?" Would not the strain of college studies undermine women's physical and mental health, render them unfit for motherhood, and, in short, upset the natural order of things?[1]

Notwithstanding such commonly held opinions, the state university had begun in 1869 as a coeducational institution. Six of the nine private colleges functioning in the state by the end of the nineteenth century accepted women. Despite this relatively open situation, in sharp contrast with that prevalent in the eastern seaboard states, opportunities for women's education beyond high school were still limited in the Minnesota of the 1890s. On the average only a little more than five women each year had earned degrees from the University of Minnesota in the 1870s and 1880s. Of the six private colleges enrolling women, only two (Hamline and Carleton) were attracting them in significant numbers. No single-sex institution had yet been created for women, although there were three for men.[2]

The decisive role in establishing colleges for women in the state was taken by members of three Catholic religious communities who were among the state's first waves of immigrants. Four Sisters of St. Joseph traveled up the Mississippi River from St. Louis to St. Paul in 1851. They were followed by a small group of Benedictine sisters who arrived in St. Paul in 1857 and, after a brief stay with the Sisters of St. Joseph in their crude log cabin convent, moved north to establish a community in St. Cloud. Sisters of St. Francis from Illinois reached the southeastern part of the state in 1877, settling first at Waseca, and finally in and around Rochester.[3]

From the academies founded by these groups of women religious between 1851 and 1894 grew the present-day colleges of St. Catherine in St. Paul, St. Teresa in Winona, St. Benedict in St. Joseph, and St. Scholastica in Duluth, all of which had become collegiate institutions by 1915. Building successful schools and effecting the transition from academy to college were difficult tasks to accomplish. The many early failures experienced in the Midwest by such eastern educators as Catharine Beecher illustrate the difficulties only too well.[4] It was group support through membership in religious communities that enabled women like Anna McHugh, Mary Molloy, Anna Borgerding, and Mary Kerst to succeed where others failed, and even then, their successes came only in the twentieth century. The story of how the efforts of these first- and second-generation immigrants resulted in expanded educational opportunities for women is exemplified in the life and career of one college founder, Mary Molloy.

Born in Sandusky, Ohio, on June 14, 1880, Mary Aloysia Molloy was the only child of a late marriage. Her father, Patrick John Molloy, had married Mary Lambe while working as a conductor on the Baltimore and Ohio Railroad. He continued in this occupation until retirement. Mary's was a sheltered childhood. An incident which remained vivid in her memory years later captured the essence of the shyness and the inhibitions such an upbringing can engender. Longing for the forbidden thrill of roller skating, she borrowed a pair of skates from a friend only to stop at the gate of the friend's yard not daring to launch forth.[5]

Fortunately, or perhaps consequently, books and almost every subject taught in school fascinated young Mamie, as she was affectionately nicknamed. Her only formal Catholic education took place at Saints Peter and Paul Parochial School in Sandusky, where she attended grades one through eight. There she was taught by "Madame Fitzgerald's Ladies," religious wearing ordinary clothes rather than clerical garb.[6]

They deepened that love of the church and things Catholic which her devout Irish immigrant parents had already instilled in their daughter. The "Ladies" evidently gave her a good founda-

Mary Molloy

tion in the educational fundamentals as well, for we next hear of
Mamie carrying off prizes in the Ohio Society of the Sons of the
American Revolution essay contest while enrolled at Sandusky
High School. Just a hint of awe over the superior scholarship of
the young lady emerges from a newspaper summary of her high
school graduation ceremony, where one of her essays was read to
the great admiration of those assembled: "Suffice it to say that the
vocabulary at her command is the most extensive and elaborate in
the high school."

Sandusky High School by no means satisfied Mamie Molloy's
appetite for learning, but women who wanted to go to college in
1899 encountered serious obstacles in terms of both social custom
and financial support. It was not considered entirely suitable for
men, much less women, to work their way through school, but
Mamie was undeterred by these problems. She secured admission
to Ohio State University at Columbus and found enough odd jobs
to meet the expenses of a four-year classical education leading to a
bachelor of philosophy degree.

A full-page spread in the *Ohio State Journal* for Sunday, June
21, 1903, featured graduates for that year who belonged to various

sororities. Mamie's name was not among them. Instead, in a short article tucked away in the bottom right corner, she appeared as a human interest item which explained that "many of the girls at O.S.U. have earned their own way through college, either wholly or partly. Though the girls must in a certain degree be subservient to conventionalities, yet there are some who have overcome the difficulties." Such a one was "Miss Mary Molloy of Sandusky," who had "successfully acquired a college education by her own efforts and . . . leaves the university with the enviable record of having more honors to her credit than any young man or woman in the history of the college."

The month before graduation, Mamie had won a two-year fellowship to graduate school at Ohio State. Superior class standing and promise in the fields of English and rhetoric had won for her an annual stipend of $300, in return for which she was expected to assist in the English department for two hours daily. In this manner she financed her work on a master's degree in English philology. Upon its completion she was elected to Phi Beta Kappa and won an English fellowship at Cornell University for the academic year 1905–06.[7]

Although Mary Molloy was not the first woman to complete a doctorate at Cornell — one May Preston had earned that distinction in 1880 — she qualified for membership in a select group, when in 1907 at the age of twenty-seven she received her doctor of philosophy degree from Cornell "with highest distinction." As the *Columbus Citizen* had observed two years before, she was "a splendid example of what the American girl will do for education."[8]

Obviously much drawn to the life of a scholar and well trained in the tools of the trade, Mary Molloy's next important decision seems incomprehensible. Confronted in August, 1907, with a choice between a trip to Ireland and the Continent with Dr. Douglas Hyde, leader of the Gaelic revival, or responding to an advertisement seeking a competent Catholic woman to initiate college courses for a religious community in Winona, Minnesota, she chose the latter.[9]

Her choice forces upon one an awareness of how much the church and her faith had come to mean to Mary Molloy. In Columbus she had filled her spare time with catechetical work at the local penitentiary and had participated in a local Catholic literary club. Feeling a strong sense of obligation to her parents as an only

child, she had thrust to the back of her mind an earlier desire to
enter a religious community. It now appeared to her that she could
do something for the spread of the faith through education by accepting the job in Winona.

To her parents Winona seemed far more remote than Ireland.
Reassured by a quick trip to the public library where an atlas revealed the peculiarly named Minnesota town to be a significant
railroad junction on the Mississippi only 300 miles west of
Chicago, Mamie's parents finally acquiesced in her giving the job
a trial "until Christmas." [10]

What the atlas did not reveal about Winona was its boom-and-
bust history. All four of the railroads then serving the town had
laid their tracks in the 1860s and 1870s to take advantage of a
primary grain market which had placed Winona fourth in the nation (after Chicago, Milwaukee, and Toledo) by 1868, but had
peaked by 1873. A lumber industry which eclipsed both wheat
and flour by the 1890s had gone into near total decline with the
deforestation of the Chippewa and St. Croix river valleys; the last
sawmill was to close in 1909. [11] Unknown to Winona citizenry in
1907, much less to the readers of an atlas in Sandusky, the Mississippi boom town's greatest future asset was to be not wheat, flour,
or lumber, but the young people who would populate its schools
and infant colleges.

Sister Leo Tracy, the writer of the appeal relayed to Mary Molloy through an east coast teachers' agency, had already invested
nearly thirty years of her life in the cause of education in southeastern Minnesota. Born Emma Tracy, the first of three children,
to Irish immigrant parents on June 22, 1860, in Katonah, New
York, she had moved with her family to Minnesota while still a
young girl. There at the age of eighteen she began teaching in the
rural schools of Olmsted County with the aim of earning enough
money to help her parents pay off the mortgage on their farm. This
filial obligation acquitted after four years, she entered the community of the Sisters of St. Francis in Rochester, taking the name of
Sister Leo. [12]

Skilled in the arts of teaching and administration, Sister Leo had
spent over twenty years in schools operated by the Franciscans in
Rochester, Owatonna, St. Peter, and Winona by 1907, when as director of Winona Ladies Seminary she turned her full attention to
transforming that school into the College of St. Teresa. Like her

counterparts in the orders of St. Joseph and St. Benedict, Sister Leo had come to regard the sponsorship of a college for women as a natural and desirable outgrowth of her congregation's involvement in education in Minnesota. Accordingly, she bent her every effort to ensure the success of the college.

Because no Rochester Sister of St. Francis possessed a bachelor's degree in 1907, Sister Leo sought to attract one of the all-too-rare educated Catholic laywomen of her day to introduce college-level work at Winona Seminary. There was no particular cause for discouragement in the lack of degrees among the sisters; when Bryn Mawr was founded in 1885, women were teaching at Wellesley, Mount Holyoke, and Smith without even so much as a single college course behind them.[13] Admittedly, higher standards prevailed by 1907, standards which Sister Leo Tracy was determined to uphold.

In Mary Molloy, Sister Leo found a woman extraordinarily well qualified by moral convictions, temperament, and scholarly credentials to begin a college worthy of the name. Sister Leo had herself studied for several summer sessions at the University of Minnesota and had spent a full year at Trinity College in Washington, D.C., which had opened its doors in 1900. There she observed the work of the Sisters of Notre Dame of Namur whose college had the distinction of being the fifth institution of higher education established in the United States by religious orders of women.[14] From her contacts on the east coast, Sister Leo had a fair idea of what was wanted in the organizing of a college. She also had a persuasive manner when it came to implementing her ideas.

In Winona her recruit, Mary Molloy, had little time to theorize about what must have been one of the most unusual jobs assumed by a graduate of Cornell or any other university that fall. Scarcely off the train, she singlehandedly undertook to teach by tutorial methods the entire freshman curriculum for St. Teresa's first students. These were four Sisters of St. Francis whom the community had freed for full-time study. Three had had some college experience during the preceding summer, Sisters Adelaide Sandusky and Blanche Sexton at Harvard, and Sister Blandina Schmit at the University of Minnesota. In 1908 the intrepid philologist added the second-year courses to her repertory and was named assistant principal of Winona Seminary.[15]

Some uncertainty regarding Molloy's continued commitment to the institution seems indicated by the fact that she maintained an

active placement file at Cornell. In the spring of 1909 she applied
to the University of Minnesota for a position as assistant professor
of English. The seven-member university English department, as
distinct from the department of rhetoric where Maria Sanford had
found an outlet for her talents, then included no women with faculty rank. The department evidently was in a hiring mood for it
expanded within a few years by adding new personnel at the pro-
fessorial level. Molloy's qualifications were outstanding, especially given the fact that several of the department's men lacked
the doctorate. Her recommendations from Ohio and Cornell were
glowing.[16] Despite all these favorable elements in the situation,
the response to her inquiry was negative. Even Alta Churchill,
who appeared on the 1910 roster as a teaching assistant with a
bachelor degree, had disappeared by 1912, leaving the men of the
department to themselves.

Perhaps this rebuff was just as well. It is difficult to imagine that
a good college would have emerged from Winona Ladies Seminary without Mary Molloy's leadership. Under her direction a
single-page folder published in place of a catalogue in 1910 outlined the four-year course of study in clear and uncompromising
terms.[17] In addition to required classes in physiology and civics,
the schedule for freshmen specified that no more than five, and no
less than three, "heavy" subjects were to be taken each quarter.
These were to be chosen from courses in Latin, English, mathematics, French, and German. Depending on their preference for a
classical, Latin-scientific, or modern language track, second, third,
and fourth year students developed the initial language and
mathematics base and branched out into the fields of history,
chemistry, physics, botany, geology, Greek, or Italian.

This curriculum closely resembled Mary Molloy's undergraduate classics program at coeducational Ohio State. The
physiology-civics requirement was distinctive, as was the absence
of the economics, sociology, and psychology which she had taken
at Ohio. The strict classical dimensions of the curriculum were a
forthright expression of her belief that women should have an
education equivalent to that of men. For her equivalent meant
identical.

As for the stated aims of the new college, the goals formulated in
1895 for Winona Seminary were allowed to stand for several years
in the absence of any college publication beyond the brief 1910
outline of courses. The 1895 declaration was an unequivocal asser-

tion that education had for its goal preparation of women for homemaking: "Women's influence is best exerted not at the polls or on the rostrum, but in the sacred precincts of the Christian home. There, by her mental attainments, her gentleness, her purity, her devotedness, whether as daughter, sister, wife, or mother, she may obtain and exercise a limitless power for good. Hence her education should be such as to enable her to realize her responsibilities. . . . To afford its patrons such an education, is the aim of the Ladies Seminary." [18]

However, the aims of the college as Mary Molloy visualized them went well beyond these conservative claims. Moreover, the studies Sister Leo had hired her to introduce were explicitly designed to enable women to acquire bachelor degrees and to qualify fully for teaching as a profession. The distinctive purpose which was ultimately set for the College of St. Teresa when it was incorporated in 1912 reflected the personal convictions of Sister Leo Tracy and Mary Molloy. Background and training had influenced both to expect from the educated women zeal for religion and a commitment to teaching. These expectations were intensified by certain incidents of bigotry which took place in Winona during the initial years of college operation.

Secret societies such as the American Protective Association and the Guardians of Liberty were active in Rochester and Winona from the 1880s up to the time of World War I and after. Much of their anti-Catholicism took the form of vandalism perpetrated by youth gangs against the college, whose buildings and clientele offered a conspicuous local target. Obscene posters were left by night on the gates and fence of the college grounds. Boys taunted and even physically attacked women from the town, chasing one employee, who regularly removed posters from the gates on her way to a night job at the college, and pushing her into a mud puddle. [19]

Things took an even more serious turn as far as Molloy and the sisters were concerned when in 1914 the Guardians of Liberty sponsored a lecture series in Winona by one Anna M. Lowry, billed as a former nun. Her qualifications included editorial work "for some time" on the staff of the *Menace*, a rabidly anti-Catholic newspaper published in Missouri, and authorship of a book entitled *The Martyr in Black*. An advertisement in the *Winona Republican Herald* announced the platform appearance of Anna, alias Sister Justina, who would deliver an exposé of Rome's "Slave

Pens" in which she had been a prisoner behind convent bars for
twenty long years. Addresses were to be given on March 12 and 14
in Winona's Philharmonic Hall, entrance fee only twenty-five
cents — "Ladies Especially Invited." This pitiful woman's lecture
tour appears ludicrous from the vantage point of the 1970s. In
1914, it was no laughing matter for local Catholics, much less the
Sisters of St. Francis, to have her appear in nun's garb at the
podium of a respectable public hall to detail supposed horror
stories about nun's lives and Catholic beliefs and practices.[20]

Molloy and her friend Mary O'Brien tried unsuccessfully to prevent the lectures from being given. They then attended the first
one and promptly swore out a complaint against Lowry for using
obscene language; one must admit to a slight regret over the failure of the press to give the text of the complaint, which was considered unprintable. Although Lowry left town before a warrant
could be served, an arrest was made two months later when she
again ventured into Minnesota to keep a speaking engagement in
Rushford.[21]

The *Menace* rushed to the support of its hapless editor-lecturer,
protesting her arrest by "dupes of Rome in fear of exposure." The
lead article on August 1, 1914, proclaimed, "The enemy is at your
door!" and it went on to urge the Scandinavians of Minnesota to
wake up to the menace in their very midst. Anna Lowry's cause
was not markedly helped by this propaganda. Her trial led to a
guilty verdict, which was eventually upheld by the state supreme
court, and to a fine of thirty-five dollars. Meanwhile the mayor of
Winona had issued a prohibition forbidding Miss Lowry access to
Philharmonic Hall for the purposes of disseminating her ideas.[22]

This incident fitted into a context of heated debate during the
first decades of the century over the intentions and rights of
Catholics in education. Specifically at issue was the nature and
function of the nation's public school system. The masthead of the
Menace neatly portrayed the issue with its drawing of a brick
building, an American flag waving from the cupola, labeled "Public School." Captions above and below proclaimed the school to
be "The Antidote For Papal Poison."

Such was the atmosphere in which Mary Molloy and her Franciscan collaborators took counsel and arrived at a description of
the College of St. Teresa. Their experience of intolerance in
Winona had convinced them that the days of immigrant dependence on the clergy to safeguard their religious liberties were past.

Nor could they hope to be defended by Catholics who had won a degree of prominence in American business, social, or political life by the opening decade of the twentieth century. As Molloy observed with her usual forthrightness, fear of losing status often inhibited such men from fighting in unpopular causes. "There is a vast difference in many cases," she noted, "between 'leading Catholics' and Catholic leaders." The anti-Catholic offensive carried on by the Guardians of Liberty and the *Menace* was guerrilla warfare best combatted by ordinary men and women familiar with the local terrain: "The situation does not yet demand the pomp and circumstance of glorious war and the great leader — the demand is rather for a warfare under many leaders who should spring up wherever a wrong exists that needs to be redressed. Let local situations be met promptly by definite effective action. Let those who are 'willing to do something' set out and actually begin to do." From such local skirmishes would emerge "heroes and heroines" who would truly lead. Winona Seminary had educated its students on the assumption that woman's place was in the home; the new collegiate institution would have as its goal the turning out of "apostolic women thoroughly trained in every department of secular learning, militants to uphold the ideals of Christianity in society to-day."[23]

Sister Leo, as president of St. Teresa's from 1912 to 1928, and Mary Molloy, first as her dean and then her successor in the presidency, worked together to implement this apostolic theme. Sister Leo's hiring of a laywoman to initiate the college-level work had been more than the purely pragmatic action of one forced by circumstances to look beyond her own religious order for help. Sister Leo believed in encouraging lay leadership and regarded lay-religious collaboration as a necessity for a successful Catholic college. "The Faculty," stated the first catalogue in 1915, "is made up of Religious and lay women. The object of this arrangement is to secure to the College the peculiar spirit demanded by the needs of the present time."[24]

Sister Leo's practical concern and broad experience in the area of teacher preparation led to a singular emphasis on "public service" as a second major goal of the young college. She interpreted the upgrading of elementary and secondary teaching, whether in the public or parochial school system, as a service which her congregation could render to the Midwest. Reflecting these ideas of

Sister Leo's, Mary Molloy once observed, "There is no such an institution as a private school. Every teacher is a public servant, because the teacher trains by virtue of his [sic] profession boys and girls or men and women for public service." [25]

Sister Leo's determination to begin a college had, in fact, stemmed from her work in 1905 on a committee charged with developing plans for improving the education of the Franciscans' teaching sisters. [26] The summer after Mary Molloy got college work under way, Sister Leo inaugurated normal school courses on campus. Regular summer sessions followed, during which she made it a point to deliver weekly addresses to the sisters in attendance, holding up to them the ideal of excellence in teaching. Circular letters, sent to the various Franciscan convents during the school year, likewise defined and promoted an ideal of service through teaching. This ideal, focused at the beginning on the Franciscan sisterhood, was broadened over a span of twenty years to become as integral a part of Teresan purpose as apostolic zeal.

In 1928 Dean Molloy distributed to the faculty a letter entitled "A Statement of Purpose and a Pointing of Aims," in which she set forth her mature reflections, based on twenty-one years' involvement, on the purposes of the college. "There is not a single student in the institution who does not 'know what she is going to do,'" she observed, since her work was directed to one of two vocations — scholarship or public service. "We are very desirous," she continued, "that our students go out into the public high schools and do really distinguished teaching. We are equally desirous that many go on for advanced degrees." [27]

Students had been advised in their Blue Book that "attending college is a business. Collegians therefore should be consistent and make their dress conform to business demands." [28] Faculty were now reminded of their primary responsibility for the success of the entire enterprise. Kindling in students the spirit of the teacher or scholar was the college teacher's vocation. Always practical, Molloy interpreted this ideal in terms of actual daily classroom routine. Each faculty member, she noted, "must lead and speed the classes" rather than be led by the students. Each member of the faculty should take thought of his or her department work in the light of two questions; namely, "(1) Is the work I am giving sufficiently well rounded and thorough so that on it, as a foundation, successful high school teaching may be done by my students? (2) Is the work I am giving sufficiently complete so that students who major in my department may secure a Master's degree in one year after graduation?" The college, she concluded, was a "co-operative organization in which every one connected with it profits directly in proportion to his or her effort at making its influence stronger."[29]

Feminists of a later generation would appreciate the nicety of Dr. Molloy's "his or her" idiom. The consciousness-raising with which she was concerned as a determined, if somewhat conservative, feminist had to do with upholding college standards and with what she called "keeping trust." A favorite expression of hers, "keeping trust," constituted the bedrock ethic of her approach to the administration of an institution of higher learning. It was, she believed, the business of a college to keep trust with parents, with students, and with society at large by giving them the best possible quality of education.[30]

This belief was not, in her view, incompatible with a highly magisterial administrative style. Much to Molloy's displeasure, a representative sent by Phi Beta Kappa to inspect the college in the early 1930s insisted on the necessity for administrative consultation with the faculty as a prerequisite for chapter consideration.[31] Dr. Molloy had never held a faculty meeting nor did she intend ever to do so. Plans for Phi Beta Kappa were summarily dropped.

By this time, under her leadership and that of Sister Leo, the College of St. Teresa had attained an enviable reputation among Catholic four-year liberal arts colleges for women. Finance and recruitment generally fell to the Franciscan community and to Sister Leo, who was president until 1928 and superior general of the community from 1915 to 1933. Acquisition of nearby houses and property as well as the construction of five major buildings on campus had extended classroom and residence facilities to accommodate 400 students by 1930.[32]

The importance of the sisterhood in terms of personal and financial resources was as great for St. Teresa's as for St. Catherine's, the women's college in St. Paul founded by the Sisters of St. Joseph, and for Minnesota's two Benedictine-sponsored women's colleges. All capital accounts for St. Teresa's were kept by the Rochester mother house throughout the tenure of Molloy as dean and president. Moreover, an endowment of $500,000 was obtained in the early 1920s by a loan secured through the Franciscan community. For its part, the college met operating expenses from tuition income without the help of any major donors or fund drives until the

1950s. Sisters, who constituted 50 per cent of the faculty when Sister Leo relinquished the presidency in 1928, allotted their summer weeks to graduate study, largely at community expense, and to recruiting trips through Minnesota and neighboring states. These junkets were vacations of sorts, involving hours of train travel, stopovers at homes of friends or at convents, and house-to-house canvassing among prospective students at town after town.[33]

Not surprisingly, these activities brought the Winona college into direct competition with its St. Paul sister institution, the College of St. Catherine, founded in 1905. This fact of life, along with other inevitable frictions, is said to have made it difficult for the president-builder of St. Catherine's, Sister Antonia (Anna) McHugh, to apply to Dr. Molloy the gospel dictum that "our Father's house has many mansions." There is little doubt that Mary Molloy had the moral stature and ability to rival Sister Antonia as a promoter of women's higher education in the state. Their keen awareness of each other's efforts made for the rapid advancement of both colleges along the paths of institutional quality and numerical expansion. St. Teresa's produced its first graduates in 1911, two years before the College of St. Catherine did so, and won regional accreditation in 1917, just a year after its rival. By 1920, as St. Catherine struggled to reach an enrollment of 200, the Winona college surpassed 300. And so it went with programs, facilities, and faculty development throughout the 1920s and 1930s.[34]

Unique in her day as the lay administrator of a college operated by women religious, Molloy worked hard at attracting to Winona well-qualified lay faculty. She succeeded in recruiting them in numbers almost equal to those of religious, although her aim of hiring laywomen proved difficult of attainment. Despite her consistent efforts to persuade bright young women graduates from Cornell, her alma mater, to teach at St. Teresa's, the thirteen-member lay faculty of 1928 included only two women.

Dr. Molloy herself exchanged lay for religious status, taking the name Sister Mary Aloysius, in 1922 after the death of her father, for whom she had kept house in Winona since 1919. To those who knew the forty-two-year-old woman well, the interruption of her administrative responsibilities for a novitiate period of two years at Rochester seemed just that — an interruption rather than a drastic change. By then, colleagues and students had come to esteem the short, sturdy, plain woman with the crushing handshake as an outstanding educator and scholar whose high academic goals one "necessarily adopted," so determined was she in their promotion. Those with whom she was associated soon became acquainted with her belief that the highest educational aims were within the reach of women.[35]

In 1915 she laid before Bishop Thomas Shahan, rector of Catholic University and president of the National Catholic Educational Association (NCEA), facts which she believed made imperative a special department within the organization devoted solely to the problems of Catholic women's colleges. The most serious of these problems she identified as misuse of the name "college" by institutions that were still mere finishing schools. The great unmet need for good Catholic colleges for women made the inferior quality of many schools all the more deplorable.[36]

The 1917 convention of the NCEA in Buffalo, New York, gave Molloy a public forum for her views on improving the quality of higher education for women. Her remarks concentrated on the legitimacy of women's demands: "In general, as far as graduates of schools go, undoubtedly eighty out of 100 girls find their places in the home. With college graduates, however, it is different. Only thirty-three per cent of college women graduates find their place in the home. Can we at the present ignore the claims of the sixty-seven per cent who may wish to pursue work other than that bearing directly on the home?"[37]

Although she did not necessarily endorse this attitude "of women pointing away from the home," she saw it as something to be reckoned with. "Women are restless in this generation," she pointed out. "They are taking their places side by side with men in political, economic, sociological and pedagogical fields. If a young woman wishes to become a specialist in higher mathematics, in the classics, or in history or sociology, is her ambition legitimate?" It was high time, she insisted, for the all-male clergy who ruled the NCEA and for the women religious who purported to run colleges to take their task seriously. This they could do by giving women "mathematics, the classics, even the professional courses in law and medicine" in the context of the Catholic college.

Despite these forewarnings, the broadsides she delivered a year later at the 1918 NCEA convention in San Francisco caught an audience of women's college officials unaware. Her address opened innocuously enough with the general observation that "co-operation, co-ordination, conservation and centralization" were the imperatives of the day. A hint of what was to follow came in the blunt sentence which rounded out her introductory remarks: "we are here, I feel, to get something done and not to be insincere enough to use up the precious time allotted to us in mutual admiration."[38]

But listeners were still unprepared for the hard-hitting analysis she proceeded to develop: "*We have too many small, struggling, inefficient and useless so-called colleges.* . . . We need a parochial grade school in every parish; we need at least one Catholic free high school in every city of any size; but we do not need, as we have at present, in some instances, some five or six colleges for women within the confines of every state. . . . It is not a case for gratulation or edification when we see many of our 'colleges' for women either omitted altogether from the list of any rating agencies or slipped quietly and justly into the high school block."

Dr. Molloy's solution to the proliferation of low-quality institutions was no less startling to her listeners than her candor in assessing the situation. Might there not be agreement, she speculated, on "five great geographical areas, two divisions midway of each coast and one district in the center." Within each of these regions a single Catholic college for women could mobilize resources sufficient to offer even the legal and medical training which women deserved.

This drastic solution was labeled as "ideal," but she went on to exhort those present to begin in practical ways to make the institution each one represented "one of the five great centers." Their task, she insisted, was to bring their colleges up to a "thoroughly standard" level with respect to curriculum, buildings, laboratories, and libraries. At the least, women should restrain the impulse to open new colleges and should be ethical in promoting those they currently staffed.

Little imagination is needed to visualize the reaction to a talk at once so outspoken in condemning abuses and so idealistic in proposing remedies. To his credit, Bishop Patrick R. Heffron of Winona, who had been providing encouragement and help to St. Teresa's for some years, once more demonstrated his support for quality Catholic education. He had promoted Molloy's cause in Rome, and as a result Pope Benedict XV honored the Winona dean just before the San Francisco gathering with the *Pro Ecclesia et*

Pontifice medal for distinguished service in the field of higher education for women. It was the first time this papal honor had been conferred on an American woman for educational reasons. As such, it was a signal mark of ecclesiastical approval for the direction Molloy's leadership was taking. In a characteristic gesture of erudition, she wrote her letter of acceptance in impeccable Latin.[39]

Like it or not, Catholic women's colleges found they had a crusader in the person of Mary Molloy. Partly through a vigorous speaking and writing campaign, but especially through positions she held in educational associations, she filled a long career of nearly forty years with unremitting efforts to improve standards and gain recognition for women's education.[40]

Serious literary scholarship had claimed her attention and talents for a few years after the move to Winona. In addition to published articles on the Celtic revival, she produced a study of "The Celtic Rite in Britain" and collaborated with Cornell colleagues on concordances to the works of Wordsworth and Horace. Her doctoral thesis, which established her philological reputation, had been a concordance to the Anglo-Saxon translation of Bede's *Ecclesiastical History*. Involvement in college business and in the larger concerns of higher education forced abandonment of such pursuits by 1915. She turned instead to writing articles and pamphlets on a more popular level. These included *The Lay Apostolate*, published in 1911, and *Catholic Colleges for Women*, the printed version of her 1918 address.

Beginning in the 1920s Dr. Molloy held a series of influential posts which enabled her to implement in significant ways the ideals she so vigorously set forth in her 1918 and later speeches. For twenty-five years she served on the standing Commission on Institutions of Higher Learning of the North Central Association of Colleges and Secondary Schools, the regional accrediting organization. She functioned in 1923 as the sole woman on the association's six-member *ad hoc* commission to draft new standards for North Central colleges and universities. Her services to North Central were recognized in 1943 with the granting of honorary life membership.[41]

A member of the National Catholic Educational Association from 1913, Molloy was appointed in 1923 as the first woman member of the executive committee of its College and University Department. She ultimately served as president of that section. Competence and longevity won her an ex officio lifetime membership. Election to the associate ranks of Phi Beta Kappa in 1947 placed her in a select body of only 200 persons distinguished for their records of scholarship and public service.

Despite being cofounder in 1918 of the Confraternity of Catholic Colleges for Women, the Winona dean and president never managed to become more than a peer among equals so far as other presidents were concerned. Her attempt in 1935 to close their ranks behind her illustrates her style of leadership. A long-time and active member of the American Association of University Women, Molloy took it as a betrayal of trust when the association passed a resolution favoring federal legislation to legalize the dispensing of information on contraceptives by physicians. Not only was she personally opposed to the resolution, but she was also disturbed by the fact that it had not appeared on the draft agenda circulated before the Los Angeles meeting. To aggravate the matter, distance had kept many, including herself, from attending the California convention. She reluctantly registered a protest by canceling her own membership and withdrawing the College of St. Teresa from the esteemed AAUW list of accredited institutions.[42]

During the next six months Molloy conducted an unsuccessful letter campaign to muster unanimous support for her move from the other eleven Catholic colleges with AAUW accreditation. Only four presidents agreed with her to the extent of imitating her action. Others, including the only other Minnesotan, Sister Antonia McHugh of the College of St. Catherine, argued caution.[43] They felt the Los Angeles resolution represented mainly "the group in the West" who were, after all, only a small proportion of the organization as a whole. Still others took exception, believing that they could exert more constructive influence from within the association than through withdrawal. A few admitted quite frankly that the recognition afforded their institutions by AAUW accreditation outweighed the value of standing up for principle in the manner the Winona president was urging. "Membership in an association," they argued, "does not necessarily imply approval of all the measures sponsored by the group."[44]

These arguments, and such statements as "we are waiting for a little while before we take any definite stand on the matter," struck the Winona crusader as an appalling indication of apathy. Although she was convinced of the essential rightness of her position, she resigned herself to the failure of additional support to materialize and carried on more or less alone. Further correspondence with the central office of the association eventually effected a change in the AAUW position. When she learned at last, in November, 1936, that "the final form of the legislative program proposed for the next biennium does not include the item relative to birth control," she renewed her membership and had the satisfaction of seeing St. Teresa's reinstated without compromising her principles.[45] One can debate the merits of the different points of view in this episode. But whatever one's opinions, the courage and decisiveness exhibited by Molloy set her apart from the crowd on the national scene.

At home these qualities made for progressive growth of the College of St. Teresa. Like St. Catherine's and other Minnesota colleges, the Winona institution accommodated itself to post-World War I vocational demands. With typical forthrightness, Molloy defended the adjustment on pragmatic grounds while still preserving a lofty consciousness of destiny. "We cannot ignore the appeal of the practical or vocational courses," she declared, "if we would save the college from extinction; we dare not overlook the claim of the humanities if we would save a civilization from decay."[46]

Franciscans were prominent in hospital work in southeastern Minnesota. The community had founded St. Mary's Hospital at Rochester in close collaboration with Dr. William W. Mayo in the 1880s. In 1907 the sisters had established a nursing school in conjunction with the medical facility which had grown to over a thousand beds by 1930. By 1927 this involvement and the related expertise of the sisters had led to a degree program at St. Teresa's combining nursing and the liberal arts. In the same vocational and professional area, a complete home economics sequence had developed by 1939 from isolated courses introduced during World War I. Business administration became a major in 1932.

Resources never permitted the expansion of St. Teresa's into the kind of regional university that Dr. Molloy had once dreamed of. Indeed, it is surprising to learn that such a step was ever actually envisaged. Nevertheless, Bishop Heffron, a product of St. John's University at Collegeville, at one point in the early 1920s suggested a name change to "Teresan University." Heffron evidently considered this ambitious proposal when it looked to him as though the development of a school of science would transform the Winona college into a Catholic university of the Midwest.[47]

Within the smaller college sphere which circumstances dictated,

President Molloy took satisfaction in conscientious adherence to a demanding level of scholarship. She and her faculty were proud of the diversity of professions for which alumnae qualified and in which they distinguished themselves. Occupations of the women who graduated from year to year were listed in general terms in the catalogue immediately after a notice of the "Teacher's Registry," or placement service for teacher-graduates. Juxtaposition of the two, the "Registry" and the list, constituted a subtle reminder to students of the double thrust of the college toward teaching and all the other careers engaged in by the educated woman. According to the 1928 catalogue, professions in which alumnae were represented included, among others, banking, dentistry, college teaching, high school teaching and administration, social work, music, and science. By the eve of World War II, St. Teresa's, like St. Catherine's, had produced over a thousand four-year graduates.

There was reason for congratulations, too, in the matter of faculty development. By the end of the presidency of Sister Mary Aloysius in 1946, the Franciscans paralleled the Sisters of St. Joseph in terms of advanced studies at an array of outstanding universities. The sisters composed half the total faculty, as they had in 1928. Nine had earned doctorates, whereas twenty years before only Dr. Molloy had gone beyond the master of arts degree. By 1946 a much larger proportion of the lay faculty, nearly two-thirds, were women.

Sister Mary Aloysius Molloy lived eight years after her retirement as president, dying on September 27, 1954, at the age of seventy-four. Her collaborator and friend, Sister Leo Tracy, died on May 2, 1951, at the age of ninety, after sixty-nine years in the Franciscan sisterhood. Their deaths, together with that of Sister Antonia McHugh of St. Catherine's in 1944, closed the heroic age of the "founders" in the history of Minnesota's colleges for women.

Today's Minnesota women take for granted what their sisters accomplished during the pioneer years. The colleges founded by religious orders, including those established by the Benedictines in the central and northern areas of the state, were not begun and developed without an unswerving sense of purpose, inspired personal leadership, co-operative effort, and immense cost in human energy. Progress, seemingly so inevitable from the vantage point of the 1970s, was far from guaranteed at a time when institutions of higher learning came and went with breathtaking rapidity.

Even among the ten independent coeducational or men's colleges of the state which survived the nineteenth century, progress toward the full dimensions of a liberal arts institution was often slow.[48] Difficulties in identifying purposes and securing resources frequently endangered college existence. Accreditation was consequently either not acquired for years or, once gained, was lost for frustrating periods of time. Remarkable indeed in that alternately affluent and economically depressed era was the excellence and stability achieved by colleges for women. These two traits reflected in large measure the corporate strength of the religious communities which established the four women's institutions in Minnesota. They also mirrored in no small way the personalities and individual accomplishments of women like Mary Molloy.

8. ALICE O'BRIEN
Volunteer and Philanthropist

By Eileen Manning Michels

"THE DEATH Friday of Miss Alice O'Brien, 71, of Marine-On-St. Croix, removed from the St. Paul scene its leading woman philanthropist, world traveler and art connoisseur of a past era."[1] On the basis of that 1962 obituary, a person unfamiliar with Alice Marie O'Brien might conclude that her life had paralleled those of other society women who busy themselves quietly with the usual round of activities which the wealthy traditionally have found acceptable — charity, travel, and a polite interest in the arts. The rather bare statement does not begin to suggest the full range of Alice O'Brien's activities and accomplishments, nor does it convey any idea of the zest with which she pursued them. In the diversity of her interests and in the life which she shaped for herself, she could serve as a model for the independent but nonmilitant feminist of today. Like a few other women elsewhere then living analogously independent lives, she was a force in her community during her lifetime, but, because she pursued no career, produced no famous literary or artistic work, participated in no single great historic event, she quickly receded, for all but family and close friends, into a forgotten past after her death in 1962 at the age of seventy-one. If history is indeed a richly dimensioned continuum shaped by multitudes of people, rather than a straight-line development leading from one discrete, acknowledged important event or person to the next, then the story of Alice O'Brien merits being recorded.[2]

Alice O'Brien was born on September 1, 1891, in the family residence, then at 77 Virginia Street in the comfortably fashionable Summit Hill area of St. Paul. She was the first of three children and the only daughter of William and Julia Mullery O'Brien. Her mother (1863–1944) was one of eight children of pioneer Irish

Catholic settlers of St. Paul, and her father (1856–1925), of Irish-American and Irish-Canadian Catholic background, was born in Taylors Falls. Following in the footsteps of his father, he began work as a St. Croix River Valley logger at eighteen and had established a logging business of his own by the time he was twenty-four. His lumber interests expanded in Minnesota and to Florida, South and North Carolina, and the Bahamas, and by 1910 he was involved, with other members of his family, in one of the largest lumber and sawmill business operations in the country. The fortune which he amassed ranked as one of the most substantial in the state.[3]

William O'Brien was a large, affable man, shrewd but fair in business matters, and an affectionate, indulgent husband and father. The relationship between father and daughter was close. She observed him at work, understood his business, and acquired from him a broad comprehension of business and financial matters. For his part, he encouraged her independence, intelligence, and inquisitiveness. Perhaps most significantly he seemed not to restrict his daughter to the domestic sphere of his life. For the thirty-four years of her life that he was alive, they were in fact close companions, and he was without doubt a centrally important figure in her life. In 1945 Alice O'Brien gave to the state of Minnesota as a memorial to her father 180 acres of rolling wooded land, fronting on the St. Croix River just north of Marine, for William O'Brien State Park.[4]

Alice O'Brien first attended the Backus School for Girls, one of the numerous private academies, now defunct, that existed in the Summit Hill area at the turn of the century, and then Visitation Convent, a Catholic high school for girls that is still in existence. Two years at Bennett, a finishing school in Millbrook, New York, followed. Charming photographs show her playing tennis there, a small, trim, graceful, attractive dark-haired girl in yards and yards of full-skirted, high-necked, long-sleeved, lacy tennis costume. Obviously a genteel but skillful tennis game was part of the social equipment of the well-brought-up young lady of that day. After graduation from Bennett in 1911 Alice made the extended European tour that was then an accepted and expected part of the education of the daughters and sons of affluent American families.[5]

According to today's standards, her formal education was limited in duration and in academic quality. A fine intelligence and an innate intellectual curiosity, however, led her to continuous self-education. Throughout her life she read extensively about any subject which interested her, and, since one particular topic always was succeeded by another, the accumulation of interests and information was ultimately massive. A 1937 newspaper article stated that, among other things, she would have made a good mayor, department store executive, or college president.[6] A driving intelligence and a fortune ample enough to allow her to pursue her interests seem to account for the direction of her mature life.

Alice O'Brien never married. In the militant suffragist circles of her youth, marriage was viewed increasingly as a matter of individual choice rather than the only normal adult female state of existence. Indeed, rejecting marriage was in some instances a means of making a political statement. Although Alice O'Brien was sympathetic to the cause of women's suffrage — she once recalled that her first experience as a public speaker had been to introduce Emmeline Pankhurst, the indefatigable English suffragist — there is no reason to conclude that her rejection of marriage was anything but a personal decision.[7] In fact, her niece recalls her saying with a laugh that she never met a man her own age smart enough to marry. Obviously, and with characteristic independence, she rejected the prevalent idea of a proper marriage to a proper young man from a proper family just for the sake of being married. Although single, she was part of an affectionate, extended family that included parents, brothers, maiden aunts, and cousins in early years and nieces, nephews, and their many children in her later years.

During her twenties and early thirties, seemingly motivated in about equal measure by curiosity and a sense of adventure, she traveled extensively and sometimes to unusual places or by unusual means. Traveling to China in the early 1920s was unusual for a young woman as was driving in a roadster from California to Minnesota in 1911. Her fascination with automobiles was lifelong. As a child she learned to drive and to repair and even assemble an automobile engine.[8]

Alice O'Brien's skill as a driver and mechanic led her to volunteer during World War I as a member of the Volunteer Motor Repair Unit of the American Fund for French Wounded. Originally formed as the American Branch of the French Wounded Emergency Fund, an English war relief agency, the American Fund for French Wounded became a separate organization in

Alice O'Brien

March, 1918, with headquarters in New York and local chapters in cities throughout the United States. It was one of many private relief groups that proliferated early in the war, and its main activity was shipping supplies to France and operating supply depots there. In St. Paul, it seemed initially to have been better organized administratively than the Red Cross. In actuality, the AFFW and the Red Cross were similar organizations, and in France they often worked together.[9]

Ultimately several hundred Ramsey County women volunteered their services to field and base hospitals and to relief organizations. But Alice O'Brien and her friends Marguerite Davis of St. Paul and Doris Kellogg, a classmate at Bennett, seem to have been alone in volunteering as AFFW motor repair workers. On March 30, 1918, waving good-by to families, they sailed from New York on a camouflaged ship carrying mostly volunteer war workers to the port of Bordeaux. They later learned that they were on one of the last ships to leave the United States loaded with war workers rather than with combat troops. Although the United States had entered the war in April, 1917, the rest of that year had been needed to transform the country into a war-ready society and to train and equip troops. While this was being accomplished, the allied military situation in Europe deteriorated dramatically, and in March, 1918, just nine days before the St. Paul women sailed, the Germans, numerically superior on the western front, began an offensive intended to culminate in the taking of Paris. By April, 1918, American soldiers were pouring into France, and by July the tide had turned decisively in favor of the Allies.[10]

As it turned out, the three St. Paul women spent most of the final seven months of the war either very near the war zone or actually in it. Alice, a dutiful daughter, wrote to her family about twice a week during the entire time, and fortunately many of the letters were saved. A fearless, observant, considerate, compassionate, articulate young woman with a sense of history as well as a sense of humor emerges from these letters. The one jarring note that obtrudes today is her rhetorically hateful and uncharacteristically gross manner of referring to Germans, particularly German soldiers, and her willingness to believe civilian atrocity stories. Apparently she too had accepted the anti-German propaganda that flowed from the Committee on Public Information after the United States entered the war in 1917. Her letters constitute a factually detailed behind-the-scenes documentation, previously known only to her family, that should be of value to the historians of World War I.[11]

On the ninth and last day at sea she wrote: "Everyone on deck has their life belt beside them, the nervous ones are straining their eyes for periscopes. The French gunners fore and aft are pacing up and down beside their guns which are loaded and ready, the lookout is in the top crows nest on the forward mast, he looked like a human fly climbing up the rope ladder, there are eight guards around the deck all armed with powerful spy glasses, everybody knows their lifeboat number by heart and where to go and stand for orders in case of trouble, all the life boats are supplied with beef, crackers, and kegs of fresh water and are slung over the side in place and down level with the deck, all ready to jump into."[12]

Her first letter from France describes their reception: "Twelve hours before reaching the mouth of the river, the captain received word from shore that submarines were in the vicinity so we changed our course, went due north and then came sneaking along the coast into the harbor. It was thrilling, everyone in lifebelts, etc., but we did not know our real danger until it was past. We anchored at the mouth for the night and the next day came up to Bordeaux. Never have you seen or heard of such a welcome as the old ship received on her triumphant entry — people lined the banks and shouted, waved handkerchiefs and aprons, sang, screamed, all the whistles tooted themselves into a frenzy, soldiers stood at attention, flags waved — oh! — everything happened." [13]

A few days later, in Paris, awaiting assignment, the women experienced their first air raid: "The long range gun has dropped a few shells into Paris for the last three days but no one thinks of paying any attention to it. It does not throw a bad shell, only dangerous in an eight foot circle wherever it strikes and Paris is so big that it seems more like a mosquito bite than a gun. We went thru our first air raid last night. We were just getting into bed at ten o'clock when we heard the alarm given and a second later heard the first bombs explode. Only a few machines got thru the defense of Paris and they succeeded in dropping some bombs before they were driven out [but] not many." [14]

In Paris, they learned to their disappointment that there were few motorcars to be serviced for the AFFW, and they began discussing alternate assignments with the Red Cross: "In the meanwhile we have not been idle. The Red Cross asked us if we could assemble a Ford for them. We said 'Sure, send it along,' and the next day they did send it, in a box, placed it carefully on the garage floor and left. We had a lot of fun putting it together and great was our interest when we got it all set up, cranked it and it started. We jumped aboard and ran it around the block, hanging to the thing by our teeth because there was not a body on it and the French people looked at us as [if] to say 'Three crazy Americans.' The Red Cross man came over and inspected it, found everything O.K. and said that as long as we [had] got that far with it why not go a bit farther and make an automobile out of it, so we took the body off of an antediluvian wreck that [had] stood in the corner for months, put it on the new chassis and then went for another ride." [15]

Rather than remain in Paris as chauffeurs with the AFFW, a lackluster assignment in their opinion, the three women arranged a release from the AFFW and signed for three months as canteen workers with the Red Cross. Early in June, while they were still awaiting papers which would send them to a French canteen in Chantilly, the battle of Chateau-Thierry began, and they were pressed into emergency service caring for wounded soldiers: "The wounded started to pour into Paris and in twenty-four hours the hospitals were crowded to the doors, beds in all corridors, operations going on all day and night, men's wounds being dressed in wards, hallways or wherever they could get room to lay them, the nurses and the doctors so busy that the half well patients had to wait on the others, in fact everything in pell mell shape and all organization swept off its feet by the rush. We were sent out to Hospital No. 1, used to be the American Ambulance, at Neuilly, just outside of Paris and only fifteen minutes from Place de la Concorde, and told to do whatever we could to help. . . .

"Today was our fifth as auxiliary nurses and I cannot believe that we have done all that we really have. . . . I am the auxiliary in ward 237, the nurse comes in three or four times a day, but the rest of the time I am left alone to sink or swim with ten French blesses, one Russian and four Americans whose beds are in the corridor right outside the door. If you would like to know a few of the things I did today, read the following — washed faces and hands, made beds for the ones not seriously ill — gave Dakin treatment to men whose wounds were being treated with it — removed dressings from all wounds so that they would be ready for the Doctor (some of the wounds are dreadful and some not so bad, the Russian has had his leg amputated just below the knee, one man has dreadful wounds, one has a shrapnel wound the size of a saucer in the middle of his back, one has the calf of his leg shot away, one, a poor young French boy, has a bayonet wound through the abdomen and I am afraid that he is mortally ill, and one has a gun shot wound that enters one side of his body and comes out the other) — assisted the nurse and Doctor at the dressings — bound up all wounds after dressings — made the Russian's bed — took all pulses and temperatures — gave them their luncheon — did Lord knows what all afternoon — gave them dinner and at six came home to my own, tired as a dog but thoroughly satisfied and happy with the day's work. I would have to have training and experience, in America, before I would be allowed to do half what I did today, but, over here, they tell you to do the best you can and you go ahead knowing that if you didn't do them no one else would, and, I suppose something is better than nothing. I am sorry that the men in my ward are not lucky enough to have an A number one nurse but I give them the best I have and pray for results." [16]

A few days later: "Dad always says that there is nothing in the world that human nature won't get used to and it has never seemed truer to me than in the past week. I see and do things that would raise the hair off my head if I were reading about them but nowadays I take them just as calmly as I take the rest of life. I had to hold a man down in bed yesterday, leaning my full weight on his chest and holding his hands down, while his wounds were being dressed. . . . Poor kids, I can't say enough for them. America will win the war but it will be at their expense and a lot of them won't be alive to enjoy the day of victory."

By the middle of June, the three had been transferred to a canteen in Chantilly. Preparing and serving meals for between 800 to 1,000 French soldiers at a time kept them busy for long shifts, sometimes twelve consecutive hours. One of the letters even included a crude floor plan of the canteen. Although the women had signed up for European service for only six months, they soon gave up all idea of returning home before the end of the war. They truly felt that they were needed in France: "Well, must close now, the candle is flickering out and I am nodding with sleep. Mugs came into the room last night and saw me darning my socks by the feeble light and said that she realized, for the first time, how far we were from home. You bet we're a long way off when I start darning." [17]

Late in July, Alice O'Brien became the driver of a one-ton Ford canteen truck and subsequent letters tell of her marketing coups: "Just to give you an idea of the quantities we deal in — the following is an ordinary days purchase — one thousand eggs, five hundred pounds of meat, five hundred heads of lettuce, fifty heads of cabbage, four hundred peaches, two hundred loaves of bread and all the other stuff that we receive from the Red Cross warehouses in Paris and that they ship us by railroad. It is a big job to get all the food that we need to feed as many men as we do." [18]

Throughout the summer and early autumn, the three women worked nonstop having only two days of rest in fifteen weeks. A note of physical and emotional exhaustion began to appear in Alice's letters in September. Finally, in late October, their replacements arrived at the Chantilly canteen, and the three women were released for a week of rest in St. Jean du Doight in Brittany far away from the war zone. One day before the Armistice was signed, they arrived at their new assignment, an American canteen at Toul in the war zone. On November 11 Alice wrote: "I have managed to dry my eyes and pull myself together to write this letter. I have been crying with joy over the signing of the Armistice! Of course, it is too big a thing to realize that Peace has come after four years of hideous war. All the bells rang at eleven o'clock, the soldiers shouted, and everyone is so happy about it all. . . .

"We arrived here yesterday. . . . We heard cannon booming and soon discovered that the anti-aircraft guns were firing at a Boche plane almost directly overhead. It was a beautiful, clear day, so thousands of feet over us we could see the German plane shining in the sunlight and the shells bursting all around it. Imagine our excitement when we saw it waver, knew that it had been struck, and a minute later saw it start its bumbling careen to earth. It flashed in the sun, as it fell, like a spoon hook on the end of a fish line. Suddenly a white spot seemed stationary in the sky and we realized that one man had extricated himself from the wreck and his parachute was bringing him down a prisoner in the Allied lines. . . .

"Am worried to death about the Influenza in America. For heavens sake be careful." [19]

Her wartime experience left Alice O'Brien with a deep and particular fondness for France, and she returned there from time to time in later years. Sometime between the war and 1927, when she left on a well-publicized trip to Africa, she traveled to Peking apparently to see for herself what was happening in China during that tumultuous period. No one in the family now remembers the exact date of the journey nor who her traveling companions were. Although several dozen photographs from the trip remain in the possession of her niece, none is a typical, trivial souvenir snapshot of Alice O'Brien or of any other western person. Instead, the photographs she took or acquired are of Peking, unidentified villages, machinery, peasants, tradesmen, farms, and countryside. Like the letters from France, they qualify as previously unknown documents of considerable interest to the historian or, in this instance, to the China-watcher. In China Alice met the eminent Swedish art historian, Osvald Sirén, then an internationally renowned authority on Chinese art, who was there to acquire Chinese art for the Swedish National Museum. It was a fortuitous meeting. He had expertise, and she had money. Presumably acting upon his advice, she bought, from Chinese families who were then hastily selling their treasures, several dozen paintings, sculptures, and bronzes, all of superb quality. After Alice O'Brien's death, fourteen

Chinese works from her collection entered the permanent collection of the Minneapolis Institute of Arts as a bequest.[20]

In contrast to the trip to China, an African trip is well documented by a book and by a silent motion picture. Apparently since childhood she had wanted to see the wild animals of Africa, and in maturity she developed a curiosity about its people, particularly about the Pygmy and Mangbetu tribes. In a newspaper article written just before her departure, she simply said that she wanted to see the real Africa.[21] She and Ben Burbridge, a friend and experienced African hunter from Jacksonville, Florida, spent four months planning the trip during late 1926. Part of the preparation included studying the Swahili language. Alice O'Brien, Ben Burbridge, and Charles E. Bell, a photographer then associated with Ray-Bell Films of St. Paul, sailed in October, 1927, on the "Aquitania" from New York for France. There they met good friends from Minnesota, Grace and Blair Flandrau, who had decided to accompany them. Grace Flandrau was a well-known writer, and her book, *Then I Saw the Congo*, is an account of the African adventure from beginning to end.[22]

In December the party of five, wearing helmets and impeccable safari suits made for them in France, sailed from Marseilles on the "Brazza" bound for Dakar, Senegal, the first port of call. From Dakar, a leisurely three weeks on the "Brazza" along the west coast of Africa and up the Congo River brought them to Matadi. They went inland from there by train to Kinshasa. The two-week wait at Kinshasa for the river boat which would take them one thousand miles farther upriver to Stanleyville was spent purchasing additional supplies and hiring about 200 native bearers and servants. When finally collected and packed, their baggage weighed two and one-half tons — enough to fill one freight car.[23]

From Stanleyville they set out by car and truck on a newly completed road through the Ituri Forest. Although a portion of their luggage was left in Stanleyville, it was necessary to take along complete housekeeping equipment, and each day an elaborate camp would be set up on a village clearing. At Avacubi the party changed to huge dugout canoes, each forty to fifty feet long and manned by twenty paddlers, which brought them down the Aruwimi River to a point just north of Stanleyville.[24] Once back there, the most arduous part of the journey was over, and the native bearers, no longer needed, were dismissed. The group then proceeded via the new Cape to Cairo railroad south to Kabalu, then east to Lake Tanganyika and across it by steamer. From there they went by train and truck into East Africa to see big game and finally, in May, 1928, to Nairobi and the port of Mombasa on the east coast — covering all in all about 7,000 miles in five months.[25]

Although no one in the party was a trained anthropologist, Grace Flandrau's *Then I Saw the Congo*, one of the first books in English about travel through the Congo, is a detailed day-by-day description of their adventure written with sensitivity, knowledge, and humor. It was, as a matter of fact, a far more interesting account of travels in Africa than one written for the *New York Times* in 1927 by Martin Johnson, a well-known explorer of the day. Flandrau, an excellent writer, was particularly responsive to the often incongruous juxtapositions of indigenous old and transplanted new in equatorial Africa, to the shoddiness of much white colonial culture, to the brutality which often characterized treatment of black by white, to the nature of native villages and music, and to the style, dignity, and beauty of many native people, particularly the Mangbetu tribe — a group erroneously described at that time by the *Encyclopaedia Britannica* as extinct.[26]

The trip was arduous physically. However, the travelers stressed, upon their return to the United States in May, 1928, that all popular romantic beliefs about mysterious, primitive, darkest Africa were untrue. Instead, Africa was rapidly becoming a modern, westernized continent. In fact, they pronounced it more healthful than Minnesota, more thoroughly explored than some parts of Montana, and more orderly than some parts of Texas.[27]

Fascinating visual documentation of the adventure still exists. Bell, the photographer, had carried along film for 3,000 still photographs and 28,000 feet of movie film. About four dozen still photographs were published in the Flandrau book and in the serialization of it which was carried in the *St. Paul Pioneer Press*; a few dozen more are in the possession of the O'Brien family, but the rest have dropped from sight. As in the case of the photographs of China, most of the ones which do survive qualify as serious documentary photographs.[28]

However, the most important surviving visual documentation of the trip is the feature-length silent film, "Up the Congo." Flandrau stated that the group initially had intended to make a movie about primitive native life and about travel methods in crossing equatorial Africa. En route discussion turned to the possibility of making a picture which could be shown commercially. Although opinion was divided about what kind of picture to make, eventually, over the objections of Alice O'Brien and Grace Flandrau, a loose scenario evolved. There would be sequences of Pygmies shooting at the company with presumably poisoned arrows; the two women would peer into a cannibal pot supposedly containing boiling chunks of people; elephants would charge the women, and so on. There were attempts to stage and film these and several other similarly fraudulent scenes with the full co-operation of the natives who seemed amused by most of it. Straight documentary sequences also were shot. In New York at the end of the trip, filmmakers from Hollywood became involved in producing the movie. A man cryptically identified by Flandrau as "the Biggest Cutter in the business" analyzed the situation: "All we gotta do is to graph the interest, redistribute the peaks, and potentialize the threat. We'll feature the two ladies as having made the trip alone, run a title about the danger of exploration in the forest, show the tame elephants for wild, say that Teddy Roosevelt discovered the okapi, and play up that place where the Pygmies are shooting the party with poisoned arrows." [29]

Luckily he more or less was held in check, and the film which resulted was, in spite of a few sequences of easily spotted hokum, what the travelers had intended to make all along; that is, a record of people and places. Its titles were translated into eight foreign languages. Occasionally, as at its New York showing, it was accompanied by a lecture, and it was distributed widely in 1930. Nearly fifty years later it has stood the test of time, and it too will be of value to the historian or anthropologist who discovers and uses it now. [30]

Back in St. Paul after the African adventure, Alice O'Brien at the age of thirty-seven began a different phase of her life. Although she returned to Europe from time to time in subsequent years, her days of far-flung wanderlust were over. During the next fifteen years, her time was taken up with civic and philanthropic activities, and she became a public figure in St. Paul, a force in the community. She felt, as her father before her had and as the rest of her family also would, a sense of loyalty and obligation to St. Paul and to the Washington County area of Marine on St. Croix where, after her father's death, she and her mother lived unostentatiously in a rambling, spacious, comfortable, old house overlooking the St.

Croix River.[31] She gave her time, her organizational talents, and her money to causes which were of interest or importance to her.

For example, feeling that the Volstead Act had produced flagrant evasion, hypocrisy, lawlessness, and crime, she was active in the National Prohibition Reform movement. In 1933 she served as general chairman of the women's division representing consumers in the local campaign which urged adoption of the provisions of the National Recovery Act. She was president of the St. Paul Community Theater. She worked enthusiastically for Wendell Willkie during his presidential campaign.[32] However, two St. Paul organizations, the Women's City Club and Children's Hospital, clearly were closest to her heart during those years.

On the evening of October 15, 1931, the new building for the Women's City Club was inaugurated with a gala reception for members and guests. That a clubhouse costing $265,000 could have been built as the Depression began settling in was due in no small part to the zeal of Alice O'Brien, who from 1929 to 1936 was chairman of the building committee and from 1930 to 1932 was president of the organization.[33]

The change in the nature of women's clubs between the 1890s, when a number of them first were organized throughout the country, and the post-World War I period, when they proliferated and became important in their communities, reflects the broad changes in the position and role of women in American society during the same period. The early clubs usually emphasized literature and culture. Today it is all too easy to dismiss as unimportant the clubs which offered afternoon lectures, often prepared with more enthusiasm than knowledge, on subjects as remote from their members' lives as "Druids and Druidical Monuments in Brittany" or "Court Life and Manners in the Reign of Louis XIV." [34] Who today knows exactly what was said about any of these exotic subjects? That they were discussed at all in the many midwestern communities whose raw frontier days had ended only a few decades earlier is remarkable enough. In general such meetings and topics seem to have been but one more manifestation of the enthusiasm for self-education and self-improvement which swept over the country during the late nineteenth and early twentieth centuries. To many of the women involved in the clubs, equally as important as the intellectual and cultural aspirations must have been the relief such meetings offered from an otherwise ceaseless domesticity circumscribed by household, family, and church.

Bulletins of women's clubs indicate that by 1900 meeting topics were changing from the study of high-brow culture to the active promotion of public welfare. Specific social issues were studied methodically. Public school education, for example, was the subject of a programmed, yearlong study conducted by many women's clubs throughout the state in 1898 with guidance from the Minnesota Federation of Women's Clubs. During World War I, thousands of women whose lives previously had been lived largely in their houses ventured into public and community life as volunteer or paid workers. That experience, plus gaining the right to vote in 1920, was responsible for a further broadening of interests within women's clubs. Women began to realize that, acting collectively as an informed group, they could wield political power. By 1920 the Minnesota Federation of Women's Clubs had standing committees on art, civil service, education, home economics, industrial and social conditions, legislation, library extension, music, and public health; also, significantly, it urged adoption of a state constitutional amendment, Good Roads Amendment #1 — a far cry from concern with "Druids and Druidical Monuments." [35]

Many St. Paul women doing war work had found themselves in the downtown area of the city each day for the first time in their lives, and they noted the lack of convenient lunching and resting places. Men had had downtown clubs for decades, but there were few for women. In 1894 women had clubhouses in just five cities. By 1933 there were 1,200 women's clubs, and typically they included every facility found in men's establishments: sleeping and residential rooms, restaurants, gymnasia, showers, libraries, and recreational facilities. [36]

The Women's City Club of St. Paul reflected these general developments. In 1920 a group of thirty women, among them Alice O'Brien, met at the Ramsey House, then the residence of Mrs. Charles E. Furness, to discuss the founding of a women's club. At the meeting, they resolved to organize, conduct a membership campaign, and raise funds to open a clubhouse as soon as 1,000 women had signed application blanks. A year later their goals had been met, and, with $8,000 in hand, the group adopted a constitution and bylaws, elected officers and a board, and incorporated. The *raison d'etre* of the club was simply stated: "The purpose of this Club shall be to provide for women a center for organized work and for social and intellectual intercourse." Membership was open to any woman who was interested in the goals of the club and could pay the modest ten dollar annual membership fee.[37]

For its first eight years the club was located in renovated quarters in the old Minnesota Club building at Fourth and Cedar streets in downtown St. Paul. In 1929 that arrangement terminated when the building was razed, and the membership, in an expansionary mood typical of the period just before the stock market crash, decided to build its own clubhouse. Alice O'Brien became chairman of the building committee which was charged with authority to select a site, choose an architect, oversee the preparation of plans, and raise funds for the project.[38]

Fund-raising activities included the usual methods of soliciting pledges and conducting rummage sales, but far more grandiose and risky strategies were also employed. The Women's City Club sponsored two visits of the German Opera Company in 1930 and 1931, performances by the Ballet Russe de Monte Carlo in 1934–35, and a visit of the Salzburg Opera Company in 1937. Besides swelling the building fund, these activities added immeasurably to the cultural life of St. Paul. When presented by the Women's City Club, *Tristan and Isolde* had not been heard for the previous nineteen years, and people came from all over the upper Midwest for the completely sold-out performances. The Ballet Russe, then at its artistic height and conquering all of Europe with its dazzling performances, appeared that season in only two other American cities, New York and Chicago.[39]

Masterminding these enterprises and all other aspects of the building campaign was Alice O'Brien. Her willingness to take risks — for example, the German Opera Company demanded a guarantee of $20,000 per visit — her accurate, detailed manner of working, her ability to plan and delegate, and her broad knowledge of business methods gained from her father stood her in good stead. Her engaging flair for publicity also emerged. For example, she trained her two Great Dane dogs to deliver opera tickets held in their mouths to various city dignitaries. She donned a jump suit and threw out free tickets to the opera while flying over the city in a plane. She climbed into the cab of a steam shovel. She induced Governor Floyd B. Olson to turn the first shovel of dirt at groundbreaking ceremonies — the list of publicity maneuvers is ingenious and amusing, and all of it was photographed for the newspapers.[40]

The committee selected Magnus Jemne, a St. Paul architect, to design the building overlooking the Mississippi River at Third and St. Peter streets in downtown St. Paul. A stunning example of architecture in the style now referred to as Art Deco or Art Moderne, it was the only architecturally modern women's clubhouse in the country at the time it was finished. Four storeys high, its clear, prismatic forms, elegant detailing and furnishings, and its integral decoration by Elsa Jemne, an artist who was also the wife of the architect, were recognized nationally for over-all excellence of design. Frank Post, then the most fashionable decorator in the area, designed the interiors. By agreement, all furniture was made from local materials by local manufacturers, a gesture of support in the depressed local economy that was noted approvingly.[41]

Thus, in late 1931, St. Paul had joined the ranks of other cities which offered women a club, a centrally located clubhouse, and a variety of activities. From the beginning, meeting rooms were also made available to other local organizations. For a quarter of a century, through its facilities, many women of St. Paul kept in touch with each other and, equally importantly, with the social, cultural, and political world at large. International luminaries such as T. S. Eliot, Gertrude Stein, and Amelia Earhart lectured at the Women's City Club in the early 1930s, and local experts in politics, sociology, government, international relations, and the arts also spoke to the membership each year. During World War II the club was a focal point for recruitment of women for the services and for volunteer Red Cross work.[42]

Membership peaked at about 1,500 in the 1950s, and the social unrest of the 1960s coincided with a decline in membership. Feeling that membership might increase again if the building were air-conditioned, Alice O'Brien spent the winter of 1959–60 in St. Paul, rather than in Florida as she had been doing for many years, in order to help raise funds for air conditioning the building. However, membership did not revive. By and large, younger women by then no longer were interested in the kinds of organized activities which the club typically provided and generally instead preferred an unstructured educational and social environment. In 1972 it was apparent that the Women's City Club could no longer maintain its building, and it was sold to the Minnesota Museum of Art. Remodeled, it has since then housed the Permanent Collection Gallery of that institution.[43]

Concurrent with Alice O'Brien's interest in the Women's City Club was her interest in the Children's Hospital of St. Paul which was founded in 1923 by Dr. Walter Reeve Ramsey, a medical pioneer in the field of infant and child health. Although the first children's hospital in the United States had been established in Philadelphia as early as 1855, malnutrition, disease, and an appallingly high child mortality rate still prevailed throughout the country at the beginning of the twentieth century. During the first quarter of the century, tremendous advances were made in the conquest of many children's health problems, and many of them occurred in hospitals especially devoted to children's diseases. Children's Hospital in St. Paul was opened in 1924 with sixteen beds in an old frame house at the corner of Smith and Walnut streets. Since it was the only children's hospital between Chicago and the northwest Pacific coast, children went to it from all surrounding states. Almost immediately the need for an adequately housed and staffed facility was apparent, and in July, 1928, Children's Hospital moved into its large, new, specially designed building at 311 Pleasant Street. A dream of Dr. Ramsey had been realized, and Alice O'Brien was a member of the hospital's board of trustees which had assisted him in realizing it.[44]

Since no family with a child who needed help that Children's Hospital alone could provide was ever turned away for lack of money, the hospital steadily accumulated an operating deficit. After the crash of 1929, the hospital's fiscal situation worsened, and by 1932 its plight was desperate. Late in that year, while still actively involved in fund raising for the Women's City Club, Alice O'Brien successfully presented to the Junior League of St. Paul a plan to form a Children's Hospital Association for the express purpose of raising money for a free-bed fund. The Children's Hospital Association still carries on its work today. Another significant step taken by the board members that year was to pay out of their own pockets an accumulated deficit of $106,000 in order that the hospital might start the next year free of debt.[45]

With her fashionably short hair and her smartly simple manner of dress, Alice O'Brien was a familiar figure in St. Paul during the 1930s. Her numerous public commitments took up virtually all of her time, and, since she lived about thirty miles out of town in Marine, she needed a St. Paul base of operations. Accordingly, shortly after the First National Bank Building was opened in 1931, she rented an office in it which she maintained for the rest of her life. From it she conducted her many volunteer activities and also kept watch over her own numerous private financial affairs.[46]

After World War II, her life changed as noticeably as it had some fifteen years earlier. She began to live more privately, spending more of her time with family and friends, although she still came to her office about three days a week when she was in Minnesota. She even drifted away from active participation in the Women's City Club. While she still maintained her Marine residence for the summer months, she began living about half of each year on Captiva, an island off the coast near Fort Myers, Florida, in a house designed for her by Magnus Jemne, the architect of the Women's City Club. Beginning in the late 1930s, she also acquired the first of her three yachts, all named "Wannigan," after the river boat which in the early days of lumbering was a bunkhouse and cookhouse for the lumberjacks who accompanied the logs being floated from camp to sawmill. The pride of the three was "Wannigan III." Launched in 1950, it was seventy-two feet long and had a crew of three, but otherwise there was little of the ostentation typical of yachts of that size. Instead, it was comfortable and severely practical with aspects of both a tugboat and a shrimp boat. Needless to say, Alice O'Brien had been involved actively in the designing of it, and it was built to her specifications. During the winters of the 1950s, she enjoyed cruising in it off the Florida coast. However, shortly before her death she sold "Wannigan III." Her nephew Terence recalls her explanation that yachting, as she objectively observed and reconsidered the pursuit, had begun to seem to her an advanced form of senility. Seemingly with no regrets, she abandoned an activity which for more than twenty years had given her great pleasure.

Although her fondness for winters in Florida and for yachting might be considered self-indulgent, she still actively supported many philanthropic causes — but at this stage of her life by giving her money rather than her time and entreprenurial talents. In December, 1951, increasingly besieged with requests from people and organizations for financial support, she formed the Alice M. O'Brien Foundation in accordance with conditions established by the Minnesota Non-Profit Corporation Act, for the broad purpose of supporting charitable, educational, religious, and scientific causes. Although the foundation always supported a diversity of causes, the directors in 1962 voted to allocate funds only to Minnesota projects or organizations. The list of organizations, people, and projects which through the years have received help from the

Alice M. O'Brien Foundation is long. Children's Hospital, the Minnesota Society for Crippled Children and Adults, Our Lady of Good Counsel Free Cancer Home, Little Sisters of the Poor, the chapel at the state prison, the Minnesota Historical Society, the Washington County Association for Senior Citizens, St. Paul Academy and Summit School, and the Monastic Manuscript Microfilm Library at St. John's Abbey are but a few of the major beneficiaries. During her lifetime the foundation channeled particularly generous support to the Minnesota Medical Foundation of the University of Minnesota, which provided funds for Dr. Owen H. Wangensteen's pioneering work in surgery, and to Neighborhood House, now known as the Hallie Q. Brown Center, a youth center which has been closely attuned to the black community in St. Paul.[47]

In her later years, Alice O'Brien also became interested in conservation, particularly in erosion control in Florida. On November 8, 1962, while driving to Florida for her winter sojourn there, she stopped at Des Moines, Iowa, to attend a board meeting of the Jay N. (Ding) Darling Foundation, an organization named after the well-known political cartoonist, which was devoted to conservation. She died unexpectedly that day in Des Moines of an aneurism of the brain.[48] Given her wealth, she could have chosen to lead a totally self-centered and self-indulgent life. Instead, beginning with her volunteer service during World War I and ending only with her death forty-four years later, innumerable people, causes, organizations, and communities were the beneficiaries of her intelligent and generous support.

9. MAUD HART LOVELACE and Mankato

By Jo Anne Ray

MAUD HART LOVELACE is a writer who immortalized a town, a family, and a childhood friendship. The fictional town is called Deep Valley, the family is named Ray, and the friends are Betsy, Tacy, and Tib. To a considerable extent they are patterned after Maud Hart Lovelace's own family and her childhood in Mankato, Minnesota, during the early years of the twentieth century.

The Betsy-Tacy books, like many other fictional works based on autobiography, impel their devoted readers to seek some dimension of reality. They write to Maud to ask the names of the "real" Tacy and Tib, to find out if Betsy's Joe returns safely from World War I, and to ask if they have a daughter they call Bettina. Some travel to Mankato to walk the streets and climb the hills, to look for Lincoln Park and the Carnegie Library and the slough, and to find Tib's chocolate-colored house with the tower and pane of colored glass. This desire to give reality to fiction was recognized in a 1961 "Betsy-Tacy Days" celebration sponsored by the Mankato branch of the American Association of University Women. Maps of Mankato were distributed showing the Deep Valley landmarks, the former homes of Betsy, Tacy, and Tib, and the hills where they picnicked and played. The real-life models for some of the principal characters were present in Mankato for the event, which featured talks by Maud and guided tours of the landmarks described in the ten Betsy-Tacy books that have appeared since 1940.[1]

The volumes in which Betsy and her family and friends are central characters begin when the children are turning five, take them up through high school, and end with Betsy's wedding. The series ranks among the best-selling children's fiction of the period. The incidents and adventures that make up the Betsy-Tacy stories have wide appeal: the half-pretend, half-real world of youthful play and the whole glorious glow of happy childhood are in their pages. Young readers — almost always girls who begin the books at age six or seven — follow the older Betsy and her crowd into their own adolescence and later launch their daughters on the series. Memories of their own childhoods intermingle with nostalgia for the idyllic bygone small-town world of 1900 that is the books' setting, as indeed the author's memories were stimulated by her daughter's demands to know what it was like when her mother was a small girl. "I lived the happiest childhood a child could possibly know," Maud has said again and again.[2] From her reminiscences and from the books, it is clear that the author was indeed happy in her family, her time, her place, and in her own disposition.

Happiness, talent, ambition, and determination have characterized Maud Hart Lovelace's life. In addition to her extremely successful children's books, she has written several adult historical novels which, while not so successful as those about Betsy-Tacy, were generally well received by critics and public when they first appeared. Perhaps the best known is *Early Candlelight* (1929), a romantic story set in the early years of Minnesota's Fort Snelling. In recognition of the novel's historical accuracy and literary merit, the University of Minnesota Press reissued the book in 1949 on the occasion of the Minnesota Territorial Centennial. In all, Maud Hart Lovelace wrote eighteen children's books and six adult novels (including three in collaboration with her husband, Delos W. Lovelace).[3]

Maud maintains that she was born to be a writer. At age five, she followed her mother about asking, "How do you spell 'going down the street'?" From the time she could hold a pencil, she was writing diaries, poems, plays, and stories. "I cannot remember back to a year in which I did not consider myself to be a writer, and the younger I was the bigger that capital 'W'," she said. When she was ten, her father printed a booklet of her rhymes. And, at ten, she began sending stories and poems to magazines. She kept a record and checked off each publication when the rejection notice came back.[4]

The ten-year-old Maud who sat in her office — the backyard maple tree — composing stories with titles like "The Repentance of Lady Clinton" and "Her Secret Marriage," had much in her favor, not least of which was Mankato. "I liked Minneapolis and

Delos W. and Maud Hart Lovelace

other places I lived," she said, "but I don't feel about them like I do about Mankato. I love Mankato and I love the people." On another occasion she commented that "Mankato is a wonderful town to grow up in. It is a wonderful town to live in." What, Maud was asked in California in her eighty-second year, do you remember most about Mankato. "The hills," she answered promptly.[5]

It would be hard to overestimate the force of those hills on the young Maud Hart. They produced sights and sounds and smells to live in memory for a lifetime, stimulating her imagination. The hills of Mankato were green in Maud's time and rose up beside and behind her home at 333 Center Street. From the top of the hill Maud could look down on the whole town, on the roofs of the red-brick Pleasant Grove school and her own house, Front Street with its stores, the Big Mill, Sibley Park, and, far away in the valley, the silver ribbon of the Minnesota River. Betsy, Tacy, and Tib "had the whole hill for a playground. And not just that one green slope. There were hills all around them."[6]

The Mankato into which Maud Hart was born on April 25, 1892, was only forty years old. The natural beauty of winding rivers,

hills, and woods remained. Early settlers still talked vividly of the
Sioux Uprising of 1862, the bravery of the First Minnesota Regiment at Gettysburg, the devastation of the grasshoppers in the
1870s, and the ordeals of blizzards and floods. While Maud was
attending Pleasant Grove grade school, army veterans regularly visited on Memorial Day to tell the children about the Civil War and
the Sioux Uprising. She was enthralled by their stories, and by
those that appeared in a book entitled *Mankato — Its First Fifty
Years*. "As a child," she recalled later, "I loved its pictures of the
bearded pioneers and the views of Mankato in the early days. I
loved the stories of hardships and adventure, the struggles to start
the various churches, the opening of the first school in a
warehouse on Walnut Street. . . . After I was married and in a
home of my own I borrowed this book so often that at last, in despair, probably, my father gave it to me. It is always on my desk."
Maud did not, one feels sure, overlook the following statement in
this book: "The early pioneer hereafter will be the interesting vic-
tim of the novelist, as well as the subject of the historian. The
literary ferret will hunt their lives for romance, and their exploits
will be celebrated in story and song." Twenty-four years later, *The
Black Angels*, the first of Maud Hart Lovelace's novels dramatizing
the exploits and romances of the pioneers was published by John
Day and Company.[7]

Mankato's physical beauty and recent romantic past provided
stimulus for Maud's imagination. Most important, perhaps, was the
spirit of the time and place. In Maud's youth, people still mar-
veled at the contrast between Mankato's recent pioneer past and
its comfortable civilized present. All things seemed possible, because so much had been accomplished already. As close as Mankato was to pioneer days, however, it was hardly a rough frontier
settlement in 1900. Some 10,000 people lived there; there were
twenty-two churches, five public elementary schools, a brick-
turreted high school, two private commercial colleges, a state
normal school, two parochial schools (German Catholic and German Lutheran), and an opera house. Deep Valley, Maud has written, "was what is known as a good show town. It was a thriving
county seat, and theatrical productions, passing from the Twin
Cities to Omaha, found it a convenient and profitable one-night
stand." What had happened to Mankato in the years from its
founding in 1852 to 1902 was mainly an influx of people, people

from the East, from Ohio, Illinois, and New England. There were also Germans, Welsh, Scots, Scandinavians, and Irish, and, more unusual, a group of Syrians who arrived about 1885 and founded a small colony called Tinkcomville — named for the enterprising pioneer who first owned the land and whose heirs later sold it to the Syrians.[8]

The author herself has made it clear that the Betsy-Tacy books are a portrayal of Mankato and of the happy home life of the Hart family. "It is a great joy to me to have that dear family between book covers," she wrote in 1961. Maud, like Betsy Ray, was the middle child; Kathleen (Julia Ray) was three years older, and Helen (Margaret Ray) was six years younger. Like Mr. Ray, Mr. Hart presided at Sunday night lunches: "Sunday night lunch was an institution at the Ray House," Maud wrote in *Heaven to Betsy*. "They never called it supper; and they scorned folks who called it tea. The drink of the evening was coffee. . . . The meal was prepared by Mr. Ray. . . . No one else was allowed in the kitchen except in the role of admiring audience." A friend of Kathleen's recalled some seventy years later: "They were such a nice family. I can remember Mr. Hart coming in with this big tray of sandwiches and pot of coffee. He was so loving of his family and so proud of them all." [9]

Thomas Walden Hart arrived in Mankato from Iowa in 1883 and by 1888 was a partner in a wholesale-retail grocery business located on Front Street. About 1892, the year Maud was born, he opened a shoe store. He was successful as a merchant — "a natural born businessman" Maud later described him. He had inherited from his pioneer mother an intense respect for education. His parents had moved to Iowa from Canada. His mother "had been a school teacher in Canada, and there were always books in the little farmhouse. She had implanted in everyone of them [*her children*] a yearning for an education, and they had not been satisfied with the little country schoolhouse. There was an academy in the town nearby and to this she and her husband had managed to send the older children in turn." [10]

Mrs. Hart, nee Stella Palmer, had lived as a small girl in nearby Winnebago, Minnesota, with her parents and brother Frank. Her father, a Civil War veteran, died, and her mother, Albertine, later married Chauncey Austin and moved to Madison Lake, just outside of Mankato. There Maud's mother spent much of her girlhood — a girlhood marked by a family disagreement that was to exert a powerful influence on the writing career of her daughter.[11]

Chauncey Austin was a stern man who frowned on worldly pleasures such as the theater and dancing. For this and perhaps other reasons he did not get along with his stepson Frank. At the age of seventeen Frank ran away from home with an opera troupe and shortly thereafter married an actress as old as his mother. Stella had sympathized with her brother, and in later years she often talked about him. He became something of a legend to her children, and he was intimately associated in Maud's mind with her ambition to be a writer. Years later he was to be the model for Uncle Keith in the Betsy-Tacy books; it was also her Uncle Frank and the legend surrounding his life that provided much of the plot for Maud's first novel, *The Black Angels*. The character Alex was based on Frank, and the fictional opera troupe with which he sang, called the Angels, was based on the Andrews Opera Company with which Frank had sung for a time.[12]

Numerous other characters in Maud's fiction were also drawn from close acquaintances who lived nearby. Across the street from the Hart house on Center Street, at number 332, lived a "large merry Irish family" which included among its numerous children a girl Maud's age, Frances Kenney, or "Bick," as she was affectionately called. Bick, the model for Tacy, had long red curls which often covered her face, for she was very shy. With "Maudie," however, she was not shy. She was an enthralled listener to Maudie's fanciful stories, an enthusiastic companion on real-life and pretend adventures, a sympathetic and devoted friend with whom to share all the joys and sorrows of growing up. Betsy consoled Tacy on the death of her baby sister, just as Maudie must have consoled Bick when her baby sister died. "And she *had* comforted her. All the sore feeling was gone."[13]

There was a third playmate, a tiny girl with fluffy yellow hair and round blue eyes who despite her spritelike appearance was thoroughly practical and competent. She lived on the corner of Byron and Bradley streets in a chocolate-colored house with a pane of colored glass over the door and a tower. Her name was Marjorie Gerlach, but because of her tiny size she was nicknamed "Midge." The eldest child of architect Henry Gerlach, she was the real-life model for Tib. Many years later Maude recalled neighborhood circuses held on a knoll in the Gerlach backyard which "featured Midge on a trapeze which was put up in a big tree there. I believe she hung from her toes." Midge was "very agile and absolutely fearless. At the age of seven or so she climbed a telephone pole which had just been placed on that corner; it may well have been the first one on Byron Street. Seeing her perched at the top," a neighbor "ran to the Gerlach house in alarm, but Mrs. Gerlach took the news calmly. 'Don't worry,' she said. 'She'll get down.'" [14]

As they grew older, the three girls roamed farther from home. They often ventured to Lincoln Park to play near the fountain and rest under the big elm that spread its branches over the small pie-shaped park. The large stately homes of Mankato's most prosperous citizens were an attraction, Maud recalled fifty years later. "The Patterson house seemed to us the last word in elegance. We hoped to buy and live in it when we grew up. Another house we admired was the Judge [Lorin] Cray house. We didn't know who lived there. Midge Gerlach and I, aged seven or so, left a bouquet of violets on the doorstep as a tribute." When Maud and her friends wandered to what in Mankato is literally *down* town, they found even more attractions. There were the newly built Carnegie Library and the opera house. Free passes to matinees at the latter were the prized possession of Beulah Hunt, whose father was editor of the *Mankato Free Press*. Beulah's lucky friends, including Maud, Bick, and Midge, were sometimes invited to share these passes. The tense, almost agonizing suspense Maud felt before the curtain went up is well described in *Down Town*. [15]

Another place of great mystery and romance was Tinkcomville, the Syrian colony. Rumor had it that one Syrian child was a princess. Later, when Maud was living in New York City, she did considerable research on the Syrians and discovered that the rumor was true. In her books, Maud succeeded in bridging the gap between the Syrian culture and that of Mankato — something that never quite happened in real life. In *Betsy and Tacy Go Over the Big Hill*, the children make friends with the little Syrian girl Naifi, who because of her language and dress has been the object of ridicule and taunts by some schoolboys. Betsy's father tells the girls that Naifi is a real princess, and that the members of the colony are Christians who came to America for religious freedom. "'Most of them came from the Lebanon District,' Mr. Ray went on. . . . 'Cedars still grow in those wild Lebanon hills; and in the ravines and valleys some brave groups of people still keep their

loyalty to their native Syrian princes — in spite of the Turks.
Emeers, these princes are called, and their daughters and
granddaughters are emeeras or princesses.'" His disclosures were
met by a dazzled silence, for in Betsy's imaginative life, as in
Maud's, kings, queens, princes, and princesses held very important places.[16]

Bick, Midge, and Maud became lifelong friends. "We couldn't
have been closer if we had been sisters," said Maud. And from the
Betsy-Tacy books it is evident that the three complemented each
other nicely. "Betsy loved to think up things to do and Tacy and
Tib loved to do them." They shared another bond — the ambition
to succeed in the Great World. In high school, Betsy is "almost
appalled" to discover what fixed ideas her classmates had about
marriage. They had hope chests, embroidered towels, and were
beginning to collect their silver. "When Betsy and Tacy and Tib
talked about their future, they planned to be writers, dancers, cir-
cus acrobats." Perhaps for this reason the Betsy-Tacy books were
included in the 1974 feminist publication, *Little Miss Muffet
Fights Back*, a list of recommended books in which girls are portrayed in positive roles.[17]

For Maud, entrance into Mankato High School, long anticipated
as a major milestone, was made especially dramatic by her family's
move from the small cottage on Center Street to a larger home on
the corner of South Fifth Street and Cherry. Located only a block
from the high school and the courthouse (Mr. Hart became treasurer of Blue Earth County in 1904), the house was roomier than
the cottage. It had a large entrance hall called "the music room," a
bedroom for each of the three Hart daughters, a gas stove, a coal
furnace, and a bathroom ("no more baths in a tub in the kitchen").
Maud felt terrible about the move. "Didn't they know how much
she loved that coal stove beside which she had read so many
books while the tea kettle rang and the little flames leaped behind
the isinglass window? Didn't they know how she loved the yellow
lamplight over the small cottage rooms? And she thought it was
cozy to take baths in the kitchen beside the old wood burning
range!" Before long, however, she came to love the new house,
which became the gathering place for "the Crowd," a group of
high school boys and girls who made it their indoor headquarters.
Picnicking with Tacy near the old cottage on Center Street nearly
a year after her move, Maud's alter ego "knew that she did not

wish to come back, not to stay, not to live. She loved the little yellow cottage more than she loved any place on earth, but she was through with it except in her memories." [18]

The four Betsy-Tacy books which chronicle the four high school years are based on the author's meticulous diaries, the letters, party programs, snapshots, and other mementos she saved, as well as the memories and souvenirs shared with her by childhood friends. When she came to write of those years, Maud also pored over old newspapers, fashion magazines, collections of pop songs, and Sears Roebuck catalogs. As a result, the books are a rich source of detail about life in a small midwestern town in the early 1900s. One learns, for example, that once a year Mankatoans turned out in large numbers to hear tenor Chauncey Olcott sing "My Wild Irish Rose"; that Ouija, progressive dinners, and embroidering jabots were among the pastimes of young ladies; that barn dancing to "Morning Cy, Howdy Cy" and waltzing to "You are my rose of Mexico/ the one I loved so long ago" were the rage in 1909. The customs of the Hart family are also described: the Sunday surrey rides about town and the excursions to Sibley Park and Minneopa Falls a few miles west of Mankato; the Christmas Eve traditions with Maud reading Dickens' *Christmas Carol*, Kathleen reading the nativity story, and Helen reciting "'Twas the Night before Christmas"; and the family's annual trip to Madison Lake, Mrs. Hart's childhood home, on the Harts' wedding anniversary. "Mother would point out the second story window where she sat on her wedding day . . . looking down the driveway and waiting for Tom's horse and buggy, a rented livery rig, to drive through the big, white gate. A twin row of spicy-smelling evergreens led from the house to that gate and the property was enclosed by a white fence." [19]

The books also include a variety of characters based on real persons who lived in Mankato while Maud was in high school. Among them was the "heroic" piano teacher Kate Robb, who broke off her wedding to care for the children of her sister who had died of tuberculosis, only to have three of them die of the same disease. There was Marguerite Marsh, whose grandmother taught the first Mankato public school class in 1853. Marguerite, an orphan, was younger than Maud and lived a somewhat lonely life with her grandfather. Following graduation from high school, Marguerite was left behind while most of her friends went on to college. Later, she became the real-life model for Maud's heroine in *Emily of Deep Valley*, the story of a sensitive young girl who is not part of the carefree and self-confident high school crowd. And then there was Marion Willard, who, like Bick Kenney and Midge Gerlach, was to remain Maud's friend as an adult. Marion graduated from high school a year before Maud and went to Vassar College. Her experiences there, as well as her romance with a childhood sweetheart, are the focus of Maud's book, *Carney's House Party*.[20]

The Maud who emerges from the high school books is a fun-loving, friendly girl, struggling to grow up with dignity, but often lapsing into silliness; longing achingly to be pretty and therefore enduring the discomfort of Magic Wavers, a curling iron, and an affected, fashionable slouch; discovering boys as friends and as figures of romance with whom popularity was very important. Looking back on her high school days some forty years later, Maud recalled the pleasures of dances at Schiller Hall, private parties in the ballroom of the Saulpaugh Hotel, singing around the home piano and dancing in the back parlor with the carpets rolled up.[21]

Maud Hart completed her high school education in 1910. It had included languages (Latin and German), history (ancient and modern), sciences (biology, botany, physics), mathematics (not a favorite), and English composition and literature. As one might expect, she excelled in English and was well read in the classics: Shakespeare, Dickens, Thackeray, Scott, etc. Her graduation photograph shows a young woman with an upswept hairdo wearing a high-collared shirtwaist, and smiling somewhat wistfully, perhaps because of a conflict between a desire to smile broadly and a wish to conceal the gap between her two front teeth. The whole ritual of her senior year and high school graduation — class play, junior-senior banquet, awards assembly, class day, commencement — are well chronicled in *Betsy and Joe*. So too are her feelings on having her high school years come to a close. "You grow older in spite of yourself, Betsy thought resentfully. . . . 'I wish I were a freshman again.'" She looked at her friends as they prepared to receive their diplomas and reflected how some of them had been friends since kindergarten, and, "Now they were being blown in all directions like the silk from an opened milkweed pod." And blown they were, Maud along with them. That autumn Maud Hart enrolled at the University of Minnesota in Minneapolis. Although she didn't know it then, she was leaving Mankato as a home forever.[22]

The years immediately following her graduation from high school were not entirely happy ones for Maud. "I didn't adjust to college very well," she wrote in a letter to a reader. "I was just recovering from an appendix operation. When I went home for Thanksgiving my family saw that I wasn't well and they kept me at home until after Christmas when I went to California — and *that* was a *very* happy experience." [23]

Visiting her Grandmother Austin there, she was "dazzled" by roses in winter; she met cousins she had not known before; she renewed her friendship with Rupert and Helmus Andrews, who had moved from Mankato to California. "Best of all . . . I began to pound out my stories, and soon was greatly assisted by my Uncle Frank. He was ranching, not far from San Diego, and came to Grandma's often, and was banging the piano and making me smile and (for he was a writer as well as an actor) helping me with my writing." He suggested that perhaps her stories failed to sell because they were hand written. He loaned her his typewriter and on it she pecked out "Number Eight" and sent it to the *Los Angeles Times* Sunday magazine. She later described how she bought a copy of the *Times*, scrambled through the magazine section, and found her story there. "I had not had notification of its acceptance; they paid on publication. The moment in which I saw that story in print was one of the happiest of my very happy life." [24]

When Maud returned to Minnesota, it was to a new home in a new city. The Hart family moved from Mankato to 905 West 25th Street, Minneapolis, where their daughters could more conveniently attend college. Maud re-enrolled in the university as a special student, not working for a degree but taking courses she thought would help her as a writer. She later recalled her French class and the fascinating courses taught by Professor Richard E. Burton. Her greatest interest was the *Minnesota Daily*, on which she became women's editor and around which her social life rotated. [25]

She wrote stories for the *Minnesota Magazine*, and one attracted the attention of Professor Maria Sanford whose letter praising the story became one of Maud's deeply prized possessions. Professor Sanford wrote her in part on May 31, 1912: "Your article was indeed good and you have reason to be proud of your power. I do not say this to turn your head, but only to encourage you. Remember, literature is very exacting. The only way for a young person who has ability, is to keep modest; study hard to catch not the trick but the inspiration of the great masters; and work, work, work.

"It may not be at all wise to neglect seeking in other lines your means of support, if you must depend on yourself; but do not fail to give your gift in this line a chance to develop." [26]

Despite this triumph, Maud did not enjoy college. "I seemed to be studying things I cared nothing whatever about," she recalled. And so, like Betsy, she sailed for Europe probably with chaperones in January, 1914. She stayed about a year, spending the time almost equally in Munich, Venice, and London, apparently sometimes on her own. Her mother saved the regular and detailed letters she wrote, and they later provided the material for *Betsy and the Great World* (1952). A romance with a young Venetian also formed part of the plot. In the book, the romance ends with Betsy sailing for home, but in real life the young man later came to the United States, met Maud's family, and eventually stayed in this country permanently. He was a musician and had great charm. Maud later recalled that her sister Kathleen had wondered "how in the world you could have refused to marry him." [27]

Instead two years later Maud married Delos Lovelace. Writing brought them together. After her return from Europe, Maud was introduced to Mrs. Harry B. Wakefield, wife of the city editor of the *Minneapolis Tribune*. Mrs. Wakefield was in charge of a money-raising effort and needed someone who could write. "I went to see her," Maud recalled, "and we liked each other very much. She told me to look through the collection of articles and materials to see the kind of thing they were doing. I remember coming across Delos' name and saying, 'Why, what name is this? It sounds like a valentine.' Then I went on to read some of the things he had written, and I said, 'My, he certainly writes well.'" [28]

"Mrs. Wakefield was a great matchmaker, and she invited Delos, myself, and Helen [*Maud's sister*] to dinner at her home — I think she invited Helen because she was young enough not to give any competition. Well, we had a lovely time. Delos and I were seated across from each other and we kept eyeing each other. I remember Helen was walked home and then Delos and I walked and walked, around the lakes, and talked and talked — it was practically dawn before we reached my home. After that, whenever possible, Mrs. Wakefield would send me on assignments out to Fort

Snelling," where Delos was stationed at the First Officers Training Camp.[29]

Delos Lovelace was born in Brainerd, Minnesota, and by the time he met Maud Hart in May, 1917, he was a newspaperman of some experience, having worked on the *Fargo* (North Dakota) *Courier*, the *Minneapolis Daily News*, and the *Minneapolis Tribune*. Contrary to the Betsy-Tacy books in which Betsy has known Joe (Delos' counterpart) since her first year in high school, Maud knew Delos only a brief time before their marriage in her home in Minneapolis on November 29, 1917. The whirlwind pace in *Betsy's Wedding* is, however, a true reflection of real events, as is the book's description of the young couple's first years of marriage.[30]

The Delos who emerges from the novels is an energetic, ambitious, strong-willed man. In his ambition for himself and his wife, he and Maud were at one. He insisted that she have household help, despite the fact that both their apartment and their budget were small. "He was adamant that I have time for writing," said Maud, who was not especially domestic. How this shared desire to write set them apart from other couples is described in *Carney's House Party*.[31]

Later in life Maud once said, "I was brought up to believe that one person in a family has to have the final word, and that person should be the man. If Delos hadn't wanted me to write, I wouldn't have." When it was suggested to her that if such a conflict had seemed likely she would not have married Delos Lovelace, she said, "Well, that's probably right."

The summer after their marriage Delos was sent to the war zone in Europe, returning safely in 1919. In 1920 he and Maud decided to move to New York City, where he worked as a reporter and then copy editor and night editor on the *New York Daily News*. Illness forced him to resign, however, and he and Maud returned to Minnesota, this time to what Delos described as a "shabby, rambling, delightful home" at Casco Bay on Lake Minnetonka. There Maud's writing career took a new turn. Both she and Delos were writing short stories, but while his sold to such leading magazines as *The Saturday Evening Post, Country Gentleman, Ladies' Home Journal*, and *American*, hers were accepted mostly by such smaller magazines as *Ainslee's* and *Sunset*. Maud credits Delos with encouraging her to try a novel. In 1926 her first book,

The Black Angels, was published, receiving a generally favorable review from the *New York Times*, which described the story as "genuinely pleasing. . . . It abounds in vivacity and a not too sugary sentiment."[32]

Maud had read William W. Folwell's *History of Minnesota* while doing research for *The Black Angels*. She had been fascinated by Folwell's account of life at Fort Snelling in the early decades of the nineteenth century, by the contrast between the gay routine of dinners and balls within the fort and the wilderness and Indian country surrounding its walls. Thus the idea for *Early Candlelight* began to develop. To do the research for this novel, Maud and Delos moved into a St. Paul hotel for the winter so that she could spend her days at the Minnesota Historical Society reading diaries and letters about the years from 1800 to 1850. "When spring came we moved back to Minnetonka," she wrote. "That summer I turned my rough outline of the novel into a rough draft. My husband and I, sometimes with my father and mother, drove around southern Minnesota visiting the places mentioned in the novel. We had many adventures finding the sites of the early trading posts and settlements. I went often to Fort Snelling and, although I had long been familiar with this place, I saw it now with new eyes. Mendota took on a charm impossible to describe."[33]

The following winter of 1928 the Lovelaces returned to New York, Delos to the staff of the *New York Sun* and Maud to complete work on *Early Candlelight*. She continued her research at the New York Public Library, and she and Delos visited the American wing of the Metropolitan Museum to select from the displays there the wallpaper, chairs, and other furnishings for the home of her hero, Jasper Paige. "[We] were as excited as a bride and groom on their first shopping trip," she said later. In 1929 the novel, probably her most successful work for adults, was published. The *New York Times* reviewer commented: "Like a fresh wind sweeping in from her own breezy prairie comes this romance of early Minnesota, delightfully told by one of her native daughters." The book was also praised for its "lyric beauty of expression and consummate skill in the re-creation of a life long since vanished."[34]

The Lovelaces, settled in New York and established as writers, remained there for nearly twenty-five years, and there the couple's only child, a daughter they named Merian, was born in 1931.

Delos spent most of those years on the *New York Sun,* writing a
few books between his editorial assignments. Maud followed
Early Candlelight with two more romantic novels — *Petticoat
Court* in 1930 and *The Charming Sally* in 1932. Neither book has
a Minnesota background, although the former owes something to
Maud's family. It is set in Paris at the court of Napoleon III because "Grandpa and Grandma Austin attended the Paris Exhibition of 1889," wrote Maud, "and when I was a little girl Grandma
used to tell me about Paris and how she had seen the Empress
Eugenie, sitting in the Tuileries Gardens. I loved hearing about
this old woman in black who had once been acclaimed the most
beautiful woman in the world and so, half a lifetime later, I put
her into a novel." [35]

Maud's next two novels, written in collaboration with Delos,
used Minnesota themes. *One Stayed at Welcome* (1934) was set in
Hennepin County in the 1850s and 1860s and included in the plot
such local historical events as the opening of the Suspension
Bridge across the Mississippi River at St. Anthony, the first settling of Bloomington, and the naming of Minneapolis. *Gentlemen
from England* (1937) derived from Maud's family background as
well as from Minnesota history. This story of a British colony at
Fairmont in Martin County is based on fact interwoven with
Maud's recollections of nearby Winnebago, where her mother
spent part of her early childhood. The colony of Englishmen "had
been lured across the ocean by a promoter's assurances that they
could make a fortune raising beans," wrote Maud later. "Most of
them were wealthy; some were the younger sons of titled persons;
and many brought servants along. Leaving the beans to hired
hands, they enjoyed fox-hunting and Mother told us fine stories of
the red-coated fox hunters galloping over the prairie and also
loitering around Winnebago City for they particularly liked the
tavern there. Delos delighted in her stories and in time proposed
that we do a novel about these English gentlemen." [36]

Maud did most of the research for the books they wrote together, and Delos did most of the plotting. They amiably divided
the writing assignments, she taking the romantic parts and those
focusing on women, and he writing the sections devoted to men
and such exploits as the wolf hunt in *Gentlemen from England.*
The amiability with which the Lovelaces worked together was recalled by Maud in an interview with the editor of the *Mankato
Free Press.* "We always got along because we loved each other so

much," she said. "Some people, you know, wouldn't like to collaborate because one or the other wouldn't give in to the other — that sort of thing." Maud thoroughly enjoyed doing the research for this novel. "In addition to the usual old American newspapers, I read British sporting journals and the *Illustrated London News*. I made two trips to Fairmont, interviewing the descendants of the original British settlers, and I went through one of their old mansions and the bachelor's hunting lodge which had doors so tall that, if the whim struck them, the young men could ride their horses inside." [37]

Delos was also a great help to Maud when she was writing the Betsy-Tacy books. She wanted him to be represented in the high school series, and needed his reactions. "While I knew many boys as a child, I did not have any brothers. . . . But Delos said 'No sir!' Again I was more persistent than he, and said flatly that he would be the hero of the book. He finally gave in." On another occasion, Maud wrote: "It was so pleasant for me to have Delos really and honestly in the picture. I had always tried, in the earlier books, to have Joe walk and talk and behave like Delos, but one of my friends said to me about *Betsy's Wedding*, 'Delos walks right off the pages.'" [38]

But the person who was perhaps most influential in spurring Maud to write the Betsy-Tacy books was her daughter Merian. When Merian reached the age where she loved bedtime stories, her mother, like so many mothers before and since, told stories about her own childhood. Merian had focused her mother's thoughts on Mankato and reawakened her memories of childhood, and Maud, being a writer, then thought of putting the stories down. The first Betsy-Tacy book was published when Merian was nine, and after that a Betsy-Tacy story appeared almost every year until 1955. Besides the old letters, diaries, and other mementos, Merian was an additional resource, helping her mother remember what it was like to be a certain age. Merian graduated from high school the same year Maud was writing about Betsy's graduation from Deep Valley High School. That fall, when Merian went off to Smith College, Maud was writing *Carney's House Party*, which includes descriptions of Vassar as it was in the first decade of the century. During the writing of *Betsy's Wedding*, Merian was married to Englebert Kirchner, a young magazine editor. [39]

These were the busy, productive years in which trips to visit family and friends were included among all the other family and professional obligations. There were trips back to Mankato, of course, and to visit Bick and Midge who, like Maud, had left Mankato. Bick married Charles Kirch, settled in Buffalo, New York, and became the mother of two. Midge, after attending art school in Milwaukee, returned to Mankato, and married Charles Harris of Iowa. Later they moved to Lincoln, Nebraska. After her husband's death in 1929, Midge worked in Chicago and elsewhere as a dress designer. Although they often saw each other, only rarely did the three friends get together at the same time. When they did, said Maud, "We had an absolutely wonderful time. . . . We were such good and close friends all our lives. We loved each other." [40]

Delos retired from newspaper work in 1952, and not long after that the Lovelaces moved across the continent to California, where Maud's sisters then lived. The warm climate attracted them (despite her love for Mankato and the Middle West, Maud never liked the cold), and Maud had an abiding affection for California dating from her first visit there in 1911, when she had sold her first story. On their way to the home of Maud's sister Kathleen, the Lovelaces went through Claremont. "Delos declared immediately that this was where he wanted to live," said Maud. "He drove to a real estate office, told the man we wanted to buy a home in Claremont and that he should look for a place while we continued on to Kathleen's." The characteristic speed and decisiveness will seem familiar to those who know the Joe of the Betsy-Tacy books. [41]

Claremont thus became their home, and the Lovelaces settled into a comfortable routine of writing. There Maud finished the Betsy-Tacy series and completed another children's book, *What Cabrillo Found* (1958), a fictionalized biography of the discoverer of California. Now freed from newspaper work, Delos wrote a short novel entitled *Journey to Bethlehem,* and *That Dodger Horse,* a children's book laid on a Minnesota farm. While he found a regular routine of book writing more demanding than he had imagined, "even in my most reluctant moments, however, I feel that putting words down, in more or less sense, is preferable to any other work I might find in my semi-retirement." [42]

In 1967 Delos died of a heart attack. Midge died in 1965, and Bick some years later. In 1977 Maud continues to live in California. "Idyllic" Maud has called the Mankato of her childhood. And the happiness of her childhood is one key to the enduring popularity of the Betsy-Tacy books. A recent reviewer of children's books suggested that young adolescents are turning away from books today because there is no joy in reading about burnt-out fourteen-year-olds, teenage alcoholism, teenage pregnancy, strife with parents, and abortion. For great numbers of children and young adults the well-told pleasures and sorrows of Betsy-Tacy show them how happy a childhood can be. "I never had a crowd of high school friends like Betsy had," said one reader, "So I always enjoyed reading about hers." "I play I'm Betsy and my best friends play they are Tacy and Tib," write many young readers.[43]

For some years Maud intended to add one more book to the series, "Betsy's Bettina," which would bring Joe home safely from World War I and tell about the birth of their daughter. But she never warmed to the book. "I did a little research on it but didn't care to write it. I have always felt that the last lines in *Betsy's Wedding* were a perfect ending for the series." In that perfect ending Betsy at Tib's wedding dance felt the future and the past seem to melt together and she "could feel the Big Hill looking down as the Crowd danced at Tib's wedding in the chocolate-colored house."[44]

10. GRATIA ALTA COUNTRYMAN
Librarian and Reformer

By Nancy Freeman Rohde

GRATIA ALTA COUNTRYMAN, called the "first lady of Minneapolis" and the "Jane Addams of the libraries," served from 1904 to 1936 as head librarian of the Minneapolis Public Library. When she was appointed to that position, she was the only woman in the country to head a library the size of the Minneapolis Public, and, as of 1977, she was still one of the few women to have directed a major municipal public library in the United States. A dramatically forward-looking woman with an educational and social service philosophy of extending library service to more and more segments of the community, Gratia Countryman gained an international reputation for herself and for the Minneapolis Public Library. Over a period of fifty years her public life in Minneapolis touched almost every area of civic interest. She helped to found and lead a number of new organizations and service clubs, and at one time it was said that "No public welfare organization in the community was complete without Miss Countryman's name on its board of directors." [1]

Born on Thanksgiving Day, November 29, 1866, at Hastings, Minnesota, she was named Gratia by her father, a Latin scholar, to express his thanks. She had two older brothers, Amplius and Theophilus, and a younger sister, Lana. Her parents, Levi and Alta Chamberlain Countryman, were among the early settlers in Dakota County, homesteading near Hastings in the mid-1850s. The family farmed during the early years and Levi, who had a master's degree from Hamline University, also taught school. Following his return from service with the Second Minnesota Regiment in the Civil War, he entered the agricultural machinery business first in Hastings and later in Minneapolis. The family was a warm and affectionate one, and, with the exception of Amplius, remained close throughout their lives.[2]

Showing her promise early in life, Gratia graduated from Hastings High School in 1882 at the age of fifteen. Her commencement essay, entitled "The Vocations in Which a Woman May Engage," argued that women were capable of doing many things and should have a choice of vocations suited to their abilities and interests.[3]

After her graduation from high school, her father moved the family to Minneapolis so that his daughters could attend the University of Minnesota and live at home. Because she was so young, Gratia enrolled in the prefreshman course at the university, postponing her entrance into the freshman class until the fall of 1883. Illness forced her to drop out of school for a while, delaying her graduation until 1889.[4]

A warm, vivacious girl with many interests, she was soon involved in campus life, and her home became "a center where students, sorority members and classmates dropped in." The range of her activities was diverse. She enrolled in an otherwise all-male surveying class and found it something of a lark to carry stakes and chains around the campus on spring days. She was a member of Delta Gamma Sorority and served as vice-president of the Hermean Society, a literary organization. She loved music, taught piano, took voice lessons, and tried her hand at a little composing. Church activities were also important to her and remained so throughout her life.[5]

Two campus activities stand out as indications of a pattern she was to follow for the rest of her life: being a "first" and a "founder." In what was to be one of many firsts in her life, she inaugurated the participation of women in the annual Pillsbury oratorical contests at the university. Although she did not win any prizes, an editorial in a Minneapolis newspaper argued that she should have been awarded either second or third place. The editorial considered her essay as good as and her delivery better than those of the young men who had won.[6]

The campus organization she helped found was Company Q, a women's military drill team, a seemingly strange activity for a woman who later became a well-known pacifist. In the 1880s there was no provision at the university for physical exercise for women. Feeling they deserved some attention, the girls petitioned the faculty to allow them "some form of military drill . . . as an aid to physical culture." Although the faculty probably did not think

Gratia Alta Countryman

they were serious, permission was granted and Company Q was duly formed. The girls designed their own uniforms and selected their own officers, with Gratia serving as first lieutenant. They followed the regular *Manual of Arms* and did all of the setting-up exercises. The wooden guns issued to Company Q for weapons drill provoked a good deal of teasing from the boys, but this did not dampen the girls' enthusiasm or enjoyment.[7]

Gratia graduated from the university in June, 1889, and was elected to Phi Beta Kappa. Her abilities had come to the attention of Cyrus Northrop, president of the university and an *ex officio* member of the recently created board of the Minneapolis Public Library. He suggested to Gratia that she apply for a position in the soon-to-be-opened library and recommended her to Herbert Putnam, who had been selected as the new public librarian.[8]

During the last quarter of the nineteenth century, a relatively new American institution, the tax-supported public library, was growing slowly but steadily, particularly in the East and Midwest. Although libraries had existed in Minnesota since the creation of the territory in 1849, the foundation of the state's public library system was a law passed by the legislature in 1879. The following decade saw the establishment of thirteen public tax-supported municipal libraries, including those of St. Paul in 1882 and Minneapolis in 1885. The new Minneapolis Public Library was to house the collections of the Minneapolis Athenaeum, a subscription library supported by annual assessments, and Putnam, librarian of the Athenaeum, was chosen to head the city's new public institution. A permanent building was under construction, and Putnam was busy acquiring books in 1889 when Gratia decided to follow President Northrop's advice and give library work a try.[9]

On October 1 of that year she joined five other assistants who were helping to prepare the library for its opening on December 16, 1889. Many years later one of those assistants, Josephine Cloud, recalled their first meeting: "What I was prepared to see was a very imposing person with a superior air of whom I would stand in awe. What was my surprise when a slight little girl in a blue sailor suit and a cap with a vizor perched jauntily on top of her blond curls, very modestly announced herself as 'Gratia Countryman.' I took to her at once and we have been the best of friends for forty-seven years." Gratia's first job in the library included classifying the 30,000 volumes that made up the initial collection. Putnam was impressed by her abilities and within a year she was appointed head of the cataloguing department.[10]

Putnam resigned to become director of the Boston Public Library in 1891 and was succeeded by Dr. James K. Hosmer, who in December, 1892, appointed Gratia assistant city librarian, a position she held in addition to heading the cataloguing department. Hosmer was a scholar interested in research and writing and in building a fine central library collection, so much of the administrative work fell to Countryman.[11]

The staff was small and close in those early days, and the moving spirit in their activities was Gratia Countryman. Always a leader, she was the first among them to learn to ride a bicycle. She put this skill to good use on her first trip to Europe in 1896, when she and three other young women bicycled through England.[12]

Young as she was, and unusual as it was for women to be active in the business and professional world at that time, Countryman soon was making an impact upon the city of Minneapolis and the library world. She considered herself fortunate to have found work that was highly congenial, and from the beginning she began to develop a philosophy of reaching out and making library services available to more people. Her efforts did not go unnoticed, and the

Minneapolis newspapers soon were writing articles about her and her work.[13]

Her activities on behalf of libraries were not confined to Minneapolis. She recognized the value of library systems and the necessity for state aid to libraries if service was to be widely extended. With the encouragement of Hosmer, who considered that the library cause in Minnesota was lagging, she became the leading advocate for state library laws.[14]

In 1891 she became a charter member of the Minnesota Library Association and in 1892 became secretary. As secretary she sent out circulars and helped organize traveling town libraries. A professional spirit began to manifest itself in the state, which resulted in association membership from more communities and a growing interest in promoting state-wide library development.[15]

The largest task undertaken by the state association before 1900 was the passage of legislation in 1899 which created the State Library Commission with its system of "circulating book collections," and enabled towns and villages to establish their own public libraries. It was Gratia Countryman who in 1893 had outlined a scheme for traveling libraries similar to a program just begun in New York. The Minnesota association passed a resolution favoring the plan, but not until 1895 was a bill based on the New York law introduced into the legislature. The bill was defeated, reintroduced in 1897, and again defeated. Countryman began to rally the support of many groups throughout the state, most notably women's clubs. In his annual report for 1898, Hosmer wrote of her lectures around the state, her leadership among women's groups, and her lobbying efforts with state legislators, who, he observed, had "been approached and enlightened." [16]

When the bill was finally passed in 1899, Hosmer hailed the creation of the State Library Commission as a significant step in library development and praised the efforts of Gratia Countryman, who "more than anyone else, has carried the thing through to a successful issue." She was appointed to the commission and served as recording secretary from 1899 until 1919, when its work was absorbed by the Minnesota Department of Education.[17]

Evidence of her growing national reputation came in 1902, when she was elected to a five-year term on the council of the American Library Association, a distinct honor.[18] Thus, when Hosmer submitted his resignation in March, 1903, it was not surprising that his assistant librarian was considered a strong candidate to succeed him. The *Minneapolis Journal* of March 12, 1903, commented favorably on her qualifications and also suggested as a candidate Letitia M. Crafts, secretary of the library board and assistant librarian at the university. The *Journal* predicted that questions would be raised about whether a woman could fill the position as capably as a man and wondered whether a highly qualified man could be found for a salary within the means of the library.

As the news of Hosmer's resignation traveled outside the state, Countryman received letters from various parts of the country offering support for her candidacy. Herbert Putnam, by then librarian of Congress, wrote the board urging her appointment, mentioning that she had been the actual head of the administrative work. She had, he said, the necessary education, energy, system, and initiative for the position and had kept in touch with experiments elsewhere. In Putnam's opinion, nonconsideration of her for the position because of her sex would be unfair and not in the best interests of the library. Nor would it be fair, he said, to accept "a man's service" from a woman and not give her the salary and title a man would receive. He expressed his doubt that the board could get a man who was better qualified than Countryman for the $3,000 it was paying Hosmer. Putnam's recommendation was concurred with by Melvil Dewey, a prominent American librarian and the creator of the Dewey decimal system, who, in writing a letter of recommendation for another applicant, endorsed the appointment of Countryman, saying that leading librarians shared the feeling that she was a superior woman.[19]

By the fall of 1903 she and Letitia Crafts were among the serious candidates for the position. On November 6 the board, overcoming its reluctance to appoint a woman, voted six to three to select her chief librarian. The members decided, however, to pay her only $2,000 and to abolish the position of assistant librarian.[20]

Immediately the press raised questions of discrimination. Typical of the comments were those made by Mrs. Maud C. Stockwell, state president of the Equal Suffrage Association, who was quoted in the November 7, 1903, issue of the *Minneapolis Journal* as saying: "The action in cutting her salary and giving the new librarian the work of two persons shows a most unjust discrimination against woman [*sic*] and every high-minded citizen should protest against such injustice."

Nor was comment limited to the local press. After her appointment had been announced, Countryman began to receive letters of congratulation from all over the nation. Many of the correspondents expressed pleasure that a major library position had finally gone to a woman, and nearly all protested the board's action on salary and the assistant librarian position. Articles, editorials, and letters to the editor appeared in newspapers in other cities and in the library press.[21]

The board denied that it had discriminated against Countryman, saying, according to the *Minneapolis Journal* of November 7, that it had promoted her and given her a raise of $700. On November 13, 1903, the *Minneapolis Tribune* printed a letter from Thomas B. Walker, president of the board, refuting the charges of discrimination: "The salary was fixed before a selection was made and when it was presumed and looked decidedly as though a man from the East would be given the position; but out of respect and good will towards Miss Countryman, as a resident of the city, it was given to her, as against others whom there was reason to believe might have conducted the library on a more economical basis." Walker went on to say that Countryman had expressed no desire or need for an assistant and that the action in reducing the salary of the position was necessary to meet criticism that too much money was spent on salaries and not enough on books.

Hosmer, however, had nothing but praise for his successor, and in his last annual report he wrote: "Well endowed by nature, thoroughly equipped by education, specially trained and vouched for by the most skillful master of our profession [*Putnam*], minutely familiar with this institution, which indeed her care and counsel have done very much to shape, — what can be expected for her but the best success."[22]

Hosmer's prediction of success for Gratia Countryman was prophetic. When she officially assumed the post of head librarian on February 1, 1904, she immediately began to change the philosophy of public library service. In her first annual report she expressed the view that "A public library is the one great civic institution supported by the people which is designed for the instruction and pleasure of all the people, young and old, without age limit, rich and poor . . . educated and uneducated. . . . It should be 'all things to all men' in the world of thought."[23]

She realized that implementing her vision of library service would mean adding programs not commonly thought of in connection with libraries. Many people regarded the library only as a place where books were stored or distributed under many "objectionable restrictions" rather than the institution she was proposing: "a wide-awake institution for the dissemination of ideas . . . the center of all the activities of a city that lead to social growth, municipal reform, civic pride and good citizenship. It should have its finger on the pulse of the people, ready to second and forward any good movement."

If the library were to carry out her ambitious goal of "elevating the people," it would have to adopt new methods. No longer would it be enough to buy a fine collection, house it in an attractive building, and then wait in a dignified way for people to come. Her concern was "How to reach the busy men and women, how to carry wholesome and enjoyable books to the far-away corners of the city, how to enlist the interest of tired factory girls, how to put the workingman in touch with the art books relating to his craft and so increase the value of his labor and the dignity of his day's work."

Countryman's probationary period was up in January, 1905, and the dissident board members having been won over, she was given a permanent appointment as librarian, the position she was to hold for more than thirty years. Under her direction the Minneapolis Public Library began a period of tremendous expansion. In 1904 when she took charge, there were 43 persons on the staff and the system consisted of the main library, 3 branches, and 10 stations, mostly in drugstores. When she retired in 1936, there were 250 people on the staff (excluding WPA workers on professional projects), and over 350 distributing agencies including branches, stations, classrooms, business firms, factories, and hospitals. The book collection had grown by 500,000 volumes and the circulation from 500,000 to over 3,600,000. The budget had more than quadrupled. These figures, however, tell little of the innovations in service which helped the library earn a local and national reputation as the city's "most human institution." [24]

Even before she was appointed librarian, Gratia Countryman's influence was felt in shaping policies. It was through her efforts, for example, that a children's department was opened in 1893, complete with small chairs and tables and a special attendant — the first such department in the country. [25]

But special service to children was only one small step in making the library more accessible for everyone. Always modest,

Countryman once credited Herbert Putnam with being the guiding spirit behind the accomplishments of the Minneapolis library, and certainly the first tentative moves toward open shelves, extension of service through branches and stations, public lectures and use of the library's rooms for study groups and club meetings were made during his two-year tenure as librarian. It was Gratia Countryman, however, with her strong commitment to making the public library a vital part of the community, who expanded library services until they touched nearly all aspects of life in the city.[26]

As the city's population grew, the library expanded its service through the establishment of more branches and stations. Cooperative programs with the schools were begun. Branches in the junior high schools served adults living in the neighborhood as well as students and teachers. Stations were established in some of the elementary schools, and collections were deposited in many classrooms. The library reached out to the county also, extending borrowing privileges and providing books to residents of suburban and rural areas through parcel post and traveling libraries. In 1922 the Hennepin County Library was officially established with its headquarters in the Minneapolis library and with Gratia Countryman as librarian.[27]

Early in her tenure Countryman set about making it easier for people to borrow, renew, and return books. Not only was the number of distributing points increased but the procedures were also changed so there were not so many barriers between readers and books. Vacation cards, renewals, telephone reference service were just a few of the changes she made.[28]

As a means of introducing people to the library and making them feel it was theirs, she held an open house in the central library on New Year's evening 1905 — the first public reception in the building since its grand opening in December, 1889. Invitations were posted in various parts of the city, including lodging-houses, restaurants, and factories. It was estimated that at least 75 per cent of those who came to the open house had never been in the building before.[29]

In her attempts to reach more readers, Countryman showed an awareness of the specialized needs of the community, which she attempted to satisfy by establishing separate subject departments. The Art Department was the first such area of specialization. Putnam had laid the foundation for an important collection of art books, and in 1904 Countryman moved it into its own room. In

1911 she created two new departments, Municipal Reference and Useful Arts. Municipal Reference was formed "to collect city reports and statistics, ordinances and charters, the reports of civil commissions and civic associations, newspaper clippings and magazine articles on civic matters, in fact . . . everything relating to the government of cities or the health, happiness and morals of its citizens." In 1916 the department was enlarged to include specialized services for businessmen and moved to a central downtown location as the Business and Municipal Reference Branch, a unique combination in American libraries. The Useful Arts (later the Technical) Department provided books on such subjects as engineering, electricity, mining, building trades, manufacturing, and business for mechanics, carpenters, and other workingmen.[30]

The Music Department, long a dream of Gratia Countryman's, was next. It included not only books and sheet music, but also records and a phonograph, clippings and pictures, and a soundproof room with a piano. Then came the Parent-Teacher Room, which provided materials on such subjects as child psychology, health, and education. It was followed by a Social Service Branch, which was established in the Citizen's Aid Building, headquarters of the community's social service agencies, and was the first such branch in the United States.[31]

It was not, however, for these extensions of library service that Gratia Countryman was best known, but rather, as a newspaper reporter put it, "for her thought of the bedbound, the poverty-bound, the troublebound to whom she has given and sent and taken her greatest solace; the love of books." Believing that books were stimulating, inspiring, curative, and regenerative and that they should be freely available to anyone who needed them, she put into practice a humanitarian philosophy that saw the public library as an agency for social betterment and uplift, a force against laxness in morals, and an institution for lifelong education.[32]

The first to benefit from this philosophy were working people. Convinced that workers who spent the day on their feet would not be likely to go out of their way to get a book to read, Countryman sent collections to factories and other businesses, including telephone exchanges, railroad shops, department stores, and streetcar stations. Each collection was carefully selected with the needs and interests of the employees in mind. Next to be served were firemen, who received collections at the engine houses to help them fill their leisure hours mentally improving themselves, an experiment that did not meet with much success. Many firemen preferred to read magazines, which could be put down at a moment's notice.[33]

When the saloons were closed on Sundays in 1905, new opportunities for library social work presented themselves. In several areas of the city library hours were extended to provide the men who lived in rooming houses with a place to spend their afternoons, and more reading rooms were opened in districts where lodgers were often turned out of their rooms by mid-morning.[34]

In 1910 a branch was opened in the Bridge Square section of the city in an effort to help the jobless who congregated in large numbers near the area's employment bureaus and boardinghouses. In addition to books, tables were provided for men who wanted to write letters or answer advertisements, and paper, envelopes, and stamps were sold. In that year's annual report the branch librarian wrote: "The value of this reading room to the working man is inestimable. Many men have said to me, 'If I were not here I would be in a saloon.' The saloon to a man without a home is the only place where he seeks entertainment and relaxation after his day's work. . . . I venture to say that many a man passes his evenings here quietly reading who otherwise might be spending that time in a degrading place."[35]

When the building in which this branch was housed was demolished, it was relocated on the second floor of a nearby structure. Usage decreased somewhat, but Countryman still thought a useful social function was being performed. As she put it: "The service to the city is large; these men would, in many cases, be considered vagrants and sent to the workhouse; many of them would be drinking and doing themselves and perhaps others damage if they were not spending the evening in a warm and comfortable reading room."[36]

Continuing to reach out to all segments of the city, the library by 1915 was sending collections to the workhouse, the poor farm, the boy's detention home at Glen Lake, the city and county jails, orphanages, homes for the aged, and residences for young women. Service to hospitals was begun in 1923 as an outgrowth of the library's war effort. Later, provisions for the blind were made through an arrangement with the school for the blind at Faribault.[37]

Special service meant more than books, however. When the lack of supervised recreation facilities brought large numbers of children to the branch libraries, clubs were formed and the lecture rooms were opened for games and recreation. Recognizing that this kind of service might not be considered the province of the library, Gratia Countryman defended it vigorously, pointing out that "the Library cannot avoid this problem which is agitating all social workers." In her annual report for 1915 she wrote: "We seem to be living in a period when children must be entertained continually, when excitement is sought for and the sensational is the only thing which satisfies even the parents. It is to be deeply regretted that the home no longer takes the burden of recreational activities, but throws the burden off upon the school, the public park and playgrounds, the library, the churches and settlements, and the commercialized agencies for amusement." Acknowledging that the library was not "primarily a recreational agency," she nevertheless insisted that it was a "social agency as well as an educational one, with the avowed purpose of making and developing good citizens. . . . We cannot therefore avoid the recreational problem."[38]

Heavy immigration in the early 1900s brought a new group of people who needed library service, the foreign born, especially those who did not speak or read English. Books in foreign languages were purchased, with each branch concentrating on the nationality groups living within its area of service. Minneapolis was the first city in the country to have such collections. The library also co-operated with night schools and other agencies in working with immigrants who wanted to become naturalized citizens. In her annual report for 1916 Countryman wrote: "The sooner the new American becomes informed and educated, the better for his adopted country, and the library is holding out every inducement."[39]

The Depression of the 1930s provided more opportunities for social services. Throughout the country the demands on libraries were increasing at a time when their budgets were being slashed. Minneapolis was no exception, but Countryman continued to seek out those who needed assistance and now had time to use the library's services. Books and magazines were sent to such places as the Union City Mission, the Salvation Army Home, girls' clubs, cheap hotels, and shelters — anywhere that the unemployed gathered. A psychologist from the Minneapolis Board of Education gave vocational guidance tests at the library to help the unemployed in "a campaign to rehabilitate human lives."[40]

Drastic budget cuts nearly wrecked the library, according to Countryman. In her annual report for 1933, she wrote: "Roads and bridges, sewers and paving, have loomed larger in importance in fixing tax levies than the values of human life, the passing years of youth, the re-adjustment of older men and women to perplexing and overwhelming experiences."[41]

When her appeal to the city for additional funds in 1933 met with another budget cut, she began to rally the people of Minneapolis, who responded in great numbers with letters to the newspapers, aldermen, and members of the city's Board of Estimate and Taxation. Unsolicited speeches by citizens were made at meetings of the taxation board, and in 1934 the library was granted the full two-mill tax rate allowed by law for the first time in its history.[42]

In a period of fiscal crisis, Minneapolis residents had responded to preserve the library which was important to them as an educational as well as a social service institution. The attempts of the library to relieve human suffering were perhaps more visible and dramatically newsworthy, but it was the educational usage of the library which increased most substantially. Committed to the idea of the library as the agency for the provision of "lifetime" education, Countryman expanded programs begun by Putnam and added new educational services. "The great rank and file must learn to think clearly and to act thoughtfully," she wrote in 1918. "All of our democratic ideals rest upon the foundations of a wide education and an equal opportunity to acquire it." Early in her tenure as librarian, she began a lecture series to stimulate an interest in books and study. In 1918 she saw the imminence of women's suffrage as another opportunity for the library to help educate and inform a new group of voters so that they could better assume the obligations of good citizenship. A reader's advisory service was added in 1928 to provide individually tailored reading and education programs. A monthly magazine, the *Community Bookshelf*, was published "to stimulate distribution of our wares." Later there were weekly book-review meetings and radio book-review programs to encourage good reading.[43]

"The modern library is a great, live, working school for the education of all the people," Countryman wrote in 1918. "But the modern library is not only a great democratic school, it is a *propagandist for education.*" And she was always alert for new ways to make opportunities, especially for self-education, available. In 1934 several women's organizations donated money to the library for the purchase of a radio, and a new service was inaugurated — listening to specially selected broadcasts on educational subjects and current events. Periodicals and literature relating to the radio programs were made available, and each broadcast was followed by discussion sessions. The only complaint was that reception in downtown Minneapolis was disappointing.[44]

Under Gratia Countryman, the Minneapolis Public Library continued to be in the forefront of innovations in library service. One example of her farsightedness shows why. As president of the American Library Association (ALA) in 1934, she encouraged librarians to assume obligations and accept challenges brought about by the difficult times, including adult education programs which would "use radio, television, films, or whatever new inventions may be bent to educational uses."[45]

As an inspirational and nationally recognized leader, it was appropriate that she should be elected president of the national association at one of the most difficult periods in American library history. Her professional activities were important throughout her career. Locally, she had served in several capacities in the Minnesota Library Association, including its presidency. Nationally, in addition to her year as president of the ALA, she served several terms on its council and executive board, two terms as its second vice-president, and was active in committee work. She was a charter member of the American Library Institute, an organization of leaders in the library profession, and continued her membership until 1942, when the organization ceased to exist. Internationally, she served in 1935 as a delegate of the ALA to the Second International Library and Bibliographic Congress in Madrid, at which she presented a paper on school libraries of the United States.[46]

In great demand as a speaker, she appeared before library associations throughout the country, lectured at library institutes and schools, and often spoke to civic, cultural, business, professional, social welfare, philanthropic, educational, and religious groups. Most of her talks were on library topics, but others reflected her wide-ranging activities and interests, including women's suffrage,

American social problems, and the international peace movement.[47]

To Gratia Countryman the community and social service activities in which she participated were closely related to her work in the library, and, indeed, many of the organizations to which she belonged reflected her concerns in planning library service and the tone she set in implementing those services. She was instrumental in organizing and served as the first president of the Minneapolis Women's Welfare League, which maintained residences and clubs for young working women, convalescents, female delinquents, and "subnormal" girls. The welfare league, as she wrote in its first annual report in 1912, was "brought into existence because of the apparent moral laxness in this city, and the bad moral influences surrounding young girlhood. Its purpose was . . . to awaken among all women a strong protective sentiment toward the young women of the city." She also helped organize and was the first president of the Business Women's Club, the purpose of which was to strengthen the friendly and business relations of its members and to provide the means for mental and physical well-being, recreation, business discussion, and good fellowship. These associations were only two of at least seven groups, ranging from women's activities to adult education concerns, which she helped organize or headed or both.[48]

She was invited to serve on numerous boards, committees, commissions, and congresses which dealt with such diverse issues as crime, unemployment, malnutrition, conservation, and agriculture. Her two dozen or more memberships included civic, social service, religious, educational, literary, and fine arts organizations. She chaired the national convention of the Women's International League for Peace and Freedom when it met in Minneapolis in 1938.[49]

Her many activities and accomplishments brought her a number of honors. For her work with the foreign born, the Inter-Racial Service Council in 1931 awarded her its Civic Service Honor Medal, given each year for outstanding civic service. She was the first woman to receive this honor. Her most significant award, however, was the master of arts degree conferred by the University of Minnesota in 1932. It was only the fourth honorary degree given by the university and the first received by a woman, the other three having gone to former university presidents and a former United States secretary of state.

There were other honors bestowed upon her, the last only a few months before her death, an indication of the impact she continued to have for more than fifteen years after her compulsory retirement on November 30, 1936, at the age of seventy. By the time she left her beloved library, the Minneapolis Public Library and Gratia Countryman had become synonymous in the minds of many Minnesotans, who found it difficult to visualize the institution without her at its head — without her forward-looking policies, her interest, and enthusiasm.[50]

Gratia Countryman had set high standards for herself and her staff. She chose her professional assistants wisely and inspired them to accomplish more than they thought themselves capable of doing. She could be a hard taskmaster and severe disciplinarian who had little patience with slovenly work, but she was always considered fair. She was a capable administrator who commanded both respect and affection. She thought of her staff as her family, was concerned about their personal welfare as well as their professional development, and had been known to invite overworked assistants to her home or her summer place on Lake Mille Lacs for a weekend of rest.[51]

Efficient and businesslike, a decisive and fearless fighter for what she believed in, she accomplished much through her courage and zeal. Yet, despite all her achievements and honors, she remained modest, feeling that many chances for making the library an even greater institution had been missed. After her retirement she even wondered whether she could be useful without a job.[52]

Gratia Countryman's family also responded to her warm personality, sometimes expressing surprise that with all she had accomplished she still could remain such a lovable "family hub." Concern for orphan children led her to expand that family in 1918 when she adopted and raised a small boy named Wellington, who had come into the library expressing an interest in books.[53]

After her retirement she took up farming on land she owned near Lake Mille Lacs, but the venture was not a financial success and eventually had to be given up. She could not remain idle, however, and was recruited back to the library to head a WPA newspaper indexing project after she was told it meant jobs for two hundred people. She directed the project from 1938 to 1941, when an eye operation forced her to quit.[54]

She remained active even as her health began to fail. During the last few years of her life, she lived with a niece, Constance, and her husband, Gilbert Buffington, in Duluth. She died there on July 26, 1953, at the age of eighty-six. Her career was summed up by an editorial in the *Minneapolis Tribune* on July 28, 1953. More than any other person, it said, Gratia Countryman "placed the indelible stamp of a vigorous and far-seeing personality upon our library system. . . . [She] left countless library users in her debt because she planned so well against the future's needs."

11. CATHERYNE COOKE GILMAN
Social Worker

By Elizabeth Gilman

IN 1880 in the small town of Laclede, Missouri, Jeremiah Cook, a conductor on the Rock Island Railroad, and his wife, Aditha, brought their third child into the world and christened her Caroline Catherine. It was an unpretentious beginning for a future teacher, social worker, and feminist, who for more than twenty years played a leading role in the child welfare and social reform movements in Minnesota. The towns of Laclede and Brookfield, Missouri, and Mount Pleasant, Iowa, where the Cooks lived during the 1880s and 1890s, were small pockets of civilization. Although the railroad linked them to Chicago and Minneapolis, they were remote from both the misery and the opportunities of urban centers. As unlikely as it seemed at the time of her birth, Catherine's future lay in those cities. Like so many others who reached adulthood in the first decade of the twentieth century, she was to be inspired by the promise of urban "progress." She would devote her life to reform so that promise might be fulfilled.

Little is known about Catherine's childhood and how it may have formed the striving, dedicated woman she became. What she herself later wrote about her early life is suspect because of her tendency to romanticize. Not content with the plain name she was given, she changed the spellings of both middle and last names to make them more distinctive. She always signed herself "Catheryne Cooke," and not until fifteen years after her death did her own children discover the original spelling. She even persuaded her sisters to add an "e" to their last names, and she claimed descent from a Cooke whose name appeared on the Mayflower Compact. No one else in the family ever discovered such a connection.[1]

Although her parents were not well educated, they seem to have

190

instilled in three of their five daughters the ambition and drive necessary to secure post-high school training. Following Catheryne's high school graduation in 1898 and a subsequent yearlong teacher training course, she taught history and social studies in various Iowa schools. By 1904 she had become principal of the Keosauqua, Iowa, schools. Two years later she moved to Fort Madison, where she headed the history department and developed an innovative four-year history program. In 1911, after taking summer courses for eight years, she graduated from Iowa State Normal School in Cedar Falls, and proceeded to the University of Chicago for a year of graduate work in history and political science. This move took her to a sprawling industrial city of squalor and splendor and to a university that was a center of social thought and theory, the first in the nation to institute a department of sociology.[2]

Catheryne's year of study in Chicago provided both a break with her small-town past and an exposure to the philosophies and problems around which her future career revolved. Through a course taught by Sophonisba P. Breckinridge she was not only exposed to the issues of the feminist movement but also to Jane Addams' Hull House, where Sophonisba served on the board. Thus Catheryne learned of the relatively new profession of social work and became especially enthusiastic about settlement houses. In 1913 she went to New York City and took up residence in the East Side House Settlement, where she worked part time. In January, 1914, she described her activities as assisting the headworker of the East Side House, directing a Summer House for women and children, and conducting investigations of conditions in day nurseries. At the time she wrote she was also "occupied at the U[niversity] S[ettlement] where I am supervisor of Women & Girl's clubs and have charge of the Social Room six nights per week."[3]

The director of the University Settlement was Robbins Gilman, who, like many early social workers, came from an upper-middle-class family. His ancestors *had* been among the early white settlers in the New World, some arriving with William Penn. His father headed a modest banking firm in New York City, where Robbins had valiantly attempted to carry out the duties of a junior partner for ten years before giving up and turning to his real vocation, social work. He had a strong religious background and deep, humanitarian faith, combined with a zeal to serve and a fine, whimsical sense of humor — something Catheryne sadly lacked.[4]

Robbins was by no means a radical, but he stood up firmly for his beliefs. In the winter of 1913–14, when Catheryne first knew him, the white-goods workers of New York, backed by the Industrial Workers of the World (IWW), went on strike for improved working conditions. Both the strikers and later a group of unemployed men were made welcome at the settlement house, and in a speech Robbins suggested that the IWW protest was beneficial because it brought abuses and injustices to public attention. Relations with the board of directors soon became strained, and in the summer of 1914 Robbins resigned. Ostensibly the IWW episode had no connection with his departure, but letters from family, fellow workers, and friends all indicated that it constituted a large part of the trouble. In late September Robbins found another position as director of a newly conceived settlement, to be called the North East Neighborhood House, located in Minneapolis. A few weeks after accepting the post he and Catheryne startled their families and friends by announcing their engagement. They were married on the last day of 1914 in Carrollton, Missouri.[5]

As soon as the newlyweds had settled themselves in the third-floor apartment of North East Neighborhood House, Catheryne plunged into civic activities as if to convince herself that she had not forsworn her career by marrying. She was at the time an independent, ambitious, and talented career woman, thirty-four years old. Although she believed matrimony and motherhood were the natural states for women, she nonetheless felt they represented sacrifices. In New York she had given speeches and organized meetings about women's suffrage, and she continued the crusade in Minneapolis. At the Neighborhood House she helped start a "Baby Health Improvement Contest," a competition among neighbors for better infant health through proper nourishment and cleanliness. She also sat on the board of directors of Maternity Hospital, an institution which admitted unwed as well as married mothers and was staffed and administered by women. Notwithstanding her first pregnancy and the accompanying curtailment of some of her activities, she made many acquaintances among social workers and reformers in Minneapolis and quickly gained a reputation as an able speaker.[6]

In August, 1916, only a year and a half after she had arrived in the city, Governor J. A. A. Burnquist appointed her to the Minnesota

Catheryne Cooke Gilman

Child Welfare Commission, a newly created body charged with
the formulation of a legislative package to revise and codify laws
applying to children. The Minnesota Children's Code, presented
to the governor in February, 1917, contained forty-three proposals
dealing with four basic areas of juvenile law: general child welfare
(birth certificates, school attendance, etc.), dependency and neglect, mental and physical handicaps, and delinquency. Catheryne
served on the task force for dependency and neglect. The code
stood for many years as an outstanding example of progressive
legislation in the area of child welfare and has been termed "perhaps the greatest achievement in the history of Minnesota's social
legislation."[7]

In March, 1916, Catheryne's identification with the cause of
child welfare led her to address the Co-operative Committee of
the Minneapolis Women's Welfare League, an umbrella group
composed of some half dozen women's organizations, which had
in 1915 hired a woman as a part-time investigator to help detect
and prevent conditions contributing to juvenile delinquency in
Minneapolis. She quickly became involved in the work of this
group and was asked to organize the First Ward in which North
East Neighborhood House was located. The work of the committee at this time was carried on under a "block system" borrowed

from social workers in Chicago and New York, in which a chairman was recruited from each ward in the city. She then recruited precinct chairmen, who in turn found women in every block to observe and report on conditions in their immediate neighborhoods. These observers were to focus on saloons, dance halls, theaters, motion picture houses, rooming houses that might harbor prostitutes, and such establishments as ice cream parlors where the young might congregate and be exposed to temptation.[8]

By virtue of Catheryne's success as an organizer during the summer, she received an invitation to attend a meeting in September, 1916, to discuss the future of the Women's Co-operative Committee. "The question was what to do," Catheryne later recalled. "I suggested that they take up a program of social hygiene . . . for the development of a community program. . . . It was an educational program that I proposed." Her proposal was accepted and she was hired as the executive secretary of the organization. In the annual report for 1919, the president commented that with "Mrs. Gilman's coming the work took on system and stability and breadth. Its scope widened, its possibilities increased, . . . and under the inspiration of her leadership and guidance, the members came to see that what had been established in faith and feeling, but with little scientific knowledge, was becoming a power within the city."[9]

The Co-operative Committee provided Catheryne with a more satisfactory vehicle through which to work than did classes and clubs at the Neighborhood House. She remained with the committee, renamed the Women's Co-operative Alliance in April, 1917, during the full seventeen years of its existence. In the first year of her tenure as executive secretary the Alliance grew significantly. More than 3,000 women signed up as block, precinct, and ward workers. Between January and July, 1917, Catheryne addressed "24 Church Clubs, 25 Study or Social Clubs, and 43 Mothers' Clubs of the Parent and Teacher's Association." The investigator, who had begun on a part-time basis in 1915, now worked full time; she had received and disposed of 247 reports of "immorality." A "big sister," whose duties included befriending and helping lonely, homeless, handicapped, unemployed, or wayward girls, had been hired in December, 1916. (Eventually, a separate Big Sister Department was developed.) Four secretaries supervised the organizational work in the wards, with another nine to be hired as soon as funds permitted. They were responsible for visiting every home in their wards to reach women who did not belong to clubs and therefore had not heard an Alliance representative speak. By December, 1917, they had "secured 50 precinct chairmen out of a possible 61, and a total number of 523 block workers." In six weeks the secretaries also distributed 38,800 pieces of literature and addressed 81 groups in their wards.[10]

This phenomenal growth continued. By the close of 1920 there were 24 paid workers, a mailing list of 10,164, and 19 co-operating organizations, including the Children's Protective Society, the Council of Parents' and Teachers' Associations, Maternity Hospital, the Lutheran Inner Mission Society, and the Women's Christian Temperance Union. The publications of the Alliance had been translated into Polish, Swedish, Norwegian, and Yiddish, and "ethnic secretaries" worked with Scandinavian, Jewish, Polish, and "colored" women.[11]

The mission of the Women's Co-operative Alliance was to prevent juvenile delinquency and protect the morals of children and young women. Both purposes were served by a comprehensive program of sex education. In some way which Catheryne never truly explained in all the literature she wrote on the subject, abuses of sex by children and sexual abuses perpetrated on children by adults were assumed to lie at the root of juvenile delinquency. Although reform by means of legislation was also necessary, she believed that social hygiene and moral instruction were the measures which would most effectively reduce juvenile delinquency.

The pamphlets she wrote on sex education were far ahead of their time, encouraging parents to deal with the subject in an open and frank fashion. She felt that there had developed around human reproduction a mystique not only harmful but also obsolete in an age of scientific thinking. Thus she emphasized the need for early preschool sex instruction for both boys and girls. Maintaining a studied impartiality, she claimed, "At this time it is essential that boys and girls begin to appreciate that men and women are made to supplement each other in every way, and while there are marked differentiations between the sexes, the discussion of inferior and superior qualities is futile. Men and women are essential to the happiness of each other and to the continuance of the human race."[12]

In her pamphlets and lectures, however, Catheryne never dealt

with the emotional aspects of sex. The "simple, scientific vocabulary" she recommended did not include "desire," "climax," or
"orgasm." No one reading her pamphlets would imagine that sexual intercourse was pleasurable or even much different from an
involuntary process like digestion. Catheryne dealt with sex as
dispassionately as she might have the weather — and that is
exactly how she thought it ought to be treated by parents. "The
home cannot give what the home has not," Catheryne emphasized
over and over again. Her goal was to educate parents so that they
would and could perform their responsibilities in rearing their
children. A study conducted by the University of Minnesota
suggested that the Alliance's methods were moderately successful
in this regard. Children of 250 women with whom the Alliance
worked intensively from 1925 to 1931 received 24.83 per cent
more information about sexual matters than did children of a com-
parable control group.[13]

During the latter part of the 1920s, when the Alliance program
placed its emphasis more directly on parental education,
Catheryne suggested that every institution of higher learning
should have a department to train future parents. When the university proved unresponsive to this suggestion, she created her
own parent-training courses under the auspices of the Alliance. In
these classes, whose enrollment slid from 917 in 1926 to 339 in
1930, she lectured on parenthood as "the real goal of the whole
series of sexual and reproductive phenomena" and asserted that
"all relations should be perfected for this primary end." The family, she wrote, was the "essential control and humanizing factor in
human evolution," and the encouragement of "fit marriages" was
the primary task of "a future society which has in it any trace of
hope."

This belief reflected Catheryne's conviction that the married
state was the happy and natural one, particularly for women. The
idea was not uncommon among feminists of the period, who, as
William L. O'Neill has pointed out, did not seek social and
economic equality with men in part because they believed women
were morally superior. They reasoned that women should be responsible for making a respectable home and bringing up morally
sensitive children in order that society might continue its
progress. But women might also, if given the chance, exert as
salutary and wholesome an influence on government as they did
in the home. As Catheryne put it: "The function of the mother in

politics is identical with the function of a mother in the home. Her work is creative, productive, spiritual and moral. . . . She is working as woman for others. She is devoted to an ideal and that ideal is based on an inherent, protective conservation of health, morals and education for her children, her family and her home." Social feminists of the early twentieth century accepted their places on a pedestal but endeavored to erect their own statues in the community.

Because Catheryne viewed motherhood as a noble calling, much of her work was directed toward teaching women how to be better mothers. To women who did not have the good fortune to become parents, she recommended the development of "social and sex relationships and forms of expression . . . involving continence which carries service to humanity and satisfaction to the individual." Perhaps it was possible for Catheryne to crusade so confidently for motherhood because, like most well-to-do women of her generation, she never devoted herself entirely to child-rearing and homemaking and so did not have to endure the more dispiriting aspects of either. A governess raised her three children; domestics cared for the apartments on the third floor of the Neighborhood House; and a cook prepared the meals served by a maid, on a table laid with silver and fine linen, to all the resident social workers.

In a fund-raising letter in 1919 Catheryne wrote, "Mothers have been blamed for all of the evils that have befallen children and especially girls. It is the aim of the Alliance to overcome any part of the truth of their [*this*] accusation by giving mothers the information necessary to protect their children." [14] Catheryne was quick to point out that it was not fair to hold mothers solely responsible for their children's transgressions. Many other influences were at work in the lives of urban youngsters over which mothers, at least until they achieved the right to vote in 1920, had little control. Dance halls, pool halls, bars, speak-easies, street carnivals, and movie houses exposed children to "immoralities." Unsupervised parks and skating rinks and insufficiently lighted streets could provide loitering places for young people and might introduce them to "questionable" activities.

But an enlightened and unified band of women could bring to bear a certain amount of moral and political pressure upon the city fathers who were in a position to improve conditions. Street carnivals could be denied licenses; movie house managers could be

made to realize that decent citizens did not want suggestive films
in their neighborhoods. Above all, law enforcement could be
strengthened so that adults (implicitly assumed to be male) who
contributed to the delinquency of minors would be adequately
punished. To these ends the Women's Co-operative Alliance bent
its efforts.

The organization entered the legislative arena somewhat hesi-
tantly early in the 1920s, proclaiming that the problems it addressed were "due more to the failure of enforcement and lack of
information in reference to existing laws than to the meagerness of
legislation." Through research, "scientific" findings, and a comprehensive educational program aimed at both lawmakers and the
community, the Alliance hoped to mold public opinion for passage
of socially and morally beneficial laws. During the 1920s the organization's efforts with the state legislature and the Minneapolis
City Council resulted in the virtual elimination of street carnivals
and gambling in Minneapolis, some degree of child labor regulation in the theater, paternal support for children of divorced and
unmarried parents, an amendment of the Indecent Assault Act to
include sodomy, and the creation of a women's bureau in the
Minneapolis Police Department under the leadership of a female
lieutenant (although the bureau did not possess the powers which
the Alliance wished).[15]

Catheryne's campaign for passage of such morality laws emphasized the need for strict law enforcement. She was, however,
somewhat ambivalent about how it should be applied, expressing
considerably more sympathy and patience with youthful offenders, unwed mothers, single girls with "sex experience," and even
prostitutes than for adult male offenders. Apparently she felt that
young people and females of all ages could be helped to mend their
ways, while the men who led them astray were beyond all hope of
redemption. In 1923 one of the Alliance proposals was that the
legislature ban pardons for violators of morality laws unless the
imprisoned person could present positive proof that he had been
wrongly convicted. The Alliance evidently had little faith in the
ability of the adult male offender to change his ways.[16]

Like the supporters of Prohibition (of whom Catheryne was
one), the members of the Alliance believed that proper moral behavior was easily defined, that everyone accepted the same definition, that it could be achieved and enforced by law, and that

human beings could be saved from their baser instincts by strict enforcement of the law. Few in the Alliance doubted what was "good" and what was "bad," nor did they imagine that any offender would question their definition. But as the 1920s became the 1930s, morality laws came to be regarded as less and less relevant to the problems of a depressed economy, and progress on the legislative front grew increasingly difficult. Eventually, their uphill campaigns for strict law enforcement and social welfare legislation made the women of the Alliance bitter and mistrustful of the city and state fathers. At the beginning of their work the women believed officials would be willing to enforce the laws and to pass enlightened ones — as soon as they were made to see which laws were enlightened and had popular support. As time passed, however, their faith waned. Annual reports of the Alliance in the latter half of the 1920s abound with stories of insensitivity, patronizing treatment, broken promises, and unresponsiveness. By this time, the world had begun to question whether "good" and "bad" were absolutes. In this respect, as in others, Catheryne and her associates found themselves not directing social change, but dragged reluctantly behind it.[17]

Historians have argued that the 1920s, while they failed to engender significant reforms, did give social reformers and social workers an opportunity to formulate new theories and plans that could be implemented in the 1930s, when the mood and needs of the country changed. Considering the rapidity with which the social work profession had developed, and the chronic lack of theorizing within it, the pause to take stock was beneficial.[18] But a local group like the Alliance needed successes to stay alive, and by the end of the decade such successes had become few and far between. The women relied heavily upon the power of moral suasion, believing it to be their strongest weapon. Given the temper of the times, it is doubtful whether any other type of challenge to the political-economic *status quo* would have met with greater — or even with as much — success. However, moral suasion was effective only as long as men in positions of authority took it seriously enough to let it guide their actions.

When the group first became active, many political and business leaders were co-operative and encouraging, and their wives often served on the board of managers. Indeed, throughout its existence the Alliance was supported by funds provided by a handful of wealthy women. Moralistic social reform enjoyed widespread

popularity during the Progressive years. However, in the disillusionment that followed World War I and in the business prosperity
of the 1920s, this support lessened. Property leased to houses of
prostitution proved far too lucrative to the "respectable" businessman who owned it to allow him to support his wife's reform-
ing activities; "obscene" movies drew greater crowds than
"wholesome" ones; and liquor sold illegally produced a far larger
profit than soft drinks sold lawfully. When businessmen and government officials realized that the Alliance programs threatened
their economic interests, they became hostile, patronizing, deceit-
ful, or rude. This reversal on the part of community leaders whom
the women considered their strongest allies eventually resulted in
the financial failure of the Alliance. Some business and community leaders supported it to the end, but Catheryne never forgot or
forgave those who pressured her principal backers into withdrawing their support. As executive secretary she refused to allow the
organization to continue with an inadequate program and,
therefore, in October, 1932, the corporation voted to dissolve. Activities were suspended on January 1, 1933.[19]

By the end of the 1920s the moralism and crusading zeal of the
Alliance were not only unpopular with society at large, but were
also discredited within the profession of social work. At the height
of the Progressive era social work and social reform had gone hand
in hand; one could work with individuals who had been wronged
by society, but in order to prevent further exploitation, poverty,
and break-up of the family one had also to press for legislation
which would strike at the roots of these problems. As Freudian
psychology became popular, however, social workers began to
perceive individual problems as personal maladjustments rather
than manifestations of social ills. Casework came into its own in
the 1920s, and the definition of social work began to exclude social
reform.[20] Moreover, the Alliance was an anomalous organization.
To the extent that subdivisions and interest groups existed in the
profession — medical social workers, psychiatric social workers,
settlement workers, and so on — the Alliance fitted none but
shared something with all. Because Catheryne's own first contact
with social work had come through settlement houses and because
she lived in one during the time she led the Alliance, she undoubtedly adopted most of her philosophy from the settlement
movement. The Alliance, however, was in no sense a settlement;

nor could it easily be included in any other classification of social work.

Catheryne's personal relations with her fellow Alliance workers had their ups and downs. There is no doubt that she had the ability to lead and to inspire devotion and self-confidence. One fellow worker wrote to her: "Mrs. Gilman — you were right. I *can* talk, and when I found I could get up before large groups without *any* fear whatsoever . . . I was *thrilled* with my victory — And I owe it all to you; had it not been for your faith in me and your encouragement I would never have had the courage to try." But Catheryne's dealings were not always so cordial. She frequently threatened to resign, and her family often advised her to find another post. In the privacy of her home she gave vent to all the feelings of doubt and self-sacrifice that she hid from the world at large. Although her position as executive secretary required an enormous expenditure of time and energy, she was unhappy when anyone encroached on her territory or hinted that they might do the job better. Every time she offered to resign, she was apparently persuaded to change her mind either by the devoted and patient members of the board or by her husband.[21]

Her marriage on the whole was fortunate. Robbins Gilman endured her periodic flights into melodrama and misery with equanimity. Even-tempered and forbearing himself, he had respect for, faith in, and patience with his wife that never faltered. As their fifth wedding anniversary neared, he had written to her: "Thee asks my opinion about our marriage. I consider it the most important & successful single event in my life. I know I have not measured up to thy expectations as to what a husband should be, & that continually grieves & pains me. . . . Thee has been a counsellor and advisor to me and had thee not been, I would have been a dismal failure. But above all thee is the mother of our two children & I never could conceive of a finer one. I am proud of thee all the time, for what thee is and what thee has done."[22] There is nothing to indicate that these feelings for her ever changed.

He accompanied her when she addressed large, important groups and reassured her afterward that she had spoken well. Yet the woman seen by Robbins and the outside world as capable, forceful, and accomplished always doubted herself. In 1940 she revealed much of that doubt in a letter to her son. "I understand exactly what you mean by saying that you seem to over impress

your teachers and associates with knowledge you do not have,"
she wrote. "I have been blessed or cursed with the same all my
life. Even as a small child I was considered unusual and
more — much more — [was] expected of me than of other[s]. . . .
People have commented on me being able to appear at home in
any environment, of grasping things of which I never heard & all
of the time. . . . I have known how little I know. My method of
meeting it has been to make myself learn what ever others expected me to know. I have spent hours delving into subjects quite
foreign to my interests because I did not want any one to be mis-
led by my attitude. If they thought I knew then I must know, other
wise I would feel guilty of deception." [23]

Catheryne's effort to live up to the expectations she thought
others had of her was exemplified in her fanatical adoption of
Gilman family traditions. To the end of her life she arose at five
o'clock on Sunday mornings when the family was gathered at
home and prepared codfish balls and popovers for breakfast, to be
served at eight sharp, because it was a Gilman custom. None of
the family dared suggest that it might be a foolish custom or that
they would prefer to sleep late. When her children reached school
age, she was just as determined as Robbins that they should go to
first-class private schools and colleges. The two boys, Logan
Drinker and Robbins Paxson (both names from her husband's family), attended Williams College as their father and grandfather had
done. Her daughter Catherine was sent to Radcliffe, which had
been founded by a Gilman great-uncle.

The demise of the Alliance in 1932 came at an unfortunate time
for Catheryne, philosophically, financially, and personally. She
was suddenly left jobless in the midst of the Depression, at a time
when her husband had to accept a cut in salary. Both of them also
felt keenly the adverse effects of the economy upon their work.
Their son recalled that "More and more emphasis had to be
placed . . . on relieving the basic necessities of life of those im-
poverished by the economic conditions. . . . There was an un-
measurable psychological despondency which grew like the
yawning of a pitch black pit in front of us. Aid to the needy became a more urgent problem than the positive goals my parents
had set out to tackle. A great negativism eclipsed the horizon toward which [they] had jauntily set their course." [24] In addition her
children, growing ever closer to college age, were beginning to
assert their independence. Since Catheryne had always regarded

motherhood as an important, even sacred, task, she found it hard
to accept the fact that her role was no longer central to their lives.

As the Alliance collapsed and her private life became increasingly unhappy, Catheryne redoubled her efforts in another arena
that had engaged her concern since 1915 — the regulation of the
movie industry. An early pamphlet published by the Alliance had
instructed block workers to ascertain whether movie theaters "are
sufficiently lighted, notice whether objectionable posters are displayed, and find out . . . the character of the films shown; also
whether conditions affecting children on amateur night are un-
wholesome." In 1920 the Alliance formed a committee to work for
improvement in the films exhibited in Minneapolis.[25]

Catheryne hoped at first to encourage movie house managers to
select "wholesome" films. She soon found, however, that certain
trade practices frustrated her efforts: blind selling forced exhibitors to place orders for films by looking at their titles only; block
booking made it impossible for exhibitors to select one or two
films from a series — they must order an entire block or none at
all. "Objectionable" films could thus be mixed with "wholesome"
ones. Furthermore, since shorts, newsreels, and advertising all
formed part of the programs, a "good" main attraction might be
shown with "bad" shorts.[26]

Movie producers in the 1920s found themselves trapped between conflicting social trends. The popularization of Freudian
psychology had begun to lift some of the late-Victorian taboos
concerning sex, but the prevailing mores did not permit open discussion of its pleasures. In addition, reformers like Catheryne ob-
jected not only to sexual explicitness but to crime, unnecessary
violence, ridicule of the law (particularly Prohibition), and de-
rogatory characterizations of minority groups. Fearing the power
of the new medium, especially over the minds of children, the
reformers were not satisfied merely to eliminate negative elements. They demanded that films positively reinforce the established moral codes of the community. It was not sufficient that the
criminal or the erring spouse repent; he or she must be clearly
punished for the misdeed. This approach was, of course, doomed
to conflict with the growing sophistication of audiences and with
the first attempts to use film as an art form portraying life.[27]

The Alliance had established its citizens' committee on better
movies in 1920 with the underlying assumption that the public

had good morals and would force the producers to respect community standards. By 1925 Catheryne had concluded that morality would have to be imposed on the industry by the government, and she began to work for the creation of a federal commission empowered to rule on the suitability of film scripts, staging, and musical scores before and during production. In 1927 she became chairman of the Motion Picture Committee of the National Council of Women in the United States. The following year she was named president of the Federal Motion Picture Council, and (while still heading the Alliance) she became a member of the National Committee for the Study of Social Values in Motion Pictures. The latter organization had a generous grant from the Payne Foundation of New York to conduct a series of "scientific" studies on motion pictures. These included content, patterns of attendance, merits, educational and propaganda value, influence on the physical and emotional health of those who attended and on the attitudes and conduct of children watching them, as well as the preferences in subject matter of both movie-going and nonmovie-going children.[28]

The complete results of the Payne Fund Studies, as they came to be known, were published in 1933, as was a popular, condensed version entitled *Our Movie Made Children*. While their impartiality is questionable (since the research was undertaken by people with a considerable bias against movies), they nonetheless constituted the only systematic body of research on films then available. With all their shortcomings, the Payne studies demonstrated that films could teach children and that regular attendance influenced personal development — much as television would shape later generations.[29]

In 1932, as the Payne Fund Studies drew to a close and some six months before the Alliance officially dissolved, Catheryne became chairman of the motion picture committee of the National Congress of Parents and Teachers. In this position, she was responsible for formulating and executing a program of action for all Parent-Teacher Associations (PTA) in the country. She elected to promote educational films, putting this new medium to use in the classroom, where the knowledge it transmitted would be of the "desirable" sort, rather than the "undesirable" sort she had encountered so often in commercial theaters. She publicized educational and nontheatrical (or non-Hollywood-produced) films through the PTA's magazine, urging groups to press their school boards to buy projectors (she even published the names of companies selling suitable ones) and to show educational films in the classrooms. Further, she hoped that PTAs would exhibit nontheatrical films in community auditoriums to provide an alternative to Hollywood movies. In fact, she advocated a complete boycott of films produced by the major movie companies and urged PTA members to lobby for legislation to establish federal regulation of motion pictures at the point of production.[30]

Economic boycott proved to be the most effective weapon. Late in 1933 the Catholic archbishops laid the groundwork for the Legion of Decency campaign, which took full effect the next year. Catholics took an oath to boycott movies that the National Legion of Decency labeled "objectionable in part" or "condemned," and other religious groups followed suit. Results seemed instantaneous; a widespread boycott would have wreaked havoc with the industry at that time, since three out of the five major producers were already in serious financial trouble. By the end of 1934 the major producers had established the Production Code Administration in Hollywood and had granted it authority to pass judgment on all their films. Without that administration's approval, films could no longer be exhibited in theaters owned by the major producing companies, and a fine of $25,000 could be imposed upon members of the industry who produced, distributed, or exhibited a film which violated the production code. This form of industry self-censorship lasted for another twenty years, overseen by the Hays Office. It was an indirect and grudging tribute to the hard work and relentless campaigns of the better movie advocates.[31]

At the time, though, Catheryne was profoundly skeptical that this new promise of self-reform would be honored any more firmly than the many which had preceded it. Other board members of the National Congress of Parents and Teachers may have been more hopeful; in any case Catheryne's incessant pleas for more space in the magazine, stenographic help with her correspondence, stationery, and postage (she received no salary for her work) seem to have elicited less and less response from the national office. To preserve some of the momentum in the crusade for better films built up during 1933 and to forestall an anticipated counteroffensive from the industry, she launched an ambitious series of lectures in the fall of 1934. From September through November she presented daylong "institutes" on the movie issue to PTA and other civic groups in twenty-two cities in the East and

South. Her expenses were partly covered by the groups to which she spoke and partly by donations from friends.[32]

The following spring she set out on another lecture circuit in March with a serious ear infection. She refused to obey a doctor's orders that she be hospitalized in Washington, D.C., and traveled in the South until May. She arrived home ill and immediately underwent a mastoid operation. She spent the summer of 1935 recovering her health, quarreling over trifles with officials of the National Congress, and making life unbearable for her children. As usual, her family bore the brunt of her unhappiness, which this time amounted to little less than a nervous breakdown. At the end of the summer, Catheryne went to Washington, D.C., to head a company for the production of educational and entertaining films. The company never got off the ground, however, and she returned to Robbins in Minneapolis after Christmas $7,000 poorer.[33]

Thus twenty years of active crusading for morality and responsibility and decency left Catheryne — now in her mid-fifties — isolated, disappointed, and bitter. Her experience had also made a profound change in her own social philosophy. She increasingly perceived the concentration of economic power in large, urban-based corporations as a threat, not a benefit, to the country. At first she assumed, as many Progressives did, that large corporations could simplify a complex economic life and ensure more scientific and efficient management of natural and human resources. They could promote "progress." However, events of the late 1920s and 1930s made her see also an immense potential for abuse in the consolidation of economic power in any form. The city which had seemed to hold such promise in the first decade of the century concealed traps and pitfalls for the advocates of "progress." The struggle with the movie industry, the collapse of the Alliance, the passage of the Twenty-first Amendment repealing Prohibition (which she always attributed to the power of the liquor manufacturers), and her association with peace groups which vilified the munitions industry all contributed to her change in attitude.[34]

Catheryne spent the remainder of her life writing, lecturing, and working at North East Neighborhood House. Her writings dealt mainly with social hygiene, sexual crimes, and social work. By 1943 she had written more than 200 pamphlets and articles. Her greatest achievement, however, was a massive history of North East Neighborhood House, begun after she turned seventy and finished shortly before her death. The manuscript carefully detailed the programs and philosophies of the Neighborhood House during the thirty-three years her husband directed it until his retirement in 1948. By the 1950s the theory and practice of settlement work had come under attack within the social work profession. In her manuscript she defended both vehemently and, in essence, defended her career.[35]

Catheryne Cooke Gilman was my grandmother. She died in 1954 when I was a little over two years old. Although many of the causes for which she fought so hard now seem mistaken or outmoded, I cannot help admiring her long years of unwavering and at times truly self-sacrificing commitment to those causes she perceived as good for her fellow beings. Thus, like my grandfather, I can say: "I am proud of thee all the time, for what thee is and what thee has done."

12. ADA COMSTOCK NOTESTEIN
Educator

By Susan Margot Smith

ADA LOUISE COMSTOCK was born on December 11, 1876, into very happy circumstances. Her father, Solomon Gilman Comstock, was a successful attorney in the prairie city of Moorhead, Minnesota, and the owner of a considerable amount of fertile land in the Red River Valley. He named his daughter Ada after his sister and Louise after his mother, and she grew up knowing that her father thought she was perfect from the day she was born.[1]

Comstock had migrated from Maine to Minnesota in 1870 with a classical education, some knowledge of law, and a bit of experience with Texas and railroads. He was a man in the right place at the right time, for James J. Hill, pushing his transcontinental railroads across the prairies during the last two decades of the nineteenth century, needed lawyers. In payment for services rendered to Hill, Comstock received enough land in the fertile Red River Valley to assure his fortune. By the 1880s he was ready to carry out what he regarded as the responsibilities of a pioneering citizen.[2]

His family was part of his endeavor. He and his wife, Sarah Ball Comstock, raised their three children — Ada, Jessie, and George — to believe that the world was making progress and that their activities would be essential to it. The Comstocks believed that the steady advance of civilized men could not be prevented if certain ideals were upheld and if those who were gifted were taught to serve. Their eldest child, Ada, absorbed these beliefs and, more than the others, shaped her life and career in accord with them.[3]

Ada was a strong and independent child. The Victorian mansion in which she grew up had numerous possibilities for fun and she was full of ideas. Apples could be roasted on the furnace, corncob dolls were easy to make, and children were permitted to watch the servants dry corn and make mincemeat. For the sport of it, she carried her dog around the top of the wooden fence that enclosed the Comstock yard. She also rode horses and loved baseball. Her mother tried valiantly to reduce Ada's vigor to manageable and ladylike proportions. But her father was proud of her capacities and was determined to cultivate them. He brought her books from St. Paul to help satisfy her active imagination, and as soon as she was able, she took his place in reading to the family after supper.[4]

Education for their children was a matter of early concern to the Comstocks, and circumstances caused Ada's to be varied. Until she was eight, her mother tutored her at home. Then she was sent, with four other little girls, to the Bishop Whipple School, a local Episcopal institution for boys which her father had helped to found. The admission of girls to the institution was short-lived, however, and they were soon sent to pursue their educations elsewhere. For Ada this meant the public schools, although she did attend another private school for one year in Washington, D.C. She mastered the Moorhead public schools quickly and dutifully appeared in the closing exercises in 1887 reciting "Grandma's Love Letters."[5]

Ada was very young when she went to high school, but she already had a reputation for being bright and knowing it. School had not been very challenging to her. She thought examinations were like crossword puzzles and liked to play with them. As a result, she passed arithmetic without learning anything about percentage and even skipped several grades. She loved literature, but her tastes reached beyond public school offerings. They ranged from the leather-bound books of Kipling that her father gave her to a forbidden volume of Elsie Dinsmore which she unearthed in the Sunday school library. When the Moorhead State Normal School was built in 1887, someone is supposed to have remarked, "Now Ada will not think she is the only one who gets ahead in school." If she was guilty of that conceit, her father apparently shared it. Both took it for granted that she would go to college, and they spent hours together poring over catalogues. When Ada graduated from Moorhead High School in 1892, she was only fifteen. Although she and her father agreed that a women's college would be best, she was so young that Solomon Comstock was at first unwilling to have her go any farther away than the University of Minnesota in Minneapolis.[6]

The University of Minnesota was not very hospitable to women in 1892. How they spent their time and where they lived were mainly their own concern. Ada's father arranged for her to live with the dean of the Law School, his former Maine classmate. From that secure base, she ventured onto the campus among the other young women in long skirts, high collars, and little hats. She approached her new milieu with characteristic resourcefulness and managed quite well. At the end of two years she had made some lifelong friends.

In 1894 she transferred to Smith College in Northampton, Massachusetts. Smith offered a completely new experience and Ada was thrilled by it. Girls there were not scattered all over a campus that barely recognized them. They were gathered in an environment segregated, at least part of the time, from matrimonial prospects. Although Ada liked boys, she responded enthusiastically to what she regarded as a healthy "prolongation of little girlhood," during which young women might explore their capacities. What impressed her most about Smith was its "richness of girl companions." Its rules, however, did not always fit in with her plans. When her desire to attend the theater was threatened by a ten o'clock curfew, she moved into a room at the head of the back stairs in her Hubbard House residence. She then persuaded the night watchman to let her sneak up the back stairs with her roommate after hours in exchange for telling him about the plot of the melodrama they had just seen.[7]

Rules and imagination came together more harmoniously when Ada's class of 1897 chose for its senior play Shakespeare's *The Merchant of Venice*. Since the girls undertook to play all the male characters, a make-up expert was imported from New York, and ingenious draping created male attire for girls who could not appear on stage in pants. Ada played the role of the prince of Morocco and made a dramatic entrance to the strains of "barbaric" music that she herself picked out. At least one New York critic was lavish in his praise, dealing out superlatives to the entire cast and concluding that "the Prince himself was nobler than any of the rest of them." The high spirit of the event continued off stage. As a graduation gift, Ada received a case of champagne from a bachelor friend of her father. In the face of her housemother's polite opinion that it should be given to the hospital, she stored it in the water cooler and used it to refresh her classmates after rehearsals.[8]

Both Ada and her father thought she ought to do some sort of

Ada Comstock Notestein

postgraduate study. A Smith education was not enough to enable her to sustain herself financially, and her father was determined that she should be able to do so. It made sense for her to be certified to teach in Minnesota, and, in any case, she had not been home for a long time. So in 1897 she enrolled in the second year of a two-year graduate course at Moorhead State Normal School. She received a certificate in 1898 and left immediately for further graduate work at Columbia University in New York City. Her adviser there was Nicholas Murray Butler, dean of the faculty that supervised all the courses in education. She received a master's degree in English, history, and education in 1899 and returned home to look for a job.[9]

A friend of her father's who was a member of the board of regents at the University of Minnesota came to her rescue. He thought there must be something she could do at the university, and he raised the question with its president, Cyrus Northrop. Although there was no money left in the budget for faculty appointments, President Northrop was persuaded to give Ada a fellowship that paid $25 a month. This would do, the regents thought, because her father was able to clothe her. So Ada Comstock became an assistant in Professor Maria Sanford's department of rhetoric. In 1900 she received the rank of instructor, and in the academic year 1904–05 her promotion to assistant professor took effect while she was abroad studying at the Sorbonne in Paris.[10]

Teaching freshmen how to write was the most formidable academic challenge Ada faced during this period. She found it relatively easy to draw male scoffers out of the back row and closer to her desk, but more difficult to understand and correct the writing deficiencies of significant numbers of students. At first, she devoted herself to the more interesting members of her classes. These were often the agriculture students, because, she thought, they came to the task with interesting things to say. In her search for effective teaching methods, her pedagogy was sometimes brutal. She once asked a student to read his theme to the class so that the members might have a bad example for discussion. When they had completed their criticism, he turned to her on the verge of tears and said, "Don't ever do that to me again." She was somewhat taken aback but not really persuaded that it had been a bad idea.[11]

Eventually she came to some conclusions in writing. She did not care whether her students could recite the rules of composition as long as their writing reflected a knowledge of them. What she wanted was a clear, fluent, unaffected style. She found fault gently, but she found it in many places. Poor speech habits at home, too much emphasis on composition as a fine art, and overworked public school teachers were all part of the problem. The solution, she thought, was not to be found in one academic department but in the entire educational system. It was characteristic of her approach to problems that she should reach beyond particulars to a larger view.[12]

This same turn of mind made her aware of women students and their relationship to the university. More of them were now on campus than had been there when she was a student, but their circumstances were not much different. They were still essentially outside the life of the school, and their efforts were often not taken very seriously by the community. Ada once went to see the editor of a Minneapolis newspaper to ask him to refer to women students by some term other than coed and to write about their activities in a way that was not facetious. He only laughed at her.[13]

But the university did not laugh at her. If nothing else, it was agreed that the growing number of females on campus needed supervision. In 1907 at the age of thirty-one Ada Comstock was appointed the first dean of women at the University of Minnesota; two years later she was promoted to the rank of professor. The *Moorhead Daily News* proudly reported her appointment and the petition on her behalf signed by about a thousand students. It was, the editor thought romantically, "a striking recognition of a broadly cultured, dignified, and gracious young womanhood." [14] His assessment reflected Ada's talent for dressing change in the garb of traditional values.

The new dean immediately set out to improve the quality of university life for women. She helped them organize a cap and gown society "for the purposes of promoting a spirit of sociability," and she arranged a series of afternoon teas for the same purpose. She encouraged and sponsored women's organizations of many types. Then she turned to the matter of living conditions, personally visiting boardinghouses located near the university to give them an opportunity to be listed as approved residences for women. She asked only that the residence be limited to female boarders and that a special room be provided for callers. The effect of employment on academic performance also fell under her scrutiny. A study of university women who were self-supporting revealed that their grades were as good as those who were not working. Employment problems subsequently became a concern of the dean's office. During Christmas recess in the academic year 1911–12, Ada herself went looking for jobs for university women in Minneapolis and St. Paul. [15]

The most tangible accomplishment of the Comstock administration, however, was the funding and raising of Shevlin Hall, completed in 1906. It had been clear to the dean for some time that the mice-infested "Ladies' Parlor" in the main building was a symbol of an environment that was inadequate, even detrimental, to the needs of women. She argued persistently that intellectual attainment was inseparable from physical well-being and that the university was responsible for both. When she took her request for a women's building to President Northrop only to be told that there was a greater need for a new chemistry building, she wept. The money she needed was donated shortly thereafter. The dedication of Shevlin Hall marked a new era for women on the campus. Its meeting rooms, resting parlors, and eating facilities gave women a place of their own; their nomadic campus life was over. [16]

The author of these changes had blossomed herself. Pioneering as a dean agreed with her. She found that she liked taking a new job, a first of its kind, and building it. In 1910 she had become president of the newly organized Association of Deans of Women. Then she discovered that she was presiding over a task that she had completed. Not even the activities of a rapidly growing university could overcome the fact that Ada was bored. When she received an invitation in 1912 to become dean of Smith College, she readily accepted. In her new position, Ada announced, she would have opportunities unavailable at a coeducational institution to teach and advise young women. Perhaps the challenge mattered even more. For once again the job was a first of its kind.[17]

The Smith class of 1897 turned out for its fifteenth reunion and the commencement of 1912 in exuberant force. They were thrilled with Ada's appointment and beleaguered her lovingly throughout the festivities. At intervals they chanted:

"Sing, sing, sing to Ada Comstock
97's Dean of Smith!
For we're proud to own the college
Which displays the taste and knowledge
To make 97's Ada, Dean of Smith."

Ada ran herself ragged in a flush of excitement. She drank quantities of congratulatory champagne, went on picnics, and sat up talking late into the night. She also met with Smith's trustees, carried the standard for her class in the commencement procession, and spoke at the exercises. When they were over, she went to bed with a cold.[18]

She rose to begin a complete appraisal of student life at Smith. It was anticipated that the new dean would be interested in academic standards and educational philosophy, but no one was quite prepared for her interest in living conditions. As she had at the University of Minnesota, Ada took as her first project an evaluation of student housing. She also undertook to determine how much it cost to attend Smith by asking students to keep careful expense journals recording all their expenditures. (After surveying the journals, she was able to offer the information that a student could manage for $400 a year and meet all of her needs for $750.) Within five years Ada had taken steps to expand the housing available on campus, proposed new plans for regulating living units, and struggled to bring into being a new infirmary. All of these

activities were in accord with the conviction she had earlier formulated at the University of Minnesota that education must provide for physical well-being in order to promote intellectual attainment.[19]

Since Smith did not need to be convinced that it was appropriate to educate women, the dean was free to turn her attention to
further refinements of educational objectives. One of the most important, she thought, should be inculcating in young women a respect for themselves. She took many occasions to describe what
she meant by self-respect, and her cumulative definition was demanding. The self-respecting woman would not wish to be "conspicuous" and would follow fashion with moderation. She would
speak in a beautiful and simple way, expressing lofty thoughts.
Above all, she would "not follow blindly the behests of the mob,
or accept ideas ready-made." Although these now sound like
dated moral precepts for the socially favored, in the early years of
the twentieth century they were an assertion of faith in the integrity and individuality of women. Expressing her confidence in the
worth of that individuality, Ada told the class of 1922 "if you
sufficiently respect yourselves, if you sufficiently value the life
given you to live, I have faith to believe that your answers will be
more nearly right than ours have been."[20]

One tangible aspect of self-respect was knowing how to employ
oneself. There were many ways an educated woman might do so
without venturing outside of women's traditional sphere. Ada
Comstock always thought that colleges had a responsibility to ac-
quaint women with the full range of possibilities. A central objective of education, as she saw it, was to direct the average woman,
not endowed with extraordinary energy or cleverness, to success.
Early in her career at Smith, she wrote a pamphlet describing the
vocations available to the college woman. It suggested everything
from commercial photography to municipal research. Then uncommon professions for women such as law and pharmacy were
excluded only because they seemed to her self-evident.[21]

Above all, Ada believed a college education should inspire a
woman to play her part in shaping the world. World War I gave
her an opportunity to talk about the responsibilities of women at a
time of crisis. She knew that war caused a nation to set aside
domestic squabbles for the sake of a united front, and she
wholeheartedly approved of that. But she also knew what that
might mean for causes vital to women. People would be called to

unselfishness and sacrifice in the name of the war effort, and in the process, the arguments advanced on behalf of a new role for women would be silenced. In the face of this, she urged women to make their contributions to their country by dispassionate thinking, mental development, and continuing aspiration. They had a job to do in the world that demanded more of them than the temporary comforts they might be able to offer.[22]

Educated women active in the world were, in fact, associating under Ada Comstock's leadership. She became the first president of the American Association of University Women in 1921. In its early years, one of that organization's most ambitious projects was sponsoring the International Federation of University Women. In the wake of World War I, educated women from participating countries saw the federation as a vehicle for encouraging education among women and thereby increasing amity among nations. Ada served on the federation's council, and she returned from its first two meetings in 1921 and 1922 full of enthusiasm for a near future in which the quality of education for women would be improved. Achievement among women, she felt certain, would have a positive influence on international affairs and mutual understanding would flourish. A world war had not altered her belief that peace and co-operation among nations were logical possibilities. "In these strange days," she wrote, "idealism has come to be the only practicable cure for the very concrete ills from which the world is suffering."[23]

Ada Comstock's years of "deaning" at Smith are recorded in superlatives. Her achievements for the college were significant and numerous. So also were her contributions to the well-being of those in her charge. She was a "gentlewoman" of the sort she most admired, giving praise without clamor and encouragement without patronage. She had a gift for warmth but intimacy was something she did not permit. Even her trusted secretary never learned that she had once found her relationship with the college unsatisfactory. When the presidency of Smith became vacant in 1917, the trustees gave the operating responsibility to Dean Comstock, but they did not consider her for the position nor did they dignify her day-to-day efforts by naming her acting president. Apparently they felt it was not time for a woman to lead the college, and William Allan Neilson was named president of Smith. Ada was wounded and humiliated and never stopped feeling that it had been an insult. Nevertheless, her relationship with President Neilson became deep and affectionate and they worked together for many years.[24]

But the time came, as it inevitably did for Ada, when the task at hand was complete and the challenge was gone. Thus when she was offered the presidency of Radcliffe College in 1923, it took her only a fortnight to accept. Her decision to leave Smith brought gestures of esteem from all sides. The faculty issued a statement expressing "a deep sense of official and personal loss" as well as its "affection and admiration." The students collected $600 to be placed in her name at the bookstore of her choice. Peggy Hazen, the president of the student council, wrote on its behalf, "we only hope to give you a little happiness in return for all you have done for us." The loyal class of 1897 presented a portrait of Ada Comstock as its twenty-fifth reunion gift to Smith College. William Allan Neilson saved his farewell for her inauguration.[25]

Ada Louise Comstock was inaugurated as the first full-time president of Radcliffe College on October 20, 1923. The ceremony was simple and impressive. The inaugural speeches went elegantly to the heart of the central issue. Marion Edwards Park, president of Bryn Mawr College, spoke confidently of Radcliffe's potential and Ada Comstock's endurance. William Allan Neilson was more outspoken. He warned the Radcliffe Associates and the Harvard Corporation that everyone in the academic community would be watching the fortunes of Radcliffe and its president, who, he thought, "should be displaced only by greater opportunity." Addressing his concluding remark to Ada, he said pointedly, "If you find this household into which you have been taken intolerable, you can always come home." The laughter indicated that his gentle humor had gone straight to the mark. President Abbott Lawrence Lowell of Harvard was mild and gracious. Of course President Comstock would have his help whenever he could give it.[26]

The new president, then forty-seven years old, rose to a standing ovation. She was tall and stately, and addressed the audience in her unusually rich and persuasive voice. Like the others, she carefully skirted the pending problems. She spoke of academic standards, admissions, and the inadequacy of a fragmented education. She offered the opinion that the student had not sufficiently entered into the reckoning in educational planning. There was universal agreement, she was sure, "that education is the only means of relief in a confused world and that there is a demand for

men and women who have the capacity, the training, and the will
to think." Her remarks were addressed to colleagues or patrons
with whom she assumed a body of shared ideals, offering the essence of her educational idealism without thrusting anything radical upon her new colleagues. She was entering the arena with
quiet reasonableness. The *Radcliffe Quarterly* was jubilant, expressing the opinion that "Under such leadership, we may feel a
deep sense of security with high hopes of the future of our college."[27]

The *Quarterly's* "sense of security" may have exceeded the new
president's, for the challenge that faced her was not a casual one.
All of the inaugural speakers knew that while Radcliffe may have
had potential, it also had distinct problems. It lacked a resident
faculty of its own, its physical facilities were undeveloped, and its
finances were in a tangle. It needed Harvard, but its association
with the university could not be taken for granted. In spite of his
inaugural promises to help, President Lowell was determined
to cut what he regarded as the Radcliffe parasite away from Harvard. As far as he was concerned, the invitational lectures that
Harvard faculty members gave at Radcliffe were sapping their
academic strength. Moreover, he thought that Radcliffe was more
bother than it was worth and a nuisance to serious academic
endeavor.[28]

Serious academic endeavor was exactly what Ada Comstock had
in mind and she approached it from several directions. She
charmed the members of the Harvard Corporation with a mixture
of educational philosophy and kidney pie. She made it her business to know when a Harvard faculty member was doing something well, and then she tried to interest him in the pleasures of
sharing it with Radcliffe students. She adapted Harvard's tutorial
system for use at Radcliffe. After a few years, special tutorial
rooms were set aside and a tutorial secretary was appointed. The
president had high hopes that the system would "develop in the
young American the thoughtfulness, thoroughness, and self-
reliance which constitute independent citizenship in the intellectual world." She also hoped that it would start women tutors toward distinguished academic careers. She began to talk about the
scholarly life, the need for critical research by women, and what
part Radcliffe might play in enhancing them.[29]

Throughout most of her administration, President Comstock's
policies maintained the precarious and delicate balance between

Radcliffe's continuing association with Harvard and its independent strength as a women's college. Once she had attracted the Harvard faculty, she turned her attention to strengthening Radcliffe. She called for the formulation of a building program, indicated her own wish for a special building for graduate students, and created a new department for health education. In the 1920s she brought Radcliffe into association with six other women's colleges to consider matters of mutual concern. In that period, too, she invited four Boston and Cambridge clergymen to serve as college chaplains and conduct weekly morning prayer services at Agassiz House.[30]

Not until 1926–27 did she warily initiate a more formal claim to the services of the Harvard faculty. She pointed out to her trustees that instruction at Radcliffe was an addition to a Harvard faculty member's regular program and, as such, was most vulnerable to being eliminated in the event of professional or academic pressures upon the individual. The solution she persuaded the Radcliffe Associates and the Fellows of Harvard to accept was a plan of joint appointments secured by endowment money from Radcliffe. She was careful to add, however, that she believed the foundation upon which Radcliffe rested was Harvard instruction. It would always be Radcliffe's policy, she promised, "to preserve the relationship with Harvard which affords that foundation."[31]

Her growing reputation as an educator drew the president of Radcliffe outside of the academic community in 1929. In that year President Herbert Hoover appointed her to the National Commission on Law Observance and Enforcement. The Wickersham Commission, as the newspapers called it for its chairman George W. Wickersham of New York, was charged with analyzing the entire federal judicial system as well as problems of law enforcement with particular attention to the Eighteenth (Prohibition) Amendment, and recommending remedial action at the state and local levels. When Ada Comstock, the only woman on the eleven-member commission, was interviewed about her assignment, all she would say was that "there is an interesting piece of work to be done and I am glad to have a share in it." One political cartoonist played upon the old theme of women's inability to keep a secret by sketching the uncommunicative Ada on a pedestal somewhat after the fashion of the Statue of Liberty. When the commission issued its report in fourteen volumes in 1931, she was listed among the five who favored modification of the Eighteenth

Amendment. Reminded of her work on the commission many years later, she said, "I never had more fun."[32]

In the autumn of 1931 she took a three-month leave of absence to attend a meeting in Shanghai of the Institute of Pacific Relations, to which she was appointed for the third time as a delegate. The purpose of the institute was to conduct "a study of the conditions of the Pacific peoples with a view to the improvement of their mutual relations." Its procedures involved "a continuous process of discussion, supported by intensive research." The institute's delegates were not representatives of governments or organizations. They passed no resolutions. Presiding over the Shanghai meeting was a philosopher. Ada returned from China in a glow of renewed idealism. If such a meeting could take place with civility and good will right after the clash between China and Japan in Manchuria, it must mean that the world could be altered through co-operation to become a better place. Surely there was such a thing as progress.[33]

Unlike many institutions, Radcliffe emerged unscathed from the crash of 1929. It did not even have a deficit, and the 1930s saw many new plans and ambitious projects. A nationwide admissions program was initiated to attract students "capable of distinguished achievement." New classroom buildings appeared and steps were taken to improve student housing. The academic program was also expanded to offer a doctorate in American civilization and preparation for certification in secondary school teaching. The administration now included both a dean of the graduate school and a dean of undergraduate instruction, and a new director revitalized the school's efforts to find jobs for Radcliffe graduates in a depression economy.[34]

By the late 1930s, Radcliffe's permanence seemed assured, and in the spring of 1937, the college launched a four-million-dollar fund drive to increase its endowment and provide fellowships and expanded facilities. While the Boston newspapers were singing compliments to Radcliffe's president, she was writing her brother that "Sometimes the thought of it makes me feel like one of those witches whom they killed by heaping stones on them." About the same time, Radcliffe flourished its dawning independence in the matter of instruction. A graduate course in music offered by visiting lecturer Mademoiselle Nadia Boulanger was announced with the note that Radcliffe would accept any "properly qualified Harvard students."[35]

The cumulative effect was too much for President Lowell, and the Harvard administration assembled a "Committee of Eight" to study the relationship between the two schools. Among its recommendations in 1939 was a limitation on teaching at Radcliffe by the Harvard faculty. It was a blow to the thriving institution, but President Comstock calmly told her trustees that "whatever the difficulties of adjustment may be, nothing would be more short-sighted than for Radcliffe to quarrel with any arrangement, short of a categorical prohibition which, in the long run, promises to strengthen the Harvard faculty and to increase its effectiveness." Meanwhile she went on to write about the assured future of what she termed "the coördinate college." She counted Radcliffe a "coördinate college" because it enjoyed a co-operative relationship which gave its students the benefits of a university and a separate college. Harvard might be chafing against Radcliffe's presence, but it could not easily rid itself of a mutually advantageous association in which Ada Comstock believed.[36]

The deepening conflict of World War II in Europe displaced some of Ada's idealism and replaced it with melancholy. Her outlook was darkened by this fresh indication of how little progress the world had made. She began to reflect, as she had during World War I, on what a new war would mean for women. She was convinced that the threat to democracy offered by totalitarian governments was doubly a threat to women. Measures to limit the employment of married women reminded her of the attitudes toward women of Fascist countries, and she advised vigilance. A deficit at Radcliffe, the loss of her new dean, and the preparations for war added to her bleak state of mind. When war came, she added her efforts to the task at hand. She made speeches, organized the Cambridge Salvage Committee, and worked with the Women's Division of the Cambridge Committee on Public Safety.[37]

World War II brought many changes at Radcliffe. Perhaps most importantly it completed the work Ada Comstock had begun in the 1920s, for it brought Harvard and Radcliffe to a point of co-operation they had never before achieved. War drew off Harvard faculty members, and many women were appointed in their places. Women also filled the empty seats in graduate classes. Summer courses were introduced in order to accelerate degree programs, and both men and women were admitted to them. Ada Comstock had spent twenty years matching Harvard in quality and accomplishment. National crisis and the pressures of empty classrooms did the rest. Harvard was persuaded to accept classroom coeducation in 1943. In her annual report to the trustees, the president of Radcliffe announced that "the anomalous arrangement [between Radcliffe and Harvard] becomes a contract of specific rights and obligations . . . departments are now charged with the duty of providing Radcliffe with instruction adequate to attain degrees." Ada Comstock had completed the work she set out to do, and she retired in 1943.[38]

Her retirement marked the end of an era at Radcliffe. Her leadership had brought the institution to maturity and distinction, and the tributes to her were many and eloquent. The newspapers spoke of a grievous loss, and the trustees published a resolution of thanks and gratitude. She was flooded by compliments, reminiscences, and good will. But it was William Allan Neilson, her old friend and Smith colleague, who perhaps best summed up her accomplishment: "For years all the Harvard men who had dealings with Radcliffe and the people in Cambridge and Boston who came in touch with it, have learned to appreciate the soundness of Miss Comstock's judgment, her fairness, her breadth of view, her freedom from anything approaching faction or intrigue," he wrote. "They discerned in her a remarkable capacity for going to the heart of a situation without being distracted by non-essentials or merely conventional considerations. Radcliffe itself . . . has known more intimately her charm and dignity."[39]

Ada's own comments went unusually close to the heart of what she was thinking. At the Radcliffe commencement of 1943, she told departing graduates that she and others of her generation had been "over-sanguine about the speed and painlessness with which civilization can progress." She was no longer sure of the steady ascent toward lofty ideals, she thought. Nor did deliberate harmony and reasonable association seem to hold the answers. Experience had tempered her optimism. "I value more than anything else I have learned from life," she said in conclusion, "an increased sense of the magnitude of the human drama, and of the intrinsic blessedness of struggle."[40]

It took the freedom of afterthought, however, to provide a more candid assessment of the Radcliffe experience. "If anyone asked me," she later observed, "who caused the greatest emotional disturbance of my life, I should say Abbott Lawrence Lowell. I had the worst fight of my life there. I wouldn't have missed that period in my life for anything. When President Conant succeeded President Lowell, the excitement went out of things for me."[41] Ada Comstock may have owed her sense of purpose to an ideal, but she owed her resilience to a keen sense of a good game.

Shortly after commencement Radcliffe was electrified by the news that the president had married Wallace Notestein, Sterling professor emeritus of history at Yale University. Although she had known him since they had been faculty members at the University of Minnesota, the announcement came as a complete surprise. She maintained a private silence almost to the day itself, and then she wrote to an old friend, "I'm going . . . to New Haven to be a faculty wife! . . . I do hope you don't think it too absurd or risky."[42]

Retirement was a misnomer for her married state. She was on the board of trustees for Smith College, was working on plans for the graduate center at Radcliffe, and was inundated by educational committee work. In her seventieth year she complained especially of January, a month filled with trips in connection with the Smith board, the China College for Women, and the Institute of Pacific Relations. In February, 1949, she delivered an address to commemorate the seventy-fifth anniversary of Smith. In 1959, at the age of eighty-two, she enraptured an audience at the inauguration of Smith president Thomas C. Mendenhall. "Her brief address, which dealt with the challenges and rewards of a college presidency, was beautifully phrased, crisp, and witty," wrote one commentator. "Speaking with a vigor and presence rare in women many years her junior, she seemed to be drawing on a lifetime of leadership and reflection, distilling in her precise and pointed phrases the essence of her experience. It was a tour de force, and epitomized for the whole occasion the finest product of higher education for women." Long after her departure from Radcliffe, she received honorary degrees from both Harvard and Oxford. She seemed to be living in accord with an opinion she had expressed long before it had anything to do with her: "I cannot see why writing, painting, laboratory research or any other valuable contribution to life and living, need of necessity, be stopped by marriage."[43]

Marriage did, however, introduce significant new dimensions into her life. One was a completely different sphere, although still an academic one, in the Yale community of New Haven. Another was the endless administration of a two-career household. While the Sterling professor emeritus feverishly wrote up his research, his wife was dealing with a long procession of cooks, maids, and furnace and fence repairmen. Domestic service was far from infallible and a successful social occasion frequently required a deft balance of confusion in the dining room with tact and good conversation after dinner. She greeted these trivia of life with both incredulity and impatience. Writing to an old friend, she remarked: "Someday we must talk about the need, for a woman with a home and husband, of some quiet, sustained interesting piece of work which she can retreat into and thereby keep a thread of continuity in her life. Also I should like to write a platform for professional women which would induce them to relieve themselves of the small duties of living which men disregard so readily. I'm convinced that the superior achievement of men is due in part to their refusals (right and necessary) to be distracted by concern for clothes, foods, housekeeping, bill-paying, and all the rest. Why can't we clear the decks?"[44] It wasn't really a complaint, only an observation.

Her marriage also led to more travel abroad. Wallace's work demanded extensive research in England and they went there for several months every year. Some of her friends thought that she was being dragged exhausted and long-suffering in her husband's wake, but in fact she enjoyed their travels as much as he did. She felt at home in England, preferably from the vantage point of London, and found her own entertainment while her husband was ensconced in libraries. She had time to indulge her love for theater, gardens, and fine shops. The social pace was more moderate than in New Haven, but there was a steady flow of English and American friends to dine and visit. Once every season she traveled somewhere on the continent with her old friend Margaret Williams. In later years, she and Wallace warmed themselves by end-of-the-season sojourns in Italy.[45]

Ada Comstock had always been credited with a fresh and independent mind, one that could grasp the entirety of a situation. The same could be said of Ada Comstock Notestein, with an addition. In her later years, her sensitivity gained ascendance and she spoke more often from the lyrical and introspective side of her nature. She had always loved flowers, and frequently used metaphors from the garden to illustrate her ideas. As she grew older the metaphors and descriptions gained intensity. Her letters were filled with glimmering lakes of bluebells, pussy-willows growing fat and fuzzy, and willows turning bright yellow. She composed paragraph after paragraph of vivid word-pictures to send to her family. Silver-gray Greece, gray-green olive trees in Mycenae, Cinzano in Milan, the shattering colors of Chartres, and white oxen in Pisa stood away from her pages in a third dimension.[46]

Her lifelong interest in history and biography also took on an introspective cast as she grew older. Relationships with people assumed more significance, and she reflected upon her own. The death of her sister Jessie in 1951 seemed to revive her sense of the loss of her father, who had died in 1933. She thought of him often, of what he had stood for, and of what he had wanted for her. She also became closer to her brother and spoke sadly of Jessie's isolation in adulthood. There was in her sorrow a judgment of herself. While she had not been careless of those who loved her, she had not been on hand to take responsibility for them either. She had refused to become embroiled in the frustrations of their lives, and it occurred to her in retrospect that perhaps she used submissive and willing people badly. Perhaps her spirit had been so high, her ability to sustain herself so complete, that she had starved others of the sustenance they needed. Perhaps, she thought, her calm judiciousness was a deficiency of spirit.[47]

Ada Comstock Notestein died early in the morning on December 12, 1973. Her last words were of her father. The newspapers carried all the facts about her. She had received fourteen honorary degrees and had three residence halls named in her honor. The Radcliffe College Alumnae Fund endowed a Radcliffe scholarship in her name. She had received the Radcliffe Founders' Award and had been cited as the "chief architect of the greatness of Radcliffe." Rockford College had given her its Jane Addams Medal and Ida M. Tarbell had cited her as "one of the foremost women of the United States." Her friends spoke in memorial of her gifts and graces. They recalled her achievements at Smith and Radcliffe, her integrity, wisdom, charm, and courage. For many she was a personified ideal. For some she was little less than a goddess. The only voice that would have been raised in dissent was her own.[48]

13. ANNA DICKIE OLESEN
Senate Candidate

By Dolores De Bower Johnson

ORATORY, like soapmaking, is not a skill much admired or cultivated any more. In the nineteenth century, though, and into the early years of the twentieth, great orators were often the celebrities of their day, and the politically ambitious could hardly hope to succeed until they had mastered the elements of the art. Perhaps that is why, on a warm summer's day in 1897, twelve-year-old Anna Dickie of Waterville, Minnesota, walked across the clearing outside her family's farm home, took a deep breath, and prepared to speak to the man who watched with critical attention from the front porch. "Now say something," her coach advised, "but don't yell. Don't yell. Just speak in an ordinary voice, but let me hear you."[1]

In the years that followed, Anna Dickie was to put to good use the oratorical skills she first practiced as a young girl. Although she could not even vote until she was nearly thirty-five years old, she came to understand and enjoy the practice of politics as only a few women of her generation did, achieving national prominence in the Democratic party and becoming the first woman to run for United States senator as the candidate of a major party. The talent for public speaking she worked to develop under the tutelage of her parents' friend Judson Jones became one of her major assets. "A real spell binder," one admirer declared; "[she has] no rival in the world of public speech making," said another; "perhaps one of the five fastest talkers in the world," claimed a third.[2]

The first child of Peter Daniel and Margaret Jones Dickie, Anna was born on July 3, 1885, in Cordova Township, Le Sueur County, Minnesota. Although the family was not well off and had to struggle, especially in the early years, the members were never in great want. In addition to their daughter, Peter and Margaret Dickie had two sons: Lewis, who was born in 1891, and Owen, born in 1894. The parents belonged to the local Methodist church and were teetotalers and Republicans. Later, perhaps because of the agricultural depression of the 1890s, they switched their support to the Great Commoner, William Jennings Bryan. In a recollection dating back to the presidential election of 1888, Anna once recalled, "My first political speech . . . was for the Republican party, when at the age of three years my uncle, an enthusiastic and loyal Republican, to the delight of my family taught me to say 'Hurrah for Harrison.'"[3]

From the start, Anna loved school and she loved to talk. When she was about ten she decorated a box for a box lunch social. The unsuspecting young man of eighteen who purchased it thereby acquired a supper partner who was not only a mere girl of ten, but also one who did not stop talking. He never forgot the experience.[4]

Anna's childhood in rural Minnesota was of the kind that is easily idealized, but for her it was not entirely satisfying. Even as a small girl she was sometimes restless and discontented, yearning for the wider world beyond Waterville. Watching the trains go by, she often murmured, "Someday I'll be on your back, old train." When she was four her mother inherited $400 in gold, and Anna later recalled that she was once given the gold coins as playthings to stop her from crying — though the action shocked other members of the family. To some extent, that childhood fascination with objects of such value presaged Anna's later life. Her ambition, or so it seemed to other family members, was partly directed toward assuaging a desire for status, expensive clothes, and other material possessions.

Perhaps Anna's drive came also from her ancestry, which included some unusually strong-minded and independent women. Her maternal great-grandmother, Margaret Hughes Davis, was a member of a colony of Welsh immigrants who settled in Ohio in 1838. Later Margaret and her husband Owen moved to southern Minnesota, settling near Le Sueur. Their daughter Anne married John C. Jones and established a home across the road from her parents. Anne died in 1869 and after the death of John Jones in 1871 the three surviving children, including Anna Dickie's mother Margaret, went to live with their grandmother. A true matriarch, Grandmother Davis was the acknowledged leader who functioned as banker as well as adviser to the family. Anna regarded Grandmother Davis as "a great woman." She once observed: "The

Hughes must have been superior people — I think though that the Welsh women, like the French women, are superior to men." Grandmother Davis saw to it that her grandchildren were educated. Anna's mother taught school near the Davis home for a time, and then in 1883 exhibited her own independent spirit by marrying Peter Dickie against the wishes of the matriarch. The young couple started farm life near the town of Waterville, somewhat out of the range of her displeasure.[5]

Peter Dickie was an inordinately hospitable man who welcomed a variety of guests to his door. Judson Jones, who undertook to give Anna voice lessons, was one of them. Strangers who attended local church services were always invited to Sunday dinner, and itinerant salesmen regularly stopped at the Dickies'. A Jewish peddler once arrived on a Saturday, in tears because he was violating his holy day. Peter Dickie sent his boys to unharness the horse from the man's cart, and the peddler spent his Sabbath at the Dickies' saying his prayers. Thereafter he often stayed with the family and called Peter the only *goy* he had ever met who knew God. Her father's genuine interest in people and respect for their individuality stayed with Anna and was one reason she was later able to command strong loyalties.

Books and education were also important in the Dickie household. Volumes that had belonged to Anna's maternal grandfather formed the nucleus of the library that filled two bookcases. Among the many guests at the Dickie home was Zephaniah (Zeffie) Flowers, who arrived in a buggy with a piece of oilcloth covering the books he peddled around the countryside. Each time he left, he presented a book to the family. The Dickies attracted persons who were interested in good conversation, and their home was, in son Owen's words, known in the community as a "mental place."

Every summer there was an influx of well-to-do people who owned cottages on the lakes around Waterville, and Anna became aware of the difference between their affluent ways and the simple, almost austere style in which she and her family lived. She came to know the Andrews family, a traveling company from Mankato who presented summer opera in Waterville, and she caught a glimpse of the exhilaration of performing.[6]

After completing the eight grades of country school, Anna went to Waterville High School, commuting from the farm by foot, horseback, or buggy. She completed the course work in three years and was certified to teach in one-room country schools. Despite her

*Anna
Dickie
Olesen*

childhood desire to see the world, Anna took a position as a teacher with a salary of twenty-one dollars a month and continued to live at home until she left it for the usual reason — to marry.

Several years earlier, Peter Dickie had brought home for Sunday dinner a young man named Peter Olesen, who had emigrated from Denmark, served as a hospital orderly during the Spanish-American War, and at the time was working his way through Hamline University by selling books, mostly in the Dakotas. He kept in touch with Anna after his visit to Waterville, and they were married on June 8, 1905, when she was almost twenty.

Peter Olesen recognized and encouraged his wife's intellectual ability, guiding her reading in religion, literature, and philosophy. Nevertheless, the gregarious, ambitious Anna and the taciturn,

strong-willed Peter do not seem to have been ideal companions.
Many years later, Anna dryly observed to her daughter: "The
Uncle Tom's Cabin of marriage has never been written."[7]

The Olesens began their married life in St. Paul, where Peter
was working on a master's degree. He continued to support himself and his new wife by selling books, but the young couple had
very little money. After Peter received his degree, he obtained a
position as superintendent of schools in Pine City, Minnesota.
There he became active on the local high school debate team, and
when the debaters met at the Olesens' house, Anna observed his
coaching. Her husband willingly included her in the sessions, in
part, perhaps, to distract her from grief; their first child Margaret,
born in September, 1906, had lived only three months. More
happily, another daughter, Mary Winifred, was born the following
year.

In 1908 the Olesens moved to northern Minnesota, where Peter
became superintendent of schools in Cloquet. It was an important
move, for the town was to be the base from which Anna took her
first steps into politics. Life there also exacerbated her already
keen status consciousness. Cloquet was a lumbering town populated by a work force of immigrants of various nationalities, along
with the millowners and managers. Social distinctions were
clearly drawn. Even such a prosaic item as the kind of doorknobs
one had (were they metal or glass?) assumed enormous significance. Anna was painfully conscious that she did not have
an impressive house and that her clothes were not as elegant as
those of the wives of the businessmen who would determine her
husband's success. Peter Olesen controlled the family finances,
providing Anna with only enough money for the bare necessities,
and she often had no money of her own to spend. Peter's fiscal
management was not always prudent. He, too, wanted more of
life's goods than his salary provided, and in his determination to
become wealthy he invested whatever money could be spared
from household expenses in unsuccessful get-rich-quick schemes.
Anna, energetic and ambitious, plunged into the community life of
Cloquet. She first became active in the Mothers' Club of the local
school and later joined the Women's Club, where she volunteered
her time to teach English to newly arrived immigrants.[8]

By 1910 the cause of women's suffrage had been taken up by
Progressives throughout the country, and Minnesota was no exception. In the outstate areas work for suffrage was largely carried on

by members of the local affiliate of the Federation of Women's Clubs; it was in connection with her club work that Anna first became officially associated with the movement. Her interest in votes for women was not surprising. She was, after all, descended from a line of strong Hughes women, and on her father's side of the family there was Grandmother Dickie, who, Anna recalled, used to say that her husband had gone off to fight in the Civil War and after the war the vote had been given to the Negro but not to her. Women's suffrage was the issue that first involved Anna in politics; it was representative of the causes she was to espouse throughout her political career: Prohibition, child and social welfare programs, opposition to large corporations and special interests, and, later, support for the Social Security Act and other New Deal legislation.[9]

In 1913 Anna Olesen was elected president of the Federation of Women's Clubs in Minnesota's Eighth Congressional District. The following year she was appointed by Governor Adolph O. Eberhart, a Republican, as a delegate to the International Child Welfare Congress in Washington, D.C., and she took an active part in the passage of the Children's Code in Minnesota. In May, 1916, Anna appeared on the program of the Mississippi Valley Suffrage Conference in Minneapolis, speaking on "The Problems in Our Part of the State." That same year she was elected state vice-president of the Federation of Women's Clubs, a post she held until 1918. At the age of thirty-one Anna was now on her way, on the "back of that old train." She convinced her husband that they should hire a maid to look after the house and to care for Mary, the daughter who had been born in 1907, and she began to buy her "public" clothes from the nearest *couturière*, Madame Ward of Duluth.[10]

In 1916 Anna accepted the invitation of the Minnesota Democratic party to speak at its state convention. Apparently Judson Jones's tutelage served her well: her speech on women's suffrage was judged the most impressive at the gathering. The *Minneapolis Journal* reported that her talk had "electrified the recent democratic state convention." She continued to speak at Democratic meetings, and in 1917 she was appointed as Minnesota member of the women's advisory committee of the Democratic National Committee, on which she served until 1924.[11]

In the fall of 1918 a disastrous forest fire swept through Cloquet, completely destroying the town. The Olesens escaped with other refugees by train, and passing through St. Paul on her way to Waterville, Anna made public appeals for money, food, and clothing for the survivors. For years afterward she continued to lobby in Washington, D.C., for government reimbursement of the Cloquet fire victims. In 1934, after six years of litigation, the inhabitants received a settlement of fifty cents on the dollar for their losses. Finally, in the second administration of Franklin D. Roosevelt, Congress passed a bill for their full compensation.[12]

All these activities, however, involving travel, household help, and dressmakers' bills, began to strain a school superintendent's salary. Peter felt that his wife should help pay the expenses of her activities, and so, in the summer of 1918, Anna went with her daughter Mary to Libertyville, Illinois, to try out for the Chautauqua.[13]

The Tent Chautauqua — traveling groups of orators, dramatic artists, politicians, and humorists — was a manifestation of both the American zeal for self-improvement and a hunger for entertainment. Its forerunner, the American Lyceum Association, had been founded in 1831, and its performances had been delivered, usually with a considerable amount of dignity, in churches, schools, and libraries. Chautauqua was a more flamboyant medium, pitching its tents on wind-swept prairies and well-used pastures, and presenting to its perspiring audiences everything from low humor to no-holds-barred, issue-oriented debate. As the historian of Tent Chautauqua has observed, "Inside the big brown tents, millions of Americans first heard impassioned pleas for a Federal income tax, slum clearance, free schoolbooks, world disarmament."[14]

The platforms of the Lyceum Association had been open to males only; Chautauqua welcomed both men and women. James Redpath, manager of the lecture bureau that sent the Tent Chautauquas throughout middle America, was in favor of women's suffrage and frequently booked women who would speak on its behalf. Carrie Chapman Catt, Anna Howard Shaw, and Jane Addams all made Chautauqua appearances. By the summer of 1919, when the suffrage amendment was before state legislatures for ratification, "suffrage tents," their yellow and white flags flying, were set up just inside the gates of every Chautauqua, and women volunteers handed out literature to everyone who passed.

Olesen's audition at Libertyville was successful, and she began an association with Chautauqua that lasted more than a decade. It was a fortunate association, for it offered a platform for her oratorical abilities, made her a well-known figure throughout the South and Midwest, and provided an ideal springboard to politics. Through Chautauqua, she became a friend of William Jennings Bryan, who promoted both her lecturing and her political career.[15]

Her big chance came in January, 1920, after she had spent a full season on the circuit. She was asked to speak in Washington, D.C., at the Jackson Day banquet of the Democratic party, the first woman ever invited to do so. She chose to talk about the party's "ideals." Speaking both as a Democrat and as a woman of her times, she told the assembled guests: "The campaign of the democratic party in 1920 is not merely a political campaign; it is a crusade on behalf of the progressive forces of American life." She assured her audience that "the women of America will never forget that this Democratic Administration, true to its high ideals, threw around the army camps every precaution for clean living for the soldier, and they will never forget that intoxicating drinks were banished from American warships."[16]

The words might not bring today's Democrats cheering to their feet but on this occasion, her first before a national audience, Anna proved that she had that quality politicans still prize — charisma. Although she was a small woman, not quite five feet tall, her impact was considerable. Journalist Mark Sullivan wrote: "probably Mrs. Olsen [*sic*] left a more vivid recollection than any other [speaker]. . . . vitality, magnetism, charm — whatever you choose to call it, radiated from her small form so richly and strongly you could almost see the rays darting out over the audience." On a later occasion a reporter from the *Chicago Evening American* was similarly captivated: "I saw in the lines of her face a great purpose. Her clear, bluish-gray eyes looked right into you — unafraid."[17]

Olesen's Jackson Day speech gave her a national reputation and a rapid series of events consolidated her position as a prominent Democrat. In February the *grande dame* of the suffrage movement, Carrie C. Catt, invited her to speak at a banquet of the National Woman Suffrage Association in Chicago. A few months later she was elected a delegate to the national Democratic convention by the state party, and on June 12, 1920, the *Minneapolis Journal* printed her picture on page one. "Minnesota Woman Planned as Candidate for Vicepresidency," the caption prematurely announced.

Among the major issues facing national Democrats who met in San Francisco that summer of 1920 was one that proved troublesome for Anna as well as for many other Democrats — Prohibition. In 1920 the national Democratic party was the home of fundamentalist Bryanites as well as of urban "wets" who advocated either modification or total repeal of the Volstead Act passed in 1919. In San Francisco Olesen was a floor manager for the campaign of William G. McAdoo, a supporter of Prohibition and Woodrow Wilson's son-in-law. Anna also supported a plank endorsing Prohibition and, after being introduced to the convention by Bryan, spoke in its favor: "I come before the convention to speak in the name of the motherhood of America," she said. "The great fight is on between the home and the liquor traffic. . . . I thank the Democratic Party, for it was the Democratic Party that brought about the prohibition amendment . . ." She went on to warn the delegates of the dangers in passing a wet plank: "the women of the land will never support a wet party. You are not facing guns in this battle but you may be facing the anger of the folks at home unless you do your duty and adopt a dry platform."[18]

Her warning was unavailing. After forty-four ballots, the convention nominated the anti-Prohibition candidate, James M. Cox. "They have drowned our party in the beer keg!" Anna Olesen lamented. She proved her party loyalty, however, by announcing that she would support Cox and his running mate, Franklin D. Roosevelt. She assumed that the fall campaign would focus on the issue of ratifying the League of Nations, and she expressed the hope that the Democrats would not "court wet support."[19]

Until 1920 Anna Olesen had been spared any public criticism of her activities. Back in Cloquet, of course, there had been rumors among her neighbors that she neglected her child and was a bad housekeeper. Accusations of this sort were not at all unusual for a woman who sought a life outside the home. Now, however, Anna's compromise with the wets brought sharp and widespread criticism. Mrs. Wenonah Stevens Abbott, head of the Democratic women's committee of Hennepin County, announced that Mrs. Olesen had "killed herself politically" at the convention by voting with the drys on national questions and with the wets on state questions. Others accused her of falling in with the "wrong element" of the Democratic party, "namely the 'wets.'" Olesen denied the attacks and went ahead with her plan to campaign for the national ticket.[20]

In August, 1920 — the month that the Nineteenth Amendment granting the vote to women was ratified — Anna was asked to assist Roosevelt's vice-presidential campaign, but she was committed to three weeks of Chautauqua lectures in Ohio and Illinois. By October she was free, and she began her campaign tour with an address to 400 women of the Minnesota Democratic Women's Club. She supported the League of Nations as "one thing that has come out of the conscience of the world to stop wars." In November the Democratic presidential candidate was overwhelmingly defeated, and Republican Warren G. Harding took office, calling for a return to "normalcy."[21]

Progressivism was moribund in the nation and in Minnesota. From 1900 to 1918 both Republican and Democratic politicians in the state had given at least lip service to its programs. But in the conservative reaction after World War I, various disaffected groups seeking political power — grain farmers, trade unionists, German-Americans alienated by the wartime loyalty hysteria, left-wing progressives — could find a home in neither major party. By 1922 the dissidents had formed the coalition Farmer-Labor party, which ranked behind the Republicans as the second largest party in Minnesota. Despite Anna Olesen's progressive stand on many issues, she remained faithful to the Democrats, at least on the national level. In the 1930s she supported the administration of Farmer-Labor Governor Floyd B. Olson, whom she greatly admired, claiming that knowledge of his private telephone number was her most "precious possession."[22]

In March, 1922, the Farmer-Labor and Democratic parties held their conventions in Minneapolis at the same time, and not by accident. A committee from the Democratic party proposed that the Farmer-Laborites endorse a Democratic nominee for governor, while the Democrats in turn would support a Farmer-Labor candidate for senator. The Farmer-Laborites, confident of their strength, resisted this *quid pro quo* and nominated Henrik Shipstead for United States senator and Magnus Johnson for governor. Across the river in St. Paul, the Republicans endorsed the incumbent senator, Frank B. Kellogg, and the incumbent governor, Jacob A. O. Preus.[23]

The Democrats, spurned by the Farmer-Labor party, went on with their convention and the selection of a candidate for the Senate race. Sigmund U. Bergh of the *New York Times*, claiming "in-

side information," wrote one account of what happened: "The
story goes that the inner circle of Minnesota Democrats planned a
series of courtesy endorsements — the nominees in due time to
decline with thanks." The first nominee, former Democratic governor John Lind, "gracefully refused because of his age." A second nominee, state representative James A. Carley of Plainview
also "played his role and declined. Then an enthusiast outside the
circle thought it would be fitting to offer the senatorial nomination
to the Minnesota woman member of the Democratic National
Committee [*Anna Dickie Olesen*]. 'You never know where light-
ning is going to strike,' she said, and promptly accepted." [24]

Olesen's daughter Mary recalled the sequence of events somewhat differently. According to her account, Anna wanted the
nomination and indicated she would try for it. Her decision to do
so came about as the result of a congressional debate, which she
followed with keen interest, over the seating of Michigan Senator
Truman H. Newberry, who had been charged with violations of
the election laws. Senator Kellogg voted to seat Newberry, and
Anna gave this vote as her reason for seeking the nomination and
the opportunity to run against him. The seating of Newberry, she
declared, was "inimical to the perpetuity of free government," and
she made vigorous use of it as a campaign issue.[25]

Still another version of Olesen's selection as the party's nominee appeared in a letter to Olesen from a "Minneapolis Republican" who claimed that her nomination had been manipulated
by friends of Senator Kellogg for the purpose of displacing the
men who were candidates for the position. Olesen promptly sent
the letter to the state attorney general for investigation of the
charges, but he refused to act on it, claiming the letter must have
been written as a practical joke. Z. H. Austin, a Minneapolis
Democrat, finally owned up to writing the letter, expressing surprise that Olesen had taken it seriously. "She doesn't know how to
play the game," he said smugly.[26]

Austin was mistaken. Anna demonstrated that she knew very
well how to "play the game" in the ensuing campaign, which a
recent historian has characterized as "brilliant" and "highly professional." It was certainly determined and hard-hitting. Olesen
crisscrossed the state, speaking to as many as six audiences a day
and repeatedly attacking her Republican opponent, particularly on
his vote to seat Senator Newberry. In Washington Senator Kellogg,
asked why he did not return to Minnesota to campaign, reportedly

answered, "I've got some Swede woman running against me."
"Senator Kellogg," replied the questioner, "that's no Swede
woman, that is a Welsh woman and the devil rides her tongue.
You'd better go back to Minnesota."[27]

Accompanied by her daughter Mary, Anna toured the state in a
Ford sedan given to her by friends in Cloquet. After each talk, she
passed the hat for contributions. Her hotel bills were negligible
because she stayed with friends; altogether she spent only about
$500 on the primary campaign. Her brother Owen, who drove her
about the state, recalled a day when they began campaigning in
the Red River Valley and worked south. The candidate made
twelve speeches that day. Sometimes her audience was hostile,
but she merely pushed up her sleeves, began to talk rapidly without any notes, and soon had her listeners in the palm of her hand.
In the primary election on June 19 she won easily over her two
opponents, gaining 28,745 votes to Thomas J. Meighen's 19,941
and Homer Morris' 11,596.[28]

She was astute in the way she handled the novelty of being a
woman in politics. "I ask no consideration because I am a woman," she would tell her audiences. "I also ask that no one
close his mind against me because I am a woman." She did not,
however, contend that her gender was a matter of indifference.
"Since I am a woman," she explained, "I will admit that I am
heartily interested in everything that pertains to women and children, and thus my heart interests are there." But she also made it
clear that her concern for women and children went far beyond
the hearth. Not all women were in the home, she reminded her
listeners; nine million of them were in the work force as doctors,
nurses, stenographers, and factory laborers — yet there was not
one woman in the United States Senate to look out for their interests.[29]

"Truly understood," she declared in Duluth, "the home instinct
is the great dominant trait of woman's life," but the place of
women had now expanded and they carried their "instinct" into
every area of society. Her words must have been welcome to voters
who for years had listened to the propaganda of the antisuffragists,
warning that the home would be destroyed, babes left motherless,
and dinners uncooked if women entered public life or even cast
their ballots. Welcome too were the Democratic candidate's words
about the equality of the sexes. Where did she find endorsement of
equality? In the Bible, not in the texts of the feminists. "When I

am trying to get a correct idea about the modern women [*sic*], I read from the second chapter of Genesis," she confided. " 'It is not good that man should be alone; I will get him a helpmate.'" Now, at last, she declared, woman again stood as she had on the first day of Creation — free and equal with man.[30]

Although Olesen took pride in being a pioneer woman in politics, and sometimes tried to tell her audiences that there were important women's issues, she did not concentrate her efforts on feminist concerns. Explaining her position on broader issues, she said: "The Minnesota Democratic platform, on which I stand, is almost identical with the Progressive Republican platforms of States that have nominated candidates against present conservatives. Instead of a millionaire bloc in Congress," she continued, "we advocate a people's bloc. We stand for equal rights for all and special privileges for none. We want a lower tariff in order that the farmers of Minnesota may find a market for their product in Europe. We ask that the Esch-Cummins bill should be repealed and that the policy of subsidizing great corporate interests should stop." She opposed a sales tax, favored increased veterans' benefits, and stood against the leasing of public oil lands to "private monopolies."[31]

If there was a weakness in Olesen's campaign, it was her over-attention to national issues. In her opening speech at Crookston in September she attacked the Harding administration's foreign policy initiatives. Referring to Kellogg as the "attorney of the trust," she again assailed his vote on the seating of Senator Newberry. She pledged to support the social welfare program of the League of Women Voters and the "cause of working men and women." She promised to work for a federal child labor law. All these were worthy matters, but what concerned Minnesotans most that summer was the depressed state of agriculture. The Farmer-Labor candidates spoke to that concern and hotly criticized *state* legislative issues.[32]

Perhaps it would have been impossible for her to concentrate on local issues. In some ways she was automatically a national figure. The national press, attracted by the fact that she was the first woman candidate for the Senate to be endorsed by a major party, gave her, the state, the campaign, and the election considerable attention. "I do my own housework," she reassured the *New York Times* irrelevantly. "I think a woman can attend to her home duties and still participate in club activities or politics, measuring the extent of her participation by the time it can legitimately claim from her household duties." It is unlikely that she had forgotten her maid, but no other answer was politic for a woman of her generation.[33]

Anna's name became a matter of some controversy, and this too the *New York Times* seemed to find important. Her opponents charged that she had lost her citizenship when she married Danish-born Peter Olesen and asserted that, though she regained it when he was naturalized, she had not been a citizen long enough to meet the qualifications for senator. In fact, Peter Olesen had received his citizenship before marrying. Other opponents complained that by filing for office as "Mrs. Peter Olesen," rather than "Mrs. Anna Dickie Olesen," she was trying to run as a Scandinavian. It was a moot point, since no law stipulated which name was proper, but her husband insisted that she be referred to as Anna Dickie Olesen.[34]

The national press coverage was generally favorable. "She is a vivacious, black-haired, spirited little woman with the gift of rapid articulation," said one reporter. Most observers agreed that as a woman she would bring a freshness to the Senate but that her chances of winning the race against Kellogg were slim indeed. Noting that Olesen had declared that she was born a Democrat and was an admirer of William Jennings Bryan, the *Philadelphia Inquirer* commented, "Whether the unfortunate nominee can overcome these two handicaps is too much for a mere man to say." While acknowledging that she would have to contend with the prejudice against the election of women to public office, the *New York Globe* concluded: "Mrs. Olesen will probably not be elected, but her candidacy is a wholesome indication of the revival of liberal sentiment and of the growing acceptance of woman [*sic*] in politics."[35]

The *Ladies' Home Journal*, on the other hand, was not quite sure how to view a woman as a candidate. The magazine took pains to assure its readers that women would not dirty their skirts by becoming involved in party politics. Women's political loyalties would transcend the self-interest of the respective parties and they would vote for the candidate who would best serve the "welfare of the republic." The *New York Times* editorialized that women would eventually enter the Senate but doubted that Mrs.

Olesen would be the first. Senator Kellogg's seat was judged to be quite safe. The *Times* was correct in its first conclusion, wrong in its second.[36]

On election day, November 7, the candidate and her family planned to be in Minneapolis for the returns, but they had driven only twenty miles from Cloquet in a heavy rain when Anna insisted they turn back. At home again, she began to clean her kitchen cupboards, working until early in the morning. When she heard the election results, she went to bed and slept for several days. Farmer-Labor candidate Henrik Shipstead had swept the field, receiving 325,372 votes to Kellogg's 241,833. Anna Dickie Olesen ran third with 123,624 votes but she outpolled her party's gubernatorial candidate, Edward Indrehus, by a count of 43,721.[37]

The 1922 Minnesota senatorial election was an important one in the state's political history, for it established the Farmer-Laborites as a major party in the state, a position they held until the beginning of World War II. The effect of Olesen's candidacy on the outcome is not clear. On first consideration it would appear that her candidacy hurt Shipstead, since they both ran on progressive platforms. Kellogg evidently thought her candidacy to his advantage, for he expressed pleasure at the three-way race. His failure to campaign vigorously, however, did not reflect overconfidence but rather his general distaste for political campaigning. In August the *Minnesota Union Advocate*, official newspaper of the Minnesota State Federation of Labor and a supporter of Shipstead, voiced its fear that Anna would attract the votes of liberals. By October, however, the paper thought that Kellogg might be in trouble because of her. "Mrs. Oleson [*sic*] is a remarkable orator and has a magnetic personality, both of which are certain to attract voters to her." Anna herself claimed credit for helping to defeat Kellogg, and some years later noted ironically that she had "made" him the ambassador to the Court of St. James.[38]

The issue of Anna's sex and its effect on the campaign is also hard to measure. She described her defeat as being due to the "Republican newspaper propaganda, usually contained in this sentence: 'She is a nice little woman, but she cannot win.'" The *Union Advocate* suggested that the time had not come when a majority of voters would support a woman candidate for state-wide office. In 1922 the voters of Minnesota had, however, elected four women to the state legislature: Myrtle A. Cain, Mabeth Hurd Paige, Hannah J. Kempfer, and Sue Dickey Hough.[39]

The *New York Times*, commenting on the defeat of several women candidates, pointed out the paradoxical position they faced when they ran for office: "They promptly discover on the part of most politicians and of many if not most men voters a nearly complete lack of that special consideration which is commonly supposed and usually admitted to be their due, merely because they are women. Instead of deriving, in this particular activity, an advantage from their sex . . . they encounter as women an actual antagonism, sometimes veiled and sometimes not, and this is especially true if they are seeking an office with a salary big enough to make it seem highly desirable to masculine candidates." Journalist Chester H. Rowell perhaps summed it up accurately: "The fact that she was a woman probably lost her at least as many votes as it gained."[40]

Almost immediately after the election, Olesen was back on the lecture platform. Just as Chautauqua had once aided her political career, the reverse was now true: her Senate race as the candidate of a major political party and her excellent political connections helped her bookings. On the Chautauqua circuit her most popular address was "The Larger Patriotism," an appeal to 100 per cent Americanism, but she added several other topics as well. "Ingots from the Crucible" consisted of oratorical reflections upon the poetry inspired by World War I ("the finest human emotions are often the product of adversity"). She also spoke on "Women and Progress" — to "convey a sense of the needs and place of women in the new social order" — and "The New Social Consciousness," a "philosophical analysis of the many social problems of the day, presenting a constructive program based on the Great Master."[41]

Bolder than she had dared to be in her senatorial campaign, Olesen now predicted that as more and more women entered politics, offices, and factories there would need to be day-care centers and nurseries. She anticipated a time when the life span of Americans would increase to the point where taxation would be necessary to provide pensions for the elderly. Such pensions, she explained, would benefit the economy because they would add to the purchasing power of a large segment of the population.[42]

In 1923 Peter Olesen moved with his family to Northfield, where he became registrar of Carleton College and a teacher of German. Throughout the 1920s his wife continued to lecture and to campaign for Democratic candidates. She took little part in the life of the college where her husband taught. "You see," she told her daughter, "I can't go mincing around in Northfield as papa's wife, taking little dabs to the faculty women's clubs." She did accompany Peter on trips to Canada, Mexico, and Europe. Their stay on the Continent in 1928 was extended while Peter earned credentials in German from the University of Heidelberg.

Because of her lecture fees, Anna now had a measure of economic independence; she guarded that independence fiercely and always kept her money separate from that of her husband. At last she was able to gratify her desire for fine things: she bought their house and its furnishings; Peter paid for the expense of running it.

In 1932 Anna flirted briefly with the idea of running for office as congressman-at-large. She received the endorsement of the Democratic county chairmen but then abruptly withdrew her name, explaining that family duties prevented her from conducting the campaign that would be necessary.[43]

As the 1932 national Democratic convention approached, the state party was split over which presidential candidate to support. Olesen, again a delegate-at-large, aligned herself with the faction behind Franklin Roosevelt. At the convention she was asked to second Roosevelt's nomination, but when most of the seconding speeches were eliminated to save time, she delivered instead a speech seconding the nomination of John N. Garner for vice-president. She was once more in her element: "We of the North Star state," she declaimed, "salute you of the Lone Star state and thank you for giving us John N. Garner." After the convention she spent three months campaigning for the Democratic ticket.[44]

The lean years for the Democratic party faithful ended with Roosevelt's election in November, 1932, and Anna Olesen expected to be rewarded for her efforts on behalf of the Roosevelt-Garner ticket. Indeed she needed a job, for Tent Chautauqua was dead, its crowds lured away by automobiles, motion pictures, and, most accessible of all, radios. The Great Depression, which curtailed everyone's entertainment dollars, had delivered the mortal blow.[45] As politicians began to learn how to use a new medium of communication, the Chautauqua-style oratory of William Jennings Bryan was succeeded by the radio broadcast "fireside chats" of Franklin Roosevelt. Olesen, joining the army of political job-seekers, arrived in Washington in the summer of 1933, carrying thank-you notes from grateful Democrats she had helped. She finally got in to see James A. Farley, patronage boss of the party. In his hot, humid office, she cooled herself with the faint breeze from her sheaf of thank-you's. "Mr. Farley," she declared, "I have not come here to fan myself with this deck, but to deal."

Anna Dickie Olesen, onetime Senate candidate, ten-year campaigner, and party stalwart, was named postmistress of Northfield. The job was not quite what she had in mind, but she took it. Then in January, 1934, President Roosevelt appointed her as state director of the National Emergency Council (NEC), a federal division established to co-ordinate the programs of various New Deal agencies. The only woman to be named a state director, she unhesitatingly resigned her job as Northfield's postmistress.[46]

The new appointee announced that her job was to sell the Roosevelt program to Minnesota, and one state newspaper declared that her appointment was "proof that oratory of real quality still counts." In fact, however, there were few occasions for salesmanship or oratory in the post. Olesen had become a bureaucrat.

Her job, regarded as the plum of federal appointments in the state, was nevertheless an arduous one. To her office fell the task of co-ordinating the efforts of dozens of New Deal agencies in Minnesota. "We are all one big family," she announced hopefully in March, 1935, at a meeting of agency representatives, "the family of the Federal Government. When we come together here we are strengthened." That was the closest she came in the meetings to talking about the "expanding home," as she had done in her 1922 Senate campaign, or about the need for day-care centers or nurseries for the children of working women, as she had on the Chautauqua circuit.[47]

Perhaps, however, she still yearned for the hustings. When Ruth Bryan Owen Rohde, the daughter of William Jennings Bryan and a campaigner for the national party in 1936, broke her leg, Olesen resigned from the NEC to complete Mrs. Rohde's speaking tour. She had not lost her touch. One of her fans wrote to James Farley after her appearance in Pittsburg, Kansas: "Mrs. Olson [*sic*] made a brief speech here today. It is the best speech I have listened to since the days of W. J. Bryan. She connects the whole depression up with the Landon-Hamilton crowd where it belongs. She did it effectively and held her audience spellbound. . . . If I were president and knowing what I do about Mrs. Olson's work, I would certainly appoint her minister to some foreign country or anything else that she would desire."[48]

When the campaign was over, Anna Dickie Olesen was reappointed director of the NEC in Minnesota, although after 1936 the agency's status was never quite clear. In 1937 Roosevelt issued an order to close the office but then rescinded it. The NEC became the Office of Government Reports in August, 1939, and Olesen continued as its director. Whatever the ambiguities of her post, she oversaw the gathering of a great deal of useful information. In 1937 the NEC issued a directory of federal agencies and their departments in Minnesota. The following year, it provided a county-by-county report on the expenditures of each New Deal program in the state between 1933 and 1938. "America is on the way to better things," Olesen had said early in her New Deal career, and she continued to work to make the promise come true.[49]

Late in the 1930s Governor Elmer A. Benson appointed her to the Minnesota State Planning Board, and in 1939 Governor Harold E. Stassen named her to the Minnesota Resources Committee. Not until 1942, when the position of state director of the Office of Government Reports was abolished, did Olesen retire to private life at the age of fifty-seven. Of the original forty-eight state directors who had begun their work with the NEC in 1934, only she and Robert Cummins of North Dakota were still holding office eight years later.[50]

The following thirty years were to bring marked changes in Anna's personal life. Peter Olesen left Carleton in 1949 and took a position teaching German at Mercer College in Macon, Georgia. The Olesens lived there until his retirement from Mercer; then they returned to Northfield. Peter died in 1960 after a long illness. A year later Anna married Chester A. Burge, some nineteen years her junior, whom she and Peter had met in Macon. Burge was a wealthy, controversial, and somewhat mysterious man. Their life together was brief. In October, 1963, he died from burns after an explosion in their residence in Palm Beach, Florida, while his wife was in Northfield closing up her house for the winter.

Serenity never crowned her life. With reflection and repose came also disillusionment and disappointment. She read widely, and passages which had special meaning for her she copied and kept. From Mauriac: "To few of us is granted to know more than once that we are loved." From Alexander von Humboldt's *Personal Narrative of Travels:* "Continually haunted by fear of not executing the designs of tomorrow, we live in perpetual uneasiness." From *Son of Oscar Wilde* by W. W. Ward: "What is the use of the open door to the bird so long caged, that its power of flight is gone." From Tolstoy: "Hasty movements indicate mental restiveness. A lax body in a woman represents a soul lost in the duties of daily life." And finally, this unidentified quotation, singled out by Anna, a woman who had longed for fine things and had filled her home in Northfield with antiques from the estate of Episcopal Bishop Henry B. Whipple and furniture and *objets d'art* reputed to be from the castle of the mad King Ludwig of Bavaria:

> This I do, being mad;
> Gather baubles about me,
> Sit in a circle of toys, and all the time
> Death beating the door in.

> White jade and an orange pitcher,
> Hindu idol, Chinese God.
> Maybe next year, when I'm richer
> Carved beads and a lotus pod . . .
> And all this time
> Death beating the door in.[51]

Well along in her middle years, Anna had been converted to Catholicism, and her new religion brought her some solace. Reflection on her public life did not. She told her daughter, "Every horse has been shot out from under me."

Part of her disappointment may have come from the failure of her candidacy to open the floodgates for women in politics. The idea of paving the way for other women had always been important to her, but as the historian of Minnesota Progressivism has pointed out, her campaign and the election of four women to the Minnesota House of Representatives "failed to establish a trend in the state. . . . the highest elective offices remained a male monopoly in Minnesota as elsewhere."[52]

Anna Dickie Olesen's place in Minnesota history is secure, although smaller than she once hoped it would be. Her significance is perhaps found not in any unique contribution she made as a woman, but rather in the similarity of her career to those of many male politicians who preceded and followed her. Like them, she was moved to a career in politics by a combination of motives: a desire to serve the public good and to achieve power and status,

an enjoyment of the intricacies of the political game, and a relish
for the spotlight. Like any number of male politicians before and
since, she boarded that "old train" bound from the farms and hamlets to the big cities and centers of power, had her day of glory,
and then returned, somewhat disillusioned, to relative obscurity.

After Chester Burge's death, Olesen remained in Northfield,
where she died on May 21, 1971, at the age of eighty-six. She was
buried beside Peter Olesen in the Sakatah Cemetery in Waterville. "There will be another Anna Dickie," an old Chautauqua
friend had written her prophetically years before, " — a throwback
to you. Only this one will have a better chance. You did the
pioneer work and now the place for women has been better established. You started too early in the game . . . but you were the
first woman who had the courage to take up the banner and what a
credit you were with your youth, your God-given talent, your tireless efforts, and your great love of humanity."[53]

14. Women in the Minnesota Legislature

By Arvonne S. Fraser and Sue E. Holbert

IN 1955 Sally Luther went to a session of the Minnesota legislature with her apron on. In her rush to get to the Capitol, Mrs. Luther, who for ten years represented District 30 in Minneapolis, had simply forgotten to remove it after preparing breakfast for her husband and children. "Mrs. Sally Luther . . . usually makes the transition from housewife and mother to lawmaker without trouble," commented the *St. Paul Pioneer Press* of January 14.

Since 1922, when women first became eligible for election to the Minnesota legislature, a total of thirty-two have combined service there with traditional feminine roles. They constitute about 2¼ per cent of the approximately 1,445 individuals who have served as state senators or representatives thus far in Minnesota's history. Twenty-nine of the thirty-two women have been elected to the Minnesota House of Representatives; only three have reached the Minnesota Senate — Laura E. Naplin from 1927 to 1933, Nancy Brataas elected in 1975, and Emily Anne Staples elected in 1976.[1]

The thirty-two legislators have been unevenly distributed over the intervening decades. Seven were elected in the 1920s, four of them in 1922. Five of these women continued to serve into the 1930s, and two of them — Mabeth Hurd Paige and Hannah J. Kempfer — continued into the 1940s. But only one new feminine face joined them on the floor of the House in the 1930s (that of Bertha Lee Smith Hansen), and none were added in the 1940s. Three women won election in the 1950s, six in the 1960s, and fifteen thus far in the 1970s.

Enthusiasm engendered by the attainment of suffrage in 1920, followed by the success of women in winning four seats in the House in 1922, may account for the numbers elected in that decade. Attention to patriotic volunteer duties or possibly the entry of public-spirited women into the work force instead of politics during World War II may account for the dearth in the 1940s — a decade that saw only Hannah Kempfer and Mabeth Paige still in office. The 1950s were generally characterized, as far as women were concerned, by a resurgence of domesticity and motherhood following World War II. However, many women were active in the community and in party affairs during this period, and each session of the legislature saw scores of League of Women Voters' lobbyists in the halls of the Capitol.[2]

The appearance in the 1960s of six women elected to the House for the first time is not easily explained. The 1962 reapportionment of the legislature and League of Women Voters' activity concerning it may have generated interest and provided valuable experience and knowledge. Helen E. McMillan of Austin, a state league president, elected to the legislature in 1962, is a clear example. Esther Fox Fieldman, Alpha M. Smaby, and Virginia K. Torgerson were also members of the organization. All six were active in their political parties.[3]

The decade of the 1970s saw far more women serving in the legislature than any preceding ten-year period. Although half were avowed feminists, few ran on "women's issues." Almost all generally supported equality of opportunity and often voted with women's rights advocates. In any case, it seems probable that renewed interest in women's rights, roles, and responsibilities made seeking and winning public office more practical and more acceptable in the 1970s than it was at some times in the past. According to the Women's Education Fund, women comprised 51 per cent of the nation's population in 1976 and held 9.1 per cent of the seats in state legislatures. They increased their representation by 10.7 per cent in the 1976 election. Minnesota, with its gain of five legislators, tied for third place among the states in the greatest percentage increase.[4]

While the women legislators have been unevenly distributed in time, they have been concentrated both geographically and by political affiliation. Although the Minnesota legislature was officially nonpartisan from 1913 until the session of 1975, all the women except one — Hannah Kempfer — have associated themselves with a political party. Twenty-three were affiliated with the Democratic-Farmer-Labor (DFL) party or its predecessor, the Farmer-Labor party; eight were Republicans.[5]

Up to 1955 virtually all the women legislators represented either Hennepin County (which includes Minneapolis) or the northwestern quadrant of the state, which was the cradle of the Nonpartisan League and a center of Farmer-Labor party activity. One Minneapolis district (old 30, now the central part of District 56) has been represented by a woman for thirty-four of the fifty-four years since women first became eligible to hold legislative office. Mabeth Paige served that district from 1922 to 1944 and Sally Luther from 1950 to 1962. Three women have represented what are generally termed working-people's districts in Minneapolis. Myrtle A. Cain was elected in 1922 from District 28 (now parts of Districts 54 and 55) in northeast Minneapolis with the endorsement of the Working People's Nonpartisan Political League, and Alpha M. Smaby and Phyllis A. Kahn were later elected from the neighboring district (old 29, then 41, and now 57A). Alpha Smaby had deep roots in the Minnesota Scandinavian community as well as in the co-operative movement and the League of Women Voters, while Phyllis Kahn, a physical scientist, moved to the southeast Minneapolis area near the University of Minnesota campus with her husband, then a graduate student. She entered the House in 1973 by way of the new feminist movement of the 1960s as a result of her experience in the Minnesota Women's Political Caucus.

All of Hennepin County's women legislators had lived in the city until the election of 1972. From 1972 to 1977 the suburban areas have sent six women to the House and one to the Senate. Two have been Republicans — Mary M. Forsythe from Edina and Ernee M. McArthur from Brooklyn Center. Four have been DFLers: Joan Anderson Growe, who was elected to the legislature in 1972 from the suburban Lake Minnetonka area; Shirley A. Hokanson from Richfield; Linda J. Scheid from Brooklyn Park; and Senator Emily Staples from Plymouth.

In northwestern Minnesota, District 65 (now partly in Districts 1 and 2), then composed of Red Lake, Pennington, and Clearwater counties, has been represented in the Senate by Laura E. Naplin of Thief River Falls and in the House by Coya G. Knutson of Oklee. In keeping with the district's ethnic and economic composition, both were Scandinavian and had farm backgrounds early in life. Naplin belonged to the Farmer-Labor party with its tradition of redressing economic conditions through political activity. Knutson was a member of the successor DFL party.

Beginning in 1955 four women were elected from the south-eastern corner of the state, traditionally a Republican stronghold. The first of them, Joyce I. Lund, a DFLer from Wabasha, was followed in 1962 by Virginia K. Torgerson, a Winona Republican and the second woman lawyer to serve (Mabeth Paige was the first), and by Helen McMillan of Austin (DFL), state president of the League of Women Voters. In 1975 Nancy Brataas of Rochester became the first woman to represent that southeastern city in the legislature. St. Paul elected Margaret Mary (Peggy) Byrne in 1974, and the Duluth area sent two women — Arlene I. L. Lehto and Mary C. Murphy — to the legislature in 1976.

Only two of the thirty-two women have been widows of male legislators. Naplin was elected in 1927 when her husband, Oscar A., the incumbent senator, suffered a stroke on the opening day of the session and a special election was called after his death. Donna Jean Christianson ran for and won the unexpired House term of her husband, Marvin E., who died during the 1969 session. Naplin went on to a career in the Minnesota Senate, while Christianson retired when the term expired.

What kind of people were (and are) Minnesota's women legislators? What have been their ideas on women's role in government and other issues? Although a comprehensive study of all thirty-two is not possible here, the following nine sketches suggest the diversity of backgrounds, interests, occupations, and political affiliations that characterized members over the years.

"Four Feathered Hats Draw All Eyes as Legislature Convenes. Millinery Creations of Velvet, Ribbons and Plumes Indicate to Curious Throng Where Newly Elected Incumbents Sit in State House," the *Minneapolis Tribune* proclaimed on January 3, 1923, as the session opened with women on the floor for the first time. "It wasn't so much the hats, although they doubtless helped make for the self-assuredness of the wearers," said the newspaper, "but the fact that they were on the heads of the four women legislators — Mrs. James Paige, Mrs. Sue Dickey Hough, Mrs. Hannah Kempfer and Miss Myrtle Cain — the first to sit in the state House, that made the difference."

Three of these history-makers were from Minneapolis: Paige was a prominent civic leader, Hough was a real estate dealer and the descendant of a president, and Cain was a labor leader and Woman's party activist. The fourth, from Otter Tail County, was

Hannah Kempfer

Sue Dickey Hough

Myrtle Cain

Mabeth Hurd Paige

**Senator Laura E. Naplin with
Senator Frank Putnam**

Sally Luther

Hannah Kempfer, a Norwegian immigrant, farm wife, and schoolteacher. Two were Republicans, one a Farmer-Laborite, and
Kempfer an Independent. Of the four, Paige and Kempfer were
notable for their long tenure. Paige holds the feminine record for
the longest service thus far — twenty-two years; Kempfer is next
with eighteen years.

MABETH HURD PAIGE'S principal concerns throughout her
life revolved around people, with a special emphasis on women's
place in the scheme of things. For her time, she was an unconven-
tionally conventional suffragist who early recognized discrimination against women in politics and public life and determined to
do something about it. Born in Newburyport, Massachusetts, in
1870, Mabeth grew up in a closely knit family with a sickly
mother, an intellectual and compassionate father, and many relatives living nearby. Her father, a practicing physician, frequently
took Mabeth with him when he went to call on patients. Together
they spent hours discussing subjects ranging from science to religion to politics.[6]

After attending grammar school in Newburyport, Mabeth went
on to the local high school. Although she graduated, many of her
friends gave up classes for long hours of work in the mills. Deciding against college, she attended Massachusetts Art School in Boston. She then spent a year in Lincoln, Nebraska, taking care of her
grandmother and attending the university. During her stay in Lincoln she observed the hard life of German immigrant women.
Babies, not education, seemed to be woman's lot, she noted, and
she became dubious of marriage for herself.

In 1891 she accepted a position teaching art in the public
schools of Minneapolis. There she met James Paige, a University
of Minnesota law professor, and almost reluctantly drifted into
marriage in June, 1895. Despite her apprehensions, she accepted
Paige's conditions that she regard his interests as paramount and
that she study law "and so insure our being completely congenial." Her biographer commented that "It wasn't much fun at
home" while Mabeth was growing up with her ailing mother and
her busy father. The same proved to be true of her own married
life, for her first Minneapolis house was run tyrannically by
Paige's sister, and mealtimes were marred by constant arguments
between James and his brother, Howe. The strange, moderately
well-to-do family into which Mabeth was brought to live as a new

bride also included an invalid mother and a missionary-preacher father who appeared only occasionally. In Minneapolis, as she had in Newburyport, Mabeth turned to the outside world.

As she had promised, the twenty-five-year-old Mrs. Paige entered the University of Minnesota Law School in the fall of 1895. The couple's work there — his as professor, hers as student — helped them escape the uncomfortable home atmosphere. James Paige did not want Mabeth to pursue her law studies to the point of admission to the bar because he thought it unwomanly for her to practice or appear in court. Her father, however, insisted that she should complete her studies. Caught between husband and father, she did finish in 1899, later finding her legal training an immense help in her legislative career.

After seven years of marriage, Mabeth became the mother of a daughter, Elizabeth, whose father resented the time his wife spent with her. Gradually, as the child grew up, her mother's circle of friends widened through Elizabeth's school activities. Mabeth became a charter member of the newly formed Minneapolis Woman's Club and got involved in social service activities in the community. After her marriage, she had joined the Westminster Presbyterian Church to which her husband belonged, although she had been raised a Congregationalist. Through the Presbyterian mission programs, in which both she and James were active, Mabeth organized a young women's group and spent many hours in the Minneapolis Public Library studying all the material available on the working conditions of women and children. Constantly reading, observing politics, moving out into the community through her own interests, her husband's, and her daughter's, Mabeth Paige satisfied her need for civic and intellectual activity, but she always stayed strictly within the upper middle-class establishment.

In 1914 Mabeth was asked to become president of the Women's Christian Association in Minneapolis, an organization that ran a number of boarding and rooming houses for women. She accepted and put her administrative talents to work. The Mabeth Hurd Paige Residence Hall at Fourth Avenue and Seventh Street in Minneapolis is testimony to her efforts. From the Women's Christian Association, her activities expanded to encompass other organizations designed to safeguard children and young working women as well as groups associated with the growing movement to obtain suffrage for women. She was also one of the founders of the Minneapolis chapter of the Urban League and a board member of that organization for twenty-five years. While working with the Women's Christian Association, she advocated a separate club for "colored girls." Later she gave up the idea and instead raised money for the Phyllis Wheatley Settlement House which still serves the black community of north Minneapolis. Before and during World War I, her organizational talents, energy, interest in and ability to work with people, coupled with her desire to be away from home, gradually made her a distinguished community leader, renowned not only locally but on the national level as well.

Mabeth became active in the movement to obtain the vote for women in 1919. When Canadian suffragist Nellie M. McClung visited Minneapolis that year, Clara H. Ueland, leader of the local suffrage campaign, recruited Paige and put her in charge of arrangements. To make the most of McClung's presence, Paige organized a series of open-air street-corner meetings, using a truck as a novel speaking platform. In 1920, after approval of the Nineteenth Amendment, Paige was elected to the newly formed national board of the League of Women Voters as regional organizational chairman for seven states in the upper Midwest. In 1921 she attended the Pan-American Women's Conference in Washington at the invitation of Carrie Chapman Catt and came home determined to get more women into politics. While speaking about women's unwillingness to run for office, she was asked: What about yourself? After checking with her husband and with Fred B. Snyder, president of the University of Minnesota board of regents, to make sure her political efforts would not interfere with Professor Paige's career, Mabeth became a candidate for the state House of Representatives in January, 1922, filing under the name Mrs. James Paige at her husband's request. She was then fifty-two years of age.

Rebuffed by the regular Republican party organization, Mabeth Hurd Paige, as her name later appeared on the ballot, ran independently. A natural campaigner, and one who enjoyed it, she put to use all her previous community experience. With the help of a woman hotel operator, she personally canvassed much of the downtown hotel area. Social gatherings in family neighborhoods, personal campaigning by the candidate, and the distribution of a final remember-to-vote leaflet by residents of some Women's Christian Association homes in the district were important elements of her effort. James Paige also seemed to enjoy campaigning. He not only designed and put up his wife's campaign signs, he also helped to assemble a prestigious male committee that agreed to work in the Gateway area, then a down-and-out neighborhood near downtown Washington, Nicollet, and Hennepin avenues.

Just before the primary election in June, 1922, Mabeth — always eager to travel — fulfilled a promise to her daughter and went off with her to Europe as planned. A telegram from her husband as she sailed from New York told her that she had run first in the primary. In spite of letters from well-meaning friends who advised her to forget the election and have a good time because she wasn't going to win anyhow, the candidate, her daughter, and her traveling companions sent from Europe hundreds of post cards to constituents. Returning home that fall, she resumed her personal campaigning, won the election in November, and took her seat in the House in January, 1923.

According to her biographer, James Paige urged his wife to serve on the Taxation Committee "because he felt that women should sign up for technical and difficult legislative work and not confine themselves to committees which dealt only with matters concerning children and church and school. . . . But when she discovered that the Welfare Committee was quite looked down upon by the men and that they also took little interest in education, the need of attention to those subjects pulled her into their circle." Paige served on the Public Welfare and the Education committees throughout her twenty-two years in the legislature, chairing the Welfare Committee for six sessions and the Board of Control and State Institutions Committee in her second term. The Public Domain Committee was among her other assignments; Mabeth Paige, who had enjoyed canoeing with her husband in northern Minnesota even when she was in the late stages of pregnancy, fought for conservation interests in opposing power projects, which would have required flooding in the now-famous canoe area of Superior National Forest. She also opposed a proposed Grand Portage highway and represented the Quetico-Superior Council's position favoring federal acquisition of northern forest and lake areas. In 1933 she testified at a hearing of the Canadian-American joint commission on the boundary waters area.

During her long tenure, many of her legislative interests, like

her earlier community service, were "people oriented." She
worked for the abolishment of common law marriages, for old age
pensions, for shorter work days and weeks especially for women
and children, and for a bill to make street selling by minors a
punishable misdemeanor for employers or parents. She made a
sustained effort to establish additional mental or psychopathic
hospitals, as they were then called. Though she authored bills in
many of these areas early in her career, she soon recognized that
lawmaking often takes a long time. For example, it took ten
years — 1923 to 1933 — to pass the street-selling act and twelve
before a fourth psychopathic hospital was authorized at Moose
Lake. In the 1937 session Paige was instrumental in enacting the
Minnesota Uniform Narcotic Drug Act, and in 1941 she tried to
secure legislation permitting Minnesota to utilize federal funds for
housing. She also worked for increased payments for aid to dependent children.

Another long-term effort concerned the regulation of small loan
companies or lenders. In her work with the Women's Christian
Association, Paige had become aware of interest rates ranging
from 120 to 1,000 per cent. Because her first campaign committee
thought this a most unpopular issue, she did not emphasize it in
1922. Once elected, however, she set to work on a law that would
control interest abuses. In 1927, after five years of talking and lobbying, she was appointed to head a legislative interim commission
that studied small loan regulation in other states. Not until 1939,
however, with the help of Governor Harold E. Stassen, did she
succeed in getting her small loan interest bill passed.

In 1944, when Mabeth Paige was in her seventies, she decided
not to seek re-election. Her departure from the legislature, how-
ever, did not mean total retirement. Her community work went
on. She served as a member of the advisory council of the Minnesota Division of Employment and Security, as a member of
Governor Edward J. Thye's Inter-Racial Commission and on the
Minneapolis Charter Commission, as secretary of the Minneapolis
Police Survey Committee, as a member of the State Constitutional
Commission, and as a member of the Committee of Founders for a
Mayo Memorial, which was successful in securing funds to build a
new research center in Rochester. In addition she was active in
the Republican party, helping to create in 1945 the Republican
Workshop, an active educational arm for Republican women.

Woven throughout Mabeth Hurd Paige's career and her long life was a deep interest in women in politics and government. Her early organizing work for the League of Women Voters focused on this theme. During her legislative career, she spoke on women in government at three international women's congresses in Europe in 1923, 1926, and 1929. And she encouraged and helped other women. Her special friend in the legislature was Hannah Kempfer, whom she heard about during the 1922 campaign and looked forward to meeting upon her arrival in the legislature. The two women — Kempfer and Paige — served together for eighteen years, with Paige occasionally helping out financially and with letters of support for Kempfer's campaigns. At the age of eighty, Paige was advising another generation of women. Some six years after she left the legislature, she received a young reporter in her home and gave advice and support for her campaign in the same legislative district Paige had served so long. The young reporter was Sally Luther, who successfully continued the District 30 tradition of women representatives in the 1950s and 1960s. A widow since 1940, when her husband died of a heart attack, Mabeth Hurd Paige died on August 19, 1961, at the age of ninety-one.[7]

HANNAH KEMPFER, Mabeth Paige's special friend, was the outstate member of the quartet elected in 1922. She won re-election eight times. A description of Kempfer sounds almost like a caricature. Born out of wedlock and placed in an orphanage as a toddler, she spent much of her life struggling against hardships and ill health. She was independent, temperate, thrifty, and kind to children, animals, and the helpless. Her letters to constituents, friends and foes alike, were plain-spoken and straightforward, never ingratiating, unkind, or vindictive. Photographs portray a tall, thin, serious, resolute woman.[8]

There are really two stories of Hannah Kempfer. One is the romantic tale of her early life, her difficulties, and her determination, a tale widely publicized both locally and nationally. The other is a record of solid accomplishment in the state legislature, a record also widely acclaimed in her lifetime. Her influence was particularly felt in the areas of natural resources conservation and protection of the rights, health, and safety of children and the handicapped. It seems apparent that the two Kempfer stories are closely related. Her experiences as an illegitimate child, orphan, immigrant, hired girl, teacher, and farm wife were translated into the issues and the legislation for which she fought.

Kempfer was born on shipboard in the North Sea in 1880. Her mother was a stewardess and her father was unidentified. Somehow the child was placed in a foundling home in Stavanger, Norway. Later adopted by a Norwegian couple named Martha and Ole Jensen or Johnson, she was brought at the age of six to the United States and to Adams in Mower County, Minnesota, in 1886. The family did not prosper there, and eventually they resettled near Erhard in Otter Tail County.

From her first years in Minnesota, Hannah did chores on the farm, cooked, hired out, and generally had to be a contributing member of the struggling immigrant family. She managed, however, to attend school until she passed the state examination for teachers. She began to teach shortly before she reached the legally required age of eighteen. From 1898 to 1908 she taught in a country school in Friberg Township near Erhard.[9]

In 1903 Hannah married Charles ("Charlie") Taylor Kempfer and moved in with his Pennsylvania Dutch parents on a farm near the school. To help make ends meet, Hannah continued to teach, sold eggs, and had a fur business, trapping animals and making fur coats. She canned and sold produce; she sewed "waists," dresses, and aprons for friends and neighbors. She raised pigs and turkeys, and she also worked in the nearby country store in exchange for goods.

Childless, Hannah and Charlie nevertheless had a house full of children. They nearly always had an orphan or a child who needed a summer on a farm. And because Charlie's brother August and his family lived in a house attached to the senior Kempfers', August's daughter Margaret (Peggy) was also a daily part of their lives.

Hannah's life began a new phase when, at the age of forty-two, she decided to run for the state legislature. Encouraged by friends and neighbors, she became one of eight candidates for four seats representing District 50 (Otter Tail County). "Her election to the Legislature . . . would be an inspiration to every boy and girl in Minnesota, that in America, no matter on what seas, or under what flag or conditions a child is born, there is a chance and opportunity to make good," her volunteer committee asserted. She stumped the district in a Model T Ford and won handily, coming in second among the four elected.[10]

Although she later moved up from a Model T to a Model A, she ran as an Independent in 1922 and in all her later campaigns. Refusing the endorsement of the Nonpartisan League in her first campaign, she said: "I filed as an independent. I have never been affiliated with any political party and am not willing to be the candidate of any party or group. I would rather stand for the principle of representing all of the people of Otter Tail County and be defeated, than to be elected under circumstances that oblige me to vote according to the dictation of any party or individuals." Throughout her career, she was supported by powerful local Republican leaders such as Elmer E. Adams, businessman, editor of the *Fergus Falls Journal*, member of the House and Senate for a total of nine terms, and a University of Minnesota regent. One biographer wrote: "Her orientation . . . was that of Middle Western agrarian progressivism. If she leaned to any political party, especially in her later years in the legislature, it was to the Republicans. Still she was prepared to back many phases of Gov. Floyd B. Olson's Farmer-Laborite program during the decade of depression [in the 1930s]."

During her nine terms in the House, Kempfer served on all but one of the permanent committees. She was a member of the Game and Fish Committee continuously until her retirement in 1941 and its chairperson in 1927. Kempfer once traced her attachment to wildlife to a childhood friendship with a hen partridge whose young had been shot. The partridge later died in her lap after being attacked by a weasel. "I vowed then . . . I would make an effort to defend my helpless companions of the woods. Though the subject matter has grown in every direction I have continued to fight continuously for the dumb creatures." [11]

Dozens of laws relating to game and fish were enacted during Kempfer's years on the committee. Limits and seasons on fish, fowl, and animals were raised and lowered, opened and closed. Hardly a "dumb creature" escaped the lawmakers' attention. For example, legislation was enacted placing a bounty on wolves and forbidding the transportation of frogs outside the state. In 1925 the Department of Conservation was created, beginning the process of consolidating government functions concerning the state's natural resources now covered by the large and broadly inclusive Department of Natural Resources.

Kempfer's dedication to the cause of conservation drew praise from the American Game Protective Association in 1928, the year after she had chaired the committee. "In women's invasion of the fields of activity heretofore regarded as the peculiar prerogative of the masculine portion of humanity, game conservation is no exception," the association's *Bulletin* commented. "It is said that in the entire history of the state the legislative committee in charge of conservation legislation has never been more capably, sympathetically, or intelligently directed than under the administration of Mrs. Kempfer, whose intimate knowledge of the subject and keen interest in it peculiarly qualified her for the position." [12]

Nevertheless, Kempfer's one term in the chair caused her considerable difficulty, and she declined to serve again in that role. During her stint the 1927 legislature approved a resident fishing license law by a vote of 84 to 26. Under its terms, Minnesotans for the first time had to pay a licensing fee (fifty cents annually) for the privilege of angling. The proceeds were to be used to establish hatcheries, build dams to regulate water levels, and generally provide for fish management. The law was unpopular, however, and it became an issue in the campaign of 1928. Kempfer's constituents "severely criticized" her for supporting it, and she quickly learned that the voters of Otter Tail County were "not very friendly" about this matter. [13]

Kempfer was re-elected in 1928, however, coming in fourth (her rank among the eight candidates in six of the ten general elections in which she was a candidate) with a margin of 189 over the next contender. Two years later she lost her bid by a wider margin in a close race; six of the candidates polled votes totaling more than 6,000 while she received 5,411 to come in seventh. Her defeat is not readily explained, but her niece attributed it to lingering rancor over the fishing license law. She regained her seat in 1932. [14]

Although Kempfer's influence was perhaps strongest in the conservation area, she was also active in the fields of health and welfare. The rights of illegitimate children received her special attention — another instance of her personal involvement in the legislation she espoused. In 1923 she joined the other three women in the House in introducing bills to extend to children born out of wedlock the same rights as children of married parents in cases where the paternity of the child could be established in court. In regard to a bill allowing such children to bear the father's surname, Kempfer said in her inimitable way that men who opposed the measure were the "Tom-cats of the species." [15] The bills, although passed by the House, did not become law until 1927.

Kempfer also spent a great deal of time looking into alleged cases of neglect or abuse of the insane, retarded, epileptic, blind, deaf, delinquent, criminal, tubercular, poor, and crippled in the many state institutions, often visiting the institution in question. As a former teacher, she introduced in 1935 a successful bill requiring tuberculin (Mantoux) tests of school employees and X rays of positive reactors. Her ardent championship of the bill (which had little opposition) was again triggered by her personal background. She was outraged that "Two teachers died of tuberculosis 'on their feet' while teaching. . . . we dare not let this hazard continue," she said.[16]

Her role in health and welfare legislation was recognized in 1930 when she was invited to be a delegate to the White House Conference on Child Health and Protection in Washington, D.C. Friends paid Hannah's way to the conference, where she met President and Mrs. Herbert Hoover. She displayed her individuality once again by taking her small niece Peggy with her. According to her niece, Aunt Hannah was thrifty, as usual, and stayed at an inexpensive boardinghouse. Upon finding it inhabited by bedbugs and cockroaches, she called the District of Columbia health department. The quarters were examined by "a *covey* of officers — head officials" — and then fumigated. Hannah and Peggy stayed there throughout the conference.[17]

As delegates of the Minnesota League of Women Voters, Kempfer and her friend and colleague Mabeth Paige also attended the Conference on the Cause and Cure of War held in Washington in 1928. The two spent six weeks in the East — one of the few real holidays Kempfer ever had.

Much of Kempfer's time, particularly in 1933, when Prohibition was repealed, and in later sessions, was taken up with liquor laws. Even though she was a "dry," she raised the ire of constituents and temperance organizations by supporting local-option laws, based on her belief that "people have a right, by the constitution of the United States, and by the State of Minnesota, for self determination of government." She was permanently tinged with a "wet" label — an issue as late as her 1940 campaign. She won reelection, however, with the continued support of her faithful advocate, Elmer Adams of Fergus Falls, and others.[18]

During the legislative sessions, Kempfer lived in St. Paul, some years sharing an apartment on lower Summit Avenue with young women who worked at the Capitol. Charlie stayed on the farm, but he and Hannah carried on a regular correspondence. They seem to

have adapted comfortably to what was then an unusual life-style.
A newspaper in 1923 carried a photograph of Charlie visiting at
the legislature and quoted him as supporting his wife's position on
every issue but one. She had, he said, "voted right on every measure so far with just one exception," and he had been unable to
convince her she was wrong on that one.[19] Her niece said that
Charlie was interested in politics, and astute, but that he never
told Hannah what to do. She apparently voted "right" often
enough as far as the people of Otter Tail County were concerned.
Her retirement in 1941 was of her own choosing, and she died,
having suffered ill health most of her adult life, two years later at
the age of sixty-three.

The other two pioneers of the 1923 session were political op-
posites. Myrtle Cain, the youngest of the four, came out of the labor
movement and was affiliated with the Working People's Nonpartisan Political League and the Farmer-Labor party. Called "the
flapper legislator" because of her youth, attractiveness, and liberal, if not radical, ideas, Cain was elected when she was in her
early twenties. Sue Metzger Dickey Hough was a thirty-year-old
Republican, a businesswoman who was already well known for
her work in Minneapolis charitable organizations, the Red Cross,
and community affairs. A Pennsylvanian by birth, she was a
great-granddaughter of John Quincy Adams and a proud member
of a distinguished family that included congressmen and soldiers.[20]

MYRTLE CAIN was born in Minneapolis about 1900 of
working-class parents. As business agent for the Telephone
Operators Union, she was a leader in its first strike there in 1918–
19. She became active in the equal rights campaign through association with Alice Paul, ardent woman suffragist and national
leader of the Woman's party. Cain served as a board member of
the National Woman's party, and she also worked with the Wom-
en's Trade Union League of Minneapolis, the Farmer-Labor party,
and the League of Catholic Women. After passage of the
Nineteenth Amendment, at the suggestion of Henry G. Tiegan,
national Nonpartisan League secretary, and others, Cain decided
to act on her belief that women should run for office. Her labor
background was fitting for a representative of District 28, a
working-people's neighborhood between East Hennepin Avenue

and the Mississippi River with some additional precincts across the river bordering on the northern edge of District 30 represented by Paige.

Cain's campaign platform called for a reduction of taxes on homes, a tax on iron ore mining royalties, enforcement of the minimum wage law, better protection for all workers, especially women, and "relentless warfare upon any law establishing a state constabulary or any system of state police" — a response to the earlier excesses of the Minnesota Public Safety Commission during World War I when Nonpartisan League members and officers were called traitors and occasionally jailed. Once elected, Cain worked for the planks in her platform. She gained nationwide attention in 1923 by introducing an anti-Ku Klux Klan law that made it a misdemeanor to appear in public masked or concealing one's identity.[21]

She was also one of seven House members to sponsor in the 1923 session a bill "Granting Equal Rights, Privileges and Immunities to Both Sexes." This early attempt to pass an equal rights law split the four women legislators, as it did the public. An impressive array of organizations and prominent citizens lined up on both sides of the issue. The varying attitudes of the four women legislators have a familiar ring. Kempfer said, "This is not the time for a bill of this kind . . . and besides, the bill is too sweeping. If there are any laws discriminatory against women these can be remedied by separate bills, not by one that takes in everything and would lead to endless litigation." She successfully killed the measure by moving that it be indefinitely postponed. Paige supported her motion; Hough was absent but was quoted as saying she would also have voted to kill the bill. Cain not only supported the 1923 measure, she still supported the idea it embodied fifty years later. In 1973 she appeared at the Capitol to speak for ratification by Minnesota of a similar, but national law. In that year the Minnesota legislature voted to ratify the Equal Rights Amendment to the United States Constitution.

Cain was defeated in 1924, when she came in thirty-nine votes behind Farmer-Labor candidate John F. Bowers. She was never again elected to public office, but she remained active in the labor movement and politics for over forty years. In 1977 Cain, unmarried and still politically aware, lived in the same house in northeast Minneapolis from which she was elected in 1922.

SUE DICKEY HOUGH'S parents had moved from Pennsylvania to Minneapolis when she was two years old. She had lived there ever since, except from 1912 to 1916 when she and her husband Frank, an employee of the Thomas Edison Company, resided in Chicago. Returning in 1916, she opened a real estate office, dealing in farm and city properties and investments. Because of her involvement in charitable organizations and community affairs, friends urged Sue Hough to file in 1922 for one of the District 34 seats in the House. According to her own account, she did not seriously consider doing so until her father commented that "that's the first time I've ever seen a white-livered Dickey." She won and "loved every minute" of her term in the legislature.[22]

One-term legislators typically have little influence, and Hough served only in the 1923 session. She cosponsored twenty-nine measures, of which two became law. One allowed women to be removed from penal institutions for childbirth and the other established permanent voter registration in cities with populations of 50,000 or more. Among the defeated measures were several favored by all four women, including three to give certain rights to illegitimate children. Other proposals cosponsored by Hough dealt with the improvement and supervision of county tuberculosis sanitariums. One of her pet ideas, making Minneapolis a separate county, was revived in 1947; she reminded the public then of her 1923 efforts.[23]

Hough ran again unsuccessfully in 1924, 1926, 1930, and 1934. Her campaign slogan in the later races was "a business woman for a business position." She believed, she said, that "a woman is not qualified to hold a political office until she forgets her sex and has some business experience." Drawing an analogy between government and a home in which a man and a woman co-operate she said, "It's good to have a woman's point of view." A lifelong Republican, Hough supported some positions, such as the need for capital punishment, generally associated with the conservative point of view. On the other hand, she has been an advocate of gun control since 1923. She was employed in the Minnesota Department of Public Welfare for twenty years, retiring in 1959. Alert and active, she still lived in Minneapolis in 1977.

The middle period of women's service in the legislature — the 1950s — saw the election of Coya Knutson and Sally Luther to the House after six years in which no women served. The attitudes and personalities of the two were quite different. Both were liked by constituents and colleagues and were reasonably successful legislators. Luther served her district for twelve years until she lost a race partly by a fluke. Knutson sought higher office — she was the state's first and thus far its only female representative in the United States Congress — and in the process breached party discipline and offended tradition by her "flamboyant" behavior in Washington.[24]

COYA KNUTSON was born Cornelia Gjesdal of Norwegian parents on a farm near Edmore, North Dakota, on August 22, 1912. As a small child she called herself "Coya" and the baby name stuck. A deep interest in music pervaded her life. Graduated from Concordia College in Moorhead in 1934, she went on to Juilliard School of Music in New York. Returning to North Dakota, she began teaching at Penn and then moved to Minnesota, where she taught at Plummer and later at Oklee. There she met and in 1940 married Andrew Knutson, a local hotel and cafe owner. They had one son, Terrence.

In addition to teaching school, Coya found time to help Andy run the hotel and cafe, to be the organist and choir director for the Zion Lutheran Church in Oklee, act as agent of the Red Lake County Agricultural Adjustment Committee in 1941–44, serve on the Red Lake County Welfare Board in 1948–50, and become a worker in the DFL party. In 1949 she was asked by county DFL leaders to run for the legislature in 1950. She accepted, and she won, after personally campaigning throughout District 65. Made up of Red Lake, Pennington, and Clearwater counties, this same district earlier had elected the first woman to the state Senate.

In the legislature, Knutson got along well with her fellow lawmakers and she and Sally Luther became friends. Like all minority members, she could express her committee assignment preferences but had no real choice. She held no chairmanships and sat on no interim commissions. In her first session in 1951, she was appointed to the Elections, Co-operatives, Public Institutions, Reapportionment, and University committees. After her reelection in 1952, she served on the Elections, Health, Towns and Counties, and University committees. She was interested in agriculture and Indian affairs, both of which related closely to her district. She was a supporter of fair employment practices legislation, state aid to education, and a state health program to provide

school nurses. She kept her constituents informed of her activities
through a newsletter called "Coya's Capitol Chats."

After serving two terms in the legislature, she ran for Congress
in 1954, handily defeating four men in the primary. Her closest
opponent was Curtiss T. Olson, a former DFL state party officer
and district DFL chairman, who got 5,938 votes to Coya's 11,069.
She had not been the party's endorsed candidate. In the general
election that year she upset long-time incumbent Republican
Congressman Harold C. Hagen by 2,335 votes.[25]

In Washington Knutson introduced legislation to strengthen the
family farm, aid Indians, expand the school lunch program, and
establish student loans, continuing the interests she had exhibited
in the legislature. She also supported Senator Estes C. Kefauver's
presidential ambitions and campaigned actively for him in Minnesota's presidential primary in 1956, speaking frequently on the
question of bossism — whether the state DFL could dictate to the
voters by imposing its endorsement of Adlai E. Stevenson. The
Kefauver forces won, carrying all but two Minnesota congressional
districts.

Knutson also won re-election to Congress that year, but she paid
for her defiance of the party. Among all those who had supported
Kefauver, Coya in particular was singled out for criticism by DFL
district and state party leaders. After moving to Washington, Coya
scandalized state and national leaders by her dress and behavior;
for instance, she took her accordion with her and played wherever
she went. Her opponents criticized her attire, her attitude, and her
style, but never her voting record. Her administrative assistant,
William Kjeldahl, who had also been a party maverick, was accused of "'running' her and her congressional office."

The most famous incident in Knutson's career was the so-called
"Coya, Come Home" letter, purportedly written by her husband
and widely publicized in 1958 urging the congressman to return
to her home duties. Opponents inside and outside the party
made political capital of the implication that she had deserted
her family; Knutson claimed that enemies had conspired
with Andy to discredit her. In November, 1958, she lost the congressional race by 1,390 votes to Republican Odin Langen, a
farmer-legislator with whom she had served in the state House.[26]

In 1960 Knutson challenged the DFL-endorsed candidate, Roy
E. Wiseth, in the district's primary. Senator Hubert H. Humphrey,
Governor Orville L. Freeman, Lieutenant Governor Karl F. Rol-

vaag, and state DFL Party Chairman Ray Hemenway all campaigned for Wiseth but Coya won. Then, during the general election, Governor Freeman joined Knutson in campaigning for the DFL ticket. Although Democratic presidential candidate John F. Kennedy carried Minnesota that year, both Freeman and Knutson lost to Republicans. After her defeat, Knutson worked in Washington for the Civil Defense Agency in the Department of Defense until 1970. Divorced in 1962, she ran unsuccessfully in the special 1977 primary for the Seventh Congressional District seat vacated by Robert Bergland.

Although Knutson seemed to fit the prescribed pattern of wife and mother and, according to some accounts, had a good grasp of legislative processes, she did not follow the rules of the political game which required adherence to certain conventions and acknowledgement that a politician — of either sex — must have some help and co-operation to attain and hold leadership. In her bids for Congress, she challenged the DFL party regulars by running against endorsed candidates, a cardinal sin especially in the highly disciplined, tough-minded party of the 1950s. Her support of Kefauver was only a last straw.[27]

SALLY LUTHER, on the other hand, not only had almost ideal qualifications for office but observed the unwritten rules of the legislative "club." Born and raised in Mabeth Paige's district, Luther's legislative biography reads like Mrs. Community Service Volunteer: "Graduated Vassar College. Married, three children. Newspaper reporter prior to election to Legislature in 1950. . . . Member of Board of Directors of Minneapolis Family and Children's Service and of Council House for Senior Citizens. Member of the Citizens League of Minneapolis and Hennepin County, the League of Women Voters, and American Association of University Women. Presbyterian."[28]

Luther had been active in the League of Women Voters, had followed politics through her association with highly regarded, long-time Minneapolis political reporter Matthew W. (Mike) Halloran, and by 1948 had become an active DFL party worker recruited by Blanche L. McIntosh, veteran political organizer in District 30, and Emily R. Kneubuhl, DFL candidate for secretary of state in 1946. Luther made her decision to file in District 30 in 1950 after incumbent legislator Alf L. Bergerud moved out of the area and was declared no longer eligible to run there.

Recalling her decision, Luther noted that after filing, "Mabeth Paige was the first person I went to see . . . she had a wonderful old house down on Dell Place and she was a friend of my family's and of my mother's for years. She immediately welcomed me in her tight Maine [*sic*] way with her Maine accent but she told me . . . 'Now you must do this . . . you must visit every home in the district, you must on two days before the election remind them of your candidacy with a flyer that covers your entire area,' and then Emily [Kneubuhl] said, 'you've got to get a block worker in charge of every block,' and I was just devout in doing these things. I had a map and I would go to doors block by block and ink the block off on my map. You know, I quit working [as a reporter] the end of June so I had July, August, September, and October to do this and I . . . found that maybe 10 per cent of the people were home . . . so I'd leave a note at the other places . . . a practice widely copied by other legislative candidates as the years went on. . . . 'Sorry I missed you' . . . and my signature. I'd sit at night and sign hundreds of these things and that was the technique . . . just to meet people. They were so stunned to meet a candidate . . . every candidate always says he does this but very few really do it."

Luther carried this same thoroughness and independent spirit into the legislative sessions. In early January, 1951, she attended the liberal (DFL) caucus and met Coya Knutson there. She recalls feeling rather useless in that first session, but found that many of the others also did not know what to do — about one-third of the legislature was new each time. "It was like kindergarten . . . you spent hours choosing seats," she said. With her seat mates Lawrence R. Yetka and Vladimir Shipka, representatives from northern Minnesota, she then spent many more hours with chief clerk George H. Leahy learning the rules of the House. She believes that she was placed on the Education Committee because Mabeth Paige wrote a letter on her behalf to the House speaker or to Roy E. Dunn, majority leader.

Of her first term, Luther observed: "I introduced an amendment that lawyers who were members of the legislature could not practice before regulatory bodies of the state. I was shouted down, beaten down . . . by my colleagues as well as others. The hit-or-miss seating arrangement prevented any sense of solidarity. And Roy Dunn was so eager to be sweet to us [women] that on February 14 we came in and Coya and I had big boxes of candy on our desks. I think this was the session that Prudence Cutright was proposed for the [University of Minnesota] board of regents. . . . I took courage . . . it was something for a freshman, to say nothing of a freshwoman, to speak in that House . . . when men spoke nobody listened but as soon as they heard the timbre of the voice it was different — utter silence — you suddenly had the attention of absolutely everybody . . . and I didn't even do this in a House session, I did it in a joint session . . . so that the senators were equally stunned. . . . They had never heard a woman's voice since when — 1939? — and I got up and got the attention of the clerk or whoever it was and told what a terrible thing it was that they were electing once again all men to the board of regents. I nearly fainted, and I was a strong person, I thought."[29]

As she learned about the legislature, Luther became "the lady from Hennepin and I found you had an allegiance to a county like you had an allegiance to a nation." In later sessions she chaired the Welfare Committee for two terms and the Civil Administration and Education committees for one term each. As a member of the Appropriations Committee she became an expert in state aid formulas, education legislation, and state institutions. She worked for aid to junior colleges, favored the establishment of a Fair Employment Practices Commission, and worked for fair housing legislation, sensitive issues in the 1950s. Her interim commission appointments, relating to welfare laws, school aids, and housing discrimination, reflected these interests.

Luther served her district and her state for twelve years, but "She was part of the leadership and yet she was not part of the leadership," according to an assistant to Governor Freeman, who worked with her. "I never thought of her as a woman in the legislature," he added, "but as a legislator . . . a DFLer . . . and one of our people." Elected and re-elected, she lost her seat in 1962 when she came in third, partly because of a realignment of the names on the voting machines, where hers seemed to be listed in the Republican column in the Democratic precincts just often enough to make the difference between winning and losing a close election.[30]

After her defeat Luther worked as an aide to Minneapolis Mayor Arthur E. Naftalin and then moved back to the Capitol, where she became a valued legislative assistant to Governor Rolvaag. In 1968 she returned to Vassar College in Poughkeepsie, New York, to become director of off-campus studies. She also taught high school subjects at the Poughkeepsie Day School from 1970 to 1974, and in the latter year she received a master of arts degree from the State University of New York. She is currently living in Poughkeepsie with her second husband, John J. Neumaier, whom she married in September, 1969, and her daughter, Sara Lee Luther, a Vassar student. Sally and Charles H. Luther were divorced in August, 1963, but she has kept her legislative name — Sally Luther — as her own.

The impact of the League of Women Voters upon political awareness and legislation in Minnesota during the twentieth century would lend itself to more thoughtful study than space permits here. But its importance in the careers of women lawmakers is clear. The training, experience, contacts, and self-confidence gained in such activities serves as preparation. Furthermore, participating in league work evidences a political outlook and a sociable nature, requisites for political candidates. HELEN E. McMILLAN, who was elected to the House in 1962, is perhaps the best Minnesota example of a league alumna.[31]

A native Minnesotan, McMillan was born Helen Elvira Davis on July 6, 1909, in Ortonville but spent most of her childhood in Minneapolis. After graduating from Marshall High School, she did not — despite her mother's pleas — immediately go on to college but toured the country as a dancer with the Albertina Rasch Ballet Troupe. Returning home at the age of twenty-one, she tried the University of Minnesota but shifted to a secretarial course and then worked in the office of a St. Paul physician. In 1938 she married Kenneth McMillan, who practiced law in Minneapolis for three years and then went off to World War II. After the war the couple decided to settle in Austin, a meat-packing center in southern Minnesota not far from the Iowa border.

There Helen was an active member of the Presbyterian church and of the Red Cross, secretary of the Governor's Human Rights Commission, and vice-president of the United Council of Church Women. She also began the League of Women Voters career that took her from neophyte to state president at about the same time legislative reapportionment made the city of Austin a separate district. As state president, McMillan spent considerable time at the Capitol, testifying and explaining league positions before numerous legislative committees. Observing that she had enjoyed the experience, her husband suggested in 1962 that she run for the

House in the new Austin district. She had not yet made a decision on this suggestion when it was repeated by DFL and league friends.

Elected in 1962 by less than 600 votes, she was subsequently re-elected five times with substantial majorities. During her ten years in the House, McMillan understood that much of the work of the legislature is done in committee. A well-liked, respected, and capable member, she did not often speak on the floor, but she worked hard behind the scenes on the Health and Welfare Committee for all six terms, the Employee Compensation Committee for four terms, the Recreation and Water Resources Committee (which had varying names during the period) for three terms, the Reapportionment Committee in 1965, and the Legislative Retirement Study Committee in 1971. She also chaired the Crime Prevention and Corrections Committee in 1973.

McMillan believes that many more women should be running for the legislature and that the goal of human rights is "the right of each human being to have a good life." Although she did not consider herself a feminist, she moved during her years in the House from the fairly predictable role of a civic-minded woman to that of a quiet but forceful proponent of legalized abortion, divorce reform, and equal rights for women. Her courage and steadfastness on one emotionally charged issue — abortion — were not widely known, but the passionate advocates on both sides of the question were aware that she was a mainstay of repeated attempts to liberalize Minnesota's restrictive law.[32]

In the 1969 session, McMillan and Representative Robert C. Bell of Roseville introduced a bill to legalize abortions; Leo D. Mosier of Minneapolis introduced a similar measure in the Senate. The House proposal was considered realistic because it tied abortion to approval by a panel of physicians. The halls of the Capitol were filled with dedicated lobbyists for and against the measure. McMillan carried the House bill in committee, but neither it nor the Senate measure reached the floor. In 1971 she introduced a bill to repeal the existing abortion law. Dr. Vernon L. Sommerdorf, representative from St. Paul, introduced a more moderate reform measure. Again opponents, led by the well-financed, tax-exempt Minnesota Citizens Concerned for Life, were able to keep both proposals from the floor.

Because of her support of liberalized abortion laws, antiabortion groups mounted a strong campaign against McMillan when she ran for re-election in 1972. Despite it, she won by a large majority. In her last session Helen McMillan cosponsored a number of bills with newly elected Phyllis Kahn, Mary Forsythe, Ernee McArthur, and Linda Berglin. Widowed in 1970, she decided not to run for re-election in 1974, for the office was now almost a full-time job with new and different responsibilities, and her health was not as good as it once had been. Besides there were now younger women — she was then sixty-five — to carry on the work.

Only three women have thus far been elected to the Minnesota Senate. LAURA EMELIA JOHNSON NAPLIN of Thief River Falls was the first. She represented the three counties of District 65 — the same district that elected Coya Knutson to the House a quarter of a century later. A former teacher, she was thirty-four years of age when the voters sent her to fill the post vacated by the death of her husband early in the 1927 session. A Farmer-Laborite, she pledged to "carry out the policies favored by her husband."[33]

She soon achieved a reputation of her own, concentrating on the uses of state lands, the administration and organization of state, county, and local governments, and taxation and other economic matters. Naplin served two four-year terms from 1927 to 1935 in the depths of the Depression. In that period of unprecedented economic hardship, she introduced bills that would have provided a moratorium on mortgage foreclosures, extended the redemption period of property lost through foreclosures, and established a state-owned and -operated bank. All of these measures were unsuccessful. The mortgage foreclosure moratorium bill, however, was especially popular. She later recalled that it was mentioned favorably for years afterward by her constituents.

After two terms, Naplin chose not to run for the Senate in 1934. From 1937 to 1939 she headed the Division of Hotel Inspection in the Minnesota Department of Health, an appointive position. In 1940 she ran for Congress from the Ninth District. She carried her concern for the plight of farmers into her congressional campaign; part of her platform called for refinancing farmers at an interest rate not to exceed 1½ per cent. Despite the endorsement of the district Farmer-Labor convention, she was unsuccessful in her bid.

After her defeat Naplin, who was in her early fifties, moved to California, where she entered the insurance business. In the late

1960s she switched to real estate, and at eighty-two she said she had "no ambition to retire — that would be the dullest thing in the world." Reflecting on her days in the legislature, she believed that she did a "good job." She was interested, she said, in "all phases of legislation," and she did not recall having any special advantages or handicaps as the only female senator.

NANCY BRATAAS, then forty-seven years old and a Republican from Rochester's District 33, became the state's second woman senator in February, 1975, when she defeated Thomas H. Resner in a special election to fill the seat of Harold G. Krieger, who resigned to become a county judge. Her election followed twenty years of political experience as Olmsted County Republican chairwoman, state GOP first vice-chairwoman, and then state chairwoman (1963–69) and state finance chairwoman. "She became so adept at running political campaigns that in 1973 she organized a consulting firm, Nancy Brataas Associates, specializing in data processing, systems analysis and administrative planning for charitable and political fund raising, and voter contact programs," according to the *St. Paul Pioneer Press.* Her firm was employed by President Gerald Ford's election committee to conduct telephone campaigns in three states holding primaries in the spring of 1976.[34]

Brataas represented two minorities, Republicans and women. Discussing the latter in 1975, she said: "As for being a woman . . . I don't know why more women haven't run for the Senate. But that will change. Twenty years ago, a woman was expected only to be a volunteer on behalf of candidates; now she can be a candidate herself." In other interviews she expressed her attitude toward her role in the legislature: although she felt strongly about "women's issues," she would not concentrate only on them, she said, but would like to show that women can deal with the whole wide range of matters that concerns state legislators.

Her 1974 campaign focused on economic issues and she supported a 10 per cent reduction in state income taxes. She later criticized the state's bonded indebtedness and corporate tax policies, which she called "absolutely punitive." As a member of the Education Committee, she was interested in getting a "fair share" of state school aids for nonmetropolitan districts. She voted against the 1976 schools aids measure, however, claiming that it did not provide enough funds for basic educational needs. She was a member of the Labor and Commerce Committee and the Select Committee on Nursing Homes; she authored one of a package of bills recommended by the latter committee. In 1975 she cosponsored a proposal to ban discrimination on the basis of sexual preference. The next year she authored a bill, approved by the Senate but defeated in the House, to eliminate unemployment benefits for persons voluntarily leaving their jobs. Brataas voted against raising the legal drinking age to nineteen ("you can't legislate to eliminate the drinking problem"), but the solons adopted the legislation in 1976. She voted for a reduction of the penalties for possession of small amounts of marijuana, a measure which was defeated.[35]

Brataas was re-elected in 1976, when she was joined in the Senate by the state's third woman senator — Emily Anne Staples of Plymouth. Staples, forty-seven, was a Republican who became a DFLer because she thought that party offered more opportunities for women. She was a cofounder with Arvonne Fraser of the Minnesota Women's Political Caucus; was formerly chairperson of the Women's Advisory Committee to the Minnesota Department of Human Rights; served on the board of the Interstate Association of Commissions on the Status of Women; and was a counselor on mid-life careers in the University of Minnesota's Women's Center.[36]

Of the sixteen women serving in the House and Senate in the 1970s, one House member, DFL representative Helen McMillan, was elected in the 1960s; she retired in 1972. In that year, five female representatives were elected. They were Linda Berglin, Minneapolis, DFL; Mary Forsythe, Edina, GOP; Joan Growe, Minnetonka, DFL; Phyllis Kahn, Minneapolis, DFL; and Ernee McArthur, Brooklyn Center, GOP. Growe and McArthur served only one term, but the others were re-elected in 1974 and 1976. Joan Growe, a former teacher, became the fourth Minnesota woman to be elected to state-wide office when she assumed the post of secretary of state in 1974. The occupations of the representatives were varied: Berglin was a graphic designer, Forsythe was a teacher, Kahn held a Ph.D. in biophysics from Yale University, and McArthur was executive secretary of the Brooklyn Center Chamber of Commerce.

Others elected to the House in 1974 were Peggy Byrne, St. Paul,

who specialized in criminal justice in her undergraduate work;
Janet Clark, Minneapolis, an elementary schoolteacher; Shirley
Hokanson, Richfield, a social worker; and Claudia Meier Volk,
Rice (Benton County), a nurse. All were members of the DFL
party. Volk did not run in 1976, but the others were returned to
office along with Senator Nancy Brataas.[37]

Elected in 1976, in addition to Staples, were four more DFLers:
Arlene I. Lehto, Duluth; Mary C. Murphy, Hermantown; Linda
L. Scheid, Brooklyn Park; and Ann J. Wynia, St. Paul. Lehto,
cofounder and president of the Save Lake Superior Association,
is also a partner-manager in a Duluth printing business, Murphy
is a high school history teacher and labor leader, Scheid resigned
from her position as a teacher in a secondary school to assume
her post in the House, and Wynia is an instructor in political
science at North Hennepin Community College.

In their attitudes toward "women's roles" and women's rights,
these legislators of the 1970s were generally more inclined than
their predecessors to work for the elimination of sex discrimination
and for the establishment of equal opportunities for women.
Volk, Forsythe, and Byrne did not call themselves feminists but,
like Brataas, they were "equalists." Byrne was taught to prize independence "before the term feminist was ever mentioned." Berglin
did not run on women's issues but was considered a supporter of
women's causes. Clark, Hokanson, Kahn, Lehto, Scheid, Staples,
and Wynia identified themselves as feminists; Clark, Kahn, Lehto,
Staples, and Wynia were influenced to seek public office by their
activities in feminist organizations. The six women in the House
in 1973 voted for ratification of the Equal Rights Amendment, and
when an effort to overturn the ratification was made in the Senate
in the closing minutes of the 1975 session, Brataas voted to support ERA. Every vote was critical, since the effort to rescind was
killed by virtue of a tie.

In the House Berglin and Kahn championed feminist causes.
Berglin was responsible for passage in 1975 of a bill to reduce
veterans' preference in civil service jobs, a measure supported by
the Minnesota Women's Political Caucus and other groups. Kahn
authored a successful divorce reform act in 1974 and in 1975 saw the
enactment of laws eliminating discrimination in name-change procedures (and providing women the option of retaining their birth
names after marriage), and requiring equal opportunities in school

athletics. In the Senate Brataas supported the veterans' preference, birth names, school athletics, and uniform credit and insurance measures.

The legislators' interests are broader than women's issues, of
course. In 1976 Kahn was the only woman serving as a House
committee chair or vice-chairperson. She was vice-chairman of the
State Departments Committee. Berglin's bills to establish work activity programs in sheltered workshops for the handicapped and to
eliminate dangers caused by hazardous buildings were enacted in
1973. In 1975 Kahn was successful in establishing nonsmokers'
rights in public places and in providing for the accelerated acquisition of additional recreational lands by the state. She was also
chief sponsor of a bill which would have required builders of nuclear power facilities to obtain certificates of need and to assume
financial responsibility for any damages or disasters. Although it
foundered in the House in the 1976 session, Kahn was re-elected
and planned to try again. She felt that one of her most challenging
assignments was as chairperson of the computer subcommittee of
the House Appropriations Committee. She was interested in establishing legislative oversight of computer acquisition and use in
state departments and educational institutions.

In her first year as a representative, Byrne successfully carried a
controversial measure that provided for withholding state aids
from school districts violating state and federal laws prohibiting
discrimination. Clark, who claimed that a woman "must do twice
the job a man does to gain credibility as an elected official," was
interested in social legislation, especially that relating to the elderly, handicapped, and children. In this field two measures she
introduced were adopted; they concerned discrimination in insurance laws and annulment of adoptions.

Forsythe was an author in 1973 of the successful measure to include party designation on state legislative ballots, and she
worked for passage of bills protecting the rights of the handicapped and fostering community facilities for them. She said there
was "some prejudice" against women in the legislature but that
there were also advantages: "Visibility for women legislators is
desired in some instances and may be a factor in some extra and
interesting assignments." She was named in 1973 to the powerful
Appropriations Committee, "a plum not ordinarily given to a
freshman member of the minority caucus."

Hokanson has been especially concerned with human services — good programs and effective delivery — and saw some measures enacted as part of the Omnibus Welfare and Corrections Act in 1975. She coauthored the measure requiring uniform accident and health insurance forms. Volk's special interests were in health legislation; in 1975 she worked for enacted bills expanding nutritional supplements for the elderly; in 1976 she was similarly successful in enacting community health services measures. She was influential in nursing home reforms and helped create the Health Care Facilities Complaints Office.

One of the few serious studies of that relatively uncommon creature — the American woman in politics — was published in 1974 under the title *Political Women*. Its author, Jeane J. Kirkpatrick, attempted to draw a composite portrait of the "political woman" using as her base discussions, questionnaires, and confidential interviews with forty-six legislators from twenty-six states who were selected to attend a conference sponsored by Rutgers University in 1972.

Since only a very small number (1 or 2 per cent) of Americans ever compete for public office and the number of women who do so has been less than the number of men, Kirkpatrick regarded a decision to run for legislative office as "deviant behavior." She found, however, that in other regards, the women who participated in the study were not nonconformist nor were they in most respects different from men who seek office. In brief, Kirkpatrick contended that successful female politicians, like most successful male ones, had a conservative personal style and reflected traditional values. For women this meant they had "respected conventional norms, have been good wives, mothers, homemakers as well as office holders. Measured by conventional norms, they are virtuous and successful and have worked their way to the top of the female status hierarchy. Their conformity to fundamental cultural requirements may be a prerequisite to success in their unconventional political careers." Once in office, Kirkpatrick said, both men and women (but especially women) must live by unwritten rules of legislative behavior, which included bans on exhibitionism and self-aggrandizement.[38]

Kirkpatrick found that most of the women in her study were from small-town backgrounds, were geographically stable, were middle class, had parents who participated in community life, had some higher education, and had a background of volunteer community service before their entry into elective office. The "average" woman legislator, according to Kirkpatrick, was also fairly attractive, forty-eight years old, the mother of two nearly grown children, rarely worked outside the home, lived in the small town where she was born, and was supported financially by a reasonably successful husband, who encouraged her political ambitions. The women studied were confident in their ability and comfortable with their feminine role. Most did not resent male dominance in politics and did not seek to challenge the established leadership or use their legislative service as a steppingstone to higher office. Most criticized the "women's liberation" movement.[39]

The Minnesota women discussed in this chapter confirm Kirkpatrick's findings in some respects and diverge from them in others. Generally speaking, the Minnesota women legislators who remained in office for some time and who seem to have been "effective" fit many characteristics of Kirkpatrick's portrait. Participation in community work was common to most women in her sample, and 40 per cent had worked in the League of Women Voters. In Minnesota, the figures are higher; of thirty-two legislators, fifteen — or nearly half — have been members of the league. Kirkpatrick cited law, journalism, real estate, insurance, and farming as the vocations of most male legislators. Of the women elected to the Minnesota body, almost all had been employed outside the home. Only five were primarily housewives, and of those one was an active partner in farming. Two had law degrees; two were journalists; one was in real estate; four others were businesswomen; ten had been teachers. The others had such varied vocations as designer, student, labor union official, social worker, research scientist, executive secretary, nurse, and public relations officer. The Minnesotans confirm Kirkpatrick's findings also in that the two women who succeeded their husbands were not "put" into office by friends of their late husbands — a stereotype Kirkpatrick contended was false.[40]

Other Minnesota legislators, especially the younger, more recently elected ones, do not confirm Kirkpatrick's findings. Two reasons for this divergence may be suggested. One is the openness and volatility of Minnesota politics which has allowed leaders from a wide range of political persuasions (including mavericks and extremists) to succeed. The other is that times change rapidly, and the 1972 statistics upon which Kirkpatrick's work was based are already in some respects outdated. Perceptions of appropriate roles for women have widened in the five intervening years.

The Minnesotans have been more geographically mobile than Kirkpatrick's subjects and they have far more frequently represented larger cities rather than small towns. Kahn and Fieldman, for example, were born in New York, Paige in Massachusetts, Hough in Pennsylvania, and Kempfer was an immigrant. Nearly half (fourteen) of the women legislators have represented Hennepin County, and of those, eight represented Minneapolis, the state's largest city. Five others represented such major population centers as St. Paul, Duluth, Winona, and Rochester. Moreover, their average age was younger than Kirkpatrick's forty-eight years. The average age of nineteen women Minnesotans elected in the fifty years from 1922 through 1972 (when Kirkpatrick's study was made) was 43.1 at the time of election, five years younger than Kirkpatrick's average. For those elected since 1972, the figure drops to 37.6.

Perhaps the Minnesota woman who diverged most significantly from Kirkpatrick's model — Coya Knutson — is proof of the unsatisfactory nature of "averages" applied to human beings in general and to Minnesota politics and its practitioners in particular. Coya did come from a small town, and in various other ways seemed to fit Kirkpatrick's portrait. But she diverged from it in that she was the one Minnesota woman legislator thus far who went on to national office, challenged the established party hierarchy, and ignored the unwritten rules of legislative behavior.

In 1977 a total of twelve women were sitting in the Minnesota House and Senate, the largest group to serve at any one time. And the number of women running for office has also increased during the decade. In addition to those elected, at least thirty-five more ran for legislative office in 1976 and were defeated. If this trend continues, it appears that more women in the future will play direct roles in making the laws that affect us all.

WOMEN IN THE MINNESOTA LEGISLATURE, 1923–77

Name	Birth Date	Death Date	Terms in Legislature	District	Res. During Terms	Political Affiliation
Linda Berglin	Oct. 10, 1944	—	H 1973—	59A Hennepin Co.[2]	Minneapolis	DFL
Nancy Osborn Brataas	1928	—	S 1975—[1]	33 Olmsted Co.[2]	Rochester	R
Constance Burchett	June 1, 1911	—	H 1963–1965	51 Anoka Co.	Coon Rapids	DFL
Margaret Mary (Peggy) Byrne	Dec. 17, 1949	—	H 1975—	64B Ramsey Co.[2]	St. Paul	DFL
Myrtle A. Cain	ca. 1900?	—	H 1923	28 Hennepin Co.[2]	Minneapolis	FL
Donna Jean Andrae Christianson	Oct. 17, 1931	—	H 1969[1]	66A Norman, Polk counties[3]	Halstad	DFL
Janet Jean Hoff Clark	June 13, 1941	—	H 1975—	60A Hennepin Co.[2]	Minneapolis	DFL
Esther Fox Fieldman	1916	—	H 1961	63 Hubbard Co.	Park Rapids	DFL

Name	Born	Died	House service	District	City	Party
Mary Elizabeth MacCormack Forsythe		—	H 1973—	39A Hennepin Co.[2]	Edina	R
Joan Ruth Anderson Growe	1936	—	H 1973	40A Hennepin Co.[2]	Minnetonka	DFL
Bertha Lee Smith Hansen	July 18, 1882	Jan. 20, 1966	H 1939	12 Lincoln Co.	Tyler	R
Shirley Ann Fogle Hokanson	Feb. 8, 1936	—	H 1975—	37A Hennepin Co.[2]	Richfield	DFL
Sue Metzger Dickey Hough	Nov. 22, [1893?]	—	H 1923	34 Hennepin Co.[2]	Minneapolis	R
Phyllis Ann Lorberblatt Kahn	Mar. 23, 1937	—	H 1973—	57A Hennepin Co.[2]	Minneapolis	DFL
Hannah Johnson Kempfer	Dec. 22, 1880	Sept. 27, 1943	H 1923–1929, 1933–1941	50 Otter Tail Co.	Erhard	I
Cornelia (Coya) Gjesdal Knutson	Aug. 22, 1912	—	H 1951–1953	65 Pennington, Red Lake, Clearwater counties	Oklee	DFL
Arlene Ione Lind Lehto	Sept. 14, 1939	—	H 1977—	8A St. Louis Co.[2]	Duluth	DFL
Joyce Ireton Lund		—	H 1955	3 Wabasha Co.	Wabasha	DFL

Name	Birth Date	Death Date	Terms in Legislature	District	Res. During Terms	Political Affiliation
Sara Lee (Sally) Fletcher Luther	Dec. 6, 1918	—	H 1951–1961	30 Hennepin Co.[2]	Minneapolis	DFL
Ernee M. McArthur	Dec. 29, 1933	—	H 1973	45B Hennepin Co.[2]	Brooklyn Center	R
Helen Elvira Davis McMillan	July 6, 1909	—	H 1963–1973	5 (1963–1965) 5A (1967–1973) Mower Co.[2]	Austin	DFL
Mary Catherine Murphy	Oct. 25, 1939	—	H 1977—	14B St. Louis, Carlton counties[2]	Hermantown	DFL
Laura Emelia Johnson Naplin	Feb. 14, 1893	—	S 1927–1933[1]	65 Pennington, Red Lake, Clearwater counties	Thief River Falls	FL
Mabeth Hurd Paige	1870	Aug. 19, 1961	H 1923–1943	30 Hennepin Co.[2]	Minneapolis	R
Rosanna Catherine Stark Payne.	Mar. 19, 1884	Oct. 31, 1954	H 1927–1931	52 Itasca Co.	Deer River, Ball Club	FL

Name	Born	Died	Served	District	City	Party
Linda Jayne Longabaugh Scheid	June 16, 1942	—	H 1977—	45A Hennepin Co.[2]	Brooklyn Park	DFL
Alpha Mathilda Sunde Smaby	Feb. 11, 1910	—	H 1965–1967	41 Hennepin Co.[2]	Minneapolis	DFL
Emily Anne Mayer Staples	May 3, 1929	—	S 1977—	43 Hennepin Co.[2]	Plymouth	DFL
Virginia Katherine Gillespie Torgerson	Sept. 24, 1911	—	H 1963	2 Winona Co.[2]	Winona	R
Claudia Marie Meier Volk	Nov. 6, 1947	—	H 1975	18A Benton, Mille Lacs, Isanti, Sherburne counties[2]	Rice	DFL
Harriet Hildreth Weeks	Feb. 28, 1874	May 24, 1939	H 1929–1931	63 Becker Co.	Detroit Lakes	R
Ann Louise Jobe Wynia	July 29, 1943	—	H 1977—	62A Ramsey Co.[2]	St. Paul	DFL

[1]Elected in special election.
[2]Part(s) of county or counties.
[3]All of Norman, part of Polk County.

15. FANNY BRIN
Woman of Peace

By Barbara Stuhler

WHEN FANNY FLIGELMAN arrived in Minneapolis from
Romania in 1884, the nation's prevailing mood was optimistic.
America was on the move; it was a good place to live in or to come
to. And people had been arriving in droves, most of them from
western Europe. Minnesota had earlier attracted many German
and Scandinavian immigrants, and with the opening of the ore
mines in the 1880s and 1890s, eastern and southern Europeans
also found their way to the state's iron ranges and to the Twin
Cities of Minneapolis and St. Paul. The Romanian Jewish community in Minneapolis to which his brother Herman had moved
earlier was John Fligelman's choice for a new home for his wife,
Antoinette, and their children, including Fanny Xeriffa, then three
months old.[1]

Fanny Fligelman grew up with ties to the new country rather
than the old. "Talk United States!" her father admonished
whenever any of his seven children lapsed into Yiddish. Fanny's
childhood in the household of an immigrant family, struggling to
make it in America, was apparently uneventful. She acquired an
early orientation in politics from her father, and by the time she
entered South High School in Minneapolis, she was beginning to
show interest in the communications skills that would distinguish
her in later life. She was active and successful in the high school
debate league, and at the University of Minnesota she became the
first woman to succeed in the famed Pillsbury oratorical contest,
winning a second prize of $50 for the seemingly perennial topic,
"Russian Bureaucracy and the Jews." The man who took first
place with "Patrick Henry, the Agitator" was her classmate and a
future governor, Theodore Christianson.[2]

A serious and able student, Fanny was active in the Minerva

Literary Society and was elected to Phi Beta Kappa in her senior year (when she dropped to third place in the oratorical contest with a speech on "Back to Democracy"). Both her ability and serious mien are no doubt accurately, if somewhat unkindly, described by a limerick accompanying her graduation picture in the university yearbook for 1907:

> Fannie's all kinds of a shark
> In everything gets the top mark
> But to her that nice word
> Suggests a mere bird
> For she has never been on a lark.[3]

From the few options then available to women with liberal arts degrees, the young graduate chose to teach. Her courses included a potpourri of Latin, civics, literature, and English, which she taught for six years, first in Northfield and later at West High School in Minneapolis. On March 19, 1913, she married Arthur Brin, a prosperous businessman, and set about filling the traditional roles of wife and mother. Three children, Rachel, Howard, and Charles, commanded her attention but she was never homebound. By 1924 she had launched what would become a second, full-time career — that of professional volunteer. The choice was not an uncommon one for intelligent women of means. Fanny's husband, who had started working at the age of fourteen as an office boy, was then owner of the Brin Glass Company. More conservative than she, he was supportive of her endeavors and asked only, when she became involved in suffrage activities, that she not picket. The Brins had a cook and an upstairs maid, and Fanny, who had a close and caring relationship with her husband and children, was frank to say she was not too keen on cooking as a regular chore.[4]

In the Brin family, leisure was used not for idleness or frivolity but for service. And Fanny had the time. Arthur Brin once said, "We must give ourselves to our fellow men. We cannot live for ourselves alone." Fanny often made the point that the obligation of Jews was not to render charity (for which there is no word in Hebrew) but to promote justice. An issue that consumed some of her time and service was the women's suffrage movement, in which she was active but not prominent.[5]

She traced her interest in women's rights to her undergraduate days at the University of Minnesota. Years later, she reminisced,

Fanny Brin

"When I was quite young I heard notes which sang to women to seek their full development in the educational, the professional, the political world." Among those who influenced her involvement in "every good cause affecting the welfare of women" were her mother, who was determined that she be educated, and Frances Squire Potter, an English professor in the university who was also corresponding secretary of the National American Woman Suffrage Association. "It was good to follow . . . such fine women as Mrs. [Maud C.] Stockwell, Mrs. Andreas Ueland, Mrs. Frances Squire Potter," Fanny recalled. (Stockwell had been president of the Minnesota Woman Suffrage Association, treasurer of a Minnesota disarmament committee, and chairwoman of the Minnesota section of the Women's International League for Peace and Freedom. Clara H. Ueland was a founder of the Woman's Club of Minneapolis in 1907, president of the state suffrage association in 1918–19, and the first president of the Minnesota League of Women Voters in 1919.)[6]

These women stirred Fanny's sense of what could be achieved.

Even though, as she noted, "we seem to be moving very slowly, I have faith that women will some day make a great contribution to civilization. The need for women's participation grows daily. . . . I believe they can do more than they realize. . . . women working side by side with men can push forward for a better world." Fanny Brin understood that women's long dependence had given them a sense of inferiority. She had great confidence that education, including adult education, would dispel that inferiority.[7]

She scoffed at narrow definitions of woman's function and loved to recall the occasional horrified responses to the invention of the perambulator — it would destroy the whole fabric of family life by permitting a mother to go outside the home! She did not believe that domesticity was necessarily woman's destiny and pointed to such single women of achievement as Jane Addams, Mary E. Woolley, and Dr. Alice Hamilton. She was wont to ask, "How can we be in the world and not of it?" Nor did she view the feminist movement as a disparagement of men. With women assuming a larger place in society, they should be concerned with building and changing that society "so that men and women will have a world in which they can live happily, creatively, securely." As long ago as 1933, she perceived a future movement arising out of the need for orderly planning of "a new social order in which men and women shall share alike."[8]

Women's rights and Fanny's three other commitments — to world peace, the Jewish heritage, and democracy — all came together in the National Council of Jewish Women (NCJW), founded in 1893 by Mrs. Hannah G. Solomon as an outgrowth of the World's Parliament of Religions at the Columbian Exposition. The organization provided a platform for Fanny Brin and she used it wisely and eloquently. Initially attracted to the Minneapolis section by its founder and president, Bertha W. Weiskopf, she soon found its significant influence to be Nina M. Cohen, whose study classes provided intellectual fare. For Fanny the NCJW "accomplished two important things. It united Jewish women for the first time in a program important to themselves as Jews; it provided also a means by which Jewish women could work side by side with non-Jewish groups on programs of common welfare and world problems." In its early years, the NCJW was concerned with the cultural needs of its members, religious education for

Jewish children, social service for the underprivileged, and legislation of civic and national interest. With the influx in the early
1900s of growing numbers of Jewish immigrants from eastern
Europe, the NCJW made a pioneering contribution to the development of services, especially educational ones, for the foreign
born.[9]

The council's first involvement with international affairs was a
petition of 1898 urging President William McKinley to seek a
peaceful resolution of the Spanish-American War. With the outbreak of that conflict, the NCJW resolved to attend to problems of
war and peace. Initially, the activities of its Committee on Peace
and Arbitration were ineffectual and naïve — books on peace in
the public libraries, sporadic study groups, occasional meetings,
and an annual celebration of International Good Will Day. After
World War I the council became more active, joining with other
organizations to support American membership in the League of
Nations. With the winning of votes for women in 1920, many of
the prominent suffrage leaders turned their attention to the hard
questions of organizing a world at peace. Chief among these was
Carrie Chapman Catt who, speaking at the NJCW's convention in
St. Louis in 1923, galvanized the organization to resolve: "That
war shall be abolished as an institution for settlement of international disputes and it shall be outlawed by international agreement." This set the stage for Fanny Brin's debut in council leadership circles.[10]

By 1921 she had been a director of the Minneapolis Woman's
Committee for World Disarmament, part of a national network of
organized support for the Washington disarmament conference.
Her concern with militarism was manifested in her service as secretary of the Minneapolis Committee for the Elimination of Military Training from the city's high schools. (A decade later, she was
to exert an even more forceful influence as one of the leaders of
the State Committee in Behalf of Elective Drill at the University
of Minnesota.) She was also becoming increasingly active in the
Minneapolis section of the NCJW and was elected its president in
1924.[11]

Shortly before Fanny's election, Rose Brenner, the national
president of the council, had appointed her chairman of its national subcommittee on peace. On May 1, 1924, on one of her first
trips to Washington, D.C., in her new position, she wrote to her
husband "Arie and Children," saying, "I feel very sure that some-

thing must come of this peace movement. Just as the despised abolitionists and suffragists finally won their cause — just so these Pacifists will." In her view, the winning of that cause would require moving along a continuum from a vague yearning for peace, to a knowledge of the mechanics for peace, to the political support of institutions that would make peace a reality.[12]

The years of the mid-1920s were not a time of great expectations for those who did not fit the isolationist temper. The United States had rejected the League of Nations and was foot-dragging on the World Court, two organizations of paramount priority to internationalists of that era. On both these issues, the NCJW had joined with other associations urging American participation. Yet there is evidence to suggest that its members were not of one mind on either substance or tactics. Fanny was surprised that the NCJW was not associated with the Women's International League for Peace and Freedom, of which she was a member. Indeed, she wrote in an exchange of correspondence with President Brenner that she did not think the Women's International League radical: "I cannot find a single point which I can consider in any way extreme."[13]

On April 6, 1927, French foreign minister Aristide Briand, in a public address directed to the American people, announced France's willingness to join the United States in a bilateral mutual commitment to outlaw war. After several months of hesitation, the United States responded by proposing instead a multilateral pact involving other nations as well. It seemed reasonable to expect, in view of the 1923 NCJW resolution to outlaw war, that the idea of such a pact would be supported. But the organization was more timid than Fanny Brin had anticipated, arguing that it "was committed only to an educational campaign and not to the endorsement of the proposal itself." Fanny's impatience was thinly veiled: "More and more confusion! Why should we participate in an Educational Campaign for something which we do not endorse per se?"[14]

By 1928 the council board, previously labeled by Fanny as "ultra-conservative," had come around to her point of view. It joined eight other women's organizations under the leadership of Carrie Chapman Catt in a united campaign for the multilateral treaty, which was then before the Congress for ratification. Fanny chaired the Minnesota committee, which produced 1,200 resolutions of support (more than any other state) and brought together

over 700 participants in a one-day conference designed to
mobilize opinion. Her accolades included a telegram from one of
the treaty's negotiators, fellow-Minnesotan Secretary of State
Frank B. Kellogg, and a letter from her old classmate, Governor
Christianson, who wrote, "Your effective interest in behalf of the
abolition of war has come to my attention and I want to assure you
that I am entirely in sympathy with this exceedingly worth-while
movement." The agreement known as the Kellogg-Briand Pact
was ratified on January 15, 1929. Well aware of its shortcomings
— most particularly its failure to establish a mechanism
for enforcement — Fanny commented before its ratification,
"We have delivered ourselves of a noble and pious sentiment.
Beyond that we do not go." [15]

The successful campaign was a high-water mark in the history of
the singular organization headed by Mrs. Catt, the National Committee on the Cause and Cure of War. Although its membership
changed from time to time, the big women's groups remained the
hard core. For some of the fifteen years of the committee's existence, Fanny Brin served on the executive board and missed only
one of its annual conferences. She believed it essential to collaborate with non-Jewish groups on legislation and peace work, and
her personal involvement with this organization suggests that she
thought it of supreme importance. Mrs. Catt, in turn, valued the
NCJW's association because, as she once wrote, "I still adhere to
the opinion that the Jews are the one people to whom is assigned
the chief task of bringing peace in the world. I am just beginning
to realize how wonderful it is that away back, before history really
began, the old Jewish prophets, the greatest of whom was my dear
friend, Micah, began saying things about peace and that no one
since has said anything better." [16]

This support in turn helped Fanny Brin press her contention to
the council that "peace should be made a major activity for some
time." She argued that the local sections wished it and that "Mrs.
Catt and others were looking to Jewish women to make a definite
contribution." Mrs. Catt recognized Brin's talents of persuasion
and organization, "It will seem to you that we turn to you for any
work in the field of international relations, but your real interest in
peace and your leading position makes it inevitable." [17]

As chairman of the NCJW's Committee on Peace and Arbitration, Fanny Brin made education, co-operation, and legislation the
thematic elements of the organization's peace activities. She be-

lieved that "Only informed women can be interested. Only interested women can have convictions. We need women with convictions." But public opinion was not an end in itself: "Nothing we can do is of more immediate importance than developing leadership which can educate and crystallize public opinion and guide legislative and political action." She deplored the platitudes of the passionate haters of war and lovers of peace, of the sentimental supporters of world organization who dismissed complexity and ignored reality. Under her leadership, the council continued to support the World Court, endorsed various disarmament proposals, and advocated the development of international institutions. It is a measure of her impact that by 1930 more sections of the NCJW were engaged in peace work than in any other activity.[18]

On October 26, 1931, Fanny Brin headed the organization of a meeting of the Minneapolis Committee for World Disarmament. Designed to demonstrate public sentiment in favor of the conference that was to meet in Geneva, Switzerland, the following February, it was even more widely attended than the 1928 gathering to support the Kellogg-Briand Pact. Grace E. Ford, whose husband, university president Guy Stanton Ford, had chaired the meeting, wrote Fanny: "I was much moved to think that without your courage and tireless *work* supported by your unfailing good judgment those 8000 persons might have been deprived of that opportunity. You have done us all a great service." [19]

It was ironic that while peace worker Fanny Brin served as the ninth NCJW president from 1932 to 1938, various national aggressions and inadequate responses would provide the grist for World War II. Japan invaded Manchuria in 1931. The League of Nations took no action to stop it, and Italy was emboldened to attack Ethiopia in 1935. From 1936 to 1939 civil war raged in Spain. The duly constituted Republican government was overthrown by General Francisco Franco's rebels, with the aid of Germany and Italy. "Peace in our time" was proclaimed in 1938 in a short-lived pact consummated at Munich in which England and France consented to Hitler's partial occupation of Czechoslovakia — a hoped-for end to his territorial appetite which had already consumed Austria. But that was not to be and Britain and France, pressed to the limits of compromise and accommodation, declared war on Germany on September 3, 1939.[20]

Yet, throughout the 1930s, while the world moved closer to war,

Fanny Brin remained a fervent partisan of peace. She believed that Jewish women, whose prophets and sages taught them to believe in a warless world, had a special obligation to make peace their central concern. War, she said, does not make the world a better place. "We believe that boundaries cannot be drawn satisfactorily with the sword," she told a New Orleans audience in 1935. "That disputes cannot be settled by sacrificing young men on the battlefield. That a nation which spends four-fifths of its income on war and preparation for war cannot advance the civilized arts of life. . . . We believe that our generation must further perfect the collective system . . . which outlaws war and treats a nation which violates the peace as an aggressor."[21]

Most shattering, however, to an organization of Jewish women was the Nazi government's persecution of the Jews in Germany. When Adolf Hitler came to power early in 1933, his personal anti-Semitism became public policy. He issued laws barring Jews from public service, the universities, and the professions. On April 1, 1933, he decreed a national boycott of Jewish shops. As William L. Shirer wrote in his classic history of the Third Reich, Hitler's "burning hatred, which would so infect so many Germans in that empire, would lead ultimately to a massacre so horrible and on such a scale as to leave an ugly scar on civilization that will surely last as long as man on earth." But before then, German Jews and later Jews from Austria and Czechoslovakia would seek haven in friendlier lands — 537,000 of them between 1933 and 1941.[22]

In response to Hitler's proclamations, the NCJW agitated for programs of relief and refuge. It was the only women's organization represented on the Committee on German Jewish Immigration Policy; it was also involved with the Committee for Aid to German Jewish Children; and it was developing a long-term educational program to combat prejudice in the United States. In Minnesota Fanny Brin and attorney Amos S. Deinard worked with a university faculty chapter of the National Committee in Aid of Displaced German Scholars. From the mid-1930s to the late 1940s, she headed the Minneapolis co-ordinating committee for aid to refugees and emigrants and later chaired the state refugee committee. A good deal of both Fanny and Arthur Brin's time (nearly fifteen years), energy, and money were devoted to the care and placement of Jews displaced because of Hitler, World War II, and its aftermath.[23]

Despite an occasional outburst about "our 'ostrich' citizenry" holding seventeenth- and eighteenth-century ideas, Fanny had great faith in the principles and institutions of democracy. In her view, the welfare of Jews was inextricably linked with a flourishing democracy: "To us the triumph of democracy means liberation from the Ghetto and emancipation." She had been brought up to believe, she confessed, that the "dreams of the nineteenth century were bound to be fulfilled" and that the "great democratic movement was only beginning to bring its boons to mankind." With the achievement of universal education and the doctrine of political equality, "man, simply through his mere humanity, could claim from society a share of all the good society has acquired." And a good society was a secure one, made secure by personal liberty and equality before the law. The roots of democracy were nourished in the Old Testament "which was alive with the spirit of liberty and resistance to absolutism" and in the teachings of Jesus, emphasizing the importance of the individual, the fatherhood of God, and the brotherhood of man.[24]

Until the Nazi attack on the Jews, she had been sympathetic to Zionism but not active in its cause. In 1937 she had said that the NCJW had not declared itself on Zionism and that she preferred the question to be neither raised nor answered. Her interest in Judaism was also a later development, secondary, as Ruth Brin has written, "to her overriding concerns with peace and humanitarian goals." The position taken by many American Jews in the 1930s was a moderate one, dictated perhaps by their insecurity in the face of anti-Semitism. While Fanny Brin recognized that the United States was "a country of many ethnic groups . . . and therefore our existence depends upon our acceptance of the concept of a cultural pluralism," it was also true that for many Jews, their chief desire was to Americanize, to lose their differentness — and the hostility which attended it — in the famed melting pot.[25]

In 1935 at the fourteenth NCJW convention in New Orleans, Mrs. Brin was elected for a second term as president. In her address she noted that "our destiny as Jews is once again taking a new turn." She cited Holland and England as places of refuge for the Jews during the Spanish Inquisition and "so there is today Palestine." Five years later, a similar convention unanimously approved a statement drafted by Fanny and two other board members which supported the unrestricted immigration of Jews into Palestine. It endorsed the development of Palestine in the spirit of the Balfour Declaration of 1917, which had affirmed the British government's support of a national home for the Jewish people and offered its good offices to that end. The council added, however, that this "does not commit the organization to the idea of a state nor does it preclude the idea." It was the first statement ever made on the issue by the National Council of Jewish Women and, clearly, it had been a heatedly debated compromise.[26]

But in the early 1930s, neither the council's understandable preoccupation with the Jews in Germany, nor the Depression, nor the ominous signs of war, distracted Fanny Brin from her central concern with the building of a new international system. With striking prescience, she perceived in 1931 the world's "closely and delicately woven" interdependency as well as the struggles between the philosophies of nationalism and self-sufficiency and internationalism and interdependence which had yet to be resolved.[27]

In 1935 she had presided over her first NCJW convention, and as she concluded her term of office at the Pittsburgh convention in 1938, she spoke again of the need for new mechanisms "to remedy grievances and settle disputes in an interdependent world." After six years as national president, she agreed to serve in her old capacity with the council as chairman of the renamed Committee on International Relations and Peace. Probably she did so because, as she said, "we stand at the crossroad," and she wanted to be instrumental in determining that the road taken would be that of collective action to prevent war and maintain peace with justice. On a tour of Europe in the summer of 1938 she talked with officials of several nations, including Germany and Russia. This firsthand view of an area "so troubled and bewildered" reinforced her commitment to world organization.[28]

The peace movement, heretofore a unifying force among diverse organizations, now split into two factions — the pacifists who renounced the use of force for whatever reason, and those who felt force was a justified response to nations using it to advance their own ambitions. The NCJW was in the latter group; it urged the removal of the embargo on supplies to provide assistance to an established republican government in the Spanish Civil War. By 1940 Fanny Brin was reversing her long-standing opposition to a big American defense program. With the collapse of France and the indications of a German victory, she said it was unreal for the

NCJW to talk of "collective security . . . molding world organization, demobilizing armaments." She predicted that the council's opposition to war "may become an increasingly difficult position to hold." In September she wrote Mrs. Maurice Goldman, NCJW president, that she preferred not to be reappointed as the chairman of the National Committee for International Relations and Peace. "I took up the work . . . at the beginning of a period in the peace movement which is now drawing to a close," she wrote. She thought it a logical time for a change in the chairmanship and while it had been a privilege to serve, she had not anticipated "what years of hope and of inspiration and of despair were ahead of me." But she was persuaded to accept reappointment, perhaps because she felt so strongly that "Everything depends on who emerges victorious from this conflict — those nations that support the values of force or those which support the values of reason." [29]

Following the Japanese attack on Pearl Harbor on December 7, 1941, the council's "International Relations Digest" included this message from Fanny Brin: "We are at war. . . . We must never forget the lessons we have learned, that isolation does not protect us, that it breaks down [and] ends in intervention. . . . that we can only avoid intervention by setting up agencies which make possible collective action. We must learn and teach the lesson of cooperation and search for the form it must take. We must build up now safeguards against an upsurge of isolationist thinking after the war. Unless we can we shall go through the same cycle of isolation and intervention." [30]

Throughout World War II she kept articulating the precepts which she felt council members and others should subscribe to, the understandings they must possess: "War is global, peace is global, and prosperity is global.

"We must go foward in our work for a world organization with a realism that is courageous and a faith that is daring, and a steadfastness that is never failing.

"Peace is a condition of survival for Democracy, therefore, Democracy must find a way of guaranteeing peace.

"All the good will in the world will not avail us unless we have established, recognized institutions to which men will turn by habit to settle problems and secure change." [31]

On March 16, 1943, four United States senators introduced Senate Resolution 114, soon nicknamed B2H2 for its authors Joseph H. Ball (Republican, Minnesota), Harold H. Burton (Republican,

Ohio), Lister Hill (Democrat, Alabama), Carl A. Hatch (Democrat, New Mexico). The statement was an expression of congressional support for American participation in an international organization to be formed after the war and endowed with powers to combat aggression and resolve conflict. Fanny regarded Senator Ball's resolution as a "first step towards a system of collective security." She protested the wishy-washy statements of political figures who opted for "cooperation without commitment," saying "We stand for commitment." By the end of 1943 that commitment had been made by the United States Congress and by the president.[32]

Thus it was that on April 25, 1945, representatives of fifty-one of the world's nations came together in San Francisco to write a charter for a new international organization. Fanny Brin was present. She had proudly agreed to be an official alternate for the Women's Action Committee for Lasting Peace which, in 1943, had succeeded the National Committee on the Cause and Cure of War. Forty-two nongovernmental organizations had been invited by the Department of State to be present. Five were women's groups: the American Association of University Women, the Business and Professional Women's Clubs, the General Federation of Women's Clubs, the League of Women Voters, and the Women's Action Committee, which Fanny represented. She was also an observer for the NCJW. This was a new kind of public diplomacy, facilitating civic participation in the writing of the charter, and she regarded the San Francisco conference as the capstone of her career. It symbolized her beliefs, her hopes, her dreams, her faith that this was a perfectable world.[33]

In an interview published in the *San Francisco Chronicle* in 1943, Fanny again restated what she regarded as the prerequisites for the participation of women in international affairs: "Women must be informed if they are to take their places with men. If they are not thoroughly conversant with the questions at issue, they tend to become silent partners. They must have information before taking their stand and making their wishes known." In keeping with this prescription, Fanny Brin, relieved of her NCJW obligations in 1944, had called together thirty-six Minneapolis women's groups for the purpose of organizing a city-wide women's rally on "Dumbarton Oaks — Road to Lasting Peace." (Dumbarton Oaks, an estate in Georgetown, D.C., had been the site of preliminary work on the United Nations Charter.) That rally on February 2, 1945, started something. In the years that followed, what is now

called the Women's United Nations Rally has been the focal point
of UN Week activities in Minnesota. It is a lasting legacy of the
high priority Fanny Brin put on education and co-operation. An
inspiring leader of commanding presence, she received countless
sincere letters of admiration from women in many walks of life.
Helen Duff, president of the League of Women Voters of Minnesota, spoke for many when she wrote, "May I say again how
much I admire your masterful handling of the Rally. You made it a
success, and your leadership made the committee work a stimulating and enjoyable task." [34]

The first anniversary of the rally found Fanny saying, "Last year
we were considering a *blueprint* for a new world order with all
the hope and exhilaration that goes with projecting plans for the
future. This year we are examining soberly and anxiously the organization that has come out of those plans." She referred to the
growing hostility among the big powers, notably the United
States and the Soviet Union, and to the atomic bomb that "ticks
beneath the peace table around which the leaders of nations
gather." [35]

It was no wonder that recognition and honor came her way. She
was one of thirty-eight women named by the *American Hebrew*
for their outstanding contributions to Jewish life in 1932. In the
next year she was one of fifty-two appointed by Eleanor Roosevelt
to a national women's committee organized to respond to the
human needs and harsh conditions of the Depression. And in 1934
Carrie Chapman Catt named her one of ten outstanding women of
the year — an honor she especially cherished. As she neared the
end of her six turbulent years as head of the NCJW, the Minneapolis section honored her at a special luncheon attended by
500 women. There was high praise from distinguished persons
such as Gratia Countryman, who said "very few women in Minneapolis . . . can equal her brain power and superior character;"
others called her "a Deborah among women," one who "made
Jewish women peace-conscious"; and Mrs. Catt described her as
"one of the country's most valuable women. . . . May she live
long to serve this suffering old world." [36]

A spellbinding speaker, she was invited to serve in many
capacities and her list of appointments, organizational offices, and
memberships indicates the breadth of her interests and the depth
of her commitment. Later her energies were weakened by Parkin-

son's disease and she was forced to decline invitations for service
as, for example, the NCJW's representative on the Committee on
World Affairs of the International Council. The president of the
council, regretting her decision, wrote, "There is no Jewish
woman in the United States who could have brought to this Committee more wisdom and more experienced judgment."[37]

Fanny Brin was admired not only for her leadership but for her
social graces as well. The Brin home was the scene of many parties, and she enjoyed afternoons of card games with her friends.
There were inevitably a few critics who thought her pedantic,
puritanical, schoolteacherish, bossy, and too intellectual for their
taste. She in turn suffered fools silently if not always gladly and
was not preoccupied with personalities or troubled by trivia.
Friends remark on her courtesy and modesty, her warmth, and her
gentle yet firm manner. Over the years, she occupied important
positions and served as a role model for women who absorbed her
ideas and learned how to be effective organizers and leaders. In
both her public and private lives, Fanny Brin was a commanding
presence.[38]

She was a prolific letter writer, perhaps because NCJW business
took her so frequently from home (sixty-three days in one year of
her presidency). She has also left behind hundreds of speeches,
some of them neatly typed, others scrawled on cards, scratch paper,
Western Union blanks, and the stationery she found in hotel
rooms. In an undated letter to her daughter Rachel, she displayed
a rare touch of humor: "The two *presidents* [*Arthur was with her*]
are sitting at our table in a hotel room. . . . Having been
banqueted — corsaged — compared to Abraham and Sarah on a
mission to the Jewish people they feel pretty lofty this morning."[39]

Arthur Brin was a distinguished civic leader, active in many
Jewish organizations and the first Jewish chairman of the Minneapolis Council of Social Agencies, later the United Fund.
Friends have described the Brins' relationship as "special" and "a
true partnership." They shared a community of interests, a common bond of service, and pride in each other's achievements. On
April 1, 1932, Arthur surprised Fanny by appearing in Detroit to
see her installed as NCJW president, and he congratulated the
women on their choice. The measure of Arthur Brin is vividly described in a letter from former university president Ford to Fanny
after Arthur's death in November, 1946: "Minneapolis won't be
the same to us with your good husband gone. In his quiet way he

had made himself the city's most useful and public minded citizen. The good things about Minneapolis are better because he lived and labored there." [40]

Fifteen years later, on September 4, 1961, Fanny Brin died. Long before, in 1945, she had said in a speech that "If one hundred years ago the women had been called before that bar of judgment and the good Lord had said to them . . . what have you done [to prevent] suffering, injustice, poverty and war," they could reply "Ours is not the guilt"; for so long as they were denied the right to higher education, to hold property, and to vote, they could not be held responsible. Now, she said, they could not evade the question; they were responsible but had not assumed responsibility. And then in 1948 Fanny Brin noted, "Today's world is a difficult one for women to find their place. But someday there will be a truer integration of women's abilities and contributions . . . and it will be a better world." [41]

Fanny Brin's ideas were typical of liberal thinkers who took their civic responsibilities seriously and paid attention to international events of the day; her sense of universality and her sensitivity to global interdependencies were not. Believing in change, she once referred to herself as a "militant pacifist." She was not a radical but a political realist. She was confident that she could influence opinion — and she did. Like many women in positions of leadership in important voluntary associations, she served as a transmission link between scholars and the attentive public. If her style was that of a bygone era, the issues she addressed were not. If, to some, her preoccupation with peace seemed extreme, it was because she conceived of peace not narrowly but as "an expression of the way of life and the type of civilization we aspire to." [42]

Her achievements must be assessed in the context of her time — a period when women had few opportunities for self-expression except as volunteers. But, throughout American history, voluntary associations have served as agents of change, and Fanny Brin understood this. Her leadership in the NCJW was directed at enhancing that organization's political effectiveness. She was not always successful; frequently she took her text from the Indian poet, Tagore, who wrote "I have stars in my sky but oh the unlit candles in my house." [43]

Central to Fanny Brin's perceptions of her own efforts were these frequently quoted words of a Talmudic sage: "It is not encumbent upon us to finish the work; neither is it permitted to us to desist from it." She knew that "the winning of . . . peace is a matter of generations." And though she would have been dismayed at the banner headline on the front page of the *Minneapolis Morning Tribune* which also carried the news of her death — "Kennedy Orders U.S. to Resume Nuclear Tests" — to Fanny Brin it would have been a call to action.[44]

16. THE LARSON SISTERS
Three Careers in Contrast

By Carol Jenson

AGNES, HENRIETTA, AND NORA LARSON, daughters of a southern Minnesota farmer-businessman and a gentle homemaking mother, have among them given more than a century and a half of service to education and research. That three women from the same family attained sufficient stature to be listed in *Who's Who of American Women* is cause for wonder.[1] What were the circumstances that produced three such prominent figures? In the case of the Larson sisters much of the answer would seem to lie in the institutions which molded their early lives.

The Larson sisters grew to young womanhood in a stable family setting where the parents impressed upon their children the importance of education and a sense of responsibility to the community. Strong family ties linked the sisters throughout their lives. As they pursued three distinct careers, often separated by great distances, they continued to look to one another for advice, emotional support, and at times financial assistance.

As children, the sisters were reared in an atmosphere of Norwegian-American Lutheranism where religion played a significant but not a domineering role. They sustained a quiet religious faith through church attendance all of their lives. Their training taught them that "a Christian can be inquiring, can look at life objectively and realistically, and can act and fight in a positive and constructive way for what he believes in."[2] This belief, reinforced by the Scandinavian ethic of hard work, encouraged the sisters to develop their talents in secular professional fields. For the Larson family, as for many others of immigrant background, the Lutheran church, together with the Norwegian language and a strong family recollection of the Norwegian past, provided an ethnically based institutional structure which combined with American opportunity and experience to produce a Norwegian-American culture.

The story of the Larson sisters is thus in part the story of nineteenth-century Norwegian immigration to the United States. The pressures of increased population upon a limited land supply made Norway second only to Ireland in the percentage of its people who emigrated to America, and among the thousands of Norwegians who moved to the Midwest in the 1850s were two freeholding farmers from the vicinity of Hurdal in the Hedmark district of eastern Norway. Lars and Martha Gullickson left their homeland in 1854, and Lars Hansen and Lise Norgaarden set out for America in 1857. Both families were bound for Muskego, Wisconsin, a dispersion point for Norwegian settlement in the Midwest. The Norgaardens moved on almost immediately to southern Minnesota, where in 1858 they joined other farm families of Bloomfield Township, Fillmore County, in organizing a church. Their oldest American-born child, Karen Maria, was the first baby baptized in the new parish.[3]

Although Muskego served only as a brief stopping place for the Norgaardens, the Wisconsin immigrant community became the permanent home of the Lars Gullickson family. Their youngest child, Hans Olaf Larson, born on March 10, 1859, left Muskego at the age of nineteen with $500, his share of his father's estate. His education at the Rochester, Wisconsin, Seminary and at a La Crosse commercial college prepared him for a business career, and he ventured westward with his brother Christian with the idea of going into the Indian trade in South Dakota. En route the young men stopped in Minnesota to visit their mother's friend, Lise Norgaarden. Members of the Bloomfield settlement persuaded the brothers to stay in Fillmore County, and in 1879 they opened a general store which they named Hurdal after the Norwegian community where many of the Bloomfield settlers had originally lived.

In 1883 H. O. Larson and Karen Maria Norgaarden were married at the Bloomfield Lutheran Church in a grand country wedding. Settling on a farm in Bloomfield Township, they began to raise a family. Five children survived to adulthood: Lela M., born on December 29, 1885; Melvin C. on March 5, 1889; Agnes Mathilda on March 15, 1892; Henrietta Melia on September 24, 1894; and Nora Leona on September 19, 1901.[4]

In Fillmore County H. O. Larson prospered as a farmer, politi-

Henrietta, Agnes, and Nora Larson

cian, and businessman. In 1888 he was elected register of deeds and moved his family to the county seat at Preston, where Agnes was born. The family returned to Bloomfield late in 1892 and a few years later built a large farm home with two bathrooms, a luxury almost unheard of in the rural Minnesota of the 1890s. An energetic and capable man, Larson persuaded fellow farmers to unite in several ventures — a bank at the nearby town of Ostrander and three co-operatives, a creamery, an elevator, and a livestock-shipping association. In addition to his farm and business enterprises, Larson held offices in town government, served on the school board, and was a member of his church council. With his business skill, adventurous spirit, and intellectual curiosity, he provided a model of self-reliance, farsightedness, and determination which served his children well.[5]

The Larsons' family life in the Bloomfield-Ostrander community was busy and pleasant. Parents and children enjoyed music and reading sessions and later traveled and camped in the north woods. Everyone participated in the activities of the Bloomfield Lutheran Church. Both parents wanted a sound education for their children, making no distinction in this respect between their son and their four daughters, and the sisters grew up with the assumption that they would go to college and pursue careers of their own choosing.

In 1911 the Larson family, partly to facilitate the education of their younger daughters and partly to escape the burden of the father's heavy responsibilities in Ostrander, moved to Northfield, Minnesota. There they took a house within walking distance of St. Olaf College, from which Lela and Melvin had already graduated. The parents' selection of a Norwegian-Lutheran college for their children was a natural one. Opened in 1874, St. Olaf had gained a reputation for the quality of its liberal arts program and had accepted women students from its inception. The college had operated at first on private donations, but in 1890 it began to receive financial support from the newly formed United Norwegian Lutheran Church, which represented theological moderation within Norwegian-American Lutheranism.[6]

Between 1912 and 1923 Agnes, Henrietta, and Nora attended St. Olaf. Sharing the same household, each sister could observe the others' progress; even at that time they were beginning to shape the course of each others' lives. Young Nora watched Agnes and Henrietta receive their degrees from St. Olaf and then move on into graduate school and teaching. Agnes was Nora's history teacher at Northfield High School. For a classroom assignment at St. Olaf in 1922 Nora wrote a family history which included candid and perceptive descriptions of her sisters. She characterized Agnes, then in graduate school, as "energetic, very generous, somewhat tactless, very ambitious, quick-tempered, sensitive, original." She was also, in Nora's judgment, an "independent" person who "liked leadership." Nora described Henrietta, already teaching college in South Dakota, as "ambitious, studious, keen (the brains of the family)," but also as "reserved, considerate, generous, sensitive." Finally, Nora made an assessment of her own outstanding traits, finding herself to be "reserved, industrious, generous, cheerful, sympathetic" as well as "sensitive, emotional, affectionate, dependable, [and] systematic."

When Nora made these observations, Agnes was already giving evidence of her independence and ambition. She had graduated from St. Olaf in 1916 with a bachelor of arts degree in history and English. Responding to the Progressive era's call for reformers, she left immediately for a summer's study of social work at the University of Chicago. Before long, however, her enthusiasm was "dampened by work in the Chicago slums," and she decided on a career in teaching. Her first job took her to Walcott, North Dakota, where for a year she taught English, German, ancient history, and botany. After another year as high school principal in Harmony, Minnesota, Agnes was back in Northfield, teaching history at the high school and greatly impressing students with her ability. "We never had a dull moment and we always went away refreshed and inspired," one of them later wrote to her.[7]

By 1921 Agnes was twenty-nine and had spent five years in high school teaching and administration. Determined to pursue further study in history, she followed her younger sister Henrietta to graduate school at Columbia University. When she received her master's degree in 1922, she joined the faculty of the State Teachers College at Mankato, Minnesota. Four years later she returned once again to Northfield and to St. Olaf, where she was to spend the rest of her professional life. In accepting an appointment in the department of history, she wrote to President Lars W. Boe, "I feel that I am making quite a sacrifice in salary but the opportunity of serving my alma mater and my church quite outbid the difference in salary." With this goal in mind Agnes joined her former mentor, department chairman Carl A. Mellby, in the fall of 1926 to teach courses in medieval and modern English history as well as the European survey course.[8]

In 1929 Agnes decided to do further graduate work, this time at Radcliffe College, where she pursued her old academic loves, political theory and European culture, and also branched out into American history, a field the St. Olaf department wanted her to develop. When she completed her second master's degree, President Boe encouraged her to remain in school and work for a doctorate. At the same time he expressed the hope that she would continue her interest "in things applicable to administration." Boe may have been anticipating her long tenure as chairman of St. Olaf's history department.[9]

No account of Agnes Larson's career at St. Olaf would be complete without reference to her close working relationship with Lars Boe. In his own rather dictatorial manner, Boe believed wholeheartedly in the future of St. Olaf as an institution of academic excellence. He was able to bring the college through the Depression of the 1930s without once defaulting on a faculty salary, however meager the stipend may have been. Eager to develop a faculty of high quality, he saw graduate school support as a way of retaining promising young staff members whom the college could no longer afford to hire as full-time instructors. For a few hundred dollars a year they could be maintained at an eastern school, and eventually loyalty to college and church would bring them back to St. Olaf.

Agnes had planned to return to the campus in the fall of 1931, but in February of that year she learned that the history department was expecting her to teach several sections of modern European, rather than American, history. She complained to Boe that her new specialty was being ignored and that her salary of $2,000 was inadequate, offering to resign if her complaints were unreasonable. Before these differences could be resolved, however, the American Association of University Women awarded her a $1,500 regional fellowship which allowed her to stay on at Cambridge for another year. Competition for the grant had been keen, especially in the midst of the Depression, and the selection of Agnes as recipient of the award was a recognition of her potential as teacher and scholar.[10]

After accepting the fellowship, Agnes again offered her resignation, but Boe refused to hear of it "under any circumstances." He wrote to her: "St. Olaf must build up its faculty from a group of men and women who are well qualified scholastically and who have personality and a vision of what can be accomplished in our Norwegian group here in the Northwest." Boe added, "You are one of the chosen. I do not say this as a compliment."

In November, 1931, Agnes passed the preliminary examinations for the doctorate and then began work with Frederick Merk of Harvard University on a study of the white pine industry in Minnesota. Her choice of thesis topic was based partly on her regard for her native state and an interest in business learned from her father, but it also showed the influence of Henrietta, who in 1928 had become a research associate in the Harvard Graduate School of Business Administration.

Back at Northfield in the fall of 1932, Agnes faced three responsibilities: teaching, research for her thesis, and cataloguing the Norwegian-American Historical Association archives. A strong supporter of the Norwegian association when it was formed in 1925, Boe was eager to have its collections housed at St. Olaf. The project lay dormant until Agnes, with the help of her friend Esther Gulbrandson of the St. Olaf Norwegian department, took in hand the job of organizing the chaotic materials. Although Agnes felt the archives project was outside her area of expertise, she nevertheless recognized its value for maintaining the Norwegian heritage.[11]

In the first year after her return to the campus, Agnes worked very hard on two new courses — the history of American immigration and the West in American history. Also deep in thesis research, writing articles, and delivering papers at meetings of historical associations, she was beginning to earn a reputation as an expert on the history of lumbering in Minnesota. In addition to using traditional research methods in archives and libraries, she tramped the northern woods during the summer of 1933 to talk with lumberjacks. She also interviewed influential lumber families such as the Weyerhaeusers and the Lairds. The next four summers were spent in a continuation of her hectic research ventures, and by mid-1937 she had nearly finished the work for her doctorate. That August President Boe granted her a last-minute leave with pay for the fall semester so that she could study for her final examinations and complete her thesis, but he solicitously warned her against overpreparation. "Your sense for thoroughness," he wrote, "may be getting the best of you." [12]

On January 12, 1938, to no one's surprise Agnes wired Boe from Cambridge, "Passed very comfortable examination." Her St. Olaf friends helped celebrate her achievement by commissioning Arnold W. Flaten, a sculptor well known in Norwegian-American Lutheran circles, to create a plaque depicting her thesis subject. Flaten's "White Pine" commemorated not only a contribution to historical literature but also the devotion of a college community to one of its members. [13]

Not one to rest on her laurels, Agnes began working with Frederick Merk to prepare her dissertation for publication. She spent some of her summers in Washington, D.C., studying economics at the Brookings Institution and researching land titles at the Department of the Interior. In other vacations in the 1940s she returned to Cambridge to consult with Merk and with Henrietta, who had by then become an authority in business history. During the academic year, she somehow salvaged precious writing time from a heavy teaching schedule and the duties as department chairman which she assumed in 1942. Ten years of hard work were rewarded in 1949. While she enjoyed a well-deserved sabbatical year of travel in South America and Europe, the University of Minnesota Press announced publication of the *History of the White Pine Industry in Minnesota*. [14]

The book, which was eighteen years from inception to publication, was well received. The words of praise which perhaps meant the most to Agnes came from her Harvard adviser. Merk wrote: "I know of no other book in the field that approaches it in integrity of research, in clarity of analysis, and in the mastery of the subject."

The book was indeed meticulously researched and well written, successfully combining economic, business, and social history. It took a sympathetic approach to the industry which Agnes considered to have been the vanguard of settlement of the state. With a romantic, nineteenth-century attitude toward history, expressed in her teaching as well as in her scholarship, Agnes searched for a hero in the north woods and found him in Frederick Weyerhaeuser, whom she considered as the Andrew Carnegie of lumber. Although she described the lumberjacks and their food, tools, and living arrangements in great detail, her real heroes were the entrepreneurs of lumbering. In this analysis she reflected the views of Henrietta, who for years had been emphasizing the role of the administrator in business history.

Publication of *White Pine Industry* was only part of a broader professional career which centered on Agnes' commitment to her college. Many years later she confided to St. Olaf President Clemens M. Granskou that at the time she completed her doctorate she had received a "tantalizing offer" from an eastern women's college. But, she said, she had declined because "St. Olaf was the place where I wished to give my services. There were *my* people and this was *my* church. I have not for one moment regretted that decision." [15]

During her thirty-four years at St. Olaf Agnes perfected ideas about learning and teaching which she had formulated early in her career. Her standards were high, as some 4,000 students learned in her courses where a hard-earned 97 was a mere A minus. Some students came to avoid her thorough, old-fashioned, narrative approach in favor of the interpretive historical analyses offered by younger professors. As the early rumbles of student dissent were felt on the campus in the late 1950s, other undergraduates expressed dissatisfaction with her hero-praising, probusiness view of American development, made so evident by her repeated expressions of admiration for American capitalism during the cold war period. [16]

Despite such criticism her classes were always filled to capacity with students who admired her command of her discipline. Her lofty academic standards were deeply intertwined with a belief that faculty members must be as well prepared as possible if they were to create an atmosphere where learning could thrive. "Teaching to me is a great art that one should strive to perfect," she wrote. "And I want to know that my students are as well prepared as they are at Swarthmore, Dartmouth or Vassar." She repeatedly emphasized her belief in the importance of a liberal arts education. "I get a bit weary of these people who stress only the fact that we educate ministers in our church schools," she once said. "The church would be sadly lacking if we didn't have a few lay people too who did things."[17]

Although her doctoral research was in the area of American history, Agnes never relinquished her love for the Renaissance and European culture. Her theory of history was illustrated by the image of a stream affected at certain times by certain people who opened "a sluice-way through which eventually mighty waters flow." She saw classical Greece, the Renaissance, the Reformation, and the American and French revolutions as critical periods when, as she characteristically put it, through "able leadership mankind was shifting his viewpoint." The same attitude was reflected in her admiration for outstanding figures of the American past — Columbus, Washington, Jefferson, and Lincoln, as well as Carnegie and Weyerhaeuser. Even after the praise of national heroes became unfashionable in professional circles or was discounted by scholarship, Agnes continued to honor Washington and Lincoln in chapel addresses.[18]

She saw the interpretation of the past as a difficult task, especially when it involved teaching one's own national history. The professor of American history, she believed, must create a constructive, not a crisis, interest in understanding the nation. During Hitler's rise to power in the 1930s and the period of World War II, she was concerned particularly that the American educational system be used not to inculcate an official historical position, but to produce responsible and thoughtful citizens in and out of the classroom. In keeping with that precept, she taught several of her courses over St. Olaf radio station WCAL in the 1940s and, to judge by the reaction of her audience, they were well received.

Above all, Agnes saw American history as a tapestry of ethnic, political, economic, social, and cultural threads, emphasizing this theme in an often-repeated phrase, "the European heritage in and with the American environment." One of her favorite assignments, a research paper on the student's family history, encouraged undergraduates to understand the fabric of their own cultural background. Beyond that, she challenged them to think, to analyze, to synthesize. Her approach was humanistic. The historian's goal, she believed, was "to evaluate and tell us what elements in life are worthwhile and have a bearing upon the welfare of men." As she so often said, "We are interested in making life more interesting for you, and to make good people out of you."

Agnes Larson's concern for her students extended far beyond the classroom. She was the recipient of numerous personal confidences. On many occasions she found ways to keep able students at St. Olaf and encouraged many of them to attend graduate school. Never one to mince words, Agnes once revealed much about her struggles in a male-dominated profession when she told a prospective woman graduate student, "You know, of course, in history graduate school a woman student must work three times as hard as a man." [19]

During her eighteen years as department chairman from 1942 to 1960, St. Olaf survived declining wartime enrollments, the return of veterans to campus, and the student influx of the 1950s. As the number of history majors increased, the department slowly began to add new staff. Although she had been on the faculty since 1926, Agnes' salary was only $3,500 in 1949, and during the 1950s the administration was at times offering young Ph.D's more money than it was paying the department chairman, a salary differential indicating that unfair advantage may have been taken of Agnes' deep commitment to her college and her church. [20]

In spite of heavy academic responsibilities, Agnes found time for off-campus activities. An active member of the American Association of University Women at the local and state levels, she lectured to chapters throughout the Midwest on the importance of their fellowship program, which had been of such help to her at a crucial period in her career. During 1950–51 she chaired the Midwest History Conference, and out of a conviction that history was for everyone — not just scholars — she lent her stature to the support of the Rice County Historical Society.

In the spring of 1960, at the age of sixty-eight, Agnes Larson left the St. Olaf faculty because of ill health. What she thought was a long-standing heart ailment proved to be cancer, and from 1961 until her death on January 24, 1967, she underwent treatment by surgery, radiation, and chemotherapy. Agnes typically did not waste those final years. Shortly before her death she completed her second book, *John A. Johnson: An Uncommon American,* the biography of a pioneer Wisconsin businessman whose life personified the blending of European heritage and American environment that had been the theme of Agnes' entire teaching career. Although the book was not the contribution to business history that *White Pine Industry* had been, it was written in an easier, faster-moving style, demonstrating careful scholarship and a thorough familiarity with the subject.[21]

Agnes Larson might have achieved greater financial reward and scholarly acclaim elsewhere, but she chose to dedicate her professional life to her alma mater. Her firm sense of identity with her church and with her ethnic heritage made it possible for her to become a living example of a definition she coined herself: "A teacher is a person who makes learning an adventure."

While Agnes earned her greatest reputation as a teacher, Henrietta, two years younger, became best known for publications which pioneered a new field of scholarship — business history. Reflecting on her endeavors nearly thirty years after she began her work at the Harvard Graduate School of Business Administration, Henrietta saw a moral and institutional purpose in business history: "Essentially, the function of the business historian is that of all historians which I take to be somewhat as follows: The historian is the memory, the interpreter, and the conscience of the past, as such . . . he can do much to stimulate thinking and to create attitudes and feelings which have a part in molding the future. This implies that the historian at best may add to the effectiveness and stature of history as a social institution, which, I believe, should be the ultimate objective of business history."[22]

Henrietta's views on the role of the historian and her interest in business history developed in a number of ways. From her early years she possessed an inquiring mind, "questioning ideas and institutions under which we have been reared and live." After graduation from St. Olaf in 1918, she taught high school for a year at Wheaton, Minnesota. Then, attracted as Agnes had been by social work, she left for Columbia University and courses which would prepare her for admission to the New York School of Social Work. However, after receiving a master's degree in sociology, she too changed her mind about the profession and remained for another year of graduate study in history. She enrolled in courses at both Columbia and the New School of Social Research, and her professors included such notables as William R. Dunning, Charles A. Beard, B. B. Kendrick, and Carlton J. H. Hayes.[23]

Henrietta returned to the Midwest in 1921. After a year on the faculty of Augustana College in Sioux Falls, South Dakota, she began further graduate work at the University of Minnesota. Deciding to write her thesis "close to home," she chose as her topic "The Wheat Market and the Farmer in Minnesota, 1858–1900." Undoubtedly influenced by her father's business ventures, she was attracted to the subject because, contrary to the views of the Progressive historians, she did not feel that farmers had been exploited in the ways emphasized by protesting Grangers and Populists during the 1870s and 1890s. Published in 1926, her careful study of the growth of the wheat-marketing system in Minnesota became an authoritative work in its field.[24]

The two years at Minnesota were to prove crucial to Henrietta's future. In addition to working with such well-known historians as Guy Stanton Ford, August C. Krey, George M. Stephenson, and Lester B. Shippee, she also studied in areas essential to her thesis topic: history of the West, money and banking, agricultural marketing, and economic history. In the latter course Henrietta became acquainted with N. S. B. Gras, a medieval historian who was already developing the germinal idea of business history and the study of individual business enterprises and functions. It was this association which was to lead to her long career at Harvard.[25]

Despite the urgings of Ford and others to remain at Minnesota, Henrietta had decided to finish her graduate work at Columbia. In June, 1926, she became the first alumna of St. Olaf to receive a doctorate. During the previous year she had taught at Bethany College in Lindsborg, Kansas, but, feeling that her twenty-five-hour weekly classroom load was excessive, she applied for a position at Southern Illinois State Normal School at Carbondale. In the process she had her first encounter with sex discrimination, a problem she had not experienced in the graduate schools of the early 1920s. The president of Southern Illinois wrote that he would consider her application if he could not find a man. His search was apparently unsuccessful, and Henrietta arrived at Carbondale in the fall of 1926 to discover that she was the only member of the faculty with a doctorate. Her department chairman, whose education had ended with the eighth grade, saw little need for Henrietta's devotion to the syllabus, essay examinations, and research papers. During the year he failed no one; at the end of the first semester Henrietta failed 20 per cent of her students and expected to be fired immediately. Instead, the school's president praised her teaching methods and added administrative responsibilities to her already heavy load. Fortunately, she was not to remain at Carbondale for long.[26]

In 1928 N. S. B. Gras, who had gone to Harvard to occupy the nation's first chair of business history, asked Henrietta to join him as a research associate in developing the first course and research program in the field. She considered the offer carefully. It meant leaving the Midwest, giving up teaching for a job that was primarily in research, and taking a one-third cut in salary. But she found the challenge irresistible. When she had done research for her dissertation in Minnesota, farmers and elevator managers had expressed astonishment that anyone, particularly a woman, should be interested in their contracts and records. Now that earlier work had become part of a new field of scholarship. She accepted Gras's offer and moved to Boston in the summer of 1928.[27]

Reflecting the probusiness climate of the 1920s, the study of business history as a separate discipline had begun in the United States with impetus supplied by Wallace B. Donham, dean of the Harvard Graduate School of Business Administration. Donham wanted business school students to develop a broad foundation and gain a historical perspective. In 1927 he persuaded Harvard to establish a chair in business history and hire N. S. B. Gras as its first occupant. Gras's study of the market area of Minneapolis and St. Paul was the earliest research in the field, and he had also started to include business materials in his basic economic history course. Applying the inductive approach of turn-of-the-century German historical economists, he investigated specific business and administrative functions, rather than using the theorizing overviews employed by most economic historians. Gras saw business history as an offshoot of economic history, not a part of it. At the Harvard business school he and Henrietta, his chief assistant, led students to view the field as one "concerned with business men and units at work rather than with the description of the general development of industries, economic institutions, and organizations."

Henrietta's duties at Harvard were chiefly editorial, involving journals, monographs, and textbooks. In 1928 Gras and Edwin F. Gay established the *Journal of Economic and Business History*.

Until its demise in 1932 Henrietta carried full responsibility for preparing the journal for the press and also contributed three articles of her own. Gras and his colleagues also initiated the *Harvard Studies in Business History*, and the first volume, Kenneth W. Porter's *John Jacob Astor*, appeared in 1931. The series developed slowly because of limited financial resources, but in 1936 a second volume appeared — *Jay Cooke, Private Banker* by Henrietta Larson. A balanced, thorough study, the book portrayed the human side of Cooke as well as his banking career. In prose which was direct and flowing — unlike the romanticized style of her sister Agnes — Henrietta sounded the persistent theme of the early years of business history: the long-neglected role of the administrator in economic life. As Gras put it in his introduction to the book, "Our recent national pastime has been to judge without studying." Henrietta took the analytical case approach she and Gras were developing and applied it to a book-length analysis of investment banking. The work became a classic in its field.[28]

Along with the development of journals and monographs, Gras and Larson were preparing other materials to be used in basic courses in business history at Harvard and elsewhere. Perfecting the case method pioneered by Gras, they compiled the *Casebook in American Business History*, which was published in 1939. The work included forty-three studies of individual men and companies, ranging from the colonial period to the twentieth century and repeatedly utilized case analysis techniques. In addition it provided instructors with an outline for a three-hour college course in business history. In putting the book together, the authors drew to some extent on the expertise of colleagues in the business school, but all the cases required rewriting, usually by Henrietta, who was also in charge of preparing the manuscript for the printer.

Gras and Larson hoped the book would lead students to look at individual businesses not only in terms of "abstract ideologies or systems but of what works best." Eventually, they believed, the case-study methodology, with its emphasis on administration, policy, management, and control, would permit them to draw conclusions about the operations of business and economic life.

In 1938, when the *Casebook* was well on its way to publication, Henrietta assumed the editorship of the *Bulletin of the Business Historical Society* which Harvard had been issuing since 1926. By this time she had acquired an assistant who relieved her of routine editorial work and enabled her to devote more time to manuscript selection and to her own writing. A number of her articles appeared in the *Bulletin,* sometimes under her name and sometimes not. One in the October, 1942, issue on American railroad history not only reflected her long-time interest in railroads but also embodied a number of critical judgments about the conduct of American business. She felt that railroad executives, like many other administrators, had not adjusted quickly enough to social change nor been sufficiently concerned about careful management. These deficiences she saw as largely responsible for the Depression of the 1930s. In her view the railways had grown so rapidly in the boom years that administrative, ethical, and political checks were neglected. The result was the beginning of government regulation, which she felt had never been very successful.[29]

During the late 1930s and the early 1940s Henrietta began at last to receive recognition for her years of scholarly achievement. In 1939 Harvard advanced her from research associate to assistant professor of business history, a promotion which might have been made earlier had it not been for the Depression and Harvard's attitude toward women faculty members. In 1942, after fourteen years at Harvard, she was made an associate professor, the first woman in the business school to achieve that rank. The next year St. Olaf awarded her an honorary doctorate with a citation which praised her accomplishments but was traditionally patronizing about her work in a field dominated by men: "In keeness [*sic*] of analysis and clarity of judgment she can well hold her own with the best of her masculine colleagues."[30]

In these same years Henrietta was turning her attention to an evaluation of developments in the writing of business and economic history. Some of her reflections can be found in reviews of books by other scholars — particularly economic historians. For example, she criticized Louis M. Hacker's Marxist-oriented work, *The Triumph of American Capitalism,* as "unscholarly in its warped fitting of history into a philosophy" predetermined by the author, a charge she often leveled at economic historians. In an important article published in 1944, she again pointed to neglect of the role of the administrator. She also took economic historians to task for overemphasizing "bigness, monopoly controls, evils in business, and the irresponsible and notorious businessmen." On the other hand, she felt the business historian should not overlook the "serious wrongs in American business, not only the misdeeds

of the individual but general policies and practices which have
been injurious both to business and to society as a whole." In conclusion she wrote: "What business needs from the historians is not
defense but some understanding of how business has operated,
the reasons for its methods, what it has accomplished in producing
goods and services, what has been the effect of its work on society. . . ."[31]

Events in the late 1940s were important to Henrietta Larson's
career. In 1948 Harvard University Press published her *Guide to
Business History*, which had been under way since the early
1930s. A monumental reference book, the *Guide* provided annotated references to 5,000 works and became an indispensable tool
for research in the field. As Gras observed in the book's introduction, "Hidden in the years of drudgery that have gone into such a
compilation as the *Guide* has always been the idea of service to
the other fellow." In 1948 Henrietta also became associate editor
of the *Harvard Studies in Business History* and two years later,
after Gras's retirement, she became editor. It was in this period
too that she became involved in a project which occupied most of
the remainder of her professional life.[32]

In her 1944 article on the status of business history Henrietta
had mentioned that no thorough and comprehensive study had
been made of any major American corporation. Executives of
Standard Oil of New Jersey responded to the challenge and approached Professors Gras and Larson about preparing a possible
history of their company. As a result of these discussions the Business History Foundation was established in 1947 and Jersey
Standard became the first major American corporation to grant
scholars unrestricted access to company records. Gras and Larson
served on the foundation's original board of directors, which undertook as its first major projects a multivolume history of Standard
Oil of New Jersey and a one-volume study of Humble Oil and
Refining Company.[33]

As the work went forward, it became apparent that the task was
far more extensive and difficult than originally expected. (Even
before the project was launched, Henrietta had spent eleven
months surveying the records of Standard Oil to determine that
sufficient materials were available.) In 1955, the year the first volume was published, Gras died and Henrietta was left with full
responsibility. In addition to directing the entire project, Henrietta was senior author of two of the individual volumes — the

Humble Oil book, published in 1959, and the final part of the Standard Oil study, published in 1971.

The project provided the most complete historical treatment ever given to a major American industry. The three volumes were ·in a sense an extended application of the Gras-Larson case approach to the three stages of Jersey Standard's growth — childhood, adolescence, and maturity. As the editors and authors stressed again and again, the arrangements between the Business History Foundation and the companies had given them complete scholarly freedom. Although executives read and criticized the manuscripts and engineers reviewed technical descriptions, they never tried to censor materials. Some reviewers felt the series was too sympathetic to the oil companies and unduly critical of the political reaction against Jersey Standard, but the overall response of the profession was to acknowledge at last the legitimacy of business history and to recognize the works as historiographical landmarks.[34]

Henrietta's career centered on research and publication, but her interests in education cannot be overlooked. After several years at Harvard, she began limited teaching duties, although during her tenure there, the university did not allow a woman to conduct a course in her own name. Henrietta's first assignments involved the supervision of masters' theses and doctoral dissertations. Beginning in the late 1930s, she occasionally taught the graduate course in business history, taking more responsibility in that area after Gras retired in 1950. But even then the course was officially listed in the name of a young man in the department. She served frequently as the business history examiner for orals, since business history was a requirement for all doctoral candidates in the business school. After Gras's retirement she was also responsible for all doctoral dissertations and the work of postdoctoral fellows.[35]

Despite the fact that her professional interests lay in a specialized field of history, Henrietta's basic educational philosophy was similar to that of her sister Agnes. She believed firmly in the value of the liberal arts curriculum. "The primary concern of education," she said, "should be to strengthen the students' capacity to handle data, to think, to understand, rather than to rely on memory; to stimulate curiosity and wonder, rather than to accumulate a store of facts; to arouse enthusiasm for the search for truth rather than to earn enough credits to get a degree." Her work in business history taught her the importance of the indi-

vidual as the "creative factor in economic life" and of the need for
a firm system of values based upon fairness, hard work, and a
sense of duty to society.[36]

In 1960 the Harvard University faculty belatedly recognized
Henrietta's contributions to business history and her thirty-two
years in the School of Business Administration by promoting her
to the rank of full professor, a somewhat anticlimactic action which
came only a year before her retirement. She was, however, the
first woman in the business school and only the sixth in the 324-
year history of the university to achieve that distinction.[37]

While Henrietta never regarded herself as a crusader for wom-
en's rights, she has recognized the problems encountered by
women in fields dominated by men, particularly in academic and
historical circles. Her own success she attributes to hard work and
her good fortune in attracting the attention of N. S. B. Gras. Discrimination in colleges and universities, she believes, has been
not only unjust to women but "bad for the institutions themselves." She has observed that during the early years of the century many women professors pursued successful careers, particularly on the faculties of women's colleges. But as their numbers
increased, she feels, they presented a threat to the professional
security of their male colleagues who then used academic politics
as a weapon against women's advancement. As she wrote in 1961,
"society has not yet called forth the best efforts of our college
women, but there is no question but that their role is changing and
with it their responsibilities."[38]

Henrietta Larson's busy career did leave her some time for outside activities and relaxation. In addition to work in professional
associations she was active for many years in the American Association of University Women, the University Lutheran Church in
Cambridge, and the Boston chapter of the Scandinavian-
American Foundation. During the three decades she lived in the East
she remained close to members of her family and spent most of her
vacations with them.[39]

Partly out of concern for the health of Agnes, Henrietta retired
from the active faculty of Harvard in 1961, but she continued to do
part-time research and editorial work. She hoped that her retirement would make it possible for her "to reflect and write more
broadly on the history of business when my research responsibilities become lighter." That hope was realized at least in part
with the 1971 publication of *New Horizons*, the third and final

volume in the Jersey Standard series, which Henrietta wrote jointly with Evelyn H. Knowlton and Charles S. Popple.[40]

Since her retirement Henrietta has spent most of her time in Northfield, while maintaining an active interest in the Business History Conference and continuing on the board of directors of the Business History Foundation. In 1963 she served on the advisory curriculum committee for the newly created Southwest State College at Marshall, Minnesota. In 1965–66 she spent several months in Ahmedabad, India, as Ford Foundation consultant to the Indian Institute of Management's program in business history. In 1976, at the age of eighty-two, the quiet, gentle woman who never forgot her midwestern and Scandinavian roots remained, in the words of her friend and long-time colleague Ralph W. Hidy, "the 'deaness' of business historians in the United States."[41]

Nora, the youngest of the Larson sisters, pursued a career in bacteriology, a field very different from that of her historian sisters. She has shared with them a love of learning, a penchant for hard work, and a high regard for family and heritage. During her childhood on her parents' Bloomfield farm she was more interested in red wagons and animals than in dolls. Like her sisters she acquired a fondness for the out of doors and in her seventies still enjoyed camping trips. However, her interest in nature and sports did not interfere with a love of reading. Among her girlhood favorites were *Little Women*, the "Little Colonel" series, and the adventure stories which were then considered books for boys. At St. Olaf she majored in chemistry, enjoyed literature, and participated in women's intramural sports, earning letters in field hockey and basketball. In an undergraduate essay she summed up her interests as follows: "I am especially attracted by ideas and thoughts but I also enjoy excellency of form and perfection of expression. I prefer problem stories and I enjoy heated debates and spirited argument."[42]

Following her graduation from St. Olaf in 1923, Nora spent a year teaching biology and physical education at Aitkin, Minnesota. Her fondness for sports had led to a concern for physical fitness, and she saw a need for the "balancing of body, mind, and soul." In 1924 an interest in medical research took her to Rochester, Minnesota, and a job as technologist in the bacteriology laboratory of the Mayo Clinic's clinical pathology section. Much of her work there was routine clinical testing, but she also performed experiments on bacterial growth factors, a subject that became central to a lifetime of research in microbiology. Beginning in 1926, she took advantage of the Mayo Foundation's affiliation with the University of Minnesota to work toward a master of science degree, which she received in 1933. After a three-year interlude in Boston, where she lived with Henrietta and worked as a bacteriologist for the Lahey Clinic, Nora returned to Rochester and the Mayo Foundation's Institute of Experimental Medicine. There she spent two years as a research assistant to Dr. Henry F. Helmholz, an early investigator of the effects of sulfonamides on bacteria, and thus became involved in the first stages of experimentation with the use of sulfa drugs. In 1941 the Lahey Clinic, impressed by the caliber of her work as a laboratory bacteriologist, asked her to come back. She spent another two years in Boston, again living with Henrietta.

Nora was not, however, totally satisfied with the quality of the work at Lahey and she began to think about further graduate study. Early in 1943 she wrote Dr. Arthur T. Henrici, a professor of bacteriology whom she knew at the University of Minnesota, to inquire about the availability of jobs for graduate students. Henrici replied that the university needed an additional researcher in a project dealing with the effect of antibiotics on war-wound infections. Nora discussed the opportunity with Henrietta, who encouraged her younger sister to return to school and to work in the developing field of antibiotic research. "Within a month," Nora recalled, "I was on the train." In 1944 she became an assistant bacteriologist, working with H. Orin Halvorson, who supervised her doctoral research. She received her degree in 1947 with a dissertation entitled "An Inhibitary Factor Isolated From Growing Cultures of Yeast."

Shortly before she received her doctorate Nora went to the east coast, for the third time, to take a position as chief bacteriologist at the Takamine Laboratories in Clifton, New Jersey. Her research there was concerned primarily with the production of amylase and protease enzymes in fungi. She also worked again with antibiotics, studying the production of the enzyme penicillinase in certain species of bacteria. Nora concluded her three years at Takamine with a combination professional and pleasure trip to Europe, first attending a congress of biochemists in England, and then visiting laboratories and conferring with scientists in Sweden, Denmark, France, and the Netherlands.

In 1950, at the age of forty-nine, Nora ended the peripatetic phase of her career and settled in Minnesota. She moved to Austin, where she was to live for the next ten years, working at the University of Minnesota's Hormel Institute as a research fellow. Established in 1942, the institute was originally concerned with organic chemistry and problems of rancidity in fats and oils; later it branched out into animal nutrition and veterinary medicine, particularly the diseases of swine.[43]

At the Hormel Institute, where she did research on swine diseases, Nora was the only woman among the thirteen principal scientists. She has recalled that she suffered "no particular discrimination." Her colleagues included her in their golf games, and as far as she could determine there was no discrimination in salary. While her fellow scientists accepted her, she remembers too that when it was necessary to go into Hormel's meat-processing plant, workers often gawked at the sight of a woman researcher.[44]

Continuing to follow her principal research interests, she investigated antibacterial agents and antibiotics, especially their effects on the enzyme systems of bacteria. One of the projects in which she participated involved the effects of antibiotics on the growth rate of swine. During the summer of 1953 she worked with Dr. Gordon Davis at the Rocky Mountain Laboratory in Montana on the possibility that some insects, particularly wood ticks, might be the carriers of disease organisms to baby pigs.[45]

In 1956 Nora was promoted from research fellow to assistant professor of veterinary medicine. That her promotion was belated is suggested by the fact that three years earlier, her professional colleagues had shown their respect for her work by electing her president of the Henrici Society, the Minnesota organization of microbiologists. She spent her last years at Hormel on experiments related to the development of a disease-free, fast-growing strain of swine. This type of research was important in producing hogs which would yield the greatest amount of meat at the lowest cost, potentially of benefit to farmer, processor, and consumer alike.[46]

During the ten years she lived in Austin Nora held a number of offices in the American Association of University Women. An interest in international affairs involved her in programs supporting the United Nations. She also developed her teaching skills in the nursing program at Austin Junior College, maintained her active membership in professional societies and in Austin's St. Olaf

Lutheran Church, and pursued her hobbies of photography, camping, and canoeing.

In the fall of 1960, at the age of fifty-nine, Nora moved to Northfield to join Agnes, who had recently retired, and to become associate professor of biology at St. Olaf. In the next twelve years she managed to carry a heavy teaching load, continue her research, and participate in professional organizations. She was active in the Minnesota Academy of Science and during her more than twenty years in that organization served as a judge at numerous high school science fairs.

For fifteen months in 1964–65 she took part in a special work-study program for undergraduates at the Argonne National Laboratories near Chicago, advising and teaching the students who worked as laboratory assistants. Since the program also offered the participating faculty an opportunity to further their own projects, Nora conducted experiments on bacterial lipids, and presented a paper on the results to the American Society for Microbiology in 1965.[47]

In addition to pursuits directly associated with science Nora again became active in the American Association of University Women. She chaired a number of local committees and served as a delegate to national conventions in Miami and Chicago. In 1962 she attended the conference of the International Federation of University Women held in Mexico City and worked as a liaison officer between the United States delegation and other groups. Perhaps her most satisfying responsibility was her membership from 1963 to 1969 on the AAUW's national committee on fellowships and awards, which selected the annual recipients of graduate and postdoctoral grants. In reviewing her participation on this committee, Nora described the applicants as "intellectually superior, creative and committed," a judgment sustained by follow-up studies conducted in 1968 which demonstrated that 76 per cent of the beneficiaries of the award program begun in 1888 had continued in their professional fields.[48]

Nora Larson's observations on her experience as a woman in what is generally regarded as the male-dominated scientific field provide an interesting contrast to the sex-discrimination problems encountered by her sisters. Nora does not believe that she personally suffered discriminatory treatment. Feminist observers of her career might conclude otherwise on the basis of her slow advance up the promotional ladder, but Nora's frequent job changes are, of course, the most obvious explanation for this lack of rapid progress despite excellent educational and research credentials. Nora feels that the field of microbiology has always dealt favorably with women because they were involved at high levels from the beginning. When she joined the American Society for Microbiology during the 1920s, for instance, women composed one-third of the membership, and in 1929 a woman was elected president of the national organization. By contrast, no national professional historical association has yet had a woman president.[49]

Nora believes, however, that with the emphasis on early marriage in the 1950s and 1960s, the role of women in the scientific professions diminished. It is also her view that when men returning from World War II came into competition with women, discrimination became increasingly apparent. Despite her satisfaction with the professional treatment she received, Nora feels strongly that women must be encouraged to seek higher education and high-level jobs. At St. Olaf Nora found that a number of well-qualified women received graduate fellowships at good schools only to drop out later — some of them to get married. She expressed her own sense of responsibility when she commented, "Apparently, we don't inspire them enough."[50]

When Nora retired from the St. Olaf biology department in the spring of 1972, she brought to a close the third of three distinguished careers. Like her sisters, Nora worked in a competitive field dominated by men. Like Agnes and Henrietta, she was sustained by an attachment to such basic institutions as family, community, and church, by a traditional view of the American system which believed in hard work, improvement, and excellence, and by pride in a Scandinavian heritage. Together the three Larsons achieved a sense of sisterhood which went beyond the coincidence of birth to provide firm and crucial support for one another's endeavors. Within the security established by an institutional framework, each of the Larson sisters succeeded in her individual career because, first of all, she knew who she was.

Agnes, Henrietta, and Nora Larson belonged to the generation of professional women who completed their basic education in the early years of the twentieth century, at a time when it was assumed that women had to choose between a career and marriage and when career women expected to work harder than men in order to succeed. Most of them were willing to devote their total lives to their professions without directly challenging the male-dominated authority of their respective fields. Although none of the Larson sisters was a crusader for women's rights, each in her own way furnished the proof of female accomplishment which feminist activists down through the years have attempted to state to the world. By hard work and quiet persistence they helped pave the way for the day when women who pursue careers will be evaluated by the same criteria as men.

17. BRIEF BIOGRAPHIES
Of Other Minnesota
Women

Compiled by Patricia C. Harpole

FROM the many possible candidates, the compiler has selected for inclusion here a cross section of over 100 Minnesota women both living and dead. While no attempt has been made to be inclusive or to list all the accomplishments of those named here, it is hoped that these brief sketches will suggest something of the range of Minnesota women's activities over the years and will inspire others to undertake further research. The source material from which the following information was drawn may be found in the Minnesota Historical Society's library, where an annotated file is also maintained for consultation.

ALDRICH, DARRAGH, *pseud.* (Clara Chapline Thomas) (Mrs. Chilson Darragh Haynes Aldrich), author, b. Dec. 31, 1884, Richmond, Ind.; d. Mar. 31, 1967, Minneapolis. Novelist, playwright, poet, teacher, and newspaper reporter; first novel, *Enchanted Hearts* (1918), produced on Broadway, later made into a movie, *A Prince There Was;* radio commentator, 1941–56.

ANDERSON, EUGENIE MOORE (Mrs. John Pierce Anderson), diplomat, b. May 26, 1909, Adair, Ia. Democratic national committeewoman, 1948–49; first American woman ambassador: ambassador to Denmark, 1949–53; first woman recipient Grand Cross of the Order of Dannebrog, 1953; first woman diplomat to an iron curtain country, Bulgaria, 1962–64.

APPLEGATE, IRVAMAE VINCENT (Mrs. Dwain William Applegate), educator, b. Sept. 18, 1920, Beulah, N. Dak.; d. Mar. 5, 1973, St. Cloud. School of Education dean, St. Cloud State College, 1962–73; president Minnesota Educational Assn., 1963–64; president National Education Assn., 1966–67.

ARTH, JEANNE MARIE, tennis player, b. July 31, 1935, St. Paul. Ranked fifth in U.S. women's singles, 1958; winner of women's doubles title, 1958, 1959; Wimbledon doubles champion, 1959; member U.S. winning Wightman Cup team, 1959.

AUERBACHER, JEANNE BRAUNSCHWEIG (Mrs. William Auerbacher), fashion co-ordinator, b. Dec. 1, 1898, Strasbourg, France; d. Jan. 28, 1975, Minneapolis. Major figure in Twin Cities fashion; manager of Dayton's Oval Room for many years.

BALENGER, LILLIAN MATTIE PARKS (Mrs. Russell T. Balenger), minority rights leader, b. Aug. 17, 1909, Ft. Scott, Kan. Playground instructor, 1928–30; statistician; since 1945 inspector for Western Electric; national president Council of Urban League Guilds, 1954–57; board member of St. Paul Urban League, 1958–65.

BANNING, MARGARET CULKIN (Mrs. Archibald Tanner Banning; later Mrs. LeRoy Salsich), novelist, b. Mar. 18, 1891, Buffalo. Graduate of Vassar College (1912), and trustee of that college, 1936–44; director of Duluth Social Center, 1913–14; first woman in Duluth Hall of Fame; member of British Information Service in World War II; author of over 30 books.

BEDARD, IRENE REDMAN (Mrs. Alexander J. Bedard), journalist, b. Mar. 10, 1901, Palmer Rapids, Ont., Canada. Writer for *Hibbing Daily Tribune* since 1921; its business manager and secretary-treasurer 1943–; past president Minnesota Press Women; only woman director Northwest Daily Press Assn.; named press Woman of Achievement, 1957; named Woman of Achievement by the *Minneapolis Star* and *Tribune*, 1952; received national recognition for articles on foreign countries; awarded the President Cortines Trophy in 1956 for articles on Mexico.

BERG, PATRICIA JANE, golfer, b. Feb. 13, 1918, Minneapolis. Winner of more than 80 amateur and professional golf tournaments; leader in organizing the Ladies Professional Golf Assn.;

one of 13 charter members World Golf Hall of Fame, Pinehurst, N.C.; named Associated Press outstanding woman athlete, 1938.

BOARDMAN, ANNE CAWLEY (Mrs. Charles W. Boardman), author, teacher, b. July 20, 1899, Sistersville, W. Va. Teacher, chairman of the English department, University of Minnesota, 1931–34; author of books, *Such Love Is Seldom* and *Shepherd's Fold*, articles, and short stories in Catholic and secular magazines.

BOYNTON, RUTH EVELYN, public health physician, b. Jan. 3, 1896, LaCrosse, Wis. University of Minnesota Student Health Service director and professor of public health, 1936–61; member State Board of Health, 1939–61; author of over 85 articles and several books on student health, defense workers' health, tuberculosis, and menstrual problems.

BRINK, CAROL RYRIE (Mrs. Raymond Woodard Brink), author, b. Dec. 28, 1895, Moscow, Ida. Writer of children's stories since 1925; winner of Newbery Medal, 1936, for *Caddie Woodlawn*; editor of yearly collection, *Best Stories for Boys and Girls*, 1934–40.

BROOKS, GLADYS SINCLAIR (Mrs. Wright W. Brooks), politician, b. June 8, 1914, Minneapolis. Chairperson of Governor's Human Rights Commission, 1961; president World Affairs Council, 1942–44; delegate national GOP convention, 1952; member Minneapolis City Council, 1967–73; member Metropolitan Council, 1975–.

BURR, JANE HUMBIRD, suffrage leader, b. Apr. 23, 1869, Md.; d. Aug. 26, 1944, St. Paul. National Democratic Executive Committee member, 1920; first president Ramsey County League of Women Voters, 1919; one of the first women members St. Paul Assn. (now the St. Paul Chamber of Commerce).

CAIN, MYNDALL (Mrs. William A. Wicklund), beauty authority, b. Apr. 22, 1901, Cass Lake; d. Jan. 30, 1964, Minneapolis. Opened her first salon in Minneapolis during the 1920s; assumed operation of the Donaldson-Golden Rule salons, 1948; manufactured beauty supplies under the "Myndall Cain" label.

CHUTE, BEATRICE JOY, author, b. Jan. 3, 1913, Minneapolis. Writer of boys' sports stories; since 1950 has written almost exclusively in the adult field; youngest of three writing sisters; her book, *Greenwillow*, became a Broadway musical, 1960; associate professor of English at Barnard College, New York City, since 1966.

CHUTE, MARCHETTE GAYLORD, author, b. Aug. 16, 1909, Wayzata. Most of her works are biographical, chiefly published in England; president of the American P.E.N., 1955–57; recipient University of Minnesota outstanding achievement award, 1957.

CHUTE, MARY GRACE (Mrs. Frank Smith), author, b. Aug. 25, 1907, Wayzata. Wrote under the initials M. G. Chute because her writing was for a masculine audience; her popular short stories about Sheriff Olson appeared in the *Saturday Evening Post*.

CLAPESATTLE, HELEN BERNIECE (Mrs. Roger Wallace Shugg), editor, writer, b. Nov. 11, 1908, Fort Wayne, Ind. University of Minnesota Press assistant editor, 1937–39; editor, 1939–50; editor-in-chief, 1950–53; director, 1953–57; author, *The Doctors Mayo* (1941).

CLARK, KEITH, educator, suffragist, b. June 4, 1879, St. Peter; d. Oct. 6, 1951, New York City. Author of two travel books: *The Spell of Spain* (1914), *The Spell of Scotland* (1916); editorial writer *St. Paul Dispatch*, 1898–1917; professor of history and political science Carleton College, 1923–42.

CLOSE, ELIZABETH SCHEU (Mrs. Winston A. Close), architect, b. June 4, 1912, Vienna, Austria. Moved to U.S., 1932; student, Massachusetts Institute of Technology; partner with husband in Minneapolis architectural firm since 1938; has performed as cellist with the Minneapolis Civic Orchestra and served on its board of directors, 1951–68.

COLVIN, SARAH TARLETON (Mrs. Alexander R. Colvin), nurse, suffragist, b. Sept. 2, 1865, Green County, Ala.; d. Apr. 21, 1949, St. Paul. Minnesota Nurses Assn. member; founder Minnesota Congressional Union; suffrage activities led to two jail sentences in 1918, one for burning Woodrow Wilson in effigy; member State

Board of Education, 1935; resigned, 1941, in protest over political control of the board; author, *A Rebel in Thought* (1944).

CURRIE, CONSTANCE, social worker, b. Mar. 18, 1890, Mousamin, Sask., Canada; d. Nov. 14, 1957, St. Paul. Neighborhood House director, St. Paul, 1919–57; U.S. delegate International Conference of Settlement Houses, 1931; consultant to U.S. Children's Bureau; cited by government of Mexico for work with Mexican-Americans.

DAHL, BORGHILD, author, b. Feb. 5, 1890, Minneapolis. Despite blindness, high school principal in Minnesota schools, 1912–22; professor Augustana College, Sioux Falls, S. Dak., 1926–39; author of 13 books for young people, 1935–68; awarded the St. Olaf medal by King Haakon of Norway in 1950.

DAVIS, GRACE FAYETTE KAERCHER (Mrs. Edward A. Davis), attorney, b. June 17, 1887, Auburn, Ia.; d. Sept. 27, 1965, St. Paul. Associated with her father in insurance, law, and land businesses and on his newspaper, the *Ortonville Independent*, 1910–22; active in women's rights movement; first woman elected clerk of any state Supreme Court, served 1922–34, 1938–41.

DAVIS, IDA BLEHERT (Mrs. Harry Davis), community worker, b. Dec. 15, 1895, St. Paul; d. Mar. 16, 1970, Duluth. Daughter of Russian-Jewish immigrants; graduate of the University of Minnesota in sociology; settlement house worker and community leader; author, *Fun with Yiddish* (1967).

ELLIS, MARY JACKSON (Mrs. Carter V. Ellis II), educator, b. Mar. 21, 1916, W. Va.; d. Mar. 3, 1975, Minneapolis. Minneapolis' first full-time black teacher; nationally recognized innovator in teaching young children; author of three children's books and 70 teaching-aid publications.

ENDRESON, GURI (Mrs. Lars Endreson), pioneer heroine, b. Mar. 26, 1813, Hugen, Norway; d. June 20, 1881, Dovre. Immigrated to Kandiyohi County, 1857; during the Sioux Uprising of 1862, her husband and a son were killed; she displayed great courage, rescuing three wounded men with whom she escaped to safety.

ENRIGHT, ADELAIDE MARY (Mrs. Charles H. Loomis), business executive, political activist, b. Chicago, Ill. Sales manager, 1922, of James C. Enright (father) milling business, Enright's All O' the Wheat; president of the company, 1940–70; member National Woman's party; first woman on St. Paul City Charter Commission, 1953–65.

FIRKINS, INA TEN EYCK, librarian, b. [June 9, 1866?]; d. July 16, 1937, on a steamer off the coast of Norway. University of Minnesota reference librarian, 1889–1932; compiled indexes to collections of short stories and plays and published a bibliography on Henrik Ibsen in 1921; first president Minneapolis College Women's Club.

FLANDRAU, GRACE C. HODGSON (Mrs. W. Blair Flandrau), author, b. St. Paul; d. Dec. 27, 1971, Farmington, Conn. Published six novels and numerous short stories; *Being Respectable* (1924) became a movie; honorary degree in literature Hamline University, 1947; established Charles E. Flandrau Research Fund at the Minnesota Historical Society.

FOSSEEN, CARRIE SECELIA JORGENS (Mrs. Manley Lewis Fosseen), civic leader, b. Jan. 30, 1875, Fergus Falls; d. Mar. 23, 1963, Long Lake. First woman advocate of trade schools in the regular school system; first chairman of the Women's Welfare League; chairman of Republican women's activities in Minnesota; first woman delegate-at-large to GOP convention, 1920; first woman to be given the floor at a national Republican convention; named Minnesota Mother of the Year, 1947.

GÁG, WANDA HAZEL (Mrs. Earle Marshall Humphreys), illustrator, author, b. Mar. 11, 1893, New Ulm; d. June 27, 1946, New York City. At fifteen submitted illustrations to the *Minneapolis Journal;* first published work, *Millions of Cats* (1928), created a demand for her children's books; her woodcut drawings are in a number of major museum collections.

GASKINS, LAURA MARY GREVIOUS (Mrs. Ashby U. Gaskins), social worker, b. Sept. 19, 1916, Jessamine County, Ky. Twin Cities section president, National Council of Negro Women, 1967–69; vice-president Minneapolis Urban Coalition, 1968–70;

first black president Minnesota Adoption Council, 1968–69, and Minnesota Social Services Assn., 1974–75; first black social worker (1945) and supervisor of family counseling, Hennepin County welfare department, 1947–. Governor Wendell R. Anderson proclaimed Oct. 13, 1976, as Laura Gaskins Day.

GIESEN, MARY DREIS (Mrs. Peter Joseph Giesen), businesswoman, b. [1844?]; d. Mar. 20, 1929, St. Paul. Founder of oldest theatrical costume house in Northwest, 1872, a family business until 1960; costumer for 1883 procession celebrating completion of the Northern Pacific Railway; retired, 1903.

GLENDENNING, LOUISE M. DALY (Mrs. W. Gordon Glendenning), businesswoman, b. July 30, 1906, Cottage Grove. Established trucking firm in 1924 with her husband; after his death in 1948, president of the growing trucking firm — one of the nation's largest in 1977 — and operator of a 1,100-acre dairy farm.

HARDING, MARGARET SNODGRASS (Mrs. Samuel Bannister Harding), editor, b. Jan. 6, 1885, Chicago, Ill.; d. Mar. 13, 1976, Grand Rapids, Minn. Coauthor of books with her historian husband; first head of the University of Minnesota Press, 1927–53; vice-president American Assn. of University Presses, 1951–52.

HAUSER, NANCY McKNIGHT, teacher-choreographer, b. Nov. 20, 1909, Bayside, Long Island, N.Y. Performer with Hanya Holm dance troupe; instructor in dance Carleton College, 1944–46, 1952–54, and Macalester College, 1946–49; founder Dance Guild, St. Paul, 1951, and Guild of Performing Arts, Minneapolis, 1968, which now participates in two national touring programs.

HEFFELFINGER, ELIZABETH E. BRADLEY (Mrs. Frank Peavey Heffelfinger), civic leader, b. Nov. 12, 1900, Lafayette, Ind. National Republican committeewoman for Minnesota, 1948–60; secretary Republican national committee, 1957–60; member U.S. National Commission for UNESCO; U.S. delegate to three UNESCO conferences.

HEILBRON, BERTHA LION, historian, writer, b. May 11, 1895, St. Paul; d. Nov. 21, 1972, St. Paul. Minnesota Historical Society research assistant, 1919; editorial assistant to Theodore C. Blegen on *Minnesota History* magazine, 1922–39; its editor, 1939–60; research fellow for the society, 1961–72; author, *The Thirty-second State* (1958); editor of Henry Lewis, *The Valley of the Mississippi* (1967) and other works.

HILGER, SISTER MARY INEZ, historian, b. Oct. 16, 1891, Roscoe. College of St. Benedict teacher, 1925–32, and dean, 1925–28; ethnological field worker among Woodland, Plains, Southwest Indian tribes of North America, Chile, and Argentina, 1932–52; author of books on child life and cultural backgrounds of the Chippewa, Arapaho, and Araucanian; lecturer on Indian cultural life throughout the U.S. as well as in many foreign countries.

HOLM, VIRGINIA PAUL (Mrs. Mike Holm; later Mrs. Arthur L. Bye), state official, b. Mar. 14, 1902, St. Paul. Appointed to succeed her husband in 1952 as Secretary of State, the first woman in Minnesota's history to hold that office; elected for a two-year term, 1954–55.

HUGHES, JOYCE ANN (Mrs. Henry T. Smith), attorney, b. Feb. 7, 1940, Gadsden, Ala. First black governor of Minnesota Girls' State, 1956; first black woman to obtain law degree from the University of Minnesota, 1965; named Outstanding Young Woman of America, 1967; associate professor University of Minnesota Law School, 1971–74; associate professor, Northwestern University School of Law, 1975–.

HUSTED, MARJORIE CHILD (Mrs. K. Wallace Husted), advertising executive, b. Minneapolis. Head of Home Service Department of General Mills for twenty years; known to millions of Americans as "Betty Crocker," the character she originated on radio in 1927; named Woman of the Year, 1949, by the National Press Club.

JACOBSON, DOROTHY HOUSTON (Mrs. George W. Jacobson), educator, government official, b. Nov. 13, 1907, Herman. Assistant professor of political science Macalester College, 1945–55; administrative assistant to Governor Orville L. Freeman; policy adviser and speech writer for U.S. Secretary of Agriculture Freeman, 1961; assistant U.S. Secretary of Agriculture, 1964, the highest ranking post to be held by a woman in the Agriculture Department.

JAQUES, FLORENCE PAGE (Mrs. Francis Lee Jaques), writer, b. Mar. 7, 1890, Decatur, Ill.; d. Jan. 1, 1972, North Oaks. Coauthor with artist-husband of books about the outdoors and wildlife, notably *Canoe Country* (1938), *The Geese Fly High* (1939), *Snowshoe Country* (1944).

JOHNSON, HILDEGARD BINDER (Mrs. Palmer Oliver Johnson), educator, b. Aug. 20, 1908, Berlin, Germany. Assistant professor Macalester College geography department, 1947–52; associate professor, 1952–56; professor and chairman, 1956–75; author of numerous articles in the fields of geography and immigration movements.

JOHNSON, JOSIE ROBINSON (Mrs. Charles W. Johnson), civic leader, regent, b. Oct. 7, 1930, San Antonio, Tex. First president Minneapolis chapter, National Council of Negro Women; board member League of Women Voters of the U.S.; special assistant on community affairs to Minneapolis mayor, 1967–68; community services director Minneapolis Urban League, 1971; first black regent University of Minnesota, 1971–73.

JONES, ELIZABETH McLEOD (Mrs. Lewis R. Jones), journalist, publisher, b. Feb. 5, 1883, New Richmond, Wis.; d. Feb. 25, 1958, St. Paul. Editor of family newspaper, the *Le Sueur Sentinel*; reporter *Daily News and American* (Aberdeen, S. Dak.); head of women's department *Minneapolis Tribune*; publisher *Stillwater Post-Messenger*, 1932–41, and *Northfield Independent*, 1954–56.

JONES, PERRIE, librarian, b. Mar. 22, 1886, Wabasha; d. Nov. 7, 1968, St. Paul. Librarian of Wabasha Public Library, 1911–15; hospital librarian St. Paul Public Library, 1921–28; supervisor of state institution libraries, 1928–37; associate professor University of Minnesota, 1937–48; chief librarian St. Paul Public Library, 1937–56.

JOSEPH, GERI MACK (Mrs. Burton Morris Joseph), civic worker, journalist, b. June 19, 1923, St. Paul. Staff writer *Minneapolis Tribune*, 1945–53, and in 1977 contributing editor; Democratic-Farmer-Labor party chairperson, 1958–60; national Democratic committeewoman, 1960–71; vice-chairperson of the committee and director of women's activities, 1968–70.

KERST, MOTHER SCHOLASTICA, educator, b. June 21, 1847, Mueringen, Germany; d. June 11, 1911, Duluth. Superioress of St. Benedict's Convent, St. Joseph, 1880; founder of parochial school, Duluth, 1881, the nucleus of the parochial school system there and the forerunner of the College of St. Scholastica; Superioress, province of the Sisters of St. Benedict, Diocese of Duluth, 1889–1911; helped found St. Mary's Hospital, Duluth, 1888, and its school of nursing, 1908.

KNEUBUHL, EMILY ROSE, educator, civic worker, b. Aug. 16, 1883, Burlington, Ia.; d. Mar. 23, 1967, Minneapolis. Minneapolis elementary schools principal, 1908–17; lecturer and organizer Minnesota League of Women Voters; headed campaign to establish a city manager form of government in Minneapolis, 1926; educational director Rural Electrification Administration, 1935; served on mayor's advisory commission for Minneapolis city charter revision, 1944–46.

KOHLER, KATHERINE, suffragist, civic leader, b. June 7, 1875, Waconia; d. Jan. 2, 1967, Minneapolis. Director of adult education for Minneapolis public schools, 1920–43; first president Minneapolis Council of Americanization, 1925–45; pioneered naturalization civics classes and English classes for foreign-born mothers.

KYLE, MARY JAMES (Mrs. Earle F. Kyle, Sr.), journalist, b. St. Paul. Columnist, free-lance writer, and radio and television commentator, 1948–; member Minneapolis mayor's committee on juvenile delinquency, 1957; president Minnesota Press Club, 1975; numerous journalism and human rights awards; editor and publisher, *Twin Cities Courier*, 1967–.

LAWRENCE, RUTH ELIZABETH WILLIAMSON (Mrs. James C. Lawrence), art educator, b. June 9, 1890, Clarksfield, O.; d. Jan. 25, 1977, Santa Barbara, Ca. Designer, business manager North Country Guild, 1920–25; gallery curator, art instructor University of Minnesota, 1934–39; gallery director, assistant professor, 1939–57.

LE SUEUR, MERIDEL, author, poet, b. Feb. 22, 1900, Murray, Ia. Student and teacher of dance and theater groups; writer and poet; first published work, 1927; author of more than 10 books and over 150 articles; lecturer University of Minnesota and other colleges.

LINTON, LAURA A., teacher, scientist, and doctor, b. Apr. 8, 1853, Alliance, Ohio; d. Apr. 1, 1915, Rochester. Graduate of University of Minnesota, 1879, and its medical school, 1900; in 1879 carried out the analysis that established lintonite as a mineral, the only one thus far named for a woman; teacher Minneapolis Central High School, 1887–97; chemical researcher University of Michigan, 1898–99; physician in charge of female section, Rochester State Hospital, 1900–15.

LUND, RHODA SYNNEVA BERGE (Mrs. Russell T. Lund), civic worker, b. Dec. 6, 1904, Butternut Valley. Minnesota Republican Central Committee, chairperson, 1953–54; delegate Republican national convention, 1956, 1964, 1968; Republican national committeewoman, 1960–72; member Minnesota advisory commission to U.S. Commission on Civil Rights, 1964–72.

MacARTHUR, LAURA, educator, b. Oct. 18, 1879, England; d. June 18, 1964, Duluth. Teacher and principal Duluth public school system, 1896–1935; school board member, 1937–40; Laura MacArthur Elementary School, dedicated in 1957, only Duluth public school named for a local woman.

McDANIEL, ORIANNA, public health physician, b. Oct. 2, 1872, Barrington, N.H.; d. Mar. 12, 1975, Minneapolis. First woman physician Minnesota State Health Department, 1896–1946; head of its division of preventable diseases, 1921–46.

McFARLAND, MARY ELLEN HANSON (Mrs. Keith N. McFarland), home economist, b. July 2, 1921, Buhl. Governor's Commission on the Status of Women member, 1963–67; first woman appointed to Independent School District 621 board, 1965–71; board member of first Vocational-Technical School District 916, 1969–71; American Home Economics Assn. treasurer, 1972–74, and president, 1976–77.

McHUGH, SISTER ANTONIA, educator, b. May 17, 1873. Omaha, Neb.; d. Oct. 11, 1944, St. Paul. St. Joseph's Academy teacher, 1891–1904; dean College of St. Catherine, St. Paul,

1914–29; president there, 1929–37; recipient Pope Pius XI *Pro Ecclesia et Pontifice* medal, 1931; LL.D., University of Minnesota, 1936; University of Chicago Alumni Award, 1943; considered founder-builder of College of St. Catherine.

McWATT, KATHLEEN CURRY (Mrs. Arthur Chandler McWatt), civic worker, b. Feb. 8, 1931, Minneapolis. Vice-president St. Paul League of Women Voters, 1961–62; vice-chairwoman Ramsey County Democratic-Farmer-Labor party, 1968–70; community services director St. Paul Urban League, 1967–.

METZGER-ZIEGLER, MADY (Mrs. Ludwig Metzger), mezzo-soprano, b. Dec. 5, 1897, Munich, Germany. Royal Conservatory of Munich student; graduate Institute of Vocal Art, Milan; emigrated to U.S., 1931; founder St. Paul Opera Workshop, 1932; taught extensively in St. Paul area; appeared in concert Carnegie Hall, 1960; soloist with U.S. Army band, 1965–69.

MEYERS, SISTER ANNA MARIE, educator, b. Feb. 23, 1891, Sioux City, Ia.; d. Sept. 6, 1975, St. Paul. Founder of Christ Child School for Exceptional Children; pioneer in teaching of mentally handicapped; paralyzed from waist down in auto accident in 1932; named Handicapped Minnesotan of the Year, 1967.

MEYERS, MARY (Mrs. Michael E. Berger), speed skater, b. Feb. 10, 1945, St. Paul. National title holder in every age bracket competed in; gold medalist in 1967 World Games; silver medalist in 1968 Olympics.

MILLETT, KATHERINE MURRAY (Kate) (Mrs. Fumio Yoshimura), author, educator, b. Sept. 14, 1934, St. Paul. English instructor University of North Carolina, 1958; sculptor in Tokyo, 1961–63; English teacher Barnard College, 1964–68; distinguished visiting professor Sacramento State University, 1973–; author, *Sexual Politics* (1970) and *Flying* (1974).

MOORE, SISTER ANNE JOACHIM, educator, b. Nov. 9, 1916, Loretto. Founder and president St. Mary's Junior College, Minneapolis, 1963–; served three years with the Army Nurse Corps during World War II; director St. Mary's School of Nursing, 1957–64, reorganized as junior college, 1963.

MORAN, MARIA VIRGINIA RANGEL (Mrs. Louis Moran), Mexican cultural consultant, b. Sept. 21, 1928, St. Paul. Participant with Mexican community groups, Festival of Nations, 1944–; active with the Mexican Club of St. Paul, an affiliate of the International Institute of St. Paul, and its program chairman, 1954–68; private consultant to agencies and organizations on the customs, culture, and traditions of the Mexican peoples; teaching assistant, Mexican American Cultural Resource Center, 1973–.

NASH, KATHERINE FLINK (Mrs. Robert C. Nash), sculptor, b. May 20, 1910, Minneapolis. Director of junior programs Camp Fire Girls, 1935–39; head of art program Northrop School, Minneapolis, 1945–47; assistant professor of sculpture University of Nebraska, 1947–52; director of exhibitions Joslyn Art Museum, Omaha, 1952–57; acting director University of Minnesota Gallery, 1958–59; visiting professor San Jose College, 1961–62; professor of sculpture University of Minnesota, 1963–76.

NELSON, CYNTHIA LEE (Cindy), skier, b. Aug. 19, 1955, Lutsen. First U.S. winner, World Cup downhill race, Jan., 1974; winner U.S. Alpine Slalom race, 1976; bronze medalist, 1976 Olympics.

NELSON, JULIA BULLARD (Mrs. Ole Nelson), teacher, suffragist, temperance advocate, b. May 13, 1842, High Ridge, Conn.; d. Dec. 25, 1914, Red Wing. Through auspices of American Missionary Assn., taught freedmen in Texas, 1869–73; taught black children, Athens, Tenn., 1875–77; principal Warner Institute, Jonesboro, Tenn., 1878–82; organized the Congregational Church of Jonesboro and preached there, 1883–88; vice-president Minnesota WCTU, 1889–90; president Minnesota Woman Suffrage Assn., 1890–96; editor of *White Ribbon*, a WCTU paper.

NUTE, GRACE LEE, historian, b. Oct. 13, 1895, North Conway, N.H. Curator of manuscripts Minnesota Historical Society, 1921–46, and research associate, 1947–57; professor Hamline University, 1927–60; lecturer in history University of Minnesota, 1939–40, and Macalester College, 1956–59; author of many books and articles on the fur trade, including *The Voyageur* (1931), *Voyageur's Highway* (1941), *Caesars of the Wilderness* (1943), and *Rainy River Country* (1950).

NYE, KATHERINE ANN, physician, b. Feb. 27, 1887, Zumbrota;
d. Mar. 2, 1967, St. Paul. Examining physician Ramsey County
Juvenile Court and St. Paul YWCA; specialized in the health of
young women.

NYE, LILLIAN LYDIA, physician, b. Apr. 22, 1885, Zumbrota; d.
July 28, 1972, St. Paul. Instructor of inorganic chemistry Johns
Hopkins University; pediatric instructor University of Minnesota
Medical School, 1921–53; first woman physician for St. Paul public
schools; helped establish family nursing service clinic at Ancker
Hospital, St. Paul.

OSTENSO, MARTHA (Mrs. Douglas Durkin), author, b. Sept. 17,
1900, Bergen, Norway; d. Nov. 24, 1963, Seattle, Wash. Emigrated
to U.S., 1902; published numerous short stories and some 25
novels, many with Minnesota farm settings; her novel *Wild Geese*
(1925) won $13,500 prize and was made into a movie.

OWEN, MARY GWEN (Mrs. Edward F. R. Swanson), dramatist,
educator, b. Sept. 27, 1900, Ellsworth, Wis. Teacher in North
Dakota, Pennsylvania, and Minnesota until 1928; assistant in
speech department Macalester College, 1928; head of its speech
and drama department, 1950–68; formed the Drama Choros in
1928, continuing to direct it for several years after her retirement
in 1968.

PALMER, NELL O'BRECHT (Mrs. Arthur V. Palmer), actress,
businesswoman, b. June 23, 1893, Madison; d. Dec. 22, 1970,
Stillwater. Member, with parents and four sisters, of John Sullivan
Stock Company, 1920s; married Arthur Palmer, a pianist, 1927; the
Palmers purchased the Lowell Inn in Stillwater in 1930, which Mrs.
Palmer managed until her death.

PEAKE, EMILY LOUISE, civic worker, b. May 28, 1920, Min-
neapolis. Vice-chairman Twin City Chippewa Tribal Council, 1960;
director Indian Citizens' Community Center, 1968–69; member
Urban Indian Federation, 1969–70; member Minnesota State In-
dian Affairs Commission, 1970–71; member Minneapolis Human
Relations Commission, 1971–73; first chairperson Minnesota Native
American Center, 1971; housing commissioner Minneapolis
Housing and Redevelopment Authority, 1972–; member Minnesota

Indian Affairs Inter-tribal Board, 1976– and Metropolitan Inter-tribal Directors Council, 1976–; associated with the Upper Midwest American Indian Center since its founding in 1961 and its executive director, 1972–.

PICCARD, JEANNETTE RIDLON (Mrs. Jean Piccard), aerospace scientist, Episcopal priest, b. Jan. 5, 1895, Chicago, Ill. First woman to enter space in a record-breaking 11-mile balloon ascent, 1934; instrumental in development of aerospace equipment such as pressurized planes and frost-free windows; consultant to NASA; recipient Gilruth Award, 1970, for personal contributions to manned space flight; deacon of Episcopal Church, 1971; one of the first group of women ordained as priests in controversial ordination in July, 1974.

POWELL, LOUISE MATHILDE, nursing educator, b. Mar. 12, 1871, Staunton, Va.; d. Oct. 9, 1943, Staunton, Va. Established first five-year nursing course leading to R.N. and B.S. degrees at the University of Minnesota Nursing School, 1910–26; acting director University Hospital during World War I; head of nursing Western Reserve University, 1926–36.

QUINLAN, ELIZABETH C., retailer, realtor, b. Feb. 15, 1863, Madison, Wis.; d. Sept. 15, 1947, Minneapolis. Founder, with Fred D. Young, of retail department store, Young-Quinlan, opened March 17, 1894, Minneapolis; president of the firm until 1945; owner Elizabeth C. Quinlan Realty Company.

RAYMOND, EVELYN L., sculptor, b. Mar. 20, 1908, Duluth. Won numerous awards for her sculptures; selected to create a bronze statue of Maria L. Sanford for permanent placement in the nation's Capitol, 1958; head of sculpture department Walker Art School, Minneapolis, 1938–50; active in promoting sculpture in the Midwest; best known for her architectural sculpture.

RELF, SISTER ANNETTE, social worker, b. July 12, 1849, Lexington, Ky.; d. Feb. 16, 1915, St. Paul. Matron of Cottage Hospital, Minneapolis, 1870; founder Sheltering Arms, Minneapolis, 1882; director of new facilities for the Church Home, St. Paul, 1895, which combined with the Deaconess Home, 1909.

RIORDAN, LOUISE PARKS (Mrs. Albert Riordan), union organizer, b. Nov. 19, 1886, England; d. Aug. 7, 1916, Minneapolis. Waitress who began unionizing women workers, 1911; secretary-treasurer Trades and Labor Assembly of Minneapolis; member advisory board Minimum Wage Commission of Minnesota; a founder of the waitresses' union.

RIPLEY, MARTHA GEORGE ROGERS (Mrs. William W. Ripley), teacher, suffragist, and doctor, b. Nov. 30, 1843, Vermont; d. Apr. 18, 1915, Minneapolis. Boston University School of Medicine graduate, 1883; president Minnesota Woman Suffrage Assn., 1883–[87?]; crusader for public health measures in Minneapolis; founder and head physician Maternity Hospital, 1888–1915.

ROLLINS, JOSEPHINE LUTZ (Mrs. Richard Rollins), artist, educator, b. July 21, 1896, Sherburne. Associate professor of art University of Minnesota, 1928–57; professor, 1957–65; codirector Stillwater Summer Art Colony, 1933–50; president Minnesota Artists' Assn., 1963–66; founder, with six other women artists, of West Lake Gallery, Minneapolis, 1964.

ROOD, DOROTHY BRIDGMAN ATKINSON (Mrs. Frederick G. Atkinson; later Mrs. John Rood), civic leader, b. June 22, 1890, St. Paul; d. Mar. 7, 1965, Tobago, British West Indies. Board member Minneapolis Public Library, 1949–62, and president 1955–62; trustee Hamline University, 1954–65; associated also with the Walker Art Center, Minneapolis Institute of Arts, and Minnesota Historical Society.

ROOD, FLORENCE, teacher, union leader, political activist, b. Sept. 25, 1875, Mitchell County, Ia.; d. Apr. 13, 1944, St. Paul. Kindergarten teacher and supervisor of teacher's training St. Paul Normal School, 1894–1920; secretary-treasurer St. Paul Teachers Retirement Fund, 1920–44; president American Federation of Teachers, 1923–25, and vice-president, 1925–35; organizer and president Ramsey County Farmer-Labor Women's Club.

SATTERLEE, FRANCES MAE HOWE (Mrs. August N. Satterlee), radio personality, consumer affairs activist; b. Sept. 11, 1889, Nashville Twsp., Martin County; d. Dec. 31, 1974, Minneapolis. Piano and voice teacher, 1912–15; research analyst, 1915–16; comparison shopping manager, 1934–41; broadcaster, public service programs on Twin Cities radio stations, 1939–50; president of Consumer Interest of Minneapolis, 1945–.

SCOTT, VERNA HOVEY GOLDEN (Mrs. Carlyle MacRoberts Scott), impresario, orchestra manager, b. Apr. 30, 1876, River Falls, Wis.; d. Dec. 8, 1964, Minneapolis. Founder and director University Artists Course, 1919–44; manager Minneapolis Symphony Orchestra, 1930–38; Minnesota Mother of the Year, 1954.

SEELEY, MABEL HODENFIELD (Mrs. Kenneth Seeley), author, b. Mar. 25, 1903, Herman. Editor-in-chief *Minnesota Quarterly*, 1925–26; advertising copywriter for 10 years; mystery novelist; author nine books that consistently used Minnesota backgrounds, of which her first, *The Listening House* (1938), is probably the best known.

SMITH, JOSEPHINE WERNICKE (Mrs. Richard Keene Smith), law librarian, b. Feb. 6, 1900, Appleton, Wis.; d. June 2, 1953, St. Paul. Staff member Minneapolis Public Library, 1931–45; appointed by Governor Edward J. Thye as first woman state law librarian, 1945–53.

STAGEBERG, SUSIE WILLIAMSON (Mrs. Olaf O. Stageberg), educator, political activist, b. Jan. 30, 1877, Webster County, Ia.; d. Mar. 15, 1961, Red Wing. Farmer-Labor nominee for secretary of state, 1922, 1924, 1928; congressional primary candidate, Farmer-Labor party, 1932; active in Progressive Voters League, League of Women Voters, and president WCTU, Red Wing; editor *Organized Farmer* (Red Wing), 1927–28.

STOCKWELL, MAUD CONKEY (Mrs. Silvanus Albert Stockwell), suffragist, civic leader, b. Jan. 3, 1863, Wis.; d. Jan. 2, 1958, Minneapolis. Founder of Woman's Economic Study Club; president of the Minnesota Woman Suffrage Assn., 1900–10; member National Child Labor Committee and Minnesota Disarmament Committee; founder and president Minnesota branch Women's International League for Peace and Freedom, 1922–34.

SULLIVAN, BETTY J., scientist, b. May 31, 1902, Minneapolis. Assistant chemist, 1922–27; chief chemist, 1927–47; vice-president and director of research, 1947–54, at Russell Miller Milling Company, Minneapolis, and at Peavey Company, 1954–67; Experience,

Inc., vice-president, 1967–69, president, 1969–73, board chairperson, 1973–75, and vice chairperson, 1975–.

TILDEN, JOSEPHINE ELIZABETH, botanist, b. Mar. 24, 1869, Davenport, Ia.; d. May 15, 1957, Lake Wales, Fla. First woman scientist hired by the University of Minnesota, 1895, retiring in 1937 as professor of botany; completed 13 field trips to the Pacific during her career; a leading authority on algae, writing more than 50 botanical publications, including *Minnesota Algae* (1910).

TYLER, ALICE HELEN FELT (Mrs. Mason Whiting Tyler), historian, educator, b. Mar. 12, 1892, Galesburg, Ill. University of Minnesota faculty, 1927–60, professor of history, 1955–60; author, *The Foreign Policy of James G. Blaine* (1927) and *Freedom's Ferment* (1944).

UELAND, CLARA HAMPSON (Mrs. Andreas Ueland), suffragist, teacher, b. Oct. 10, 1860, Akron, Ohio; d. Mar. 1, 1927, Minneapolis. Established Minneapolis Kindergarten Assn. and its training school, 1892, and the first Minneapolis public kindergarten, 1897; member of first governing board State Art Commission, 1903; founder Woman's Club for Minneapolis, 1907; organized Minneapolis Equal Suffrage Club; president Minnesota Woman Suffrage Assn., 1914–19; first president Minnesota League of Women Voters, 1919.

VAN CLEVE, CHARLOTTE OUISCONSIN CLARK (Mrs. Horatio Phillips Van Cleve), suffragist, civic leader, b. July 1, 1819, Prairie du Chien, Wis.; d. Apr. 1, 1907, Minneapolis. Spent childhood at Fort Snelling; married Lt. (later General) Van Cleve, 1836; moved to Minneapolis, 1861; active in many civic organizations; founder and first president of the Sisters of Bethany; honorary vice-president National Suffrage Assn.; autobiography, *Three Score Years and Ten* (1888).

WARREN, ALICE AMELIA ROCKWELL (Mrs. Frank M. Warren; later Mrs. Oscar Gaarden), civic worker, b. Sept. 19, 1881, Kingston, Ont., Canada; d. July 1, 1962, Encampment Forest. Member of Hennepin County Republican Women's Club and the National Federation of Women's Clubs; first woman appointed to University of Minnesota board of regents, 1922.

WASHBURN, BETTY WHITLOCK (Mrs. Malcolm MacDonald Willey), municipal judge, b. Apr. 23, 1916, Terre Haute, Ind.; d. June 16, 1962, Minneapolis. Hennepin County court commissioner, 1947–50; appointed a Minneapolis municipal judge, 1950 to fill an unexpired term; elected 1951 first woman judge in Hennepin County, re-elected in 1957.

WELLS, MARGUERITE MILTON, political worker, b. Feb. 10, 1872, Milwaukee, Wis.; d. Aug. 12, 1959, Minneapolis. Second president Minnesota League of Women Voters, 1920–32; president National League of Women Voters, 1934–46.

WEYERHAEUSER, VIVIAN O'GARA (Mrs. Frederick King Weyerhaeuser), civic leader, b. Oct. 10, 1900, Chicago, Ill. Member Minnesota Federation of Women's Republican Clubs and Citizens for Eisenhower-Nixon, 1952; chairman National Council of the Metropolitan Opera Assn., 1955–57; chairman and founder Minnesota Historical Society's Women's Organization, 1949.

WILLIAMS, CLARA, singer, voice teacher, b. Mar. 4, 1870, Wales; d. Jan. 27, 1975, Minneapolis. Graduate of Royal College of Music, London; teacher University of Minnesota, Hamline University, and, beginning in 1916, MacPhail School of Music, where she was active until the age of 99; gave many national concerts on tour; frequent guest soloist with the Minnesota Symphony Orchestra.

WOOD, JULIA AMANDA SARGENT, author, pioneer editor, b. Apr. 13, 1825, New London, N.H.; d. Mar. 9, 1903, St. Cloud. Settled in Sauk Rapids, Minnesota Territory, 1851; editor *New Era* (Sauk Rapids), 1859–63; numerous articles, poems, and stories written under pen name, "Minnie Mary Lee"; author of seven novels on Catholic themes.

WOOD, STELLA LOUISE, preschool educator, b. Sept. 2, 1865, Chicago, Ill.; d. Feb. 10, 1949, Minneapolis. Moved to Minneapolis, 1896, as supervisor for Minneapolis Kindergarten Training School, popularly known as "Miss Wood's School"; founder of kindergarten section National Education Assn.; president International Kindergarten Education Assn., 1917.

REFERENCE NOTES

INTRODUCTION — *pages 1 to 6*

[1] Betty Friedan, *The Feminine Mystique* (New York, 1963).

[2] For the eight, see Edward T. James *et al.*, eds., *Notable American Women, 1607–1950: A Biographical Dictionary*, 1:151; 2:1, 327; 3:162, 232, 415, 498, 646 (Cambridge, Mass., 1971). Information on Gág and Ripley may also be found in Alma Scott's biography, *Wanda Gág: The Story of an Artist* (Minneapolis, 1949); Richard W. Cox, "Wanda Gág," in *Minnesota History*, 44:238–254 (Fall, 1975); Winton U. Solberg, "Martha G. Ripley: Pioneer Doctor and Social Reformer," in *Minnesota History*, 39:1–17 (Spring, 1964).

[3] Minnesota Historical Company, *Men of Minnesota* (St. Paul, 1902); Mary Dillon Foster, ed., *Who's Who Among Minnesota Women* (n.p., 1924); Theodore C. Blegen, review in *Minnesota History*, 6:390 (December, 1925).

Chapter 1 — HARRIET E. BISHOP — *pages 7 to 19*

[1] On Harriet Bishop's arrival in Minnesota, see Harriet E. Bishop, *Floral Home; or First Years in Minnesota*, 60 (New York, 1857); Christopher C. Andrews, ed., *History of St. Paul, Minn.*, 451 (Syracuse, N.Y., 1890); J. Fletcher Williams, "A History of the City of St. Paul, and of the County of Ramsey, Minnesota," in *Minnesota Historical Collections*, 4:169 (St. Paul, 1876); and Zylpha S. Morton, "Harriet Bishop, Frontier Teacher," in *Minnesota History*, 28:136 (June, 1947).

[2] For a description of preterritorial St. Paul, see August L. Larpenteur, "Recollections of the City and People of St. Paul, 1843–1898," in *Minnesota Historical Collections*, 9:367–371, 378 (St. Paul, 1901). On the need for a teacher and the role played by Williamson in acquiring one, see Williams, in *Minnesota Historical Collections*, 4:169, and Morton, in *Minnesota History*, 28:132.

[3] On Catharine Beecher and on the organization of the National Board of Popular Education described in the paragraph below, see Kathryn Kish Sklar, *Catharine Beecher: A Study in American Domesticity*, 168–183 (New Haven, 1973).

[4] Sklar, *Catharine Beecher*, 174, 178.

[5] Sklar, *Catharine Beecher*, 156.

[6] Sklar, *Catharine Beecher*, 163–172. For nineteenth-century attitudes toward family life, here and in the paragraph below, see William R. Taylor and Christopher Lasch, "Two 'Kindred Spirits,' Sorority and Family in New England, 1839–1846," in *New England Quarterly*, 36:23–41 (March, 1963); Kirk Jeffrey, "The Family as Utopian Retreat from the City: The Nineteenth-Century Contribution,"

in Sally Teselle, ed., *The Family, Communes, and Utopian Societies*, 21–41 (New York, 1972); and Richard Sennett, *Families Against the City: Middle Class Homes of Industrial Chicago, 1872–1890* (Cambridge, Mass., 1970).

⁷ Biographical information is taken from Winton U. Solberg, "Harriet E. Bishop," in Edward T. James et al., eds., *Notable American Women, 1607–1950,* 1:151 (Cambridge, Mass., 1971); Morton, in *Minnesota History*, 28:134; and William Cathcart, ed., *The Baptist Encyclopedia*, 101 (Philadelphia, 1881).

⁸ Williamson's letter to Slade appears in part in Williams, in *Minnesota Historical Collections*, 4:162. See also Andrews, *History of St. Paul*, 451; Bishop, *Floral Home*, 54.

⁹ Morton, in *Minnesota History*, 28:135.

¹⁰ Bishop, *Floral Home*, 60, 61.

¹¹ The quotations here and in the paragraph below are from Bishop, *Floral Home*, 51, 83, 84.

¹² Thomas M. Newson, *Pen Pictures of St. Paul, Minnesota, and Biographical Sketches of Old Settlers*, 63 (St. Paul, 1886).

¹³ Cathcart, *Baptist Encyclopedia*, 102; Williams, in *Minnesota Historical Collections*, 4:170.

¹⁴ Bishop, *Floral Home*, 85, 113.

¹⁵ Bishop, *Floral Home*, 105, 106.

¹⁶ Bishop, *Floral Home*, 105.

¹⁷ Bishop, *Floral Home*, 108; Harriet E. Bishop, *Minnesota, Then and Now*, 15 (St. Paul, 1869). On temperance legislation, see Minnesota Territory, *Laws*, 1852, p. 12.

¹⁸ Bishop, *Floral Home*, 341.

¹⁹ Ethel E. Hurd, *Woman Suffrage in Minnesota: A Record of the Activities in Its Behalf since 1847*, 7 (Minneapolis, 1916).

²⁰ Bishop, *Floral Home*, 101; St. Paul Baptist Sewing Society records, in St. Paul First Baptist Church Papers, Minnesota Historical Society, hereafter abbreviated MHS.

²¹ On the organization of the group, see Minutes, September 11, 1867; on the house purchase, see Minutes, April 11, May 4, 1869 — both in Ladies Christian Union of the City of St. Paul Papers, MHS. The house was the beginning of the Home for the Friendless, later the Protestant Home, and presently Wilder Residence East; see Ethel McClure, *More Than a Roof: The Development of Minnesota Poor Farms and Homes for the Aged*, 39–45 (St. Paul, 1968).

²² Newson, *Pen Pictures*, 63.

²³ Bishop, *Floral Home*, 71.

²⁴ Bishop, *Floral Home*, 71.

²⁵ Bishop, *Floral Home*, 241, 259, 296.

²⁶ Harriet E. Bishop, *Dakota War Whoop: or Indian Massacres and War in Minnesota of 1862–63*, 18 (St. Paul, 1864).

²⁷ Newson, *Pen Pictures*, 64.

²⁸ *New York Evangelist*, September 17, 1846, p. 4.

²⁹ For the information here and in the following paragraph, see Rebecca Marshall Cathcart, "A Sheaf of Remembrances," in *Minnesota Historical Collections*, 15:531 (St. Paul, 1915).

³⁰ Bishop, *Floral Home*, 129, 322.

³¹ Bishop, *Floral Home*, 321.

³² *St. Paul Pioneer Press*, August 9, 1883, p. 7.

³³ See Ann D. Wood, "The 'Scribbling Women' and Fanny Fern: Why Women Wrote," in *American Quarterly*, 23:3–24 (Spring, 1970).

³⁴ Barbara Welter, "The Cult of True Womanhood: 1820–1860," in *American Quarterly*, 18:151–174 (Summer, 1966).

Chapter 2 — KATE DONNELLY — *pages 20 to 33*

[1] [Ignatius Donnelly], *In Memoriam: Mrs. Katharine Donnelly*, 4–6, 10, 14, 42 ([St. Paul], 1895). Portions of this chapter appeared in *Ramsey County History*, Fall-Winter, 1976, pp. 14–18, and are used here with the permission of the Ramsey County Historical Society, St. Paul.

[2] Donnelly, *In Memoriam*, 10, 11.

[3] See especially Barbara Welter, "The Cult of True Womanhood: 1820–1860," in *American Quarterly*, 18:151–174 (Summer, 1966).

[4] Kate Donnelly (hereafter abbreviated KD) to Ignatius Donnelly (hereafter abbreviated ID), December 25, 1868, roll 40, frames 229, 230, Ignatius Donnelly Papers, Minnesota Historical Society. All letters hereafter cited are in the Donnelly Papers.

[5] KD to ID, September 8, 13, 1859, roll 7, frames 153, 160.

[6] KD to ID, July 8, August 28, September 25, 1859, August 29, 1864, roll 7, frames 9, 132, 172, roll 20, frame 212.

[7] KD to ID, July 26, 1859, August 5, 1864, roll 7, frame 46, roll 20, frame 16.

[8] Donnelly, *In Memoriam*, 16, 19, 20.

[9] Martin Ridge, *Ignatius Donnelly: The Portrait of a Politician*, 12 (Chicago, 1962); KD to ID, September 14, 1864, roll 20, frame 364.

[10] Salutations in letters from Ignatius to Kate always read "Dear Wifey," and she addressed him as "Dear Hubby." Comments of friends and relatives alluding to "Wifey" suggest that Ignatius called her that in conversation as well as in correspondence. Kate is quoted in Ridge, *Donnelly*, 17.

[11] Ridge, *Donnelly*, 23–25.

[12] See KD to ID, August 10, 28, 1859, October 11, 1861, roll 7, frames 95, 131, roll 9, frame 28.

[13] KD to ID, May 15, 1861, March 15, 1864, roll 8, frame 478, roll 16, frame 684.

[14] Ridge, *Donnelly*, 34–42; KD to ID, July 20, 1859, roll 7, frame 36.

[15] KD to Caddie [Caroline McCaffrey School?], July 23, 1862, roll 10, frame 331.

[16] KD to ID, March 2, August 24, 1862, roll 9, frame 473, roll 10, frame 614.

[17] ID to KD, August 28, 1862, roll 10, frame 630.

[18] KD to ID, October 11, 1861, September 22, 1862, roll 9, frame 30, roll 10, frame 731.

[19] Ridge, *Donnelly*, 73, 74, 124; KD to ID, November 28, 1863, roll 13, frame 796.

[20] KD to ID, December 22, 1863, April 25, May 2, 1864, roll 14, frame 329, roll 17, frame 797, roll 18, frame 125.

[21] KD to ID, and ID's note on reverse of letter, January 26, 1864, roll 15, frame 385. It is a commentary upon the incidence of infant mortality that Kate's sister Mary wrote a letter of condolence, saying she knew this loss would be hard on Kate because it was her first, but hoping that she was not "foolishly fretting over her loss but taking it as a Christian mother acepting [*sic*] God's will." See Mary Faiver to KD, February 7, 1864, roll 15, frame 647.

[22] KD to ID, February 4, October 28, 1864, roll 15, frame 589, roll 20, frame 606.

[23] KD to ID, April 28, 1864, roll 18, frame 47.

[24] KD to ID, September 19, November 1, 1864, roll 20, frames 434, 616.

[25] KD to ID, May 20, 1864, roll 18, frame 429. After Lincoln's assassination Kate Donnelly's cousin Kate Ferris observed that the president's death had been bad for business. See Kate Ferris to KD, May 23, 1865, roll 23, frame 696.

[26] Ridge, *Donnelly*, 66, 93, 94; KD to ID, January 7, 1869, roll 40, frame 319.

[27] Ridge, *Donnelly*, 116–125, 128, 130; ID to KD, February 12, 1870, roll 42, frame 319.

[28] KD to ID, August 25, 1866, January 7, 10, 1869, March 1, 1870, roll 29, frame 316, roll 40, frames 319, 330, roll 42, frames 466, 467.

²⁹ KD to ID, August 5, September 14, October 2, 1864, roll 20, frames 17, 363, 520.

³⁰ KD to ID, September 14, 15, 1864, Kate Ferris to KD, July 7, 12, 1870, roll 20, frames 364, 380, roll 43, frames 597–599, 633.

³¹ Ridge, *Donnelly*, 145, 149, 155–160, 168, 181–187; KD to ID, September 26, 1870, roll 44, frames 171, 172.

³² KD to ID, July 23, 1878, roll 61, frame 729.

³³ Ridge, *Donnelly*, 214–219; KD to ID, May 7, 1884, roll 72, frame 385.

³⁴ KD to ID, August 14, 1864, January 15, 1891, roll 20, frame 88, roll 95, frame 774.

³⁵ KD to ID, February 1, 1861, February 7, 1864, February 9, 1870, December 12, 1890, roll 8, frame 240, roll 15, frame 644, roll 42, frame 303, roll 95, frame 156.

³⁶ KD to ID, December 12, 1890, January 8, 1891, roll 95, frames 154, 678.

³⁷ Ridge, *Donnelly*, 227–244; KD to ID, December 8, 1890, roll 95, frame 55.

³⁸ Ridge, *Donnelly*, 287, 302–309; Donnelly, *In Memoriam*, 23–26.

³⁹ ID to KD, November 19, 1868, roll 40, frame 29; italics added.

⁴⁰ ID to KD, July 14, 1859, roll 7, frame 27.

⁴¹ ID to KD, February 3, 1870, KD to ID, February 8, 18970, roll 42, frames 257, 296.

⁴² ID to KD, February 27, 1870, roll 42, frame 457.

⁴³ The essays and clippings mentioned are on roll 133, frames 38–53, 94, 95, 98–105. Other examples are "Memorial of the American Equal Rights Association to the Congress of the United States," 1866, and "The Farist Community," February 8, 1866, an announcement of a communitarian experiment in which men and women would have the same rights, roll 25, frame 259, roll 26, frames 126–131.

⁴⁴ For this and the paragraph below, see Donnelly, "The Woman Question," roll 133, frames 101, 103, 104, 105.

⁴⁵ KD to ID, September 17, 1862, August 14, 1864, February 8, 25, 1870, roll 10, frame 691, roll 20, frame 88, roll 42, frames 295, 449.

⁴⁶ KD to ID, February 25, 1870, roll 42, frame 449.

⁴⁷ KD to ID, February 14, 1870, roll 42, frame 339.

Chapter 3 — JANE GREY SWISSHELM — *pages 34 to 54*

¹ Arthur J. Larsen, ed., *Crusader and Feminist: Letters of Jane Grey Swisshelm, 1858–1865*, 1–9 (St. Paul, 1934); Jane Grey Swisshelm, *Half a Century*, 123 (Chicago, 1880).

² Larsen, *Crusader*, 1, 10.

³ Larsen, *Crusader*, 12–30.

⁴ Larsen, *Crusader*, 31.

⁵ Swisshelm, *Half a Century*, 296.

⁶ *Half a Century*, 297.

⁷ Obituary in *St. Cloud Journal Press*, July 24, 1884, cited in Larsen, *Crusader*, 31.

⁸ Quotations here and in the paragraph below are from *Half a Century*, 3, 4.

⁹ *Half a Century*, 7, 8, 10.

¹⁰ *Half a Century*, 9.

¹¹ *Half a Century*, 11.

¹² *Half a Century*, 12, 14.

¹³ *Half a Century*, 15, 16.

¹⁴ *Half a Century*, 19, 20, 28, 29.

¹⁵ *Half a Century*, 32.

¹⁶ *Half a Century*, 34, 85, 86.

[17] *Half a Century,* 39, 40, 41, 50.

[18] *Half a Century,* 50.

[19] *Half a Century,* 41.

[20] *Half a Century,* 42. William B. Mitchell, the nephew who served as Jane's assistant editor on the *St. Cloud Democrat,* offered the following assessment of her marriage: "Her husband . . . I knew very well. He was a big, coarse-grained, rather good-hearted sort of a man, and while their natures were wholly dissimilar, he and his wife would have gone through life amicably, if not very happily, had it not been for his mother, who lived either with them or quite near to them, and who was a scheming, jealous meddlesome old woman, and had her son under her thumb and kept him there." Letter of W. B. Mitchell to J. L. Washburn, March 4, 1915, in the front of the Minnesota Historical Society library's copy of *Half a Century.*

[21] *Half a Century,* 47, 48.

[22] *Half a Century,* 48, 49; italics added.

[23] *Half a Century,* 46.

[24] *Half a Century,* 40.

[25] Thorp, *Female Persuasion: Six Strong-minded Women,* 61 (New Haven, 1949); Woodward, *The Bold Women,* 87 (New York, 1953); *Half a Century,* 165, 168.

[26] Larsen, *Crusader,* 3; *Half a Century,* 52, 53.

[27] *Half a Century,* 54, 57.

[28] *Half a Century,* 59, 60.

[29] *Half a Century,* 46, 65.

[30] *Half a Century,* 66, 67.

[31] *Half a Century,* 72.

[32] *Half a Century,* 103.

[33] Shippee, "Jane Grey Swisshelm, Agitator," in *Mississippi Valley Historical Review,* 7:206 (December, 1920).

[34] *Half a Century,* 146, 147.

[35] *Half a Century,* 36, 37.

[36] *Half a Century,* 93.

[37] *Half a Century,* 109.

[38] *Half a Century,* 169, 170.

[39] *Half a Century,* 171–173, 179.

[40] *Half a Century,* 182.

[41] Shippee, in *Mississippi Valley Historical Review,* 7:217.

[42] *St. Cloud Visiter,* March 18, 1858, quoted in Larsen, *Crusader,* 15.

[43] Sergeant, *Short as Any Dream,* 160, 164, 172 (New York, 1929).

[44] *Half a Century,* 173.

[45] The public meeting is described in *Half a Century,* 185–189.

[46] Larsen, *Crusader,* v, 81, 82.

[47] *St. Cloud Democrat,* December 9, 1858, quoted in Larsen, *Crusader,* 26; *Half a Century,* 206, 234, 235.

[48] Thorp, *Female Persuasion,* 98; *Half a Century,* 238–359; the injured soldier is mentioned on p. 289.

[49] On Swisshelm's role in the university's founding, see James Gray, *The University of Minnesota, 1851 to 1951,* 22 (Minneapolis, 1951).

Chapter 4 — EVA McDONALD VALESH — *pages 55 to 76*

[1] Annie L. Diggs, "The Women in the Alliance Movement," in *The Arena,* 6:172 (July, 1892); *Great West* (St. Paul), October 17, 1890, February 13, 1891.

[2] Donnelly Diary, May 19, 1891, Donnelly Papers; Reminiscences of Blanche MacDonald, 3; Eva McDonald Valesh to Albert Dollenmayer, July 19, 1891, Dol-

lenmayer Papers — all in the Minnesota Historical Society, hereafter abbreviated MHS.

³ See "The Reminiscences of Eva Valesh," 2. These reminiscences were recorded in a series of interviews made by the Oral History Research Office of Columbia University in 1952 (Copyright, 1972, by the Trustees of Columbia University in the City of New York). A microfilmed transcript is on file in the MHS. All quotations from these interviews are used with permission. Facts not otherwise credited in this chapter are drawn from this source, which provides the basic fund of information on Eva McDonald's life and offers many insights into her feelings and views. These reminiscences, however, must be used with extreme care, since Eva was eighty-six years old when they were recorded, and they contain many inaccuracies and misleading statements. For example, she gives her birth date as 1874 and consistently places the events of her early life at a much younger age than they occurred.

Other sources on her life are the reminiscences of her sister Blanche, cited above, also inaccurate in some details, and a sketch published in Frances E. Willard and Mary A. Livermore, eds., *A Woman of the Century: Fourteen Hundred-Seventy Biographical Sketches Accompanied by Portraits of Leading American Women in All Walks of Life*, 729 (Buffalo, Chicago, and New York, 1893). This sketch was written by Eva's close friend, Albert Dollenmayer, a Minneapolis journalist; it is cited hereafter as "Dollenmayer sketch." Her letter to him of July 19, 1891, cited above, gives a brief outline of her early life and has been taken as authoritative on the date of her birth. The family name was spelled "McDonald," and Eva followed this throughout her years in Minnesota. Later, however, both she and her sister adopted the spelling "MacDonald."

In the Minneapolis city directory for 1883–84 her father's occupation, which formerly appeared as carpenter, is changed to grocer. He apparently continued in the grocery business until 1888–89, when he is once again listed as a carpenter.

⁴ "Reminiscences of Eva Valesh," 23.

⁵ *St. Paul Globe*, October 28, 1888. In her reminiscences Eva recalled that the superintendent told her to come back in a few years, when she had grown up.

⁶ George B. Engberg, "The Rise of Organized Labor in Minnesota, 1850–1890," 52–75, 121, an unpublished dissertation in the MHS library; Minnesota State Federation of Labor, *Year Book*, 1915, p. 13.

⁷ Engberg, "Organized Labor in Minnesota," 69, 125.

⁸ Herbert Y. Weber, "The Story of the *St. Paul Globe*," in *Minnesota History*, 39:330–332 (Winter, 1965); Minnesota State Federation of Labor, *Year Book*, 1915, p. 13.

⁹ "Reminiscences of Eva Valesh," 21.

¹⁰ The strike received ample and sympathetic newspaper coverage; see *Minneapolis Tribune*, April 19, 22, 26, 27, 29, 30, May 11, 12, 13, 19, 1888. "Eva Gay's" account of attending a strike meeting was published in the *Globe*, April 29, 1888. See also Minnesota State Federation of Labor, *Year Book*, 1915, p. 31.

¹¹ *Duluth Daily Tribune*, June 8, 1888.

¹² "Reminiscences of Eva Valesh," 4.

¹³ "Reminiscences of Eva Valesh," 15.

¹⁴ "Reminiscences of Eva Valesh," 14.

¹⁵ *Globe*, October 28, 1888.

¹⁶ The last "Eva Gay" articles appeared on July 28 and August 4, 1889; Dollenmayer sketch; Minnesota State Federation of Labor, *Year Book*, 1915, p. 27. The strike received front page coverage in the *Globe* and other Twin Cities papers from its beginning on April 13 through April 24. Rioting occurred on Easter Sunday, April 21. For the eight-hour-day movement, see "The World of Work" in *Globe*, December 12, 15, 1888; July 28, August 11, 18, September 15, 1889.

[17] "Reminiscences of Eva Valesh," 19, 23; *Globe,* August 11, 18, 1889.

[18] "Reminiscences of Eva Valesh," 19, 23.

[19] Minnesota State Farmers' Alliance, *Declaration of Rights* (n.p., 1886). A copy of this pamphlet is in the MHS library. For general discussions of third-party politics in Minnesota during this period, here and below, see Donald F. Warner, "Prelude to Populism," in *Minnesota History,* 32:129–146 (September, 1951); Martin Ridge, *Ignatius Donnelly: The Portrait of a Politician,* 245–261, 267–269 (Chicago, 1962).

[20] For the material here and in the paragraph below, see *Great West,* February 13, 1891.

[21] *Great West,* February 13, 1891. Eva's response in "Reminiscences," 37, is given in a somewhat different context but is taken here to reflect her general attitude. Her rambling recollections of her Alliance activities are confused and inaccurate.

[22] *Great West,* February 7, 1890. The column appeared seven times in all: February 7, 21, 28, March 21, 28, April 18, 25, 1890.

[23] *Great West,* March 21, 1890.

[24] *Great West,* April 24, 1891. Donnelly's letter book, May 28, 1890, contains letters to both Fish and Eva, trying to make peace between them. For the quotations here and below, see Donnelly Diary, June 18, 1890, Donnelly Papers.

[25] *Industrial Age* (Duluth), June 21, 1890.

[26] Engberg, "Organized Labor in Minnesota," 115–117.

[27] Engberg, "Organized Labor in Minnesota," 117–120; Minnesota State Federation of Labor, *Year Book,* 1915, pp. 14, 16.

[28] Ridge, *Donnelly,* 271–278.

[29] Donnelly letter book, Donnelly Papers.

[30] *Great West,* January 9, 1891. Eva's reminiscences give the impression that her election to the office was a casual affair and her presence at the convention almost accidental. Contemporary evidence shows the reverse. In an interesting sidelight, Kate Donnelly, who was a shrewd political observer in her own right, wrote to her husband: "I am so sorry that Miss McD is state lecturer. She will be 'tanky' and troublesome and she will have a vote — and you have too many of the opposition on the executive committee." Kate Donnelly to Ignatius Donnelly, January 8, 1891, Donnelly Papers.

[31] *Great West,* January 9, 23, 1891.

[32] *Great West,* February 6, May 29, 1891; *Globe,* January 28, 1891; "Reminiscences of Eva Valesh," 41.

[33] In her reminiscences she states that she was clerk to the Senate finance committee, and *Great West,* January 30, 1891, also states that she had been appointed clerk to a Senate committee. However, Bjorge served in the House and was in 1891 chairman of the House appropriations committee. See Minnesota, *House Journal,* 1891, p. 57; "Reminiscences of Eva Valesh," 40; *Great West,* February 13, 1891.

[34] *Globe,* January 25, February 1, 1891; *Great West,* February 13, 1891. For a previous unsuccessful attempt to get rid of Fish, see Ridge, *Donnelly,* 274.

[35] John D. Hicks, *The Populist Revolt,* 113–127, 205–212 (Minneapolis, 1931).

[36] Ridge, *Donnelly,* 285; *Globe,* May 20, 1891.

[37] Ridge, *Donnelly,* 285; Donnelly Diary, May 19, 1891, Donnelly Papers; *Great West,* May 29, 1891.

[38] Ridge, *Donnelly,* 286–288; McDonald to Dollenmayer, July 19, 1891, Dollenmayer Papers. A wedding announcement is in the James C. Christie and Family Papers, MHS.

[39] Ridge, *Donnelly,* 288; Hicks, *Populist Revolt,* 218; McDonald to Dollenmayer, July 19, 1891, Dollenmayer Papers.

[40] McDonald to Dollenmayer, July 19, 1891, Dollenmayer Papers.

[41] Diggs, "Women in the Alliance Movement," 172. Quotations here and below are from McDonald to Dollenmayer, August 20, 1891, Dollenmayer Papers.

[42] Ridge, *Donnelly*, 292, 308.

[43] *Great West*, June 5, November 13, 1891.

[44] McDonald to Dollenmayer, November 24, 1891, Dollenmayer Papers; Ridge, *Donnelly*, 293.

[45] McDonald to Dollenmayer, February 25, March 23, April 2, 1892, Dollenmayer Papers; Eva McDonald Valesh, "The Strength and Weakness of the People's Movement," in *The Arena*, 5:727, 731 (May, 1892).

[46] Ridge, *Donnelly*, 301–309.

[47] Diggs, in *The Arena*, 6:173; McDonald to Dollenmayer, December 3, 1893, Dollenmayer Papers. The only real evidence for the strains in Eva's marriage is in her reminiscences, but her letters to Dollenmayer reveal her increasing boredom and sense of confinement.

[48] Ridge, *Donnelly*, 319, 361–363. Eva recalled taking her young son with her on some of these later speaking trips.

[49] In her reminiscences Eva asserts (p. 48) that her husband died in the mid-1890s and that she then left Minnesota. Frank Valesh lived in Graceville until November 7, 1916. See *Graceville Enterprise*, November 10, 1916. Blanche MacDonald states that Eva divorced him about 1910. For the quotation, see McDonald to Dollenmayer, December 3, 1893, Dollenmayer Papers.

[50] "Reminiscences of Eva Valesh," 72.

[51] "Reminiscences of Eva Valesh," 75.

[52] A complete file of the *American Club Woman*, beginning with the issue of January, 1911, and ending with that of December, 1917, is in the New York Public Library. Throughout its existence Eva was listed as editor, and beginning in June, 1913, the name of B. Franklin Cross appeared as business manager. During the last year of publication the title was changed to *American Club Woman and Modern Housewife*. Eva's work in organizing a "War Children's Christmas Fund" and a "War Children's Relief Fund" is reflected in the issues of late 1914, 1915, and 1916.

[53] In her reminiscences Eva states: "In 1923 my husband died suddenly" (p. 225). According to her sister, they were divorced. See Blanche MacDonald to Lucile Kane, June 11, 1957, in accessions files, MHS Division of Archives and Manuscripts. An obituary for Captain Benjamin F. Cross appears in the *New York Times* of November 13, 1950, p. 27. He died in Williamstown, Mass., at the age of eighty-two.

It seems likely that Eva had for some years given the false birth date of 1874, which she recorded in her reminiscences. In that case her age would have been on record as seventy-seven at the time of her retirement.

[54] Reminiscences of Blanche MacDonald; MacDonald to Kane, June 11, 1957. Eva's presence in Minneapolis was noted by the *Minneapolis Labor Review*, November 10, 1910, p. 5. No record of her divorce from either Valesh or Cross has thus far been located.

Chapter 5 — MARIA SANFORD — *pages 77 to 93*

[1] Helen Whitney, *Maria Sanford*, 270, 313–320 (Minneapolis, 1922). Whitney, a colleague and long-time assistant of Maria Sanford, was one of the literary executors of the Sanford Papers before they were donated to the Minnesota Historical Society. Sanford's unfinished autobiography, first serialized in the *Minneapolis Journal* on Sundays beginning May 2, 1920, sec. 4, p. 1, and ending June 2, 1920, sec. 4, p. 1, was incorporated in Whitney's book, pp. 1–43, as well as other contem-

porary newspaper accounts. The phrase "best-known and best-loved woman in Minnesota" is included in the inscription on a seven-foot bronze statue of Maria Sanford erected in the nation's Capitol in Washington, D.C., in 1958, the year of the Minnesota statehood centennial. Sanford was the second woman in the United States to be so honored. See *Acceptance of the Statue of Maria L. Sanford Presented by the State of Minnesota*, xix, 29, 30, 49, 70 (86 Congress, 2 session, *Senate Documents*, no. 134).

[2] Whitney, *Sanford*, 1–3, 7, 10, 45.

[3] Whitney, *Sanford*, 13, 18, 30, 32–35, 47, 50.

[4] Whitney, *Sanford*, 23–26, 35, 48; Maude S. Shapiro, "A Rhetorical Critical Analysis of Lecturing of Maria Louise Sanford," 16, Ph.D. thesis, University of Minnesota, 1959.

[5] Whitney, *Sanford*, 30, 50, 51.

[6] Whitney, *Sanford*, 52, 54, 62, 64, 66.

[7] Woodruff to Sanford, June 15, 1909, Maria Sanford Papers, Minnesota Historical Society; Whitney, *Sanford*, 68.

[8] Woodruff to Sanford, August 15, 1868, Sanford Papers; Whitney, *Sanford*, 70, 71.

[9] Whitney, *Sanford*, 72–75.

[10] Whitney, *Sanford*, 76–78.

[11] Whitney, *Sanford*, 83, 87, 91; Magill to Sanford, December 11, 1892, Sanford Papers.

[12] Whitney, *Sanford*, 91–94; Sanford, form letter, 1876, Sanford Papers.

[13] Magill to Sanford, September 27, 1904, and Magill to "Dear Clem" (Clement Biddle?), May 2, 1876, Sanford Papers; Whitney, *Sanford*, 97–100.

[14] Whitney, *Sanford*, 63, 84, 105; Shapiro, "Analysis," 36; Sanford to Magill, July 2, 1875, Sanford Papers.

[15] Whitney, *Sanford*, 58–60, 103–109; Magill to Sanford, June 4, 1881, Sanford Papers.

[16] Whitney, *Sanford*, 104, 107–109; Magill to James B. Angell, August 16, 1877, and Sanford to the Instruction Committee, March 3, 1879, in Sanford Papers.

[17] Whitney, *Sanford*, 110, 111; Folwell to Sanford, July 9, 1880; Folwell to Magill, July 31, 1880; Richard Chute to Sanford, August 6, 1880; and Emily L. Hough to Sanford, May 5, 1871 — all in Sanford Papers; Shapiro, "Analysis," 61.

[18] Whitney, *Sanford*, 111–115.

[19] Whitney, *Sanford*, 121, 125, 126; "Home Hits & Happenings," in *Ariel*, 6:41 (November 28, 1882).

[20] Whitney, *Sanford*, 111, 116; Magill to Sanford, April 17, 1884, Sanford Papers; Shapiro, "Analysis," 122n.

[21] Sanford to Northrop, March 17, 1884, Sanford Papers.

[22] Whitney, *Sanford*, 132–134; the Sanford Papers contain many letters relating to the repayment of this debt, 1890–1916.

[23] Whitney, *Sanford*, 131, 141–144, 153; Ina T. E. Firkins, "My Miss Sanford," in *Acceptance of the Statue*, 16.

[24] Whitney, *Sanford*, 119, 133, 134, 141, 142, 145, 146; Firkins, in *Acceptance of the Statue*, 18–20.

[25] Magill to Sanford, July 8, 1890, and Northrop to Sanford, November 17, 1890, Sanford Papers; Firkins, in *Acceptance of the Statute*, 16; Whitney, *Sanford*, 167.

[26] Shapiro, "Analysis," 88–91, 126; "Interesting Work," in *Ariel*, April 18, 1896, p. 11; Whitney, *Sanford*, 155; Otto K. Folin to Sanford, May 22, 1893, and Oscar W. Firkins to Sanford, March 5, 1895 — both in Sanford Papers.

[27] On the debate program, see Thomas Trueblood to Sanford, December 6, 1897; G. W. Smith to Sanford, November 9, 1898; Edward Winterer to Sanford,

November 10, 1898; Mrs. E. C. Gale to Sanford, November 10, 1898; Fred B. Snyder to Sanford, November 11, 1898; Edward Meyers to Sanford, May 19, 1902; Sanford to Stephen Updike, October 24, 1906 — all in Sanford Papers. On her classes, see Shapiro, "Analysis," 77, 80; Whitney, *Sanford,* 200.

²⁸ Northrop, certificate, October 7, 1894, Sanford Papers.
²⁹ C. M. Jordan to J. A. Foshay, December 13, 1899, Sanford Papers; Whitney, *Sanford,* 156–161.
³⁰ "The Journal Contest," in *Ariel,* 22:385 (April 15, 1899); Whitney, *Sanford,* 174–178.
³¹ Northrop to Sanford, March 31 and April 10, 1900, Sanford Papers; Whitney, *Sanford,* 179.
³² Florence Bramhall to Laura R. Linsley, May 6, 1900, David P. Jones to Sanford, May 2, 1900, and Woman's Council of Minneapolis to Sanford, May 28, 1900, all in Sanford Papers. The following letters were addressed to the regents of the University of Idaho from Pillsbury, [May], 1900, Magill, May 19, 1900, and J. P. McCaskey, May 23, 1900; and to Governor Frank Steunenberg from James Gray, May 26, 1900, Cyrus Northrop, May 28, 1900, William M. Liggett, May 29, 1900, and William Lochren, May 30, 1900 — all in Sanford Papers. See also Whitney, *Sanford,* 182.
³³ Whitney, *Sanford,* 182; Northrop to Sanford, July 13, 1901, and Sanford to Board of Regents, October 1, 1903, Sanford Papers.
³⁴ Sanford to Thomas Wilson, April 24, 1905, and to Board of Regents, May 26, 1905, Sanford Papers.
³⁵ Sanford to John A. Johnson, May 21, 1907, and John F. Downey to Sanford, May 7, 1907, Sanford Papers; Whitney, *Sanford,* 199.
³⁶ Whitney, *Sanford,* 131; William W. Folwell, *A History of Minnesota,* 4:461, 462 (Reprint ed., St. Paul, 1969).
³⁷ Samuel R. Van Sant to Sanford, June 25, 1903; Howard Dawson to Sanford, December 11, 1905; and S. D. Catherwood to Sanford, January 12, 1906 — all in Sanford Papers.
³⁸ Whitney, *Sanford,* 196; list of contributors, December 19, 1906, Sanford Papers.
³⁹ C. D. Decker to Sanford, June 17, 1909, and William W. Norton to Sanford, June 10, 1909, Sanford Papers; Whitney, *Sanford,* 201, 204–214.
⁴⁰ Whitney, *Sanford,* 220–222, 224; Proctor to Sanford, August 5, 1909, and January 17, 1910; Lucy C. Laney to Sanford, February 22, 1910; Taft to whom it may concern, February 28, 1910; and additional correspondence for February and March, 1910 — all in Sanford Papers.
⁴¹ Schedule of payments; Sanford to Woodruff, September 1, 1903; and James Murray to Sanford, August 17, October 13, 1910 — all in Sanford Papers; Whitney, *Sanford,* 225–231.
⁴² Whitney, *Sanford,* 234–238, 242; Edith M. Brooks to Sanford, February 29, 1912, and Sanford to Mary Kirtland, June 24, June 30, 1912, Sanford Papers.
⁴³ Whitney, *Sanford,* 232, 249; Adolph O. Eberhart to Sanford, February 10 and February 20, 1914, Sanford Papers; Shapiro, "Analysis," 174.
⁴⁴ Whitney, *Sanford,* 232–258; Sanford to Kirtland, August 14, December 1, 1915.
⁴⁵ Whitney, *Sanford,* 145, 258, 283, 296. Many letters to Sanford refer to her financial support of relatives. See, for example, those from Emily L. Savidge, December 21, 1902, Rufus Sanford, October 14, 1904, May 22, 1913, and James Murray, March 5, 1912, Sanford Papers.
⁴⁶ Whitney, *Sanford,* 261–271, 274.
⁴⁷ Whitney, *Sanford,* 282, 284–286, 289–291, 293, 305–309.
⁴⁸ Whitney, *Sanford,* 238–240, 244; Shapiro, "Analysis," 401, 405–410.

Chapter 6 — FRANCES DENSMORE — *pages 94 to 115*

¹ For the history of the Densmore family, see C. A. Rasmussen, *A History of the City of Red Wing, Minnesota*, 284 (n.p., 1933), and Franklyn Curtiss-Wedge, ed., *History of Goodhue County, Minnesota*, 757 (Chicago, 1909).

² "Chronology of the study and presentation of Indian music by Frances Densmore from 1893 to 1944," 1, Archive of Folk Song, Densmore Papers, Library of Congress. Hereafter cited as "Chronology." Throughout her life Frances Densmore kept meticulous professional and personal records. In addition to her publications, these include diaries, complete in 46 volumes for the years 1907–33, scrapbooks, correspondence, several retrospective accounts of her experiences, and various unpublished manuscripts, including the texts of several early lectures.

³ For information here and in the paragraph below, see Charles Hofmann, comp., ed., *Frances Densmore and American Indian Music*, 1 (Museum of the American Indian Heye Foundation, *Contributions*, vol. 23 — New York, 1968).

⁴ Densmore, "[Auto]biography," n.d. but written not earlier than 1952. Densmore Personal Papers, National Anthropological Archives, Smithsonian Institution. Fletcher's study, originally published as *Archaeological and Ethnological Papers of the Peabody Museum*, vol. 1, no. 5 (Cambridge, Mass., 1893) was reprinted as a monograph in 1967.

⁵ In 1952 Densmore noted in her scrapbook: "when a child, I was taken to an exhibit, or demonstration, of a recording phonograph that had recently been invented. This was probably in 1878 or 1879." Archive of Folk Song, Densmore Papers, Scrapbook 8, 1949–54, Library of Congress. Densmore's library contained a copy of Emile Berliner, *The Gramophone by its Inventor: Paper Read before The Franklin Institute, May 16, 1888* (Washington, D.C., 1894). Berliner had invented a recording instrument in 1877, the same year Edison invented the phonograph. Densmore noted in her copy of Berliner's book that he had given it to her about 1913, six years after she had made her own first sound recordings.

⁶ "Chronology," 2.

⁷ Hofmann, ed., *Densmore*, 2.

⁸ "Chronology," 3.

⁹ Schubert Club (St. Paul), *Programs, 1899–1924*, December 4, 1895, in Minnesota Historical Society (MHS) Library.

¹⁰ See a note by Densmore in 1945 attached to "Manuscript of a Lecture on Indian Music," dated before 1899, in Archive of Folk Song, Densmore Papers, Library of Congress. The manuscript is essentially the same as a lecture delivered in Chicago in 1899; the complete text is in Hofmann, ed., *Densmore*, 2–12. No dated manuscripts of lectures given before 1895 have survived, but a "Partial list of lectures, addresses and papers on Indian music and customs," may be found in Densmore Personal Papers, National Anthropological Archives, 4250 Box 2, Item 7, Smithsonian Institution. See also "Chronology," 3, 4. Topics are listed in printed programs for her lectures.

¹¹ Farwell, who had a strong interest in Indian music, in 1901 founded the Wawan Press at Newton Center, Mass., to promote the publication and performance of works by American composers and compositions based on American Indian melodies.

¹² *Minneapolis Journal*, May 23, 1903, p. 11. See also Hofmann, ed., *Densmore*, 11.

¹³ Hofmann, ed., *Densmore*, 25; Densmore, "Three Indian Types," in *Indian School Journal*, November, 1906, p. 35.

¹⁴ Densmore, in *Indian School Journal*, p. 36.

¹⁵ See Densmore, "Prelude to the Study of Indian Music," in *Minnesota Ar-*

chaeologist, 11:28 (April, 1945), reprinted in Hofmann, ed., *Densmore*, 21–24. The two articles by Densmore are "The Song of Minagunz, the Ojibwa," in *Indian School Journal*, pp. 23–25; "An Ojibwa Prayer Ceremony," in *American Anthropologist*, new series, 9:443 (April–June, 1907).

[16] Densmore, "Two Dakota Songs," in *Indian School Journal*, April, 1907, pp. 32–34; "Chronology," 1.

[17] Densmore, in *Minnesota Archaeologist*, 11:30.

[18] A number of the recordings made at the White Earth Reservation in 1907 were deposited with the Bureau of American Ethnology. They are now in the Archive of Folk Song, Densmore Papers, Library of Congress. For a list of these recordings, see "Catalogue of Phonograph Records of Indian Music in the Archives of the Bureau of American Ethnology," 3–6, in National Anthropological Archives, Smithsonian Institution.

[19] Densmore, in *Minnesota Archaeologist*, 11:31.

[20] Densmore, "The Study of Indian Music," in Smithsonian Institution, *Annual Report, 1941*, 529 (Washington, D.C., 1942), reprinted in Hofmann, ed., *Densmore*, 101–114. The series of events associated with the death of Flat Mouth are recounted in Densmore's first major publication, *Chippewa Music*, 51–55 (Bureau of American Ethnology, *Bulletin 45* — Washington, D.C., 1910). This volume and other Densmore books cited in this chapter were reprinted by Da Capo Press in 1972.

[21] Bureau of American Ethnology, *Twenty-ninth Annual Report, 1907–08*, 19 (Washington, D.C., 1916).

[22] Bureau of American Ethnology, *Thirtieth Annual Report, 1908–09*, 21 (Washington, D.C., 1915); Densmore, "Lecture on the Music of the American Indians before the Anthropological Society of Washington, April 26, 1909," p. 1, Densmore Personal Papers, National Anthropological Archives, Smithsonian Institution.

[23] Densmore, *Chippewa Music — II*, 35 (Bureau of American Ethnology, *Bulletin 53* — Washington, D.C., 1913).

[24] These studies appeared as Bureau of American Ethnology, *Bulletin 80* and *165* (Washington, D.C., 1923, 1957). On the elimination of tabulated analyses, see, for example, Densmore, *Cheyenne and Arapaho Music* (Southwest Museum, *Papers*, no. 10 — Los Angeles, May, 1936). For the study mentioned in the paragraph below, see Densmore, *Teton Sioux Music* (Bureau of American Ethnology, *Bulletin 61* — Washington, D.C., 1918).

[25] See, for example, Densmore, in *Indian School Journal*, April, 1907, pp. 32–34.

[26] Densmore, *Chippewa Music*, 3. For the special signs, see p. xix.

[27] On pitch discrimination, see Densmore, "American Indian Music," in *Journal of the Washington Academy of Sciences*, 18:398 (August 19, 1928); Densmore, "The Use of the Term 'tetrachord' in Musicology," in *Journal of Musicology*, 1:16 (March, 1940); and "Regional Peculiarities of Indian Songs," 1, typescript of a paper read by Densmore before the American Association for the Advancement of Science (AAAS), Minneapolis, June 28, 1935, in Archive of Folk Song, Densmore Papers, Library of Congress.

[28] Densmore, *Teton Sioux Music*, 51; Densmore, *Chippewa Music — II*, 50–58. For another example of Densmore's graph transcriptions, see *Mandan and Hidatsa Music*, 34. Later scholars have used graph notation to provide more detailed transcriptions than are possible with conventional notation.

[29] Densmore, *Chippewa Music*, 5.

[30] "Department of Physics, Case School of Applied Science," a report by Dayton C. Miller, in Archive of Folk Song, Densmore Papers, Library of Congress; Densmore, in Smithsonian Institution, *Annual Report, 1941*, 543.

[31] Densmore, "Methods of Recording Indian Songs," 9, typescript of a paper read before the AAAS, St. Louis, January, 1936; Densmore, in Smithsonian Institution, *Annual Report, 1941*, 543.

[32] John C. Fillmore, "The Harmonic Structure of Indian Music," in *American Anthropologist*, new series, 1:308 (April, 1899).

[33] Densmore, "A Plea for the Indian Harmonization of All Indian Songs," in *Indian School Journal*, February, 1906, p. 14. The works of contemporary Indian composers such as Louis Ballard, who uses traditional Indian melodies in writing for ensembles of Western and traditional Indian instruments, are in a sense fulfillments of Densmore's vision. Even more prophetic was her view that the Native American by virtue of his ethnic inheritance is himself the best interpreter of Indian culture.

[34] Densmore, in *Indian School Journal*, April, 1907, p. 34; Fillmore, in Fletcher, *Study of Omaha Music*, 61.

[35] Fillmore, in *American Anthropologist*, 1:315; Densmore, *Chippewa Music*, 8.

[36] Densmore, *Chippewa Music — II*, 3; Densmore, *Choctaw Music* (Bureau of American Ethnology, *Bulletin 136*, Anthropological Paper No. 28 — Washington, D.C., 1943).

[37] Densmore, "Recent Developments in the Study of Indian Music," in *Proceedings of the Nineteenth International Congress of Americanists*, 298 (Washington, D.C., 1917), reprinted in *Scientific American* (supplement), 85:253 (April, 1918) and *Etude*, 38:267 (October, 1920).

[38] Densmore, *Nootka and Quileute Music*, 44 (Bureau of American Ethnology, *Bulletin 124* — Washington, D.C., 1939).

[39] Densmore, *Yuman and Yaqui Music*, 18 (Bureau of American Ethnology, *Bulletin 110* — Washington, D.C., 1932).

[40] Densmore, *Music of the Indians of British Columbia*, 95 (Bureau of American Ethnology, *Bulletin 136*, Anthropological Paper No. 27 — Washington, D.C., 1943).

[41] Densmore, *Music of the Indians of British Columbia*, 98.

[42] Densmore, *Music of the Indians of British Columbia*, 97.

[43] Mary Eastman's book was published in New York in 1849. Densmore, *The Collection of Water-Color Drawings of the North American Indian by Seth Eastman in the James Jerome Hill Reference Library, Saint Paul*, 11 (St. Paul, 1954).

[44] "Handbook of the Smithsonian-Densmore Collection of American Indian Sound Recordings in the National Archives," unpublished manuscript dated 1943 listed in Hofmann, ed., *Densmore*, 127, now located in Archive of Folk Song, Densmore Papers, Library of Congress. In the same archive is Densmore's letter to Duncan Emrich, July 20, 1951.

[45] Densmore to Biederman, March 24, April 26, 1954, in Densmore Papers, Goodhue County Historical Society, Red Wing.

Chapter 7 — MARY MOLLOY — *pages 116 to 135*

[1] The remarks were occasioned by news that the Sisters of St. Joseph intended to found a college for women in the Midway district of St. Paul; *North-Western Chronicle* (St. Paul), April 10, 1891, p. 4, in Archives of the St. Paul Catholic Historical Society and in the Minnesota Historical Society.

[2] The six coeducational colleges were Hamline, Gustavus Adolphus, Carleton, St. Olaf, and Concordia (Moorhead); Macalester joined them in 1893 with a decision to try coeducation for a five-year trial period. See Merrill E. Jarchow, *Private Liberal Arts Colleges in Minnesota: Their History and Contributions*, 9, 19, 22, 30, 31, 42, 37 (St. Paul, 1973). Figures for the University of Minnesota are derived from

E. Bird Johnson, ed., *Forty Years of the University of Minnesota*, 243 (Minneapolis, 1910). Hamline possesses an unusual collection of alumni data in Henry L. Osborne's *Alumni Record of Hamline University* (St. Paul, 1924); for Carleton and other independent institutions, see Jarchow, *Private Liberal Arts Colleges*. Hamline had graduated 39 women by 1891, or slightly over 45 per cent of total degrees granted; Carleton had produced 62 women graduates by that same year, or 35 per cent of its total. While the numbers may not be entirely exact, it would seem likely that existing records reflect proportions of women and men with fair accuracy. The men's colleges were St. John's, St. Thomas, and Augsburg. Augsburg became coeducational in the 1920s, and St. Thomas decided to admit women starting in September, 1977.

[3] Sister Helen Angela Hurley, *On Good Ground: The Story of the Sisters of St. Joseph in St. Paul* (Minneapolis, 1951) narrates the history of the Sisters of St. Joseph of Carondelet in Minnesota, North and South Dakota. Parallel references for Benedictine and Franciscan history are Sister M. Grace McDonald, *With Lamps Burning* (St. Joseph, Minn., 1957); and the master's theses of Sister M. Francis Ann Hayes, "Years of Beginning, A History of the Sisters of the Third Order Regular of St. Francis of the Congregation of Our Lady of Lourdes, Rochester, Minnesota, 1877–1902"; and Sister Mary Caedmon Homan, "Years of Vision, 1903–1928" — both completed at Catholic University of America, 1956.

[4] Catharine, sister of Harriet Beecher Stowe and Edward Beecher, made numerous ill-fated attempts to found academies in Wisconsin, Ohio, and Iowa in the 1840s and 1850s. See Thomas Woody, *A History of Women's Education in the United States*, 1:319–328, 375–378, 2:143–145, 238, 456 (New York, 1929), and especially Mary M. Yeater, "Catherine [*sic*] Beecher and Midwestern Women's Education," paper delivered at the Conference on the History of Women, College of St. Catherine, St. Paul, October 25, 1975.

[5] Mary Dillon Foster, comp., *Who's Who Among Minnesota Women*, 200 (n.p., 1924); N. C. Cornwall, comp., *Who's Who in Minnesota*, 1199 (Minneapolis, 1941). The roller-skating incident and the information in the paragraph below was related by Sister Emmanuel Collins in an interview conducted by the author, January 17, 1975. Sister Emmanuel's long relationship with Molloy and the college began as a freshman at St. Teresa's in 1919. Except for those in note 21, all interviews here cited were conducted by the author and the tapes are in her possession.

[6] Clippings from the *Journal and Local* (Sandusky, Ohio) and the Sandusky High School newspaper relating to Molloy's high school and college achievements discussed here and in the three paragraphs below are preserved in a scrapbook in the Archives, College of St. Teresa, Winona (hereafter referred to as Molloy, Scrapbook). In it are clippings and letters dating from 1899 to 1927.

[7] Molloy, Scrapbook; Foster, *Who's Who Among Minnesota Women*, 200; Cornwall, *Who's Who in Minnesota*, 1199.

[8] Molloy, Scrapbook.

[9] On the sequence of events leading to the rejection of Hyde's offer and the acceptance of Tracy's, see Homan, "Years of Vision," 72–74.

[10] Homan, "Years of Vision," 74.

[11] Sister Mary David Homan, *A River Town is Born*, 7–10 (Winona, 1958).

[12] Emma Tracy's childhood and early career are documented in Hayes, "Years of Beginning"; on her later career, see Homan, "Years of Vision," 80, 90–93.

[13] This candid assessment was that of Martha Carey Thomas, then president of Bryn Mawr; see her "Present Tendencies in Women's Colleges and University Education," in *Publications of the Association of Collegiate Alumnae*, vol. 3, no. 17, p. 47 (February, 1908), quoted also in Woody, *History of Women's Education*, 2:327.

[14] Trinity had been preceded by the College of Notre Dame, Baltimore; St. Mary-of-the-Woods, Terre Haute; St. Mary's College, Notre Dame; and the College

of St. Elizabeth, Convent Station, N.J. For further information on the founding of these colleges, see Mary Mariella Bowler, A History of Catholic Colleges for Women in the United States of America (Washington, D.C., 1933).

[15] Homan, "Years of Vision," 74, 75. Molloy began instruction on the American, or group, plan of class recitation in 1909–10.

[16] J. W. T. Mack to John F. Downey, August 14, 1909 (carbon copy); G. P. Bristol to Molloy, n.d. — both in Molloy, Scrapbook. Mack, a trustee of Ohio State University, wrote that Malloy was "devoted heart and soul to her vocation" of teaching; "a complete mastership of her studies characterized her work."

[17] The brochure and other seminary and college publications cited below are in the Archives, College of St. Teresa.

[18] Winona Seminary, Catalogue, 1895.

[19] Homan, "Years of Vision," 76, 77.

[20] Winona Republican Herald, March 7, 1914, p. 10.

[21] Molloy and O'Brien contended that the lectures could not be held because the Philharmonic Hall was not licensed for lectures with an admission charge. The Guardians of Liberty forthwith claimed sponsorship of the lectures as renters of the hall. See Winona Republican Herald, March 13, p. 10, March 14, 1914, p. 6; Sister M. David Homan interview with Sister M. Loyola Gregoire, November 16, 1951; student interview, under the direction of Sister M. David Homan, with Mary O'Brien, December 31, 1953; interviews with Sister M. Aloysius, December 27, 28, 31, 1953 — all in Archives, College of St. Teresa.

[22] Menace (Aurora, Mo.), January 15, 1916, copy in Minnesota Historical Society; State v. Anna W. [sic] Lowry, 130 Minnesota Supreme Court Reports 532 (1915); Catholic Press Club, Winona, news release, n.d., copy in Archives, College of St. Teresa.

[23] Molloy, The Lay Apostolate, [4, 6, 7] (Winona, 1915), a pamphlet reprinted from America, August 22, 1914; Annual Catalogue, 1915–16, p. 12. The 1915 "Blue Book," or guide for student behavior, phrased the same goal as "to send forth broad minded, well trained, deeply religious young women."

[24] Annual Catalogue, 1915–16, p. 12.

[25] Molloy, Catholic Colleges for Women, 16 (Winona, 1918), published version of a paper delivered at the Conference of Women's Colleges, NCEA meeting, San Francisco, June 24, 1918.

[26] Homan, "Years of Vision," 38–49.

[27] "Letter to Members of the Faculty of the College of St. Teresa," February 2, 1928, reprinted in A Teresan Ideal in Service and System, 8–10, in Archives, College of St. Teresa. The issue for Dean Molloy was one which would today be called women's liberation or consciousness-raising, particularly among the daughters of first-generation immigrants whom the college served. "In one of the great cities of the country two years ago," lamented the dean in 1918, "eighty-five percent of the teachers in the public elementary schools were Catholic women," whereas the six major high schools of that same city numbered fewer than five Catholic women on their combined staffs. See Molloy, Catholic Colleges for Women, 4.

[28] Molloy herself is recalled as "the plainest kind of person" who habitually wore a trim suit for teaching and office work; Sister Helen Barden interview, January 17, 1975. On the other hand, she enjoyed fancy clothes for leisure pursuits — her outfits of shadow lace over silk and an angora jacket with hood are vividly recalled by contemporaries. She was quite capable of looking beyond clothing to the person, once defending "flappers" before a conservative audience by saying that for all her quirks of dress, the flapper of 1927 was more genuinely likable than the girl of 1907; "She is quite frank, and strange as it may seem, more idealistic than her sister of earlier days." Newspaper clipping reporting an informal talk, Catholic Women's Colleges, NCEA meeting, 1927, in Molloy, Scrapbook.

[29] Molloy, "Letter to Faculty," 10.

[30] Sister Camille Bowe interview, January 17, 1975. Sister Camille's acquaintance with Molloy began with her admission as a freshman in 1920.

[31] Collins interview.

[32] The American Association of University Women's list of fully approved colleges included only 12 of the 73 four-year Catholic women's colleges established in 28 states and the District of Columbia by 1930. Among them were St. Teresa's and St. Catherine's. Both institutions had likewise earned early recognition from the regional accrediting agency, the North Central Association, as a result of the quality of their programs and a policy change introduced in 1916. That year, Sister Antonia McHugh of the College of St. Catherine worked through a North Central committee to secure adoption of the principle that the contributed services of members of a religious community could substitute for the $500,000 endowment ordinarily required for accreditation of independent colleges. Thus persuaded of the financial stability of colleges staffed by communities of religious women, North Central granted accreditation to St. Catherine's in 1916 and to St. Teresa's in 1917. See Jarchow, *Private Liberal Arts Colleges*, 108, 116, 117; Homan, "Years of Vision," 77, 82–84; *Journal of the American Association of University Women*, 24:212 (June, 1931); Marion Talbot and Lois K. M. Rosenberry, *The History of the American Association of University Women, 1881–1931*, 429–434 (New York, 1931); *Proceedings of the North Central Association of Colleges and Secondary Schools*, 1917, p. 18.

[33] Homan, "Years of Vision," 80, 81; Sister Adele O'Neill, interview, January 17, 1975. Sister Adele went to the college in 1921 and became intimately acquainted with Franciscan community finances through her thirty-eight-year service as treasurer of the Rochester community beginning in 1931.

[34] Hurley, *On Good Ground*, 261; Jarchow, *Private Liberal Arts Colleges*, 106, 114, 116; see also Jarchow's chapters on the two colleges, 106–112, 113–117, 224–231, and 232–238.

[35] Bowe interview.

[36] Molloy to Shahan, March 12, 1915, Archives, College of St. Teresa, NCEA General Correspondence.

[37] Quotations in this and the following paragraph are from *Buffalo Courier* (New York), June 28, 1917, clipping in Archives, College of St. Teresa.

[38] Quotations in this and the following paragraph are from Molloy, *Catholic Colleges for Women*, 3, 4, 8, 10, 11, 14, 15, 16. The italics are Molloy's.

[39] Letter to Cardinal Gasparri in Molloy, Scrapbook.

[40] For her various academic activities and associations, see Foster, comp., *Who's Who Among Minnesota Women*, 200; Cornwall, *Who's Who in Minnesota*, 1199; and Archives, College of St. Teresa.

[41] *Proceedings of the Twenty-Eight Annual Meeting of the North Central Association of Colleges and Secondary Schools*, 1923, p. 9. Only 123 persons have been given an honorary life membership in the North Central Association in its entire history (through 1976), and only three of them, including Molloy, have been women; see *North Central Quarterly*, 51 (Summer, 1976).

[42] Molloy to Meta Glass, July 15, 1935; copies of this and the following correspondence are in Archives, College of St. Teresa, AAUW General Correspondence.

[43] McHugh to Molloy, August 24, 1935.

[44] Sister Marie José, (Dean, College of St. Elizabeth, Convent Station, N.J.) to Molloy, August 5, 1935. Mother M. Angelique (Dean, Our Lady of the Lake College, San Antonio, Tex.) wrote on July 29, 1935, applauding Molloy's action as being "entirely correct," but stating that she preferred to register her college's protest by work from within: "we might give courage to a large number of College Women other than Catholics, and with them form a group that would be able to have an authoritative voice in such questions."

[45] Glass to Molloy, November 19, 1936.

[46] Molloy, *Give us Teachers*, [2] (Winona, n.d.), reprinted from *Bulletin of the Association of American Colleges*, 6:125–134 (1920). A convinced classicist and humanist, fully capable of lecturing on Greek philosophy or Anglo-Saxon philology at a moment's notice (younger sisters at the college recall her doing so with aplomb in the 1930s and early 1940s), Dr. Molloy is nonetheless recalled by her contemporaries as one who adapted to the Midwest in her respect for women's need to make a living as well as for knowing how to live. Sister Lorraine McCarthy interview, January 17, 1975. Sister Lorraine, as dean of students, was a long-time associate of Molloy.

[47] Homan, "Years of Vision," 82.

[48] Jarchow, *Private Liberal Arts Colleges*, 58, 91, 99, 203.

Chapter 8 — ALICE O'BRIEN — *pages 136 to 154*

[1] *St. Paul Sunday Pioneer Press*, November 11, 1962, sec. 2, p. 17.

[2] Much of the information that follows was provided by Alice O'Brien's niece, Julia Wilcox of Marine on St. Croix, and nephews, Thomond and Terence O'Brien of St. Paul, all of whom have documents and information about the O'Brien family as well as innumerable personal recollections of their aunt and grandfather. I am grateful to them for providing me with quantities of information and for sharing their fond remembrances of their aunt with me. A trunkful of personal letters, photographs, and miscellaneous mementos kept by Alice O'Brien is now in the possession of Julia Wilcox. Newspaper articles from the *St. Paul Pioneer Press*, *St. Paul Dispatch*, and *St. Paul Daily News* between 1927 and 1940, clipped and pasted into scrapbooks kept by the Women's City Club (hereafter cited as Women's City Club, Scrapbooks) are now in the possession of Thomond O'Brien. Material not otherwise credited in this chapter is based upon these family papers and memories. I would also like to thank Lucy Fricke of St. Paul for suggesting that Alice O'Brien merited inclusion in this book.

[3] On her mother and father, see obituaries in *St. Paul Pioneer Press*, April 27, 1925, p. 1, and March 8, 1944, p. 5; *Little Sketches of Big Folks, Minnesota 1907*, 295 (St. Paul, Minneapolis, and Duluth, 1907); *Duluth News Tribune*, June 30, 1910, sec. 3, p. 10; conversations with Terence and Thomond O'Brien. Alice's brother Robert, born in 1902, was killed in an automobile accident in 1924. Her other brother, William J. (born in 1895), called Jack by family and friends, began his business career in the family lumber business, but ultimately became a partner in Hannaford O'Brien, an insurance agency. He died in a plane crash in Egypt in 1958 while on a world tour; see *Minneapolis Star*, March 8, 1958, p. 1. In 1965 his son, also named William, then a state representative from District 45 North, was one of the authors of the bill to acquire the house at 1006 Summit Avenue as an official residence for the governor of Minnesota. Next door, at 1034 Summit Avenue, was the house which the senior William O'Brien had built for his family. See *Minnesota Legislative Manual, 1965–1966*, 75 (St. Paul, 1965); "A Home for Minnesota's Governor," in *Gopher Historian*, Spring, 1966, pp. 12, 13.

[4] *St. Paul Pioneer Press*, November 9, 1962, p. 23; conversation with Ruth M. Husom, Minnesota Department of Natural Resources.

[5] *St. Paul Pioneer Press*, February 4, 1934, sec. 2, p. 12, and November 11, 1962, sec. 2, p. 17; Lucy Fricke, *Historic Ramsey Hill: Yesterday and Tomorrow* (St. Paul, n.d.); conversations with Terence O'Brien. The photographs mentioned are in the possession of Julia Wilcox.

[6] *St. Paul Daily News*, December 2, 1937, sec. 2, p. 1.

[7] *St. Paul Pioneer Press*, February 4, 1934, sec. 2, p. 12.

[8] Conversations with Julia Wilcox, Terence and Thomond O'Brien, and Montfort Dunn, Marine on St. Croix.

[9] *New York Times*, March 20, 1918, p. 12; Franklin F. Holbrook, *St. Paul and Ramsey County in the War of 1917–1918*, 5 (St. Paul, 1929); Holbrook and Livia Appel, *Minnesota in the War With Germany*, 1:16 (St. Paul, 1928).

[10] Holbrook, *St. Paul and Ramsey County*, 252, 374, 498; Samuel E. Morison, *The Oxford History of the American People*, 861, 862, 865, 870–872 (New York, 1965). A fourth friend, Genivieve Washburn, sailed with the group, but became separated from the other three when they reached Paris.

[11] The letters were privately published by Thomond O'Brien in 1971 under the title *Somewhere in France*. On the Committee on Public Information, see Holbrook and Appel, *Minnesota in the War With Germany*, 2:68.

[12] O'Brien, *Somewhere in France*, 6.

[13] O'Brien, *Somewhere in France*, 8.

[14] O'Brien, *Somewhere in France*, 11.

[15] O'Brien, *Somewhere in France*, 22.

[16] Here and below, see O'Brien, *Somewhere in France*, 44, 47, 53.

[17] O'Brien, *Somewhere in France*, 83. "Mugs" was the nickname of Marguerite Davis.

[18] O'Brien, *Somewhere in France*, 101.

[19] O'Brien, *Somewhere in France*, 164.

[20] On the China trip, see *Minneapolis Journal*, October 27, 1927, p. 19. Two of Alice O'Brien's paintings, "The Gander" and "The Goose," both painted by the twelfth-century artist Wu Yüan-yü, were illustrated in Sirén's monumental work, *A History of Early Chinese Painting*, 2:plates 15, 16 (London and New York, 1933). She also assembled a collection of modern Western art, notably works of the secondary cubist painters Robert Delaunay, Gino Severini, Albert Gleizes, Auguste Herbin, Fernand Léger, and Jules Pascin, as well as works by Georges Rouault, Stuart Davis, and Walt Kuhn. Sixty-one examples from her collection of Western art are now in the Minnesota Museum of Art, St. Paul, on indefinite loan from her heirs.

[21] *St. Paul Pioneer Press*, October 26, 1927, p. 20.

[22] See *St. Paul Pioneer Press*, February 4, 1934, sec. 2, p. 12; March 23, 1930, sec. 3, p. 1; *St. Paul Dispatch*, June 8, 1928, p. 1; Women's City Club, Scrapbook; conversation with Lucy Fricke. The Flandrau book was published in 1929.

[23] Flandrau, *Then I Saw the Congo*, 6, 8, 24, 38–40, 46, 47; *St. Paul Pioneer Press*, February 4, 1934, sec. 2, p. 12.

[24] Flandrau, *Then I Saw the Congo*, 102–104, 109, 237, 238.

[25] Flandrau, *Then I Saw the Congo*, 261, 266, 267, 270, 299, 300; *St. Paul Dispatch*, June 8, 1928, p. 17.

[26] Martin Johnson, "Camera-Hunts in the Jungles of Africa," in *New York Times Magazine*, July 17, 1927, p. 4; Flandrau, *Then I Saw the Congo*, 4.

[27] *New York Times*, June 5, 1928, p. 9; *St. Paul Pioneer Press*, May 30, 1928, p. 1.

[28] Flandrau, *Then I Saw the Congo*, 98. The book was serialized in ten weekly installments in the *St. Paul Sunday Pioneer Press*, beginning on March 23, 1930, sec. 3, p. 1. The surviving photographs are in the possession of Julia Wilcox.

[29] Flandrau, *Then I Saw the Congo*, 98, 302.

[30] *St. Paul Pioneer Press*, February 4, 1934, sec. 2, p. 12; *New York Times*, January 20, 1930, p. 21; Terence O'Brien has had the movie transferred to modern 16 mm. film, and this copy is now in his possession.

[31] *St. Paul Pioneer Press*, February 4, 1934, sec. 2, p. 12. Julia Wilcox now lives in Alice O'Brien's Marine house.

[32] *St. Paul Pioneer Press*, February 4, 1934, sec. 2, p. 12; conversations with Terence O'Brien and Julia Wilcox. According to her niece, Alice O'Brien, a lifelong Republican, felt that Herbert Hoover was an unjustly maligned president and that many innovative programs credited to Franklin Roosevelt's administrations had ac-

tually been proposed by Hoover. Interestingly, revisionist historians have reached the same conclusion in recent years.

[33] *St. Paul Pioneer Press*, October 16, 1931, p. 11; Women's City Club, *Women's City Club of Saint Paul*, 4, 7 (St. Paul, 1948–49).

[34] Clio Club, *Eighth Annual Program*, n.p. (Hastings, [1899]).

[35] Minnesota Federation of Women's Clubs, *A Circular of suggestions for work and study along Educational lines, prepared for the use of the Clubs by the Education Committee* (n.p., [1898]); Minnesota Federation of Women's Clubs, *President's Letter*, October 1, 1920, pp. 5, 8–11; Women's City Club, Scrapbooks.

[36] Sophonisba P. Breckinridge, *Women in the Twentieth Century: A Study of Their Political, Social and Economic Activities*, 82 (New York and London, 1933).

[37] *Women's City Club*, 3–6; Women's City Club of St. Paul, *Constitution and By-Laws*, 1, 2 (St. Paul, 1921).

[38] *Women's City Club*, 4.

[39] *Women's City Club*, 4, 5; *St. Paul Pioneer Press*, February 4, 1934, sec. 2, p. 12; *St. Paul Daily News*, December 2, 1937, sec. 2, p. 1; Women's City Club, Scrapbooks.

[40] Women's City Club, Scrapbooks; *St. Paul Daily News*, December 2, 1937, sec. 2, p. 1.

[41] "Around Saint Paul," in *Saint Paul Magazine*, Fall, 1931, p. 5.

[42] Women's City Club, Scrapbooks; *Women's City Club*, 5.

[43] Conversations with Thomond and Terence O'Brien.

[44] Robert Rosenthal, *The Story of The Children's Hospital*, 4, 6–8 (St. Paul, 1972); *St. Paul Sunday Pioneer Press*, November 11, 1962, sec. 2, p. 17.

[45] Rosenthal, *Children's Hospital*, 9, 10; historical file in the Children's Hospital Association office, St. Paul.

[46] This and the following three paragraphs are from conversations with the O'Brien family, especially Terence O'Brien.

[47] The minutes of the foundation are in the possession of its president, Terence O'Brien, who made them available to me. For a brief period in 1962 the foundation was called officially the William Foundation in accordance with Alice O'Brien's wish for anonymity. After her death, the name was changed back to the Alice M. O'Brien Foundation.

[48] *St. Paul Pioneer Press*, November 9, 1962, p. 23, November 11, 1962, sec. 2, p. 17; the former article stated erroneously that she died of a heart attack.

Chapter 9 — MAUD HART LOVELACE — *pages 155 to 172*

[1] Interview of Maud Hart Lovelace by the author, December 10, 1974. The ten books in the series are: *Betsy-Tacy* (1940), *Betsy-Tacy and Tib* (1941), *Betsy and Tacy Go Over the Big Hill* (1942), *Down Town: A Betsy-Tacy Story* (1943), *Heaven to Betsy* (1945), *Betsy in Spite of Herself* (1946), *Betsy Was a Junior* (1947), *Betsy and Joe* (1948), *Betsy and the Great World* (1952), and *Betsy's Wedding* (1955). According to the publisher, Thomas Y. Crowell Co. all of the titles continue to sell well, and the first two were released in paperback editions in 1974.

[2] The quotation appears on the book jackets of Maud's early Betsy-Tacy books. It is echoed in *Betsy-Tacy*, 11, where her mother says, "'When Betsy is happy, she is happier than anyone else in the world.' Then she added, 'And she's almost always happy.'"

[3] Mrs. Lovelace's other books are: *The Black Angels* (1926), *Early Candlelight* (1929), *Petticoat Court* (1930), *The Charming Sally* (1932), *Carney's House Party: A Deep Valley Story* (1949), *The Tune Is in the Tree* (1950), *Emily of Deep Valley* (1950), *The Trees Kneel at Christmas* (1951), *Winona's Pony Cart* (1953), *What*

Cabrillo Found (1958), *The Valentine Box* (1966), and with Delos Lovelace: *One Stayed at Welcome* (1934), *Gentlemen from England* (1937), *The Golden Wedge* (1942).

[4] Carmen N. Richards, ed., *Minnesota Writers*, 209 (Minneapolis, 1961).

[5] Ray interview with Lovelace, December 10, 1974; "I Remember Mankato," in *Mankato Free Press*, April 10, 1952, p. 18, and "Maud Hart Lovelace at Christmas," in *Mankato Free Press*, December 16, 1974, p. 9. All newspaper articles quoted in this chapter may be found in the Maud Hart Lovelace folder in the Minnesota Valley Regional Library (hereafter abbreviated MVRL), Mankato, or in the newspaper files of the Minnesota Historical Society.

[6] Lovelace, *Betsy-Tacy Go Over the Big Hill*, 2.

[7] *Mankato — Its First Fifty Years*, 135 (Mankato, 1903); Lovelace, in *Mankato Free Press*, April 10, 1952, p. 18.

[8] *Mankato — Its First Fifty Years*, 13–62, 134–150; Anna M. Wiecking, *Blue Earth County from 1700 to 1900*, 25 (Mankato, 1957); Lovelace, *Down Town*, 57; Michael Cabaya, "Maud Hart Lovelace," master's thesis, Mankato State University, 1966. A copy of the latter is in MVRL.

[9] Richards, ed., *Minnesota Writers*, 211; *Heaven to Betsy*, 93; interview of the author with Mrs. Ogden Confer, Minneapolis, November, 1974.

[10] Ray interview with Lovelace, December 10, 1974; *Heaven to Betsy*, 215.

[11] Lovelace to Marjorie Austin Freeman, May 19, 1964, copy in MVRL.

[12] Lovelace to Freeman, May 19, 1964. On the Andrews, see Cornelia A. Du Bois, "Operatic Pioneers: The Story of the Andrews Family," in *Minnesota History*, 33:317–325 (Winter, 1953).

[13] The first quotation is from a statement by Maud on the jacket of *Betsy and Tacy Go Over the Big Hill*. See also Lovelace, *Betsy-Tacy*, 76, 97.

[14] "The Reader Writes," in *Mankato Free Press*, February 4, 1965, p. 12.

[15] Lovelace, in *Mankato Free Press*, April 10, 1952, p. 18; *Down Town*, 62.

[16] *Betsy and Tacy Go Over the Big Hill*, 148.

[17] Ray interview with Lovelace, December 10, 1974; Lovelace, *Betsy-Tacy and Tib*, 3; Lovelace, *Heaven to Betsy*, 131. *Little Miss Muffet Fights Back: A Bibliography of Recommended Non-Sexist Books about Girls for Young Readers* was published by Feminists on Children's Media (New York, 1974).

[18] Lovelace to Isadora Veigel, librarian, April 15, 1966, MVRL; Lovelace, *Heaven to Betsy*, 28, 267. The house was torn down in 1966 to make way for expansion of Mankato State University.

[19] The high school books are *Heaven to Betsy, Betsy In Spite of Herself, Betsy Was a Junior*, and *Betsy and Joe*. In Lovelace to Freeman, May 19, 1964, Maud wrote: "The family life, customs, jokes, traditions, are all true and the general pattern of the years is also accurate."

[20] Lovelace to Joelie Hicks, August 11, 1973, copy in the author's possession. The original is owned by Joelie Hicks.

[21] Lovelace, in *Mankato Free Press*, April 10, 1952, p. 18.

[22] Lovelace, *Betsy and Joe*, 249.

[23] Lovelace to Hicks, August 11, 1973.

[24] Lovelace to Hicks, August 11, 1973; to Freeman, May 19, 1964.

[25] Lovelace to Hicks, August 11, 1973.

[26] A copy of the Sanford letter is in Evelyn Deike, "Maud Hart Lovelace," appendix I, p. 41, master's thesis, University of Minnesota, 1967.

[27] Lovelace to Hicks, August 11, 1973; Ray interview with Lovelace, December 10, 1974. See also Lovelace, *Betsy and the Great World*, 15.

[28] Ray interview with Lovelace, December 10, 1974.

[29] Ray interview with Lovelace, December 10, 1974.

[30] Lovelace to Hicks, August 11, 1973.

[31] Material here and below is from Ray interview with Lovelace, December 10, 1974; Lovelace, *Carney's House Party*, 120.

[32] Richards, ed., *Minnesota Writers*, 207; *New York Times*, October 31, 1926, p. 24.

[33] Richards, ed., *Minnesota Writers*, 210.

[34] "Pioneer Minnesota House 'Decorated' by N.Y. Museum," in *Minneapolis Tribune*, May 29, 1949, sec. W, p. 8; *New York Times*, September 8, 1929, p. 7. William H. Budd, *History of Martin County*, 90, 91, 93 (Fairmont, 1897).

[35] Lovelace to Freeman, May 19, 1964.

[36] Lovelace to Freeman, May 19, 1964; William H. Budd, *History of Martin County*, 90, 91, 93 (Fairmont, 1897).

[37] Lovelace to Freeman, May 19, 1964; Lovelace, in *Mankato Free Press*, December 16, 1974, p. 9.

[38] Lovelace, in *Mankato Free Press*, December 16, 1974, p. 9; Lovelace to Hicks, August 11, 1973.

[39] Richards, ed., *Minnesota Writers*, 210; Lovelace to Freeman, May 19, 1964; *Maud Hart Lovelace*, an unpaged, undated pamphlet published by Thomas Y. Crowell Co., New York.

[40] Lovelace to "Kathleen and other Readers," May 29, 1965, copy in the author's possession; "The Reader Writes," in *Mankato Free Press*, February 4, 1965, p. 12; Ray interview with Lovelace, December 10, 1974.

[41] Ray interview with Lovelace, December 10, 1974.

[42] Richards, ed., *Minnesota Writers*, 207.

[43] Jane Thomas, "Ultra Realist Books Turn Off Some Youth," in *Minneapolis Tribune*, November 3, 1974, sec. D, p. 1; Ray conversation with a Betsy-Tacy reader, 1976; *Maud Hart Lovelace*, undated pamphlet.

[44] Lovelace to Hicks, August 11, 1973; Lovelace, *Betsy's Wedding*, 241.

Chapter 10 — GRATIA ALTA COUNTRYMAN — *pages 173 to 189*

[1] The quotations appear in newspaper clippings from *Shopper's Guide*, May 5, 1933, and *Christian Science Monitor*, April 26, 1938, both in Gratia A. Countryman Papers, Minneapolis History Collection, Minneapolis Public Library (hereafter cited as MPL). Other versions of the phrases appear in Beatrice S. Rossell to Gratia Countryman, May 24, 1938, Gratia A. Countryman Papers, Minnesota Historical Society (hereafter cited as MHS); and in *Minneapolis Tribune*, February 6, 1950, p. 6. See also Lettie Stearns to Countryman, November 12, 1903, MHS; *Minneapolis Daily Times*, January 14, 1905, p. 5, quoted in Mena C. Dyste, "Gratia Alta Countryman, Librarian," 18, master's thesis, University of Minnesota, 1965, hereafter cited as Dyste, "Countryman"; Ina T. Firkins, "Biography of Gratia Countryman, November, 1923," a typewritten manuscript, and "Woman and Her Career," an undated newspaper clipping — both in MPL.

[2] There are many accounts of the naming story. See, for example, Augusta Starr, "Gratia Countryman, 1866–1953," in *Minnesota Libraries*, 17:195 (September, 1953); *Minneapolis Tribune*, February 6, 1950, p. 6; Ruth M. Jedermann, "My Chief," an undated typescript in MHS; Christopher Morley, *Friends, Romans*, 20 (Minneapolis and St. Paul, 1940). For other biographical data, see Levi N. Countryman obituary in *Minneapolis Journal*, March 29, 1924, p. 1; Theophilus R. Countryman, "Memoirs," July, 1935, pp. 2, 7, 13, 24, MHS.

[3] The Hastings High School diploma and a copy of the essay, both dated June 16, 1882, are in MHS.

[4] Gratia Countryman, "Why I Came to Minneapolis," undated typescript in MHS; "Woman and Her Career," undated clipping in MPL.

[5] "Librarian," in *Minnesota Alumni Weekly*, 35:439 (April 4, 1936); Countryman,

"Song No. 1" and other undated music scores; Gratia to Levi Countryman, May 9, 1884, Alta to Levi Countryman, November 5, 1885 — all in MHS.

[6] Undated newspaper clippings, MHS. At the University of Minnesota Gratia met the woman who was to be a "close and loving mentor" for many years, Maria Sanford. The strong-willed and idiosyncratic head of the university's rhetoric work was the Countrymans' neighbor in Minneapolis as well as Gratia's teacher. See James K. Hosmer, "Maria Sanford," undated clipping in MPL, quoted in Dyste, "Countryman," 5, and Chapter 5, above.

[7] Many years later she made efforts to have compulsory drill abolished at the University of Minnesota in favor of elective drill. See Fanny F. (Mrs. Arthur) Brin to Countryman, December 23, 1930, and Countryman to Brin, December 26, 1930, Brin Papers, MHS. A copy of the petition and a note from Countryman about Company Q are in the Gratia Alta Countryman Papers, University of Minnesota Archives, Minneapolis. See also "Company 'Q'," [1890], typescript in MHS.

[8] Countryman's university diploma, June 6, 1889, and Herbert Putnam to Ben W. Palmer, November 30, 1936, both in MHS; "Librarian," in *Minnesota Alumni Weekly*, 35:438, 439; *Minneapolis Public Library: Fifty Years of Service, 1889–1939*, 8 (Minneapolis, 1939).

[9] Ellworth Carlstedt, "The Public Library Movement In Minnesota, 1849–1900," in *Minnesota Libraries*, 14:351–360 (September, 1945); *Fifty Years of Service*, 7–11.

[10] Dyste, "Countryman," 6; Josephine Cloud, "When Gratia Was a Girl," in *Staff Stuff*, December, 1936, p. [2], mimeographed newsletter in MPL; *Fifty Years of Service*, 7; Minneapolis Public Library, *Annual Report*, 1891, p. 4 (Minneapolis, 1892).

[11] Minneapolis Public Library, *Annual Report*, 1892, pp. 8, 9; *Fifty Years of Service*, 7, 15; Dyste, "Countryman," 7. Several letters refer to Gratia as the actual head of the administrative work of the library at this time. See, for example, Putnam to Jacob Stone, April 25, 1903, and Lettie Stearns to Countryman, November 12, 1903, MHS.

[12] Cloud, in *Staff Stuff*, December, 1936, p. [2]; Countryman, Diary, 1896, MHS.

[13] Countryman to "Sib friends," August 21, 1893, MHS. On the newspaper publicity, see Dyste, "Countryman," 6.

[14] Dyste, "Countryman," 7–10; Minneapolis Public Library, *Annual Report*, 1898, p. 14.

[15] Before 1893 the membership of the association was from the Twin Cities, Duluth, and the two colleges at Northfield. For a discussion of the early history of the association, including its legislative battles mentioned in the paragraph below, see Gratia A. Countryman, "Early History of the Minnesota Library Association, 1891–1900," in *Minnesota Libraries*, 13:322–326 (September, 1942). On Countryman's role, see the same issue, p. 321.

[16] Minneapolis Public Library, *Annual Report*, 1898, p. 14; Dyste, "Countryman," 8, 9, 40; Countryman and Carlstedt, in *Minnesota Libraries*, 13:325, 14:362.

[17] Minneapolis Public Library, *Annual Report*, 1899, p. 18; Countryman's appointments to the Minnesota Library Commission, September 1, 1899, January 16, 1907, and February 20, 1913 — all in MHS.

[18] Dyste, "Countryman," 11.

[19] See, for example, M. E. Ahern to Countryman, March 17, 1903; George E. MacLean to Countryman, March 28, April 16, 1903; Putnam to Jacob Stone, April 25, 1903; Melvil Dewey to Stone, October 8, 1903 — all in MHS.

[20] Dyste, "Countryman," 12; *Minneapolis Journal*, November 7, 1903, p. 6.

[21] See letters to Countryman for the period from November 7 to December 30, 1903, especially those of Charles A. Herpich, December 3; Alice S. Tyler, December 5; Eliza G. Browning, December 30 — all in MHS; M. E. Ahern, editorial, in *Public Libraries*, 8:463 (December, 1903).

[22] Minneapolis Public Library, *Annual Report*, 1903, p. 19.

[23] Dyste, "Countryman," 17; for quoted material here and in the two paragraphs below, see Minneapolis Public Library, *Annual Report*, 1904, pp. 25, 26.

[24] Typewritten "Biography of Gratia Countryman," 1935?, and "A Record of Achievement," program of testimonial dinner, December 10, 1936, both in MPL; *Minneapolis Tribune*, February 6, 1950, p. 6; Bess M. Wilson, "The Library and the Good Life," in *Journal of the American Association of University Women*, 27:216–220 (June, 1934).

[25] Dyste, "Countryman," 26, 27; Minneapolis Public Library, *Annual Report*, 1893, p. 10; *Fifty Years of Service*, 43.

[26] Dyste, "Countryman," 91.

[27] The growth of the library is discussed in some detail in the *Annual Report* of the institution from 1890 to 1935 and in *Fifty Years of Service*. On the Hennepin County Library, see Dyste, "Countryman," 43.

[28] Minneapolis Public Library, *Annual Report*, 1908, p. 11.

[29] Minneapolis Public Library, *Annual Report*, 1905, p. 20.

[30] Dyste, "Countryman," 44–46; Minneapolis Public Library, *Annual Report*, 1892, pp. 10–12; 1904, pp. 6, 22; 1910, pp. 18, 19; 1915, p. 21; 1916, p. 4.

[31] Dyste, "Countryman," 46, 47; Minneapolis Public Library, *Annual Report*, 1911, p. 23; *Fifty Years of Service*, 26, 38, 39.

[32] *Minneapolis Journal*, November 29, 1936, p. 15; handwritten note, 1923, in Minnesota Library Commission folder, MPL.

[33] Dyste, "Countryman," 34–38; Minneapolis Public Library, *Annual Report*, 1905, p. 20; 1911, p. 36; 1912, p. 24; "She Has Built a Great Public Service," in *Minneapolis*, May, 1928, p. 33; *Minneapolis Sunday Tribune*, October 1, 1911, sec. 2, p. 29.

[34] Dyste, "Countryman," 65, 66.

[35] Minneapolis Public Library, *Annual Report*, 1910, pp. 22, 35, 43, 44.

[36] Minneapolis Public Library, *Annual Report*, 1913, p. 42.

[37] Dyste, "Countryman," 71, 78, 80.

[38] For the quotations, see Minneapolis Public Library, *Annual Report*, 1915, p. 22.

[39] Dyste, "Countryman," 72–75; Minneapolis Public Library, *Annual Report*, 1912, p. 22; 1916, p. 4.

[40] Dyste, "Countryman," 82–84; *Minneapolis Journal*, December 8, 1935, sec. 2, pp. 1, 2.

[41] Minneapolis Public Library, "Annual Report," 1933, unpaged typescript in administrative office, MPL.

[42] Minneapolis Public Library, "Annual Report," 1934, unpaged typescript in MPL.

[43] See, for example, Minneapolis Public Library, *Annual Report*, 1908, p. 14; 1917–18, pp. 18–25, 29; 1932, unpaged typescript in MPL; Dyste, "Countryman," 51, 52, 95.

[44] Minneapolis Public Library, *Annual Report*, 1917–18, p. 26; 1934, unpaged typescript in MPL.

[45] Countryman, "Building for the Future," in *Bulletin of the American Library Association*, 28:384 (July, 1934).

[46] Dyste, "Countryman," 86, 105; Minnesota Library Association, Thirteenth Annual Meeting Program, Red Wing, October, 1905, copy in MHS; "Biography of Gratia Countryman," in MPL; American Library Institute, *Handbook*, 2 (n.p., 1938); George B. Utley, "The American Library Institute: A Historical Sketch," in *Library Quarterly*, 16:152 (April, 1946); Minneapolis Public Library, "Annual Report," 1935, unpaged typescript in MPL.

[47] The Countryman Papers in MHS and MPL contain letters asking her to speak before various organizations as well as notes for and copies of many speeches.

[48] Countryman to George Ringham, September 7, 1934, MHS; Women's Welfare League, "Annual Report," January 27, 1928, in Social Agencies Papers, MPL; Busi-

ness Women's Club, Inc. of Minneapolis, *The Club Review*, 13 (Minneapolis, 1926).

[49] Membership cards for many organizations are in Countryman Papers, MHS. See also *Minneapolis Journal*, March 1, 1938, p. 10.

[50] Dyste, "Countryman," 106, 107; Inter-Racial Service Council (Minneapolis), Recognition Day Program, November 28, 1931; and Hazel Witchie to Countryman, May 11, 1936 — both in MHS; honorary degrees, University of Minnesota Archives; *Minneapolis Journal*, June 7, 1932, sec. 2, p. 19; Minneapolis Public Library Board, Resolution, November 30, 1936, and "Memory Book of Fact and Fancy," 1937 scrapbook — both in MPL.

[51] C. L. Saxby, "The Library Loses Its Leader," in *Parent-Teacher Broadcaster*, November, 1936, pp. 3, 16; Dyste, "Countryman," 97–103, 116–127; Jedermann, "My Chief," in MHS. See also "A Polemic Against Slovenly Work," an office bulletin, November 12, 1929, and "Memo to Heads of Departments," June 21, 1933 — both in MPL.

[52] Countryman, Diary, January 1, 1938, MHS.

[53] Gilbert Buffington to Countryman, May 15, 1936, MHS; "Index of Achievements," 1939, MPL and MHS; *Minneapolis Tribune*, July 27, 1953, p. 11.

[54] Countryman, "Wetoco Lodge Log Book," 1931–47, MHS; Dyste, "Countryman," 115; Federal Works Agency, Notice of Termination of Employment, July 29, 1941, WPA file, Countryman Papers, MHS.

Chapter 11 — CATHERYNE COOKE GILMAN — *pages 190 to 207*

[1] Author's conversation with Ida Cook Kerr, Catheryne's sister, 1969. That she changed the spelling of her first name is a guess based on the fact that the grandmother for whom she was named signed herself Caroline Catherine. See, for example, Caroline Catherine Cook to Catheryne, May 15, 1898, Robbins Gilman and Family Papers, 1699–1952, in the Minnesota Historical Society.

[2] Mary Dillon Foster, comp., *Who's Who Among Minnesota Women*, 119 (n.p., 1924).

[3] Draft of job application on the back of a letter dated January 19, 1914, Gilman Papers. On Breckinridge, see Edward T. James *et al.*, eds., *Notable American Women, 1607–1950*, 1:233–236 (Cambridge, Mass., 1971).

[4] For biographical information on Robbins Gilman, see *Minneapolis Tribune*, August 6, 1955, p. 26; Lucile M. Kane, "The Gilman Family Papers," in *Social Service Review*, 39:92–95 (March, 1965).

[5] On the strike, see Winifred D. Bolin, "North East Neighborhood House: The Process of Americanization in a Midwestern Urban Community," 24–28, master's thesis, University of Minnesota, 1969; B. M. Gilman to Robbins Gilman, July 17, 1914; Aunt Lily (Mrs. Charles P. Noyes) and Georgie Leiman to Robbins Gilman, both July 19, 1914, Gilman Papers. On the marriage, see Nira Cook to Catheryne, October 24, 1914.

[6] Catheryne Cooke Gilman, "Neighbors United Through Social Settlement Services at the North East Neighborhood House," 372–396, typewritten manuscript, Gilman Papers; *Minneapolis Tribune*, September 12, 1915, sec. 12, p. 6; Foster, comp., *Who's Who Among Minnesota Women*, 119. On Maternity Hospital, see Winton U. Solberg, "Martha G. Ripley: Pioneer Doctor and Social Reformer," in *Minnesota History*, 39:1–17 (Spring, 1964).

[7] On the Children's Code and on Catheryne's role, see Edward MacGaffey, "A Pattern for Progress: The Minnesota Children's Code," in *Minnesota History*, 41:229, 232, 233, 236 (Spring, 1969); Minnesota Child Welfare Commission, *Report*, 1917, pp. 3, 8, 20 (St. Paul, 1917).

[8] On the beginnings of the organization that came to be known as the Women's

Co-operative Alliance, see Gilman, "Early History of the WCA," an interview with Chloe Owings, October 3, 1927, hereafter cited as Owings Interview; and Virginia B. Blythe, "The Origins of the Women's Co-operative Alliance Was On This Wise," undated — both in Gilman Papers. The early annual reports cited below also carry brief resumés of the organization's beginnings; copies of them may be found in the Minnesota Historical Society library. In 1915 it included such groups as the Minneapolis Women's Welfare League, the Council of Jewish Women, the League of Catholic Women, the Women's Club, the Women's Christian Association (with which Mabeth Hurd Paige was active, see Chapter 14, below), and the Industrial and Social Conditions Committees of both the Fifth District and the State Federation of Women's Clubs. On the block system, see Roy Lubove, *The Professional Altruist: The Emergence of Social Work as a Career, 1880–1930,* 175–178 (Cambridge, Mass., 1965).

[9] Owings Interview, October 3, 1927; Women's Co-operative Alliance, *Fourth Annual Report,* 1919, p. 6 — Publication 30.

[10] Women's Co-operative Alliance, *[First Annual Report]*, July, 1917 — Publication 5; *Second Annual Report,* 1917, p. 7 — Publication 7.

[11] Women's Co-operative Alliance, *Fifth Annual Report,* 1920, pp. 2, 8–11, 26, 36, 38 — Publication 50.

[12] Gilman, *Early Sex Education in the Home: When? How? What?* 31 — Women's Co-operative Alliance Publication 77, [1928].

[13] For material here and in the following three paragraphs, see undated lecture notes entitled "Period of Maturity — Marriage — Parenthood," in Catheryne's personal notebook, pp. 18, 21; Catheryne to Estelle Holbrook, editor of *Women's Forum,* May 7, 1923 — both in Gilman Papers; William L. O'Neill, *Everyone Was Brave: The Rise and Fall of Feminism in America,* 351–353 (Chicago, 1969). For the quotation, see Women's Co-operative Alliance, *Sixth and Seventh Annual Reports,* 1921–22, p. 9 — Publication 57. For a description of how the university study arrived at its conclusions, see Chloe Owings, *The Effectiveness of a Particular Program in Parental Sex Education,* 7 (University of Minnesota, Social Hygiene Bureau, *Studies in Parental Sex Education,* Paper IV — Minneapolis, 1931).

[14] Catheryne to E. S. Woodworth, Minneapolis Chamber of Commerce, April 1, 1919, Gilman Papers.

[15] Women's Co-operative Alliance, *Fifth Annual Report,* 1920, pp. 35, 43; *Sixth and Seventh Annual Reports,* 1921–22, pp. 60, 80, 81; *Eighth Annual Report,* 1923, p. 8 — Publications 50, 57, 66, respectively.

[16] Women's Co-operative Alliance, *Sixth and Seventh Annual Reports,* 1921–22, p. 81; *Sixteenth Annual Report,* 1931, p. 8 — Publications 57, 89.

[17] See, for example, *Ninth Annual Report,* 1924, p. 12; *Tenth Annual Report,* 1925, p. 13; *Eleventh Annual Report,* 1926, pp. 16, 17; *Twelfth Annual Report,* 1927, pp. 6, 25, 26; *Thirteenth Annual Report,* 1928, pp. 15, 17 — Publications 71, 74, 75, 79, respectively.

[18] Clarke A. Chambers, *Seedtime of Reform: American Social Service and Social Action, 1918–1933,* 131–150, 229–250 (Minneapolis, 1963); Frank J. Bruno, *Trends in Social Work, 1874–1956,* 7–9 (New York, 1957).

[19] Nothing in the Gilman Papers corroborates the disaffection that grew between community leaders and the Alliance women; Catheryne Gilman weeded the papers before donating them to the Minnesota Historical Society. However, oral family history bears this out; see, for example, marginal notes on a draft of this essay by Catherine Gilman Welsh to the author, in the author's possession. On the dissolution of the Alliance, see "Final Report of the Women's Co-operative Alliance, Inc.," 24, typescript of annual meeting speech by Catheryne, December 15, 1932, in MHS library.

[20] Lubove, *The Professional Altruist,* 88.

[21] Grace E. Malin to Catheryne, December 24, 1919. For an example of a res-

ignation offer, see Catheryne to Mrs. Leopold Metzger, November 26, 1920 — both in Gilman Papers.

²² Robbins to Catheryne, December 23, 1919, Gilman Papers. Robbins' mother was a Quaker, and he always used the plain speech of that sect as she did, although he never belonged to the Society of Friends.

²³ Catheryne to Logan Gilman, November 28, 1940, Gilman Papers.

²⁴ Robbins P. Gilman to the author, August 4, 1975, in the author's possession.

²⁵ Women's Co-operative Alliance, [*Publication 2*], undated. On the movement for better movies here and in the paragraph below, see *Fifth Annual Report*, 1920, pp. 50–54 — Publication 50.

²⁶ On film industry trade practices, see Ruth A. Inglis, *Freedom of the Movies: A Report on Self-Regulation from the Commission on Freedom of the Press*, 47–51 (Chicago, 1947).

²⁷ See Inglis, *Freedom of the Movies*, 3–8, 62.

²⁸ On these organizations, see Women's Co-operative Alliance, *Tenth Annual Report*, 1925, p. 8, and *Twelfth Annual Report*, 1927, pp. 9–11 — Publications 74, 79; see also undated memorandum entitled "The Motion Pictures as a Molder of the National Character," sent by William H. Short to Catheryne with a cover letter, April 2, 1929, Gilman Papers.

²⁹ On the Payne Fund Studies here and in the paragraph below, see Inglis, *Freedom of the Movies*, 21; Henry J. Forman, *Our Movie Made Children* (New York, 1933). At the beginning of the work William Short wrote that there was "little doubt that the studies will on the whole confirm the opinions we have brought together [*that movies undermined the moral, physical, and mental health of children*] but we will get further, as I know you believe, by taking an entirely objective view of the situation and getting at the facts through the study method." Short to Catheryne, August 9, 1928, Gilman Papers.

³⁰ Francis S. Pettengill to Catheryne, June 6, 1932; Catheryne to Miss B. L. Mascorich, September 20, 1932; Mrs. Bundy Allen, June 5, 1934; Mrs. C. H. Green, October 8, 1932 — all in Gilman Papers.

³¹ On the Legion of Decency and the Production Code Administration, see Inglis, *Freedom of the Movies*, 120–131, 141.

³² On her struggle with the National Congress, see Catheryne to Mrs. Martha Sprague Mason, October 17, 1932; W. Elwood Baker, November 14, 1932; Mrs. B. F. Langworthy, December 11, 1934; Mrs. A. B. Shuttleworth, May 23, 1935; Mrs. Francis H. Blake, July 17, 1935 — all in Gilman Papers. On the institutes, see Catheryne to Mason, June 4, 1934, Gilman Papers.

³³ Eleanor B. Campbell to Mrs. Edward M. Peterson, April 2, 1935; Catheryne to Francis S. Pettengill, May 10, 1935; Catheryne to Dr. Edgar Dale, May 24, 1935; correspondence between Catheryne and William Cox, July 25, 1935 — all in Gilman Papers.

³⁴ See, for example, David W. Noble, *The Paradox of Progressive Thought*, 59–62 (Minneapolis, 1958). Regarding her changed attitudes, see copy of a letter from Catheryne to Mary Sayres, March 25, 1936, Gilman Papers.

³⁵ Gilman, "Neighbors United," 77–112, 238–243, 357–359.

Chapter 12 — ADA COMSTOCK NOTESTEIN — *pages 208 to 225*

¹ This essay was made possible by the sympathetic assistance of staff members associated with several repositories; my appreciation goes to the archives of Brown University, Mount Holyoke College, Radcliffe College, Smith College, the University of Michigan, and the University of Minnesota, the Minnesota Historical Society, and the Arthur and Elizabeth Schlesinger Library on the History of Women

in America at Radcliffe College. Robert J. Loeffler, president of the Comstock
House Society, Moorhead, Minnesota, has also given me special assistance in locat-
ing letters and documents. Particular thanks are due to Frances Frazier Comstock,
Bernice Brown Cronkhite, Frances Ruml Jordan, Esther and Sidney Lovett, Cornelia Mendenhall, Alice Heeran, Edith Gratia Stedman, and Rebecca Wedgwood
who have shared personal papers and reminiscences with me.

² *Biographical Directory of the American Congress, 1774–1971,* 772
(Washington, D.C., 1971); Roberta Yerkes Blanshard, Notes on Talk of Ada Com-
stock Notestein, 1969–73, pp. 4, 8, 9, grouped by subject, Schlesinger Library,
Radcliffe College, Cambridge, Mass.

³ Themes of family purpose and objectives appear repeatedly in Ada Comstock's
recollections and correspondence. See, for example, Blanshard, Notes, 4, 7–10; letters to George Comstock, January 29, 1939, June 26, 1942, April 28 and June 23,
1952, April 20 and June 24, 1953, in Comstock House Society, Moorhead.

⁴ Blanshard, Notes, 3–6. The Comstock House is preserved and open to the public.

⁵ Blanshard, Notes, 5; Moorhead Public Schools, Closing Exercises and Gradua-
tions Program, July 1, 1887, in the files of the Comstock House Society.

⁶ Blanshard, Notes, 5; *Moorhead Daily News,* undated clipping, files of the Comstock House Society; Minnesota State Normal School, Moorhead, *Catalogue and
Circular,* 1888–89, p. 13 (Moorhead, 1889); interview of Jacquelin Van Voris with
Ada Comstock Notestein, New Haven, Conn., March 31, 1971, p. 9, in Smith College Study, Smith College Archives, Northampton, Mass., hereafter cited as Notestein Interview.

⁷ Notestein Interview, 4, 21.

⁸ *New York Tribune Illustrated Supplement,* undated clipping, files of the Comstock House Society; Blanshard, Notes, 14.

⁹ Notestein Interview, 11, 12.

¹⁰ Elmer E. Adams letter, in *Minnesota Alumni Weekly,* 40:227 (December 14,
1940); E. Bird Johnson, *Forty Years of the University of Minnesota,* 293 (Minneapolis, 1910).

¹¹ Blanshard, Notes, 16.

¹² Ada Comstock, "The present attainments of the average Minnesota Freshman
in matters of English," Comstock files, Smith College Archives.

¹³ "Ada Speaks," in *Minnesota Chats,* December 3, 1940, pp. 1, 3, a University of
Minnesota in-house periodical published from 1923 to 1956.

¹⁴ *Moorhead Daily News,* June 3, 1937, sec. 2, p. 1, quoting *Moorhead Independent* of May 10, 1907; Ada Comstock biography file, University of Minnesota
Archives, Minneapolis.

¹⁵ "Cap and Gown for Senior Girls," in *Minnesota Alumni Weekly,* October 28,
1907, p. 7; Roberta Yerkes Blanshard, "Ada Louise Comstock, The Years 1876–1943
of Ada Notestein's Life, as she recalled them," collected for reading to the Saturday
Morning Club, March 16, 1974, p. 11, in Schlesinger Library.

¹⁶ Notestein Interview, June 8, 1971, pp. 4, 5; "Ada Comstock — What Alice
Shevlin Hall Stands For," in *Minnesota Alumni Weekly,* December 10, 1906, pp.
18–20.

¹⁷ Unidentified newspaper clipping, Smith College Archives; Blanshard, Notes,
18.

¹⁸ Ada Comstock to Solomon G. Comstock, June 22, 1912, Smith College Archives.

¹⁹ Notestein Interview, 5; Ada Comstock, "Undergraduate Budgets," and "The
Elizabeth Mason Infirmary," in *Smith Alumnae Quarterly,* February, 1916, and
February, 1919, respectively; Ada Comstock, "Seventy-five Years: A Brief Re-
view," 9, a speech given on February 22, 1949, in Smith College Archives.

²⁰ Ada Comstock, "Talk to entering class," Octoer 25, 1915, pp. 8, 12; Ada Comstock, "Commencement speech," given at Ferry Hall, Lake Forest, Ill., June 13, 1921, pp. 12, 14, Smith College Archives.

²¹ "Occupations for Women Suggested by Former Dean," in *Minnesota Daily*, April 1, 1918.

²² Ada Comstock, "Qualifications Most Essential to the Woman of Today," undated speech, Smith College Archives.

²³ Ada Comstock, untitled, undated manuscript about International Federation of University Women, Smith College Archives.

²⁴ Blanshard, Notes, 20; Hubert Herring, *Neilson of Smith*, 11 (Brattleboro, Vt., 1939).

²⁵ Smith College, Memorandum from Office of the President, undated, Smith College Archives; Peggy Hazen to Ada Comstock letter, in *Smith Alumnae Quarterly*, July, 1923, p. 358.

²⁶ Inauguration of Ada Louise Comstock, October 20, 1923, formal transcript, speeches given by Marion Edwards Park, William Allan Neilson, and Abbott Lawrence Lowell, in Schlesinger Library.

²⁷ Inauguration speech given by Ada Louise Comstock, October 20, 1923, in Schlesinger Library; "President Comstock," in *Radcliffe Quarterly*, October, 1923, p. 82.

²⁸ Blanshard, Notes, 22.

²⁹ President's Report to the Board of Trustees of Radcliffe College, 1924–25, p. 7, Schlesinger Library.

³⁰ Sidney Lovett, "Words spoken at Service of Prayer and Thanksgiving in honor of Ada Comstock Notestein," January 10, 1974, personal files of Sidney Lovett, New Haven, Conn.; President's Report to the Board of Trustees of Radcliffe College, 1924–25, p. 10; 1926–27, p. 6; 1935–36, p. 6, Schlesinger Library.

³¹ President's Report, 1926–27, p. 9.

³² Unidentified newspaper clipping in Radcliffe College Archives, scrapbook and clipping file; Blanshard, Notes, 28.

³³ Ada Louise Comstock, "The Institute of Pacific Relations," in *Radcliffe Quarterly*, April, 1932, p. 53.

³⁴ President's Report to the Board of Trustees of Radcliffe College, 1933–34, p. 8; 1935–36, p. 6; 1936–37, p. 6.

³⁵ President's Report to the Board of Trustees of Radcliffe College, 1936–37, p. 7; 1937–38, p. 6; Ada Comstock to George Comstock, March 31, 1937, files of the Comstock House Society.

³⁶ President's Report to the Board of Trustees of Radcliffe College, 1938–39, p. 9; Ada L. Comstock, "The Future of the Coördinate College," in *Radcliffe Quarterly*, November, 1938, p. 6.

³⁷ President's Report to the Board of Trustees of Radcliffe College, 1938–39, p. 9.

³⁸ President's Report to the Board of Trustees of Radcliffe College, 1942–43, p. 9.

³⁹ William Allan Neilson, "The Accomplishments of President Comstock," in *Radcliffe Quarterly*, August, 1943, p. 12.

⁴⁰ President Comstock, "The Commencement Address," in *Radcliffe Quarterly*, August, 1943, p. 9, 10.

⁴¹ Blanshard, Notes, 22, 23. James B. Conant succeeded Lowell in 1933.

⁴² Ada Comstock to Frances Ruml Jordan, May 31, 1943, in Schlesinger Library.

⁴³ John W. Bodine, "Mendenhall at Smith," in *American Oxonian*, 47:8–10 (January, 1960); "Dean says many part-time marriages are successful," unidentified news clipping, files of the Comstock House Society.

⁴⁴ Ada Comstock Notestein to Frances Ruml Jordan, January 4, 1946, in Schlesinger Library.

⁴⁵ Information about the Notesteins' European travels and activities while living

in England appear in Ada's correspondence with friends and relatives between 1944 and 1968, especially her letters to Bernice Brown Cronkhite and to Frances Ruml Jordan, in Schlesinger Library, and to her brother George, in files of the Comstock House Society. The latter collection contains a specific comment about her taste for travel in Wallace Notestein to George Comstock, December 17, 1951.

[46] The lyrical side of Ada's expression may be seen in her correspondence. See, for example, letters to George Comstock, April 9, 1951, to November 8, 1957, files of the Comstock House Society.

[47] Reflections about her sister Jessie are expressed most often in correspondence with her brother. See, for example, Ada to George Comstock, April 23 and May 13, 1951, April 28, 1952, files of the Comstock House Society. See also Blanshard, Notes, 6.

[48] The announcement of Ada's death and biographical resumés of her achievements were widely carried. See *New York Times,* December 13, 1973, p. 50; Blanshard, Notes, p. 10; Lovett, "Words spoken . . . January 10, 1974"; and *News from the College,* Spring, 1974, p. 3, a Radcliffe publication in the files of the college. Wallace Notestein died in 1969.

Chapter 13 — ANNA DICKIE OLESEN — *pages 226 to 246*

[1] Material here and below on the childhood of Anna Dickie Olesen as well as other unannotated information throughout this chapter is drawn from interviews of the author with her brother, the late Owen R. Dickie, May, 1972, and her daughter, Mary Olesen Gerin of Arlington, Va., July, 1975.

[2] Twenty-eight women ran for both houses of Congress in 1922, when Olesen ran for the Senate. Of six Senate candidates, Democrat Jessie Hooper of Wisconsin also ran as the candidate of a major party. Olesen is generally described as the first such candidate because her endorsement came in May, preceding Hooper's. See Sophonisba P. Breckinridge, *Women in the Twentieth Century: A Study of Their Social and Economic Activities,* 301 (New York and London, 1933); "Women Who Won," in *Woman Citizen,* November 18, 1922, p. 9. For the quotations see Clara H. Ueland to Mrs. John L. Pyle, April 3, 1918, Mississippi Valley Conference File, in Minnesota Woman Suffrage Association Papers, Minnesota Historical Society (MHS); *Minneapolis Journal,* June 12, 1920, p. 1; "Mrs. Olesen's Bid for the Toga," in *Literary Digest,* July 8, 1922, p. 11.

[3] *Minneapolis Sunday Tribune,* September 28, 1919, sec. 1, p. 8.

[4] Material here and in the paragraph below is based on conversations with Owen Dickie and letter of Anna to Owen Dickie, August 13, 1954, in the possession of Mary Gerin.

[5] Material here and below is from conversations with Owen Dickie, Mary Gerin, and Lewis Dickie of Waterville, August, 1975; the quotation appears in Anna to Owen Dickie, August 13, 1954, in the possession of Mary Gerin.

[6] On the Andrews family, see also p. 160, above.

[7] Material here and in the paragraph below is based on Peter Olesen to Mary Gerin, May 29, 1945, in the possession of Mary Gerin, and conversation with Mrs. Gerin.

[8] Conversation with Mary Gerin; Kathryn E. Gray to the author, July 24, 1975, in Kathryn E. Gray Papers, MHS.

[9] Carl H. Chrislock, *The Progressive Era in Minnesota 1899–1918,* 3 (St. Paul, 1971).

[10] Theodore Christianson, *Minnesota, the Land of Sky-Tinted Waters: A History of The State and Its People,* 3:152 (Chicago and New York, 1935); Mary Dillon

Foster, comp., *Who's Who Among Minnesota Women,* 239 (n.p., 1924); *Mississippi Valley Suffrage Conference,* n.p. (Minneapolis, 1916), in Minnesota Women Suffrage Association Papers.

[11] *Minneapolis Journal,* April 23, 1918, p. 22; Christianson, *Minnesota,* 3:152.

[12] Christianson, *Minnesota,* 5:413. Francis M. Smith recalled that at the 1932 state Democratic convention Olesen battled for the reimbursement of Cloquet fire victims before the resolutions committee. See Smith to Sarah A. Davidson, June 27, 1938, in William Anderson and Theodore C. Blegen, comps., Minnesota Political Party Platforms, 1849–1942, in the Division of Archives and Manuscripts, Minnesota Historical Society.

[13] Conversation with Mary Gerin; Kathryn E. Gray to the author, July 24, 1975, in Gray Papers.

[14] For this and the paragraph below, see Harry P. Harrison and Karl Detzer, *Culture under Canvas: The Story of Tent Chautauqua,* viii, xvi, xvii, 217–220 (New York, 1958).

[15] Conversation with Owen Dickie, who often served as his sister's driver on Chautauqua tours.

[16] *St. Paul Pioneer Press,* January 7, 1920, p. 1; quotations from *Minneapolis Journal,* January 9, 1920, p. 13; *New York Times,* January 9, 1920, p. 3.

[17] For this and the paragraph below, see Mark Sullivan, "The Political Calendar for June," in *World's Work,* 44:190 (June, 1922); *Chicago Evening American,* June 21, 1922, p. 6; *Minneapolis Journal,* January 18, 1920, sec. 1, p. 5.

[18] On the Prohibition issue, see Richard Hofstadter, *The Age of Reform From Bryan to F.D.R.,* 287–291, 295 (New York, 1955); for the quotation, see *New York Times,* July 3, 1920, p. 3.

[19] Harry J. Carman, Harold C. Syrett, and Bernard W. Wishy, *A History of the American People since 1865,* 2:536 (2nd Ed., New York, 1961); for the first quotation, see *New York Times,* May 14, 1922, sec. 8, p. 2. The *Philadelphia Public Ledger,* June 21, 1922, p. 10, reported that she used the verb "buried." For the second quotation, see *Minneapolis Journal,* July 16, 1920, p. 1.

[20] Kathryn E. Gray to the author, July 24, 1975, in Gray Papers; *Minneapolis Journal,* July 18, 1920, sec. 1, p. 12, July 20, 1920, p. 22.

[21] *Minneapolis Journal,* August 16, 1920, p. 11, October 4, 1920, p. 1; Carman, Syrett, and Wishy, *History of the American People,* 2:536.

[22] Chrislock, *Progressive Era,* 182–184; William W. Folwell, *A History of Minnesota,* 3:548–550 (Reprint Ed., St. Paul, 1969); Olesen, Scrapbook, in the possession of Mary Gerin.

[23] Folwell, *History of Minnesota,* 3:549–551.

[24] *New York Times,* May 14, 1922, sec. 8, p. 2.

[25] Newberry was censured by the Senate and resumed his seat, but resigned later in 1922. See *New York Times,* January 13, 1922, p. 1. For the quotation, see "Mrs. Olesen's Bid," in *Literary Digest,* July 8, 1922, p. 10.

[26] *Minnesota Leader,* May 6, 1922, p. 3; *New York Times,* May 14, 1922, sec. 8, p. 2.

[27] Chrislock, *Progressive Era,* caption facing page 113, 201; conversation with Mary Gerin.

[28] *New York Times,* June 21, 1922, p. 1; *Philadelphia Public Ledger,* June 22, 1922, p. 3; conversations with Owen Dickie and Mary Gerin; Minnesota State Canvassing Board, *Report: Primary Election, June 19th, 1922,* 19 ([St. Paul], 1922).

[29] Conversation with Owen Dickie; *Polk County Leader* (Crookston), September 15, 1922, p. 3.

[30] *Fairmont Daily Sentinel,* June 17, 1922, p. 1.

[31] "Mrs. Olesen's Bid," in *Literary Digest,* July 8, 1922, p. 10. The Esch-

Cummins Transportation Act of 1920 was a compromise bill for subsidizing railroads.

[32] *Minneapolis Sunday Tribune*, September 10, 1922, sec. 2, p. 1; Chrislock, *Progressive Era*, 187.

[33] *New York Times*, May 14, 1922, sec. 8, p. 2.

[34] Undated excerpts from *Cloquet Vidette*, in Gray Papers; conversation with Owen Dickie; *New York Times*, June 21, 1922, p. 1.

[35] "Mrs. Olesen's Bid," in *Literary Digest*, July 8, 1922, p. 10, 11, quoting *Philadelphia Public Ledger, Philadelphia Inquirer*, and *New York Globe.*

[36] "Women Voters Won't Stand for Partisan Slander and Abuse," in *Ladies' Home Journal*, August, 1922, p. 8; *New York Times*, June 22, 1922, p. 14.

[37] Conversation with Mary Gerin; Minnesota State Canvassing Board, *Report: General Election, November 7, 1922*, chart facing p. 14 ([St. Paul], 1922).

[38] Barbara Stuhler, *Ten Men of Minnesota and American Foreign Policy 1898–1968*, 107 (St. Paul, 1973); *Minnesota Union Advocate*, p. 2, October 5, 1922, p. 4; Kathryn E. Gray to author, July 24, 1975, in Gray Papers.

[39] *New York Times*, November 9, 1922, p. 1; *Minnesota Union Advocate*, November 23, 1922, p. 1. On the women legislators, see chapter 14, below; Hough and Olesen were not related, according to the Dickie family.

[40] "How the Women Candidates Fared," in *Literary Digest*, November 25, 1922, p. 11, quoting *New York Times;* Chester H. Rowell, "LaFollette, Shipstead, and the Embattled Farmers," in *World's Work*, 46:414 (August, 1923).

[41] Numerous letters from William G. McAdoo and others to Olesen, and Chautauqua publicity pamphlets, in the possession of Mary Gerin; Harris and Detzer, *Culture under Canvas*, 225.

[42] Kathryn E. Graý to author, July 24, 1975, in Gray Papers.

[43] *Minneapolis Tribune*, April 30, 1932, p. 1, May 1, 1932, p. 8. All Minnesota congressmen ran at large in 1932 because the legislature's reapportionment bill was vetoed by Governor Floyd B. Olson, whose veto was upheld by the United States Supreme Court. See Christianson, *Minnesota*, 2:499.

[44] Carman, Syrett, and Wishy, *History of the American People*, 2:585; conversations with Mary Gerin and Owen Dickie.

[45] Harrison and Detzer, *Culture under Canvas*, 260–266.

[46] For this and the paragraph below, see *Minneapolis Journal*, January 19, 1934, p. 1, January 21, 1934, sec. 1, p. 3; *St. Paul Pioneer Press*, January 30, 1934, p. 4.

[47] "Stenographic Report of the Meeting of the National Emergency Council of the State of Minnesota," March 12, 1935, p. 1, mimeographed booklet in MHS Library.

[48] Olesen to Roosevelt and Eugene S. Leggett, September 22, 1936, and A. L. Scott to James A. Farley, undated, both in the possession of Mary Gerin.

[49] Leggett to Olesen, November 4, 1936, and Addison G. Foster to Olesen, November 19, 1937, both in the possession of Mary Gerin. See also "Directory of Federal Agencies and State Departments in Minnesota," January 22, 1937; "Funds Loaned, Expended and Insured in the Eighty-Seven Counties of Minnesota," August 15, 1938; "Report of the Proceedings of the Statewide Coordination Meeting Of Federal Agencies Operating in Minnesota," November 29, 1935, p. 92 (quotation) — all mimeographed booklets in MHS Library.

[50] Benson to Olesen, December 18, 1937; Stassen to Olesen, January 5, 1939; Olesen, undated handwritten note — all in the possession of Mary Gerin.

[51] These undated fragments are in the possession of Mary Gerin; attributions of the quotations are Olesen's, and the third one seems dubious.

[52] Chrislock, *Progressive Era*, 201.

[53] Conversation with Mary Gerin; *Lake Region Life* (Waterville), July 8, 1971, p. 2; Connie May Hogan to Olesen, May 4, 1957, in the possession of Mary Gerin.

Chapter 14 — WOMEN IN THE MINNESOTA LEGISLATURE
— *pages 247 to 283*

[1] Beginning in 1875 Minnesota women were permitted to vote for and hold school offices, but the full right of suffrage was extended to them only by the Nineteenth Amendment to the United States Constitution, which took effect on August 20, 1920, after the June primary for the 1921 legislative session. See Gretchen Kreuter and Rhoda R. Gilman, "Women in Minnesota's History," in *Minnesota Legislative Manual*, 1975–76, p. 18 (St. Paul, 1975).

The count of legislators is based on W. F. Toensing, comp., *Minnesota Congressmen, Legislators, and other Elected State Officials: An Alphabetical Check List, 1849–1971* (St. Paul, 1971); *Minnesota Legislative Manual*, 1971–72, 1973–74, 1975–76, and a list of House and Senate members, 1977, compiled by the Minnesota Secretary of State's office. See also table, p. 280, below. Regular elections are held in even-numbered years for terms beginning the following January. State representatives serve two-year terms, senators four years.

[2] Among the most conspicuous party activists of the 1950s were Elizabeth E. Heffelfinger and Rhoda B. Lund, Republican national committeewomen, and Dorothy H. Jacobson, Democratic-Farmer-Labor state chairwoman, and Eugenie M. Anderson, DFL national committeewoman. See pp. 325, 331, 332, 335.

[3] Betty Kane of Golden Valley, notable for the expertise and determination she showed in efforts to reapportion the legislature, is another league alumna who decided to seek office. She ran in 1962, along with eleven other women, but was defeated.

The Minnesota legislature was not reapportioned from 1913 until 1962; other reapportionments were enacted in 1966 (amended in 1967) and carried out by the federal district court effective in 1972. The latter made all House districts single-member districts. Before that time, most districts had two or more House members and one senator. Legislators ran without party designation until 1975.

[4] The year 1974 has been characterized as a "break-through" for women in politics. Nationally 130 women were newly elected to state legislatures, making a total of 600 (102 of them in New Hampshire, which has a low salary for lawmakers). See *Ms.*, March, 1975, p. 24; *Minneapolis Tribune*, November 14, 1976, p. 18A.

[5] For information on specific legislators here and in the five paragraphs below, see table, p. 280. During the nonpartisan period, the Minnesota legislature divided into two caucuses known as Liberals and Conservatives. Farmer-Labor and DFL party members generally affiliated with the Liberals and Republicans with the Conservatives. The caucus having the most members controlled the legislative body. Only members of the controlling group could become heads of committees, and the majority caucus assigned all committee seats. From 1913 until 1955 Conservatives usually controlled both houses. In the 1955 session the Liberals attained a majority of one in the House; not until 1973 did the Liberals attain a majority in both houses.

[6] Much of the material here and below is drawn from Darragh Aldrich, *Lady in Law: A Biography of Mabeth Hurd Paige* (Chicago, 1950). For the quotations used below, see pp. 26, 136, 238. See also *Minneapolis Tribune*, May 19, 1952, p. 14.

[7] Correspondence of Paige and Kempfer and other material by and about Paige may be found in the Hannah J. Kempfer Papers, microfilm in the Minnesota Historical Society (MHS), originals in the possession of Kempfer's neice, Margaret K. Miller, Erhard. See also correspondence between Paige and Elmer E. Adams, 1923–44, concerning Kempfer's health, campaigns, death, funeral arrangements, and memorial articles which Adams solicited for his newspaper, in Elmer E. Adams Papers; taped interview with Luther conducted by Arvonne Fraser, March

30, 1975, hereafter cited as Luther Interview — both in MHS. For Paige's obituary, see *Minneapolis Tribune,* August 20, 1961, Upper Midwest sec., p. 1.

[8] Much of the information here presented is drawn from undated campaign brochures, letters, and an undated biography by Bertha R. Martin — all in Kempfer Papers; and from interviews with Margaret K. Miller conducted by Sue Holbert on December 30, 31, 1974. Notes on these interviews, annotated by Miller, are in papers entitled "Women Legislators in Minnesota: Notes Compiled by Ramona Burks, Joan Forester, Arvonne Fraser, and Sue Holbert," in MHS, hereafter cited as "Women Legislators: Notes." See also *Minneapolis Times-Tribune,* January 22, 1940, pp. 15, 17; a series by Peter Gray in *Fergus Falls Daily Journal,* January 24-March 14, 1966; Edward T. James *et al.,* eds., *Notable American Women, 1607–1950,* 2:327 (Cambridge, Mass., 1971). The surname of Kempfer's adoptive parents is variously spelled Jensen or Jenson; Hannah herself used Johnson.

[9] The school building in which Kempfer taught is located on the Kempfer-Miller property; a sign proclaims it "Hannah J. Kempfer School." For Hannah's businesses, below, see earnings and expenditure accounts, January, 1909-January, [1912], in Kempfer Papers.

[10] Here and below, see *Minneapolis Journal,* October 22, 1922, women's sec., p. 3; printed statement incorporating a letter from A. G. Norby, October 17, 1922, offering Nonpartisan League endorsement; Kempfer's refusal, October 25, 1922; campaign leaflet, [1922] — all in Kempfer Papers. Kempfer did get into trouble, however, in 1934 when as a member of the Otter Tail County Relief Committee, she was said to have actively campaigned "against the present Administration" of Governor Olson. She was relieved of her position on the committee. See Grace M. Guilford to Kempfer, July 18, August 2, 1934, Kempfer Papers. The biographer quoted is Jon Wefald, in James, eds., *Notable American Women,* 328.

[11] Typed carbon in Kempfer Papers addressed to Carlos Avery, editor of *American Game* in 1928, when it was evidently written.

[12] *American Game,* April-May, 1928, p. 42, the bulletin of the American Game Protective Association, New York City.

[13] On her refusal to chair the committee again, see "Radio Talk 1929," an unsigned typed copy; on criticism of the fishing license, see James F. Gould to Kempfer, September 4, 1928, and O. P. B. Jacobson to Kempfer, November 10, 1928 — all in Kempfer Papers. For the House vote, see Minnesota, *House Journal,* 1927, p. 1323; on the provisions of the law, see Minnesota, *Laws,* 1927, pp. 636–642. Bills introduced may be found in the House and Senate files, Division of Archives and Manuscripts, MHS, or, for the most recent years, in the Legislative Reference Library, Minnesota State Capitol.

[14] Kempfer's District 50 was entitled to four representatives, so the top four vote-getters were declared elected. Elmer Adams wrote to Hannah, urging her to file again in 1930: "Everyone has counted on it. Even Coolidge gave notice. Our delegation will be shot all to pieces. You go back." The Otter Tail County delegation (District 50) was shot; only one of the area's four incumbents was re-elected. The three new legislators, however, served only one term each. See Adams to Kempfer, May 22, 1930, in Adams Papers. Election statistics used here and below may be found in *Minnesota Legislative Manual* for the year in question.

[15] Enclosure in Kempfer to Harry T. Black, January 20, 1923, Kempfer Papers.

[16] Kempfer was a member of the committees on public welfare and social legislation for seven terms (1923–29, 1933–37), public health and hospitals for six terms (1923–29, 1933–35) and chairperson in 1935, and the Board of Control for three terms (1937–41), chairperson in 1939 and 1941. For her statement on tubercular teachers, see Minnesota Public Health Association, *Everybody's Health,* April, 1935, p. 9.

[17] Here and below, see Emily Child to Kempfer, January 3, 1928; unidentified newspaper clipping, [1928]; list of contributors, [1930]; invitation, program, and

Kempfer's brief notes on the meetings — all in Kempfer Papers; *Fergus Falls Daily Journal*, November 29, 1930, p. 7; Miller to Holbert, August 28, 1975, in "Women Legislators: Notes."

[18] Miller Interview; Kempfer to Gustav Eide, April 13, 1939, and typewritten statement of Elmer Adams, [1940] — both in Kempfer Papers.

[19] Newspaper clipping, February 16, 1923, in Kempfer Papers. Living arrangements in St. Paul were described for the authors by Ardene Flynn, who was one of Kempfer's apartment mates. Correspondence between Hannah and Charlie is in the possession of Miller.

[20] On the Working People's League, see G. Theodore Mitau, *Politics in Minnesota*, 12 (Minneapolis, 1960); Arthur E. Naftalin, "A History of the Farmer-Labor Party of Minnesota," 58, Ph.D. thesis, University of Minnesota, 1948. On Cain's position in the telephone union, see *Minneapolis Labor Review*, December 20, 1918, p. 1. Information on Hough and Cain here and below is from a taped interview with Hough conducted by Ramona Burks, March 7, 1975, cited hereafter as Hough Interview; notes on two scrapbooks in Hough's possession; and notes on telephone interviews with Cain conducted by Arvonne Fraser, October 26, 1974, June 13, 1975 — all in "Women Legislators: Notes." See also Mary Dillon Foster, comp., *Who's Who Among Minnesota Women*, 44, 144 (n.p., 1924).

[21] Cain Interviews; campaign card in Cain File, Minneapolis History Collection, Minneapolis Public Library; Mitau, *Politics in Minnesota*, 11. For the paragraph below, see circular letter of Minnesota Branch, National Woman's party, March 26, 1923, and an undated printed flyer entitled "The Equal Rights Bill" written by Marian Le Sueur — both in Kempfer Papers; *Minneapolis Tribune*, March 9, 1923, p. 1; *St. Paul Pioneer Press*, March 9, 1923, p. 1.

[22] Hough Interview; newspaper clipping, February 8, 1957, in Hough scrapbook.

[23] Here and the paragraph below, see *Minneapolis Star*, January 4, 1947, p. 1; *Capitol News*, January, 1959, p. 13; campaign leaflet, 1934, and newspaper clippings, July 19, 1931, February 8, 1957, in Hough scrapbooks.

[24] On Knutson here and below, see *Minneapolis Tribune*, December 10, 1950, Upper Midwest sec., p. 11; *Biographical Directory of the American Congress 1774–1971*, 1247 (Washington, D.C., 1971).

[25] On party endorsement and for the paragraphs below, see notes on an interview with Jack Puterbaugh conducted by Arvonne Fraser, 1975; and newspaper clipping, August 29, 1960 — both in "Women Legislators: Notes"; Kefauver campaign poster [1956], in Arthur O. Reierson Papers, MHS.

[26] *Minneapolis Tribune*, July 3, 1960, Upper Midwest sec., p. 8, October 28, 1960, p. 17, February 6, 1977, 1B, February 9, 1977, 8A; newspaper clipping, August 29, 1960, in "Women Legislators: Notes."

[27] On Knutson's ability as a state legislator, see Fraser notes on interviews with Sally Luther, Jack Puterbaugh, and Thomas R. Hughes, in "Women Legislators: Notes." On requirements for political success, see Jeane J. Kirkpatrick, *Political Women*, 42, 223 (New York, 1974).

[28] Biographical sketch in *Minnesota Legislative Manual*, 1961–62, p. 87. Information and quotations here and below not otherwise attributed are from Luther Interview.

[29] Women had served on the university board from 1922–35, but none had been appointed for many years. Prudence Cutright was not elected in 1951, but in 1953 Marjorie L. Howard began eighteen years of service. There have been women on the board continuously from 1953 to 1977.

[30] Fraser notes on interviews with Luther, Puterbaugh, and Hughes, in "Women Legislators: Notes."

[31] On McMillan, see *St. Paul Dispatch*, November 19, 1974, p. 15. On the league, see also p. 278, below.

[32] *St. Paul Dispatch*, November 19, 1974, p. 15. Much of the information on abor-

tion legislation here and below was provided by Jeri Rasmussen, St. Paul. On McMillan's attitude, see *St. Paul Pioneer Press,* March 23, 1969, sec. 3, p. 6. Abortions during the first trimester of pregnancy became legal in Minnesota due to a 1973 United States Supreme Court decision. Since 1974 the Minnesota legislature has adopted several measures restricting abortions, one of which was declared unconstitutional.

[33] Biographical data on Naplin may be found in *Minnesota Legislative Manual,* 1927, p. 486, and a questionnaire response, February 25, 1975, in "Women Legislators: Notes." See also *St. Paul Pioneer Press,* February 10, 1927, p. 1. Although the mortgage bill discussed below did not pass, some of its provisions were embodied in another bill passed in 1933. See Minnesota, *Laws,* 1933, p. 514. The exact dates of Naplin's service in the hotel inspection division are not known. On her congressional platform below, see campaign card, Adams Papers; on her retirement, see *St. Paul Dispatch,* February 1, 1975, p. 12.

[34] Here and below, see *St. Paul Pioneer Press,* February 3, 1975, p. 15; *Rochester Post-Bulletin,* June 15, 1976, p. 7.

[35] Questionnaire responses in "Women Legislators: Notes." See also *Rochester Post-Bulletin,* January 20, 1975, p. 23, February 10, 1976, p. 3, March 6, 1976, p. 13 (quotation); *Winona Daily News,* August 14, 1975, p. 3a; newspaper clippings, May 3, 1975, May 21, 1976, in Senate District 33 File, Legislative Reference Library.

[36] Telephone interview with Staples conducted by Sue Holbert, November 15, 1976.

[37] Here and below, see questionnaire responses, in "Women Legislators: Notes"; *Minneapolis Tribune Picture Magazine,* January 28, 1973, p. 15. Valuable clipping files on current legislators and elections may be found in the Legislative Reference Library. On those elected in 1976, see *St. Paul Pioneer Press,* January 23, 1977, family life sec., pp. 1, 12.

Claudia Meier married Martin Volk on August 29, 1975. A son, Peter, was born in June, 1976, and Volk became the second legislator to bear a child while in office. (Donna Christianson was the first.) Volk did not seek re-election in 1976, having moved to Roy, N. Dak.

[38] Kirkpatrick, *Political Women,* 8, 41–56, 69–72, 120, 229.

[39] Kirkpatrick, *Political Women,* 29, 44–48, 52, 61, 64, 67, 73, 76, 80, 100, 152, 158, 164–167.

[40] Kirkpatrick, *Political Women,* 106–134, 160.

Chapter 15 — FANNY FLIGELMAN BRIN — *pages 284 to 300*

[1] Lowry Nelson and Hazel Clampitt, *Population Trends in Minnesota,* 13 (University of Minnesota, Agricultural Experiment Station, *Bulletin* 387 — St. Paul, 1945). On the Fligelman family in Minneapolis, see *Davison's Minneapolis City Directory,* 1886, p. 305, and interview conducted by the author with Howard B. and Ruth F. Brin (son and daughter-in-law) and Rachel and Ralph L. Helstein (daughter and son-in-law), August 8, 1975, hereafter cited as Brin Family Interview, copy in Minnesota Historical Society (MHS).

[2] John Fligelman had two children by an earlier marriage; Fanny was the oldest of the five born to the second marriage. Ruth F. Brin, "She Heard Another Drummer: The Life of Fanny Brin and Its Implications for the Sociology of Religion," 1, master's thesis, University of Minnesota, 1972, copy in MHS. On her oratorical successes, see Brin Family Interview; *Minneapolis Journal,* March 1, 1902, p. 24; and *Minnesota Alumni Weekly,* 40:248 (January 11, 1941). Fanny was one of five women among the twenty-seven district champions throughout the state.

[3] *The Gopher,* 19:34, 194 (Minneapolis, 1906).

[4] Material on the Brin family may be found in the extensive Fanny Fligelman

Brin Papers, MHS. See also Ruth Brin, "She Heard Another Drummer," 4; Brin Family Interview; *Minnesota Alumni Weekly*, 40:248. For more on Arthur Brin see p. 298, below.

[5] *American Jewish World* (Minneapolis-St. Paul), November 18, 1932, p. 18; Brin, untitled speech, April 15, 1932, Brin Papers.

[6] *Minneapolis Tribune*, March 20, 1938, society sec., p. 8; Brin to Mrs. Irving L. De Graff, February 27, 1941; Brin, untitled speech, November 8, 1937, Brin Papers. On Potter, see *Biographical Cyclopaedia of American Women*, 1:289–293 (New York, 1924); on Stockwell and Ueland, see chapter 17, below. See also Julietta B. Kahn, "Mrs. Arthur Brin, President of the National Council of Jewish Women," in *Eve*, February, 1937, p. 35, copy in Brin Papers. Fanny Brin's woman suffrage activities are listed in Ethel E. Hurd, *Woman Suffrage in Minnesota: A Record of the Activities in Its Behalf Since 1847*, 14, 22, 36 (Minneapolis, 1916).

[7] Brin to De Graff, February 27, 1941, Brin Papers.

[8] Brin to Harold M. Dudley, June 14, 1933; Brin, "On the Occasion of the 75th Birthday of Hannah G. Solomon," typescript of radio address, January 9, 1933, and speeches, "The Value of the Suffrage Movement," undated, "For Mrs. Solomon's 79th Birthday, January 11, 1937," and undated, untitled talk probably given to International Congress of the National Council of Women of the United States, Chicago, 1933 — all in Brin Papers. On Addams and Woolley, see Edward T. James *et al.*, eds., *Notable American Women, 1607–1950*, 1:16–22, 3:660–663 (Cambridge, Mass., 1971); on Hamilton, see *Who Was Who in America*, 5:301 (Chicago, 1973).

[9] On Cohen, see Mary Dillon Foster, ed., *Who's Who Among Minnesota Women*, 62 (n.p., 1924). See also Kahn, in *Eve*, February, 1937, p. 35; "Historical Data for Council Book of National Council of [Jewish] Women of the United States," April 14, 1933, Brin Papers; and Brin, "The Jewish Woman in the American Scene," in *Eve*, April, 1936, p. 31.

[10] International Good Will Day, May 18, commemorated The Hague International Peace Conference called in 1899 by Tsar Nicholas of Russia. See also NCJW, "Toward a Durable Peace," 2, mimeographed report issued by the National Committee on International Relations and Peace, August, 1941, Brin Papers.

[11] On these various activities, see, for example, Women's Committee for World Disarmament, Minnesota Branch, *Bulletin No. 1*, June, 1921; Brin to Gratia Countryman, December 23, 1930; NCJW, Minneapolis Section, *Bulletin*, [October?], 1924 — all in Brin Papers. As a result of her growing national prominence, friends urged Governor Floyd B. Olson to appoint her to the University of Minnesota Board of Regents. See Mrs. Lester Rees to Olson, April 17, 1933, copy in Brin Papers.

[12] Brenner to Brin, February 24, 1924; NCJW Department of Peace, "Triennial Report," 2 (January 13, 1930), Brin Papers.

[13] The Women's International League for Peace and Freedom, founded in 1919 with Jane Addams at its head, was an outgrowth of the 1915 International Congress of Women. Fanny Brin was an alternate delegate to its international congress in Washington, D.C., in May, 1924. Brin to Brenner, June 25, 1924, Brin Papers.

[14] For a fuller account of the deliberations on the Kellogg-Briand Pact, especially on the part played by Frank B. Kellogg, see Barbara Stuhler, *Ten Men of Minnesota and American Foreign Policy, 1898–1968*, 115–119 (St. Paul, 1973). See also Brin to Mrs. Samuel J. Rosensohn, December 14, 1927; Estelle M. Sternberger to Brin, December 20, 1927; and Brin to Sternberger, December 23, 1927 — all in Brin Papers.

[15] Brin to Mrs. Joseph E. Friend, January 12, 1928; Kellogg to Brin, November 9, 1928; Christianson to Brin, November 26, 1928; Brin, radio speech on the pact, undated — all in Brin Papers. Governor Christianson appointed Fanny Brin to the Minnesota Crime Commission and to the State Teachers College Board in 1930. See *Minneapolis Star*, September 5, 1961, p. 7A. The nine organizations originally

joining Mrs. Catt's campaign for the pact were: the NCJW, the American Association of University Women, the General Federation of Women's Clubs, the National League of Women Voters, the National Board of the YWCA, the National Women's Trade Union League, the National Women's Christian Temperance Union, the Council of Women for Home Missions, and the Federation of Women's Boards of Foreign Missions of North America.

[16] Carrie Chapman Catt to Brin, August 27, 1936; Brin, "Why We Value Membership in the National Conference," in Conference on the Cause and Cure of War, *Delegates Worksheet*, No. 3, p. 16 (January 26–29, 1937) — all in Brin Papers. See also Micah, IV:3.

[17] Brin to Mrs. Maurice L. Goldman, April 9, 1932; Catt to Brin, September 21, 1933, Brin Papers.

[18] Brin, Department of Peace, Triennial Report to the NCJW, January 13, 1930; memorandum to section presidents, December 10, 1935; Brin, "Toward a Durable Peace," 2, a report of the national committee on international relations and peace to the NCJW, August, 1941; Brin, "A Four Point Program for Peace," in *Eve*, January, 1937, clipping — all in Brin Papers.

[19] On the Minneapolis meeting, see *Minneapolis Tribune*, October 27, 1931, p. 1; Grace E. Ford to Brin, [October 27, 1931], Brin Papers.

[20] On events leading to World War II many contemporary reference works on diplomatic history are available. A useful one is Thomas A. Bailey, *A Diplomatic History of the American People* (7th Ed., New York, 1964).

[21] Brin, typescript of a radio speech on council programs, given in New Orleans, March [9], 1935, Brin Papers.

[22] William L. Shirer, *The Rise and Fall of the Third Reich*, 46, 283 (New York, 1959); Robert Payne, *The Life and Death of Adolf Hitler*, 466 (New York, 1959).

[23] On the council's activities, see NCJW, news release, March 24, 1933; Miriam B. Wolf to Mary G. Schonberg, March 25, 1933; Mrs. Maurice L. Goldman to section presidents, November 2, 1933. On the Minnesota efforts, see R. A. Gortner to Lotus D. Coffman, April 25, 1935; Minutes of the first meeting of Minneapolis chapter, National Coordinating Committee for Aid to Refugees and Emigrants, January 3, 1935; and Minutes of Minnesota Refugee Committee, May 12, 1940, copies — all in Brin Papers.

[24] Brin, "Report on the Sixth Conference on the Cause & Cure of War," 1 [1931]; Brin, "Meeting the German Situation," [1934?] and "Democracy in Jewish History and the Teachings of Jesus," undated speech — all in Brin Papers.

[25] Brin to Julietta Kahn, April 19, 1937; Brin "Be Thou Among the Persecuted," undated speech, probably 1939, Brin Papers. Ruth F. Brin, "She Heard Another Drummer," 11, 24.

[26] Brin, "Address at Triennial, New Orleans, March, 1935," p. 1; Brin, "Statement on Palestine, November, 1943." The issue remained a matter of contention; Fanny argued that while there may have been no commitment to the political form, there was an endorsement of the idea of a national home. Brin to Mrs. Joseph M. Welt, February 29, 1944 — all in Brin Papers.

[27] Brin, "Report on the Sixth Conference on the Cause & Cure of War," 1 [1931], Brin Papers.

[28] During Brin's two terms as president, NCJW membership increased from 40,000 to 60,000. See Brin, "Address to the NCJW Triennial Convention," 12, January, 1938; on the committee's new name, see Laura G. Rapaport to Brin, March 4, 1938 — both in Brin Papers. See also *Minneapolis Tribune*, March 20, 1938, society sec., 8.

[29] On the war in Spain, see Brin to Mrs. Gordon M. Pearcy, September 12, 1938, and Rapaport to Brin, May 6, 1938. On the NCJW's position, see Brin to Rapaport, May 20, 1940; Brin to Mrs. Benjamin Spitzer, June 19, 1940; and Brin, "Statement

to the Executive Committee Meeting on Monday, June 24, 1940," 1, 2; and Brin to Goldman, September 24, 1940 — all in Brin Papers.

[30] NCJW, "International Relations Digest," December, 1941, p. 1, a mimeographed bulletin issued by the council's Committee on International Relations and Peace, Brin Papers.

[31] Brin, untitled, undated speech, probably 1942 or 1943; Brin to Rapaport, June 1, 1942; and Brin, "Interpreters of Democracy," 10, typescript of speech given July 2, 1942, Brin Papers.

[32] Brin to chairmen of the NCJW's International Relations and Peace Committee, March 29, 1943; Brin, draft of an article for *Council Woman*, May 17, 1943, Brin Papers. For a fuller account of the B2H2 resolution and Senator Ball's role, see Stuhler, *Ten Men of Minnesota,* 130–136.

[33] Mildred G. Welt to Brin, March 28, 1945; Vira Whitehouse to Brin, April 14, 1945. The concept of adjunct representation is still current in United Nations conferences. On fellow-Minnesotan and former governor Harold E. Stassen, one of eight official members of the United States delegation, Fanny wrote, "His answers were always very clear and direct." See Brin, undated notes on the San Francisco conference, [5], Brin Papers; Brin Family Interview.

[34] *San Francisco Chronicle,* May 4, 1945, clipping in Brin Papers. On the 36 organizations, see program of Minneapolis Women's Dumbarton Oaks Rally, February 2, 1945, copy in Brin Papers. Fanny's attempt in 1944 to organize a state branch of the national Women's Action Committee for Lasting Peace failed, according to her, because of the well-organized United Nations committee in Minnesota. See Brin to Margaret E. Burton, April 27, 1943; Brin to Mrs. Norman de R. Whitehouse, March 7, 1944, February 3, 1945; Helen Duff to Brin, February 3, 1945 — all in Brin Papers.

[35] Brin, untitled speech to United Nations rally, 2, 3 [1946], Brin Papers.

[36] *Minneapolis Tribune,* March 20, 1938, society sec., 8; Gratia Countryman to Mrs. Felix Moses, October 25, 1937; Carrie C. Catt, message to honoring luncheon, November 3, 1937; *American Jewish World,* November 12, 1937, p. 2, copy in Brin Papers.

[37] On her memberships and offices, see, for example, *Minneapolis Star,* September 5, 1961, p. 7A; Mrs. Moise S. Cahn to Brin, December 6, 1951. On her speaking ability, see, for example, Alice L. Kercher to Brin, November 13, 1928 — all in Brin Papers.

[38] Interviews of the author with Viola Hymes, Minneapolis, August 13, 1975, and Belle Rauch, Minneapolis, August 18, 1975, copies in MHS.

[39] Brin, "National Report to the Board of Directors of the National Council of Jewish Women," 6, April 10, 1934; Brin to Rachel, undated letter from Minot, N. Dak., Brin Papers.

[40] Ruth Brin, "She Heard Another Drummer," 3; interviews with Viola Hymes and Belle Rauch. On Arthur Brin, see Brin Family Interview; Ford to Fanny Brin, November 23, 1947; newspaper clippings in Brin Papers.

[41] Brin, untitled speech, 2, 1945; undated clipping, 1948, Brin Papers.

[42] Brin Family Interview; untitled, undated speech, Brin Papers.

[43] Rabindranath Tagore was a Bengali poet and prose writer who was awarded the Nobel Prize for literature in 1913.

[44] *Minneapolis Tribune,* September 5, 1961, p. 1. The quotation is attributed to Rabbi Tarphon in *Pirke Avot* (The Sayings of the Fathers), Chapter 2, Verse 2.

Chapter 16 — THE LARSON SISTERS — *pages 301 to 324*

[1] *Who's Who of American Women,* 1:736, 737 (Chicago, 1958).

[2] Henrietta M. Larson to Lars W. Boe, November 12, 1942, Lars W. Boe Papers, St. Olaf College Archives, Northfield, Minn.

³ On Norwegian immigration see Knut Gjerset, *History of the Norwegian People*, 2:599 (New York, 1915); Karen Larsen, *A History of Norway*, 423 (Princeton, N.J., 1948); Alice E. Smith, *The History of Wisconsin*, 1:492 (Madison, Wis., 1973); Henrietta M. Larson, ed., "An Immigration Journey to America in 1854," in Norwegian-American Historical Association, *Studies and Records*. On the family's immigration here and in the paragraph below, see "Story of Nora," 4, 11, Nora L. Larson Papers in her possession, Northfield, hereafter cited as NLL Papers; Franklyn Curtiss-Wedge, *History of Fillmore County, Minnesota*, 2:1134 (Chicago, 1912).

⁴ Interviews with Henrietta M. Larson conducted by the author, June 21, August 26, November 21, 1974, hereafter cited as HML Interviews; here and below, see "Story of Nora," 4, 13, 14.

⁵ Curtiss-Wedge, *Fillmore County*, 1:523, 2:820; HML Interviews; *Minneapolis Morning Tribune*, December 28, 1960, p. 13.

⁶ Here and below, "Story of Nora," 5, 40, 41; HML Interviews; Joseph M. Shaw, *History of St. Olaf College 1874–1974*, 41–46, 88, 93 (Northfield, 1974); Eugene Fevold, "The Norwegian Immigrant and His Church," in *Norwegian-American Studies*, 23:3–8 (Northfield, 1967).

⁷ St. Olaf College Faculty Record, Agnes M. Larson, June 27, 1950, in St. Olaf College Archives, Agnes M. Larson Faculty Personnel File, hereafter cited as AML Faculty File; *Manitou Messenger*, May 20, 1960, p. 6; Reub Monson, "Dr. Agnes Larson — Scholar, Writer, Teacher," in *St. Olaf Alumnus*, May, 1956, p. 11; O. J. Lokken to Agnes, July 8, 1916, Carl Weicht to Agnes, July 11, 1926, Agnes M. Larson Papers in possession of Henrietta and Nora Larson, Northfield, hereafter cited as AML Papers.

⁸ Faculty Record, 1950; Agnes to Boe, March 23, 1926, and July 17, 1928 — all in AML Faculty File.

⁹ Faculty Record, 1932; Agnes to Boe, December 27, 1929; Boe to Agnes, March 7, 1930 — all in AML Faculty File. On Boe, below, see Shaw, *St. Olaf*, 252–275; interview of the author with Joan Olson, college archivist, April 1, 1975.

¹⁰ Here and two paragraphs below, Agnes to Boe, February 10, 14, 1931; Faculty Record, 1932 — both in AML Faculty File; Ada L. Comstock to Agnes, February 13, 1931; Boe to Agnes, February 17, 1931 — both in AML Papers; *Minneapolis Star*, February 20, 1931, p. 9.

¹¹ Agnes to Boe, September 2, 1932, AML Faculty File; Shaw, *St. Olaf*, 269; Agnes to Boe, July 1, 1933, AML Papers.

¹² Boe to Donald E. Van Koughnet, April 21, 1933, AML Faculty File. Her presentations included an article, "The Golden Age of Lumbering in Minnesota," in *Minnesota Alumni Weekly*, 32:437–439 (April 15, 1933); a paper, "On the Trail of the Woodsman in Minnesota," presented at an annual meeting of the Minnesota Historical Society and printed in *Minnesota History*, 13:349–366 (December, 1932). She also read a paper at the twenty-eighth Mississippi Valley Historical Conference. See *Mississippi Valley Historical Review*, 22:232 (September, 1935). See also Willoughby M. Babcock to Agnes, July 19, 1932; Elmer Ellis to Agnes, April 30, 1935; Agnes to Boe, July 1, 1933; Boe to Agnes, August 27, 1937 — all in AML Papers; Agnes to Boe, August 18, 1937, AML Faculty File.

¹³ Agnes to Boe (telegram), January 12, 1938, AML Faculty File; HML Interviews. Two years later Radcliffe awarded Agnes a Phi Beta Kappa key. Since St. Olaf did not have a chapter at the time Agnes was a student there, she had not previously been elected to this prestigious society. "Agnes M. Larson Receives Honors in Graduate Work," undated clipping, AML Papers.

¹⁴ Here and two paragraphs below, Agnes M. Larson, *History of the White Pine Industry in Minnesota*, ix, 72–85, 231 (Minneapolis, 1949); Agnes to Boe, August 21, 1939, September 8, 1942, Helen MacDonald to Naida Knatrold, May 9, 1949 —

all in AML Faculty File; University of Minnesota News Service press release, May 6, 1949, AML Papers; Frederick Merk to Agnes, December 17, 1949, AML Papers.

[15] Agnes to Clemens M. Granskou, May 10, 1960, AML Papers.

[16] Recollections of the author, a St. Olaf student from 1957 to 1961.

[17] Agnes to Boe, July 25, 1935; Agnes to Granskou, March 21, 1949, AML Faculty File.

[18] Here and in the two paragraphs below, see Notes, George Washington Day Chapel Address, 1952; miscellaneous talks and addresses, undated; Agnes M. Larson, "The Contribution of the Social Sciences in Training the Student for Social Responsibility," paper presented at the annual Conference of Lutheran College Faculties, Racine, Wis., October 6–7, 1944; letters from numerous radio listeners, 1943–45; Sonya Quam to Agnes, July 25, 1959 — all in AML Papers. Agnes to Granskou, July 25, 1944, AML Faculty File. The phrase "when mankind was shifting his viewpoint" was a favorite, often used in class. Recollections of the author, History 41, 42, American History 1000 to the Present, 1958–59.

[19] Merk to Agnes, March 13, 1952, AML Papers. The advice was given to the author in the spring of 1960.

[20] Here and paragraph below, *St. Olaf College Bulletin*, 37:156 (March, 1941), 56:178 (April, 1960); Faculty Record, 1950, and Granskou to Agnes, January 6, 1948 — both in AML Faculty File; Joan Olson to the author, April 8, 1975, based on data collected by St. Olaf College, Office of the Registrar; HML Interviews; "Centennial Program," Rice County Historical Society, March 20, 1958, AML Papers.

[21] Agnes to Granskou, May 10, 1960; Agnes to the Cormans, undated rough draft, probably early 1966; Lawrence M. Stavig to Agnes, June 8, 1964 — all in AML Papers; Agnes M. Larson, *John A. Johnson: An Uncommon American* (Northfield, 1969). *Northfield News*, January 26, 1967, p. 5, and February 2, 1967, p. 5, carried notices of Agnes' death. Quotation in the paragraph below from notes for speech to Mount Horeb (Wis.) Alumni Association, Fall, 1960, AML Papers.

[22] Henrietta M. Larson, "Some Thoughts on the Future of Business History," paper presented at meeting of West Coast Historians, Berkeley, Calif., 1956, p. 16, Henrietta M. Larson Papers, in her possession, Northfield, hereafter cited as HML Papers.

[23] Henrietta to Boe, November 12, 1942, Boe Papers; Ralph W. and Muriel E. Hidy, "Henrietta M. Larson: An Appreciation," in *Business History Review*, 36:4 (Spring, 1962); HML Interviews.

[24] *Minneapolis Morning Tribune*, December 28, 1960, p. 13; Hidy, in *Business History Review*, 36:5; HML Interviews.

[25] J. B. Johnston to Guy Stanton Ford, May 16, 1922; Henrietta to Ford, April 14, 1923 — both in Guy Stanton Ford Papers, University of Minnesota Archives, Minneapolis; Hidy, in *Business History Review*, 36:5.

[26] Hidy, in *Business History Review*, 36:5; HML Interviews.

[27] N. S. B. Gras to Henrietta, March 3, 1928; R. W. Hidy, "Harvard Citation of Henrietta Melia Larson, October 22, 1962" — both in HML Papers; "The Lady at Harvard," in *Newsweek*, January 2, 1961, p. 45; Hidy, in *Business History Review*, 36:6; Henrietta M. Larson, *Guide to Business History*, 6, 9–12, 16, 17 (Cambridge, Mass., 1948).

[28] Here and below, Henrietta M. Larson, Written Interview, Northfield, September, 1974, in the possession of the author, hereafter cited as HML Written Interview; Hidy, *Business History Review*, 36:6; Henrietta M. Larson, *Jay Cooke, Private Banker*, xiv, 430 (Cambridge, Mass., 1936). N. S. B. Gras and Henrietta M. Larson, *Casebook in American Business History*, v, 15 (New York, 1939).

[29] Hidy, *Business History Review*, 36:8; HML Written Interview. See also Hen-

rietta M. Larson, "Some Unexplored Fields in American Railroad History," in *Bulletin of the Business Historical Society,* 16:69–79 (October, 1942). Henrietta remained the editor of the *Bulletin* until the end of 1953 when the publication ceased and was replaced by the *Business History Review.*

[30] *Directory of American Scholars,* 1:363 (6th Ed., New York, 1974); HML Interviews and Written Interview; Agnes to Boe, September 8, 1942, AML Faculty File; "Address of Presentation of Honorary Degree by St. Olaf College," May 30, 1943, HML Papers.

[31] Henrietta M. Larson, review of *The Triumph of American Capitalism,* in the *Journal of Political Economy,* 50:151 (February, 1942); Henrietta M. Larson, "Danger in Business History," in *Harvard Business Review,* 22:318, 319, 324 (Spring, 1944).

[32] Larson, *Guide,* xxiv; Hidy, in *Business History Review,* 36:10; HML Written Interview.

[33] Hidy, in *Business History Review,* 36:8, 9; Ralph W. Hidy and Muriel E. Hidy, *Pioneering in Big Business, 1882–1911,* xix-xxii (New York, 1955); *Business Week,* April 3, 1948, p. 24. In addition to the Hidy study cited above, the Jersey Standard series consisted of George Sweet Gibbs and Evelyn H. Knowlton, *The Resurgent Years, 1911–1927* (New York, 1956) and Henrietta M. Larson, Evelyn H. Knowlton, and Charles S. Popple, *New Horizons, 1927–1950* (New York, 1971). The foundation also supported the research for Henrietta M. Larson and Kenneth W. Porter, *History of the Humble Oil and Refining Company: A Study in Industrial Growth* (New York, 1959).

[34] Major reviews of the Humble book included the *American Historical Review,* 66:239 (October, 1960) and *Business History Review,* 34:249 (Summer, 1960). The Standard Oil volumes were reviewed in *American Economic Review,* 46:492 (June, 1956) and 47:430 (June, 1957); *American Historical Review,* 61:989 (July, 1956) and 62:708 (April, 1957); and *Journal of American History,* 60:1174 (March, 1974).

[35] HML Written Interview.

[36] Henrietta M. Larson, "Some Thoughts on Education in Church-Related Colleges," address at Luther College, Decorah, Ia., October, 1961; and "Tentative Suggestions for a Preface to the Report of the Liberal Arts Subcommittee of the Curriculum Committee," presented as a member of the Advisory Committee to Southwest State College, Marshall, Minn., 1963 — both in HML Papers.

[37] David W. Bailey to Henrietta, HML Papers. The President and Fellows of Harvard College voted the appointment on October 3, 1960. It was to become effective on January 1, 1961. See also *Newsweek,* January 2, 1961, p. 45. On the other women full professors, see *Northfield News,* October 20, 1960, p. 3c. See also HML Interviews and Written Interview.

[38] *Minneapolis Morning Tribune,* December 28, 1960, p. 13; Henrietta M. Larson, "Some Thoughts on Education in Church-Related Colleges," HML Papers.

[39] HML Written Interview.

[40] Nathan Pusey to Henrietta, June 5, 1961; Henrietta to Pusey, June 13, 1961, HML Papers. See also note 33, above.

[41] HML Written Interview, September, 1974; Hidy, "Harvard Citation," HML Papers. Since the mid-1950s the Business History Conference has replaced the defunct Business Historical Society as the major academic business history organization.

[42] Here and the four paragraphs below, see "Story of Nora," 38; Nora L. Larson, Written Interview, August 19, 1974, in the possession of the author, hereafter cited as NLL Written Interview; Nora L. Larson Interview, Northfield, Minnesota, August 26, 1974, hereafter cited as NLL Interview; *American Men and Women of Science,* 4:3562 (12th Ed., New York, 1972).

[43] *Austin Daily Herald,* January 19, 1952, p. 7.

[44] NLL Interview.

[45] NLL Written Interview; Nora L. Larson and Lawrence E. Carpenter, "The Fecal Excretion of Aureomycin by the Pig," in *Archives of Biochemistry and Biophsyics*, 36:239 (March, 1952); Larson and Carpenter, "Swine Dysentery: Treatment with 4-Nitro and 3-Nitro-4-Dydroxy Phenyl Arsonic Acids and Antibiotics," in *Journal of Animal Science*, 11:290 (May, 1952); Larson and Carpenter, "Effects of Antibacterial Substances in Fecal Clostridia Populations," in *Proceedings of the Society for Experimental Biology and Medicine*, 79:229 (1952); *Western News* (Hamilton, Mont.), July 23, 1952, clipping, NLL Papers.

[46] *Austin Daily Herald*, April 29, 1953, p. 1, June 7, 1956, p. 12; NLL Written Interview; Nora L. Larson and Eldon G. Hill, "Amine Formation and Metabolic Activity of Microorganisms in the Ileum of Young Swine Fed Chlortetracycline," in *Journal of Bacteriology*, 80:191 (August, 1960). See also clippings in NLL Papers.

[47] Earl W. Phelan, "The Argonne Semester," in *Journal of Chemical Education*, 41:668 (December, 1964); St. Olaf Biology Department, *Bulletin*, Fall, 1965, NLL Papers; NLL Written Interview.

[48] NLL Written Interview; *Rochester Post-Bulletin*, March 25, 1968, p. 23.

[49] NLL Interview. On Nora's retirement, below, see "Twelve Faculty, Administrators to Retire," in *Saint Olaf*, Spring, 1972, p. 9.

[50] NLL Interview.

INDEX